DATE DUE

Winning America

Winning America

Ideas and Leadership
for the 1990s

edited by Marcus Raskin
and Chester Hartman

SOUTH END PRESS
and the
INSTITUTE FOR POLICY STUDIES

p   MAIN   nd the South End Press
c   973.927
c   Winning America :
n

                                          ?-publication:
•   31143004266772   c.| egy" in the *New Yorker*,

• by Robert Gottlieb and Helen Ingram, "The New Environmentalists" in *The Progressive*, July 1988.

• by Saul Landau, "Toward a New Foreign Policy" in *The Progressive*, April 1988.

• by Paul L. Wachtel, "Better Than Growth" in *The Progressive*, May 1988.

• by Paul L. Wachtel, "Toward a Quality-of-Life Society" in *The UTNE Reader,* July-August 1988.

Library of Congress Catalog Card Number: 88-42556
Library of Congress Cataloging-in-Publication Data
Winning America
I. United States—Politics and government—
1981-   . 2. United States—Economic policy—
1981-   . 3. United States—Social policy—
1980-   . 4. United States—Foreign relations—
1981-   . I. Raskin, Marcus G. II. Hartman, Chester W.
JK271.W655 1988   973.927   88-42556
ISBN 0-89608-344-6
ISBN 0-89608-343-8 (pbk.)

South End Press
116 St. Botolph St., Boston, MA 02115

Acknowledgements

It was a pleasure working with our contributors, who produced well and with good spirit on short notice. Several of our IPS colleagues—Ricky Bluthenthal, Joan Drake, Sue Goodwin, Margaret Gressens, Julianne Halberstein, Josh Handler, and Barbara Wien—took part in early meetings that helped us conceptualize and outline the book. Michael Phillips, Donna Harris, and Julianne Halberstein provided secretarial assistance. Ellen Herman was a most able editor and working companion at South End Press. We are especially grateful to Sasha Natapoff, a *dea cum machina* whose intelligence and general assistance over the last two months made all the difference. Finally, our thanks to the Institute for Policy Studies, a place where projects like this can happen.

Table of Contents

Provide for the Common Defense...

Promote the General Welfare...

And Secure the Blessings of
Liberty to Ourselves and Our Posterity...

Introduction

Winning America appears during the bicentennial era of our Constitution. We believe that the "ought" purposes of the Constitution's Preamble can begin to be fulfilled through the progressive ideas, programs, and leadership recommendations offered by our various authors. The Constitution's spirit and indeed its letter can never be fulfilled with the constricted and tortured policies provided by the Reagan administration or future Reagan-like administrations.

The end of the Reagan era finds the United States careening toward disaster. Our economy is increasingly based upon paper manipulation, mergers, leveraged buyouts, and spiralling debt. Income and wealth are increasingly skewed. Eight years of the largest peacetime military buildup in this country's history have bought us less national and international security—not more. And our communities have been devastated by vicious cycles of poverty and despair.

In short, the American crisis is a crisis of spirit and direction. We must redefine what national security means and find a new place among the family of nations which truly serves our people's interests. We can fashion a just and efficient economy for all of our people. Without such economic reconstruction, we will enter the 21st century as a rigid, three-class society: a few will do very well; many will just get by (with the consequent insecurity that breeds); and there will be a permanent, expanding underclass possessing grossly inadequate incomes, education, and employment possibilities. Millions will have neither adequate health care nor a permanent roof over their heads. Racial schisms are increasing, and along with them, other senseless human divisions based on bigotry and fear. Gains made by women and minorities are under attack by those who insist upon the narrowest possible view of constitutional and economic rights. Our air, water, and other natural resources are seriously, possibly irretrievably endangered.

Now is the time for new ideas and leadership. Yet in the midst of our quadrennial circus called the "presidential campaign," little is forthcoming which can help direct us in a new way. It is in that vacuum that this book is offered. We have asked leading progressive thinkers and activists to offer new (and even some old and unfortunately for-

1

gotten) ideas and new leaders in a form appropriate to the season: platform proposals, complete with short analyses, and resource lists of
people whom a new administration should consider for advice or high-
level appointment, plus lists of relevant organizations and further reading. Together,these thirty-nine presentations comprise an exciting,
visionary, yet eminently practical platform that can direct America out
of its current crisis.

We offer no rigid blueprint. We offer alternative viewpoints: an
all-out war on drugs versus legalizing them; a plan for how we can end
economic stagnation through growth versus a set of proposals for a
non-growth solution which emphasizes more equitable distribution of
our present wealth, integration of economic planning with national and
international ecological concerns, and development of quality-of-life
values. The platform proposals include both short-run measures and
long-term solutions. And categories often overlap, defying neat boundaries. Concerns about the environment, communications, technology,
international institutions, and the U.S. role in foreign affairs appear in
numerous places because the consequences of policy in these areas
are so pervasive and so interrelated.

While *Winning America* emphasizes ideas and programs, attention is also paid to governmental organization: the role of the president; costs and budgets; creation of new agencies to deal with such
issues as culture, technology, the environment, and crime.

A wide spectrum of "people" suggestions can also be found in
our lists of "Recommended Appointees for a New Administration."
Some are little-known experts who should be considered for cabinet,
subcabinet, or other high government positions. Others are quite well
known and may have served in previous administrations. The names
listed were proposed by the authors; the individuals themselves were
not notified or asked for express permission. In a few instances, authors
elected either to list organizations from which appropriate names might
be drawn or to forego a list altogether.

The immediate needs of our nation call for insightful analysis, inspired organizing, political wisdom, and sensitivity. We need to clearly identify our problems and establish why they have arisen. We need
to recognize that alternative, progressive solutions *do* exist. We need
to develop constituencies that can apply effective pressure for progressive social change.

Once such political decisions are made—that basic health care,
decent, affordable housing, effective education, childcare, and family
income supports are *entitlements/rights*, that preserving our natural environment is as important a goal as any other we seek; that our national security is best attained by mobilizing democracy at home and
respecting principles of international law abroad—we will be better
able to face the question of how to reallocate our national resources.
Tradeoffs may be necessary among many worthy goals, since limits will

surely reveal themselves. Budgetary thinking and planning that integrates grassroots participation will be badly needed.

A book represents no more or less than its ideas. It is our collective task—organizations, activists, "experts," and readers—to make democratic use of these ideas, a step that makes the noble purposes of our Constitution's preamble practical and meaningful today. There is a job to be done by a new administration, by successive Congresses, and by future governments. We offer this set of ideas as a tool for doing that job democratically.

It has been our distinct privilege to prepare this book and to show that progressive intellectual and activist communities have answers, that we can lead, and that we have the vision and strategy to bring about a democratic and affluent nation in a changing world order.

Marcus Raskin
Chester Hartman
Institute for Policy Studies
Washington, DC
May 1988

We the People...

Restoring Democracy to America

In the millions of words that issue forth from legislatures, the executive, schools, labor unions, churches, the media, the right, center, and left, few fall more positively on our ears than "democracy." Throughout the 20th century, wars have been fought in its name with words and with guns. In American politics, all sides agree: democracy must be our practical goal, our motivating vision; our society must strive to become as democratic as possible.

But what is the definition of democracy in our time, and how is that definition relevant to the way we in the United States live our lives or the way government and society function?

We believe that our nation is becoming less and less democratic, that without a more widespread understanding of the forces leading us away from democracy and a set of conscious policies to reverse those trends, the deterioration of the American democratic experiment will intensify, perhaps irreversibly.

It would be a mistake to believe that democracy was the natural or constitutional demand of the Founding Fathers. The democratic process was tolerated—not mandated—under the Constitution. Each generation since then has struggled to define and implement democracy according to its own needs and possibilities. Throughout American history, even as conservatives sought to circumscribe the meaning of democracy and citizenship, people have struggled in factories, courts, and legislatures, and paid in life and death for the idea and reality of democracy. Women have chained themselves to the White House gates for the right to vote. Blacks and whites have defied law and police force to end apartheid in America.

Nevertheless, the dominant political players in American life today do not operate in a way that assumes government or major social and economic institutions should be guided according to democratic principles. Indeed, using the movie vocabulary so appropriate to the master illusionist who has presided over our country for the past eight years, the mass of Americans are regarded as "extras," people unimportant to

5

the main plot or success of the film. Ronald Reagan's administration has woven this feature of Hollywood culture into politics. In a world of stars and extras, his policies catered to the stars.

But democracy exists only when the "extras"—who keep the society going by producing its goods and services—participate. This country's real life extras—the old, the young, the un- and under-employed, women, immigrants, farmers, workers, blacks, Hispanics, Native Americans, and other racial minorities—are increasingly disem-powered, impoverished, and dispossessed as the resources of the na-tion are squandered in pyramidal military adventures and preparations, leveraged buyouts, and other activities that are at best unproductive, at worst destructive. Only a minority bothers to vote. Political campaigns are spending contests and image-making spectacles. The absurdly lop-sided distribution of wealth and income—the top one-half of 1 percent owning 36 percent of the nation's wealth—makes a mockery of equal citizenship. Passivity and despair about our nation and ourselves replace concern and involvement.

Democracy, as we understand it, and as it appears throughout the chapters of this book, is the means for reasoned action in the service of all the people. It embraces the tenets of individual growth and freedom, public happiness, and social and economic justice shorn of racism and sexism. It must permit—indeed it requires—continuous, ag-gressive participation and decisionmaking by the citizenry in our economic, political, and social lives, so that politicians and other leaders must listen and respond. Democracy is successful to the extent that it operates as both a means and an end. It is a process which allows for the maximum participation, access, deliberation, and implementation of specific goals on the part of the citizenry. It is an end in that it seeks to fulfill the felt and changing ideals of the nation.

Democracy is not easy to obtain or sustain. While our "balance of powers" government gives the appearance of access and of account-ability, the fact is that the best organized and wealthiest elements in public life easily outmaneuver poorly organized and poorly funded voices. The liberal vision of government, as a check against powerful economic interests, has failed. Those who control private capital—though they serve only themselves—have become national models of efficiency and rationality, while it has been assumed that government (pejoratively termed "bureaucracy" since at least the Nixon presiden-cy) could only fail. Our very real failure to solve pressing and growing problems such as homelessness and environmental degradation sug-gests that the notion of government itself must be reconceptualized, and with it, the role of the people in their government.

In a modern democracy, governing itself becomes a primary in-strument for ensuring the exercise of participation and judgement as well as the discovery and protection of people's rights. This is what the Ninth Amendment to the Constitution is all about: "The enumeration in the Constitution, of certain rights, shall not be construed to deny or disparage others retained by the people." Democracy is a set of interlocking goals which are always to be kept in mind, a network of rights which defines one's social being to the society as a whole, and which reflects the needs, wants, and potentiality of human beings both as individuals and groups. Democracy seeks maximum public judgement over and participation in the life of the society through existing institutions, while including the possibility of creating new institutions to fulfill the people's objectives.

The greatest recent enemy of democracy in the United States has been the rise of the national security state, which has made an outmoded and immoral concept of "national security" the overriding consideration for determining the allocation of our human and material resources and our relations with other countries. We must redefine this concept, and with it, reshape our domestic and global policies. In this book, Richard Barnet suggests the following reformulation: "a desired state of physical safety, economic development, and social stability within which there is space for individual freedom and development." He also notes that "a really good definition can only be the product of democratic debate" which makes the necessary links between what traditionally have been regarded as "domestic" issues and what traditionally have been regarded as "international" issues.

> The sacrifice of the most basic security expenditures—fire departments, police, libraries, schools, hospitals—to pay for additions to the military forces and stockpiles of lethal hardware has changed the face of the nation. The war prevention system has caused some inner cities to look as if war had already happened, and that prime objective of modern warfare, the demoralization of the civilian population, has been accomplished in a substantial number of farming communities and city neighborhoods throughout the nation by our own efforts without outside assistance. They are the consequences of choices American leaders have made about scarce resources.

How and where can the necessary debate about our national purposes and priorities take place? The public space in our society—that psychological and geographic area where citizens can discuss and decide important questions—is rapidly shrinking (the controlled private shopping mall, with its restrictions on free speech and any activities unrelated to consumption and spending, replacing the street and the square, is a perfect symbol of this trend). Voting is sporadic and lethargic, providing limited choices, and involving a more and more unrepresentative segment of the electorate. Public opinion polls offer the illusion of participation, but they are a poor substitute, since the important ingredient—dialogue—is missing. Universal access for all our citizens, their participation, deliberation, and implementation are necessary for a democracy, and our anti-discrimination laws must be expanded and strengthened so that no one is left out of citizenship.

From time to time candidacies of those running for political office extend the frame of reference of debate, and give the appearance of shifting political power in a more humane, inclusive, and equitable direction. Electoral politics then appears really to matter. Jesse Jackson has had this effect in his 1988 run for the presidency. He has brought together two groupings of people: those who had a surplus of consciousness, in the sense of seeing the needs of the nation beyond their immediate particular interests; and those who suffered from a surplus of pain—that is, Americans who had been left out, workers who were being thrown out, and vast sectors of the society intimidated by technological upheavals caused by those who failed to take into account the social costs of their actions. Jackson became an eloquent spokesman for a large group of people who believed that no politician heard their needs or identified with them in any existential sense.

But leaders are most successful when the citizenry has knowledge. Indeed, a democracy is predicated on access to knowledge. Hence, if we are to be a modern democracy, the citizenry needs greater access to government documents, information, and processes. The number of documents that are "classified" must be drastically reduced and the operations of government agencies must be demystified. Greater access to and responsiveness by the legal system can be mandated by reducing barriers that deprive people of "standing" to bring legal actions, by increasing resources to legal services for the poor and public interest litigation efforts, and by ensuring greater human diversity in the judges appointed.

Modern technology presents new "access" challenges. Communications media can be instruments of oligarchic control or democracy. They can serve to reinforce democracy, by reinstating the Fairness Doctrine, providing adequate funding for public broadcast stations, enforcing constraints on concentrated ownership of media outlets, providing government subsidies for innovative news services and publications, and making universal telephone access a reality.

Education is a means to empowerment and full citizenship. We can begin to realize this commitment through universal entitlement to Head Start-like preschool and after-school programs to the completion of high school education regardless of age, to the development of a national community youth service corps for educationally disaffected teenagers, to expanded post-secondary scholarship and loan programs, to improved recruitment and working conditions for teachers, and to a national parent education involvement program to link schools with families and communities.

Democracy must be a means and end inside the production process as well. American workers are alienated from their work, and demands and standards of the global economy are creating new pressures on the rights of labor. Workers need rights, obtained by law or collective bargaining, thorough information about their workplaces, a role in decisions affecting health and safety, investment of their pension funds in the social sector, introduction of new technology, and determination of what is produced in their workplaces. The quality of government "bureaucrats" will improve when these workers are granted similar rights to participate in management decisions and to create more democratic relationships between those who provide and those who receive government services. Cultural policies and institutions which support a diversity of expressive forms will ignite a renaissance in the arts, fostering a dynamic rather than a passive cultural life. The chasm between technology and cultural policies would be bridged, by allowing greater economic self-sufficiency for communities, vastly expanding access to communications and information technology, and encouraging innovation and expression.

As important as process and involvement are as both means and end, more direct and immediate steps are needed to ensure what President Roosevelt termed an Economic Bill of Rights four decades ago. For forty years, decent, affordable housing for all has been a congressionally-mandated goal. To achieve this goal requires that housing no longer be produced, owned, and managed by profit-oriented actors (land speculators, developers, lenders, brokers, landlords). The housing system must be restructured, guided by a principle that upholds the right to decent, affordable housing over the right to make a profit from housing and over traditional property rights. Similarly, decent health care can and must be established as a right—not a privilege—via creation of a national health care program. Jobs too must be created for all who want them, through government planning and, if necessary, direct government investment, with the social utility of the jobs created being a key consideration. Retraining programs must be established so that workers may switch to emerging forms of economic activity as industries modernize and adjust to the new global economic order. Our economy must move toward planned, decentralized conversion from a military-centered to a peace-centered productive system in line with redefining national and world security. Job-sharing and a shorter work week can open up opportunities for employment, cultural and leisure activities, and a healthier balance between working and non-working life, for which adequate childcare and parental leave are also essential. Progressive tax policies will both redistribute wealth and income more equitably and help provide the resources needed for the social support programs that make genuine democracy possible. The other major source of revenue for enhanced social programs will be a substantial reduction in the nation's $300+ billion "defense" budget—reductions made possible, desirable, even easy by changing our understanding of what national security actually means.

A new foreign policy to make the United States and the world more secure necessitates developing common security arrangements with the major military power, the USSR. It is clear that, under Gorbachev, the Soviet Union is ready to enter into common security arrangements and a framework leading eventually to general and complete disarmament—the only way the world's six billion people can live free from the threat of war. The place to begin this process is in Europe, via mutual troop reductions, denuclearization of the continent, and a European disarmament treaty. Regional conflicts must simultaneously be addressed, most immediately in the Middle East and Central America. Resolving the former conflict involves a non-proliferation treaty, to slow the pace of arms sales to the Middle East, a peace conference among *all* parties, including the PLO, genuine economic development efforts, and a UN-sponsored plebiscite in the West Bank and Gaza Strip to determine sovereignty issues. The Central American conflict can only be resolved if the United States abandons its interventionist posture, ending support for the *contras*, substituting aid programs to all democratically elected governments in the region, and a willingness (not confined to Central America) to let other people determine their course of development and form of government.

This new concept of national security must speak to international economic as well as military issues. We can help other countries, particularly in the third world, develop in ways that respond to the needs of the majority of citizens in those countries, fostering growth based on human needs, not exports. To accomplish this objective requires greater public accountability on the part of multilateral financial and development institutions—the IMF and the World Bank—with revised bodies of this sort replacing bilateral aid programs. As in domestic affairs, technological advances can foster international cooperation and development, global cultural dialogues, and the free exchange of ideas. A technology respectful of other cultures can become part of the linkage between the United States and the rest of the world.

Environmental concerns are perhaps the most obvious proof of the fact that we all live on the same fragile planet. A sound, secure approach to fighting environmental hazards requires reducing pollution at the source, rather than after the damage has been done, and regulating the production process in the interest of ecological balance and human health. Protecting the ozone layer and preventing nuclear accidents are of concern to every country, to every child, woman, and man on the earth.

Finally, national security and the genuine democracy it permits require that the United States renew its commitment to the United Nations and to its peace-keeping and collective security functions in Africa, the Middle East, and other regions. They require too that we rejoin UN ESCO, and that we respect the role and rulings of the World Court.

For the American people to begin to understand and accept the dimensions and connotations of restoring democracy at home and abroad—sweeping aside the cobwebs of Reaganism and all that preceded it—will require a monumental effort. This process will start with ideas and leadership emerging from groups committed to social reconstruction and activism on behalf of it. There was a time in this country when political parties were the repository and engine of such political ideas and leadership. The Republican Party, for example, began as an anti-slavery and women's rights party, and the New Deal braintrusters gave energy and direction to the Democratic Party. But political parties are no longer the keepers of that spirit. Think tanks supply ideas, usually small ones that all too often are technocratic gimmicks. Political candidates, for the most part, do not embody ideas either; rather, under the tutelage of media consultants, they manipulate messages and themes to match shifting opinion.

What is offered in the following 37 chapters are both concrete ideas and proposals for change, as well as new ways of looking at important issues and problems. The time has come to analyze what has happened and is happening to democracy in America, to begin a national debate over its meaning and the programs needed for its restoration, and to inspire a process of political activism and participation that can turn such ideas into reality.

A new administration, with Congress, can help usher in this age of social reconstruction through passage of legislation that, among other things, would repeal most secrecy laws; mandate postcard voter registration, free candidate access to television for a stipulated number of hours, and a requirement that polling places be open for two days for federal elections; sponsor projects for workplace democracy in all sectors of the economy; permit class actions and taxpayer suits where any level of government does not conform to health and environmental standards, or where officials undertake secret wars without prior and public congressional approval.

Relatedly, an administration can significantly improve human rights at home by signing the UN Human Rights Covenant, regarding economic, social, and political rights, and by creating a needs-assessment list for each of our states and counties. This audit could then be presented to Congress, the administration, and other public and private groups as the basis for needed legislation and administrative actions. To tame the power of mega-corporations, their charters should be granted by Congress, not by the states, and should include provisions for public accountability, genuine worker participation, and worker ownership.

Democracy, the means for reasoned action in the service of all the people, does not have to be an empty word made hollow by militarism or economic and social inequity. Democracy can cure these blights through the energy, interest, and will of a people whose thirst for justice and freedom is very great indeed.

Marcus Raskin is co-founder and Distinguished Fellow of the Institute for Policy Studies who, for a generation, has been a major exponent of social reconstruction. He is the author of a dozen books on political philosophy, government, and foreign affairs, including *The Common Good* and *Notes on the Old System*. He is a former special staff member of the National Security Council under President Kennedy, former co-chair of SANE-Freeze, is currently on the editorial board of *The Nation*, and has advised presidential candidates and members of Congress.

Chester Hartman is a Fellow of the Institute for Policy Studies. He has served on the Executive Committee of Architects/Designers/Planners for Social Responsibility and Harvard and Radcliffe Alumni/ae Against Apartheid, co-chaired the Massachusetts Committee on Discrimination in Housing, and been a board member of the National Committee for Responsive Philanthropy and the Urban League of Greater Boston.

In Order to Form a More Perfect Union...

Reclaiming the U.S. Economy

Platform

A debate about the means to achieve a democratic reconstruction of the American economy presumes certain broad political and economic goals. These should include at least the following:

- Ensuring the priority of basic human rights, such as the right to work and the right to reasonable security, over the "free play" of market forces

- Ensuring true and fair freedom of choice and opportunity for all

- Preserving and moving beyond the achievements of the postwar period by ensuring full employment; eliminating all poverty, including that which arises from inequality, by ensuring a decent standard of living for all and reconstructing and extending the social safety net

- Reducing significantly the influence and control over our economy exerted by the large banks and corporations

- Reducing significantly the power and privileges of the richest 10 percent of the population

Against this background, the following program for democratic reconstruction of the economy is proposed. This is a transitional program.

The public should be mobilized to support, and the powers of Congress should be used to promote, measures aiming:

- To relaunch the growth of private consumption over the next ten years by using federal manpower programs such as Roosevelt's Civilian Conservation Corps to reduce unemployment to a level of less than 2 percent; by raising the minimum wage immediately to $4.25 per hour; by initiating a policy of low interest rates comparable to that pursued during World War II; by restoring social programs cut under the Reagan administration; by instituting a tax on the richest

10 percent of the population in order to begin reducing inequalities at their source

- To move toward a rational, planned use of our national resources by constituting a new Temporary National Economic Committee to study the problems and implications of flagging growth and the appropriate short-term and long-term responses to it; by preparing a National Economic Convention of elected regional delegates to analyze the problems of democratic reconstruction and to make recommendations to the Congress for such reconstruction; by establishing a National Economic Planning Office under the authority and control of the Congress, charged with responsibility for determining national economic priorities in the use of all resources; by instituting a far-reaching industrial policy to reduce federal and state subsidies to the private sector, convert defense industries to civilian production, and ensure that all productive capacity will be used for supplying useful goods and services; by regulating plant closures; by expanding public enterprise in industries dominated by a few producers

- To limit the influence of speculation in domestic financial and commodities markets by placing the Federal Reserve under the authority of the Treasury; by much closer regulation of the banking and securities industries; by barring certain types of purely speculative financial activity

- To move toward a more rational and just use of federal resources; by ensuring competitive bidding in all government contracting, thereby saving 30 percent on procurement; by withdrawing U.S. forces from Western Europe, thereby saving more than $120 billion per year; by using low interest rate policies to reduce by at least half the $200 billion annual federal transfer to upper-income families; by reducing military expenditures by 10 to 15 percent; by expanding expenditures in required social programs

- To restore and extend the principle of equity in the federal tax system by restoring the principle of a truly progressive income tax; by increasing progressiveness so as to facilitate a significant transfer of income from the richest 10 percent to the poorest 25 percent of the population; by restoring the system of more limited depreciation allowances for large corporations; by restoring higher taxes for large corporations, to at least the levels prevailing in the 1950s

- To stabilize and to ensure equity in foreign trade, finance and immigration by seeking a new international system of trade and payments capable of ensuring an orderly and equitable development of world trade, credit, and investment; by using multilateral negotiations to ensure the fair and equitable development of world trade in the short run; by seeking international agreement for the regulation of financial markets; by returning to a more stable international system for fixing foreign exchange rates; by seeking international agreements

for the reasonable free movement and fair and equitable treatment
of immigrant workers

———

The economic debacle of the last fifteen years, and in particular
the economic and social havoc wrought by the Reagan administration,
clearly mean that we need far-reaching changes in the organization of
the economy and economic policy. In the present scheme of things,
priority is being given to the narrow interests of the very rich and the
large corporations rather than to the interests of the majority of our
people: the young, ordinary working Americans, farmers, the unskilled
and unemployed, the poor, the sick and disabled, our recent immigrants, and the victims of discrimination of various kinds.

Americans want to reclaim their future. There is no doubt they
would like to see democratic policies prevail over "market forces." The
incipient collapse of the American economy is not an abstract, academic
issue. The democratic reconstruction of the economy is a vital, practical necessity. To make that possible, we need to launch a debate on the
real economic alternatives before us.

This debate should, above all things, be informed by a respect
for basic human rights and democratic principles. It should deal with
fundamental issues which have been excluded from public debate for
too long—with results that are plain to see. It should not become a
wrangle about tinkering among academics, technocrats, and cunning
propagandists.

Stagnation and the U.S. Economic Crisis

The U.S. economy is on a dangerous course. The period since
1970 has been one of almost continuous decline, marked by falling
profits, falling rates of growth, rising unemployment, declining real
wages, increasing international competition, and, most recently, financial turmoil. There have been brief periods when this decline stopped,
or was arrested, when the pace of growth quickened or unemployment
fell. But the decline then resumed.

In retrospect, we can see that levels of economic activity have
been falling for fifteen years, that the country has been experiencing a
deepening economic stagnation.

The United States, of course, is not alone. If we are experiencing
an economic crisis, so are the countries of Western Europe, and indeed
all the countries closely linked to the North Atlantic basin, including
most of the third world. This worldwide crisis, however, is primarily a
crisis of the advanced capitalist system.

If economic stagnation is allowed to continue, the consequences will be very serious. A weak American economy already faces the prospect of a severe recession. If new policies are not found to stabilize the situation, the U.S. and Western Europe could push much of the world into a prolonged depression.

The idea that we face a grave risk of worldwide depression is not taken very seriously by our political leaders or by most economists. They have so far shown a tendency to deny the reality of the present crisis. They prefer to stress what is positive in the vain hope of bolstering confidence in the future.

The future is determined by what is happening in the economy and not by what people *think* is happening in the economy. Consider the recent collapse of world stock markets. Most economists in 1986 and 1987 believed that the rise in stock prices on world markets would continue indefinitely. They did not foresee the financial collapse that occurred in October 1987. In fact, they even denied that such a collapse was possible.

Yet the crash was predictable. It was the direct result of years of economic stagnation. When corporations and banks could not earn adequate profits in the "real economy," through the production of goods and services, they shifted capital increasingly into speculative financial activity. The decline of the "real economy," however, was weakening the entire financial structure. Corporations and banks found it harder to meet cash payments. Yet speculation required and was fed by growing debt, and debtors had to meet growing cash payments. The contradiction produced a far more serious crash than had occurred in 1929.

The consequences of the crash have yet to be felt, but they will be serious. To the problems of the "real economy" have been added the new problems of the financial sector. Their interaction can only further weaken the economy as a whole. Indeed, they open the prospect of increasing instability in the midst of decline.

Although there is no indication that governments anywhere know what to do about the current economic crisis, two main lines of policy are being suggested in many western countries. The first is "improving competitiveness." The second is severe deflation.

"Improving competitiveness" is being urged by many political leaders in the United States, even though there is no way that the U.S., which has been severely weakened by years of stagnation and declining real investment, can compete successfully against countries like West Germany, Japan, and South Korea. There is not going to be an export-led boom in the United States, and any advantage that the United States does gain in particular markets will be at the expense of its principal political and economic partners.

The second policy, of severe deflation, of sharply reducing expenditure, production, and employment, is being proposed in the United States by leading business figures, although very quietly, out of fear of eliciting public opposition. This policy will not eliminate the budget and trade deficits, as its proponents claim. It will only cause the same havoc it did in 1982 and 1983, when the Reagan administration adopted a deflationary "economic recovery program" that pushed the country into its worst postwar recession. In fact, setting in motion a severe deflation after the 1988 election is likely to plunge the world into a depression.

While the economic future seems bleak, the United States remains a well-endowed, technically progressive, and rich society which can provide work, a decent and rewarding life, and reasonable security for all who live in it.

Such a vision is clearly far from the possibilities seen by most statesmen and economists today.

Why?

The main reason is that most contemporary analysis makes it difficult, if not impossible, to understand the nature of the current crisis, and to appreciate its gravity. The world has changed profoundly in the last fifty years. And conventional economic analysis has not caught up with or grasped the changes which have taken place.

We have, in fact, no accepted theory of how a wealthy, technically progressive capitalist economy develops, and changes, over time.

Lacking an adequate understanding of what is happening to us, we flounder. And we shall continue to flounder, continue to live in crisis, so long as we fail to develop an objective analysis of our economic predicament.

This analysis seeks to sketch the essential nature of the central problem in the U.S. economy today, the problem of flagging economic growth.

The Deceleration of Economic Growth

In the immediate postwar period, economists applying the work of Keynes discovered a new, dynamic formulation of the Keynesian conditions for full development. This was, to put it simply, that the maintenance of full employment requires a continuous expansion of investment, preferably at a steady rate. This, of course, means that overall output must grow, especially consumption.

Since then, this rule of growth has been more or less taken for granted among economic theorists, despite efforts to conjure up an alternative, scholastic view (the neo-classical theory of growth). Corporations, too, seem to take it for granted. Growth is the first and main long-term objective of any small, medium-sized, or large corporation worth the name. Growth is the path to profits, and most importantly to expanding profits.

A market economy, then, even one stabilized and subsidized by the state, must grow fairly rapidly in order to ensure full employment, not to mention progress. It is worth underlining the fact that something like full employment is essential to social stability in a capitalist society.

It is hard to imagine a stable and democratic society in which there is continuous 20 percent unemployment.

The difficulty facing the United States today, as well as most other capitalist countries, is that economic growth has been steadily slowing down for more than fifteen years.

During the 1950s and the 1960s, the U.S. economy grew rapidly. In the 1950s, the growth rate of the GNP was 3.9 percent per year in real terms (that is, discounting the increase in the value of output resulting from inflation). In the 1960s, the growth rate accelerated slightly to 4.1 percent per year. This created unprecedented prosperity. It was possible to maintain something near full employment; jobs were plentiful, and many of them were in industries paying high wages. Continuous, although not uninterrupted, growth in the U.S. economy also meant a continually rising standard of living that was the envy of the world. Growth and prosperity in the postwar period therefore changed the conditions in which millions of U.S. citizens lived, carrying many out of poverty and to a new and easier life.

Things began to fall apart around 1970, despite the economic stimulus of the war in Indochina. That date may be said to mark the beginning of the economic stagnation which has now plunged the economy into crisis. Towards the end of the 1960s, the U.S. profit rate began to fall, especially in manufacturing industries. Investment and growth began to falter. The United States was losing the world economic leadership it had assumed at the end of World War II.

One of the first signs of this loss of leadership was President Nixon's August 1971 decision to cut the link between gold and the dollar. This was aimed at relieving pressures arising from our weakening balance of payments. Nixon's action, however, also put pressure on oil producers, who were paid in dollars. It thus contributed to the oil price rise imposed by OPEC in 1973-1974.

Then, in 1974-1975, the United States experienced the worst postwar recession it had known. Industrial production fell by some 15 percent, output fell, and unemployment shot up to a new postwar high—8.3 percent. In retrospect, it is clear that the basic causes of this recession, which provoked widespread alarm at the time, were the falling profits and slowing overall growth. The winding down of the war in Indochina may also have contributed to the slowing of growth. The oil crisis did not, as some believe, cause the recession of 1974-1975, but it did make it worse.

Recovery from that recession was slow, and unemployment remained high. It never again went below pre-recession levels. By 1979, the economy's rate of growth had fallen to 2.5 percent in real terms.

The net result of serious recession and slow growth during the 1970s was a marked shift downward in the trend of growth established in the previous two decades. The overall rate of growth for the 1970s was only 2.9 percent in real terms, 25 percent below the average rate of growth during the years of high prosperity.

Thus, in retrospect, we can see that economic stagnation, which is so obvious today, was already beginning in the early 1970s.

The year 1980, the last year of the Carter administration, saw a further deterioration of the economy. There was a short, sharp recession. Gross fixed investment fell by nearly 8 percent and unemployment rose again by more than 20 percent, to a level of 7 percent.

What was particularly alarming at the time was that inflation seemed to be getting out of control, in part the result of the second oil price rise. The rate of inflation in consumer prices had been steadily rising under Carter, but in 1980, it seemed that the economy was caught in a descending spiral of flagging profits and slower growth and investment, with the further, alarming possibility that we would see runaway inflation.

How the Reagan Administration Made Things Worse—and Why

It is doubtful that anyone in a position of power saw clearly what was happening to the economy at the time. There had been a continual deterioration in economic performance over more than a decade. This is the situation the Reagan administration found when it arrived in office at the beginning of 1981. Conservative economists had been studying the situation for some time, preparing an alternative to the Carter drift.

As Reagan's economists saw it, taking control required a radical break with the postwar consensus on social and economic policy, which, in their view, had clearly not worked. They considered the economy's deterioration to be a result of policy rather than of the uncontrolled development of market forces. A radical, conservative policy was needed.

The Reagan administration represented, and represents, the most conservative elements of property. The continuing deterioration of the economic situation threatened the interests of many. But it especially threatened the wealth of our ruling elite, as well as its capacity for expanding enterprise, which increases that wealth. To the arch-conservatives of the Reagan administration, the gathering economic crisis presented one problem that was more important than others. That problem was the decline of property income.

Property income consists of proprietors' income, the rental income of persons, and corporate profits. During the 1970s, the share of property income in total income fell gradually, from approximately 21 percent of national income at the beginning of that decade to 16.5 percent by 1980. Corporate profits, which account for well over half of property income, grew slowly in the early 1970s, recovered after the recession of 1974-1975, and started falling in 1979. But the rate of reported profits, the concept closest to corporate book profits, fell steadily from 1973. Worst of all, many sectors of manufacturing industry reported sharply falling profits after that year as well.

The "supply-side" solution had been debated and discussed for several years in conservative circles. In practical terms, this meant that the central objective of economic policy was to rebuild profits. The proclaimed purposes, of course, were the usual worthy ones: to bring inflation under control; to raise employment; and to relaunch economic growth. Dedication to these purposes was trumpeted noisily through every channel of communication.

These flourishes, however, were designed to turn our attention from the fact that the Reaganites were preparing the Great Raid on the poor, the working class, and the middle class.

The question was, how could profits be rebuilt in a declining economy?

If the economy was expanding slowly and the profits of the rich were declining, the only way to rebuild profits was through a direct attack on the incomes of others, in particular ordinary workers and the urban underclass. The solution for restoring "prosperity" was a radical redistribution of income. If economic expansion alone could not provide enough income for the wealthy, then other people would have to be made to do so.

The Reagan administration tried to use all the instruments of policy to redistribute income in favor of the wealthy, and to create new profit opportunities. For the most part, the burden of slowing growth, of crisis, was to be shifted from property owners to ordinary working people. The respective burdens, of course, were of very different sorts.

In order to achieve a significant redistribution of income in a short time, the new economic strategy aimed to: reduce taxes, especially for the wealthy; attack trade unions rights; raise unemployment; increase part-time and short-time work; reduce or hold down wages; force down the purchasing power of households; cut social expenditures; increase military expenditures; shift activity from the public to the private sector of the economy; deregulate the economy.

Adoption of such aggressive strategies by the administration—taking a harsh stance against trade unions, full employment, high wages, and social services—created an atmosphere in which the victims were put on the defensive. Corporations were free, indeed encouraged, to go about their cutting and chopping.

The strategy was thus broad and quite coherent. It completely rejected the idea of the welfare state and instead returned to *le capitalisme sauvage.* As such, it involved a closer coordination of actions on the part of the government and the major corporations. The policy was launched as a national policy, with all the fanfare of a colonial war, which in a sense it was. The results have made painful history.

The point, however, is not to recount the horrors of the last seven years. The question at issue here is whether the "supply side" strategy adopted in 1981 succeeded. The answer is both "yes" and "no."

There is no doubt that, in short-run terms, the administration's policy of redistributing income in favor of the wealthy was partially successful. The share of property income has been pushed up slightly, though it is still far from the 1970 figure of 20.8 percent. But after falling to 15.4 percent during 1983, it rose to nearly 17 percent in 1985, the last year for which figures are available.

Corporate profits have fared less well. They fell by 30 percent from the 1980 level of $202.7 billion during the 1982-1983 recession. They moved up gradually after that. In 1984, they stood at $204.7 billion. They fell again slightly in 1985 to $191.3 billion, in current dollars. Corporate profits, without inventory valuation or capital consumption adjustments, were more or less stagnant throughout the Reagan years.

The best the Reagan administration could do was to hold the line, or perhaps achieve some small short-term improvement for property owners. Considering the radical cuts in other incomes achieved under the "supply-side" strategy, even this short-term result is less than impressive. Furthermore, these results indicate that the deflationary forces at work in the economy must be very strong. If this is the best that can be done through severe cuts, the pressures undermining property income must be considerable.

If we take a more long-term view, it is clear that the Reagan administration's economic strategy was a complete failure for two reasons. First, the "supply-side" strategy did not really confront the long-run problem of failing growth, which was and remains the central problem of the U.S. economy. Raising profits in the short run was no solution at all to this problem, as recent history attests. Second, the administration's policy was actually counterproductive. The way it raised profits undermined the expansion of demand.

The growth of the economy in 1981 was already slowing. Growth had been 0.2 percent in 1980, and the recovery from that brief recession was slow. The Reagan administration then reduced demand at every possible opportunity. During the recession of 1982-1983, output fell more sharply than it had in a generation and unemployment rose to unprecedented levels once again. During 1982 and 1983, unemployment rose to 9.5 percent and stayed there. It fell only slowly afterwards. Many states had double-digit unemployment. The industrial basin of the Midwest, already in crisis, was devastated. Growth after the recession was not strong. Industrial production at the end of 1983 was only slightly higher than it had been at the beginning of 1981. It moved up quite slowly from early 1984. Unemployment remained high.

Overall, the rate of growth of the economy fell sharply during the first five years of this decade. In the 1970s, it had been 2.9 percent in real terms. Between 1980 and 1984, in part because of the actions of the Reagan administration, it was only 1.8 percent. This represented a further deceleration, a deepening of economic stagnation. The economy was steadily losing the momentum required to maintain full employment and prosperity.

To measure the gravity of the situation, it may be recalled that the real rate of growth of the U.S. economy during the 1930s was 1.5 percent.

The final consequences of Reaganomics are well known: rising unemployment, falling wages in many industries, a shift to low-wage employment, falling purchasing power, and reduced transfer payments. These all had a further deflationary impact on the economy and held back growth, the worst thing that could have been done in the long run.

The Need for a Democratic Reconstruction of the Economy

The present economic crisis is not the result of bad decisions or fortuitous events, and it is not the fault of any particular group. It is rather the result of a breakdown of the postwar system of economic organization, in which the private sector grew through the stimulation and development of mass consumption. The essential problem of the U.S. economy today is that the possibilities of rapid growth in the leading sectors which sustained prosperity after the war have been exhausted. Rapid growth based on automobiles, consumer durables, and residential construction, etc., is no longer possible because these sectors are nearly saturated. No new leading sectors have been developed to take their place.

The corporations' postwar growth strategy has reached a dead end. It can no longer force the expansion of consumer demand as it did in the past because human wants cannot be infinitely extended at high levels of income. And much—but by no means all—of our population enjoys historically high levels of income.

Expanding personal consumption, not investment, was the driving force of postwar growth and prosperity, and we have reached a consumption limit. This means that the slowdown of growth, which is the root cause of our economic problems, is the result of institutional failure, of the breakdown of the postwar system of economic organization.

We must now look for an entirely new strategy of economic development: a strategy for the democratic reconstruction of the economy. This strategy has two objectives: relaunching private sector growth over the short and medium term; developing the economy through expansion and rationalization of public-sector activity over the long term.

The first objective can be reached by a significant redistribution of income in favor of the poorer sectors of the population. These sectors have largely unmet needs and wants. Providing them with purchasing power will fuel traditional growth for some years. However, when these sectors of the population also rise well above the poverty level, they will begin to save large amounts, as middle- and upper-income groups already do. These savings will constitute a drag on growth, and the problem we are experiencing today will recur.

In the long term, therefore, the United States cannot rely on expansion of private consumption to maintain full employment and the welfare state, a conclusion with far-reaching implications. In the future, there will be no alternative to relying on expansion of public sector activity in order to preserve anything like a democratic and civilized society.

The platform proposals offered above are meant to sketch a new strategy for confronting the real issues posed by the gradual breakdown of the postwar system. It is "democratic" because it calls for a far-reaching reduction of inequality, and it deals with "reconstruction" because it faces up to the need for far-reaching institutional change.

These proposals will be bitterly resisted by vested interests, as will any program that calls into question that modern system of sophisticated depredation which masquerades as "free enterprise." Antidemocratic elements among the wealthy, the managers of large corporations, and their academic satraps and tele-spokespeople will lash out even at the idea of a democratic reconstruction of the economy. Power will mobilize to maintain things as they are, however inequitable or disastrous the economic situation of most citizens.

The only hope of realizing such a program, therefore, the only hope of changing and democratizing an economy cracking under the weight of its contradictions, lies in mobilizing the people in support of change. This will require a broad new political coalition composed of groups and classes already seeking these and similar goals, a coalition of those who have suffered and who continue to suffer under the sway of the new "know-nothingism" paid for and launched by vested interests.

Resources

Recommended Appointees for a New Administration

- Gar Alperovitz, President of the Washington, DC National Center for Economic Alternatives and co-author of *Rebuilding America*
- Barry Bluestone, professor of economics at the University of Massachusetts-Boston and co-author of *The Deindustrialization of America*
- Samuel Bowles, professor of economics at the University of Massachusetts-Amherst and co-author of *Beyond the Wasteland*
- Robert Browne, former member of the Board of the African Development Bank and now Staff Director of the Subcommittee on International Development Institutions of the House Committee on Banking, Finance, and Urban Affairs

- Carol O'Cleireacain is chief economist of District 37, American Federation of State, County, and Municipal Employees and former advisor to Governor Mario Cuomo

- Jeff Faux, President of the Economic Policy Institute, Washington, DC and co-author of *Rebuilding America*

- Jamie Galbraith, former Executive Director of the Joint Economic Committee and now Associate Professor at the Lyndon B. Johnson School of Public Affairs at the University of Texas at Austin

- Donald Harris, professor of economics at Stanford University and author of *Capital Accumulation and Income Distribution*

- Bennett T. Harrison, professor of political economy and planning at the Massachusetts Institute of Technology and co-author of *The Deindustrialization of America*

- Arthur MacEwan, professor of economics at the University of Massachusetts-Boston

- Michael Tanzer, President of Tanzer Economic Associates and author of *The Political Economy of International Oil in the Underdeveloped Countries* and *The Race for Resources*

- Howard Wachtel, professor of economics at American University and author of *The Money Mandarins*

Organizations

- Union for Radical Political Economics, 155 W. 23rd St., New York, NY 10011; (212) 691-5722

- Economic Policy Institute, 1730 Rhode Island Ave. NW, Washington, DC 20036; (202) 775-8810

- Center on Budget and Policy Priorities, 236 Massachusetts Ave. NW, Washington, DC 20002; (202) 544-0591

- Council on International and Public Affairs, 777 United Nations Place, New York, NY 10017; (212) 972-9877

Further Reading

- Barry Bluestone and Bennett Harrison, *The Deindustrialization of America*, Basic Books, 1982.

- Barry Bluestone and Bennett Harrison, "The Great American Job Machine: the Proliferation of Low-Wage Employment in the U.S. Economy," Study prepared for the Joint Economic Committee, 1986.

- Samuel Bowles and Herbert Gintis, *Democracy and Capitalism*, Basic Books, 1986.

- U.S. Department of Commerce, *Survey of Current Business*, monthly.

- Council of Economic Advisors, *The Economic Report of the President*, annual.

- Christopher Freeman, John Clark, and Luc Soete, *Unemployment and Technical Innovation*, Frances Pinter, 1982.
- John Kenneth Galbraith, *The Affluent Society*, Houghton Mifflin, 1958.
- John Kenneth Galbraith, *The New Industrial State*, Houghton Mifflin, 1967.
- Donald Harris, "Structural Change and Economic Growth: a Review Article," *Contributions to Political Economy*, 1982.
- International Labor Office, *World Labor Report*, Vol. 1, 1984.
- John Maynard Keynes, "The Economic Possibilities for Our Grandchildren" in *Essays in Persuasion*, MacMillan, 1931.
- Angus Maddison, "Growth and Slowdown in Advanced Capitalist Countries," *Journal of Economic Literature*, 1987.
- Angus Maddison, *The Phases of Capitalist Development*, Oxford, 1982.
- Harry Magdoff and Paul Sweezy, *Stagnation and the Financial Explosion*, Monthly Review Press, 1987.
- Stephen Marris, *Deficits and the Dollar: the World Economy at Risk*, Institute for International Economics, 1985.
- Hyman Minsky, *John Maynard Keynes*, Columbia University Press, 1975.
- Organization for Economic Co-operation and Development, *The Economic Outlook*, semi-annual.
- Luigi L. Pasinetti, *Structural Change and Economic Growth*, Cambridge University Press, 1981.
- Pascal Petit, *Slow Growth and the Service Economy*, Frances Pinter, 1982.
- Susan Strange, *Casino Capitalism*, Basil Blackwell, 1986.
- Howard Wachtel, *The Money Mandarins*, Pantheon, 1986.

Sean Gervasi is a Visiting Fellow at the Institute for Policy Studies. He is Professor of Economics (on leave) at the University of Paris VIII. He has taught economics at the London School of Economics, Oxford University, and the City University of New York, and is presently completing a book titled *American Capitalism and the Limits of Growth*.

Carol A. MacLennan

Rebuilding the Esprit of Government

Platform

- Reestablish a spirit of public service in the federal workforce that encourages political independence and professional integrity, enhances the rights of federal employees, and integrates the demand for citizen participation in public programs.
- Restore the civil service to a position independent from ideological and political control by the president through creation of an independent policymaking commission that reports directly to Congress.
- Strengthen federal unions and employee organizations through expansion of bargaining rights and closed shops in agencies that choose union representation.
- Respect the political rights of federal workers through repeal of the Hatch Act.
- Establish a participative management policy that encourages worker participation in management of federal government policies.
- Legislate a comprehensive family-policy act for federal workers that serves as a model for U.S. employers, based upon proven programs in job-sharing, flexible work schedules, on-site childcare, and family leave.
- Establish worker-citizen councils in each major policy field to serve as a source of policy innovation, scrutiny of public programs, and exchange between federal workers and citizens.

Since the Nixon administration, an attitude that denigrates public service has captured the nation. Presidents, citizens, even federal workers themselves have devalued the work and accomplishments of the civil service. This impedes the success of any public program, no matter how brilliant or imaginative. The capability and morale of the federal workforce is a critical factor in creating a responsive and responsible government. If presidents, managers, and lawmakers conspire against the workforce either through public ridicule, political harassment, or legislative initiatives, employees are demoralized and the whole nation suffers.

Harassment of the civil service reached its peak in the Reagan administration. This is not surprising in an administration that suddenly fired 11,000 air traffic controllers in order to break their union. Federal workers, who are directly controlled by the White House, are an easy target for anti-union politicians. Harassment has occurred primarily through administrative means such as reductions-in-force, reassignments, political appointment of managers hostile to agency missions, contracting out of government services, backlogs in grievance and arbitration proceedings, threatening union leaders with Hatch Act violations, and other tactics. Some of these actions are directly attributable to policies designed by the Reagan administration, but much of the impetus for these policies originates from legislation and long-term policies rooted in the belief that the problems of government can best be solved through increased management control of the workforce. Economy, efficiency, and top down control of workers are considered solutions to problems that are actually about the national economy and the inaccessibility of government.

Pushing for efficiency and accountability in government through increased hierarchy, division of labor, and punitive, divisive tactics against federal workers is misguided at best and destructive of the public trust at worst. Innovative public sector management is necessary to correct this fundamental problem that plagues our public agencies. Steps taken in three broad areas can reverse this trend and encourage development of an intellectually healthy, responsive, creative, and accountable workforce.

- Enact civil service legislation that reverses the direction of the 1978 Civil Service Reform Act (CSRA) in two areas: remove civil service policies from direct presidential control; strengthen the bargaining rights and organizational opportunities of federal employee unions.

- Develop innovative policies that enhance work life and worker creativity through: commitment to participative management in decisions involving the organization of work and personnel policies; a family-based personnel program that establishes innovative policies for leave, job-sharing, education, and childcare.

- Establish worker-citizen councils in each agency for major policy areas that ensure public deliberation and exchange between federal employees and citizens and that make policy recommendations.

Passed in 1978, the Civil Service Reform Act is a misguided effort to achieve more public accountability. It replaced the Civil Service Commission (an independent policymaking body) with the Office of Personnel Management (OPM), whose director reports directly to the White House. This makes presidential and political manipulation of civil servants easy, with no check against irresponsible and ideologically-oriented actions. Since 1981, disruption, inefficiency, and low morale have been the products of this reform. Presidential control has been erroneously equated with public accountability. As several prominent figures in public administration have pointed out, presidential control of the workforce leads to increased politicization of federal work.

The remedy is a return to a commission form of civil service management. Tenure on a commission would be fixed, subject to appointment by Congress, not the president. This expands the role of Congress in federal personnel policy beyond current oversight and legislative functions and reduces presidential appointment powers. A commission would retain an independence that encourages professional rather than political management of federal employees. Public concerns about unresponsive bureaucracies (which were at the heart of civil service reform in 1978) should be dealt with directly as an issue of citizen access to government decisions and power rather than as a problem with federal employees.

Independence and professional integrity in the civil service can also be enhanced through recognition of bargaining and political rights of federal workers. The CSRA legalized federal employees' right to organize unions. But it simultaneously set the stage for weakened federal unions by mandating an open shop and including a strong management rights clause that left little room for union bargaining. In this respect, the CSRA does neither the public nor employees much good. Similarly, the Hatch Act restricts the political activities of federal workers, creating a large sector of politically disenfranchised workers. Federal workers must be accorded the same employment and political rights as other U.S. citizens.

Two legislative initiatives can correct this problem: repealing the Hatch Act and weakening the management rights clause in Title VII of the CSRA.

Fears of creating a national political machine led to creation of the Hatch Act in 1939. These fears have existed throughout the history of civil service policy and have legitimacy in two respects: first, a concern that federal workers may use their employment for political purposes, thus violating the national trust in the impartiality of the law; and second, probably more relevant for our times, worry over the vulnerability of the civil service to political coercion from the top. The Hatch Act prohibits federal employees from taking an active part in partisan political campaigns. It is unduly expansive in its prohibitions and has intimidated federal employees into believing they have no political rights short of voting. There is currently a movement in Congress to amend the Hatch Act and relax some of its political restrictions.

The important issue is whether or not the Act is in fact protecting the career service from political manipulation. Experience with both the Nixon and Reagan administrations illustrates that manipulation of civil service occurs despite the Hatch Act, through manipulation of personnel policies and appointment of individuals in non-career positions within agencies. While the Act may discourage politicization of the workforce, it does not necessarily prevent it. Solutions to this problem lie in measures that remove presidential control over personnel policy, placing it back in the hands of Congress. Specific steps must be taken to limit presidential appointment powers in positions below the top levels (what are often called Schedule C positions). In addition, abuse of government employment for political purposes can be addressed more directly through personnel rules rather than through expansive legislation that discourages political participation.

Recognition of the role of employee organizations and bargaining rights is also important to a healthy civil service. Too often, public sector unions are viewed as a hazard to the public interest. In fact, they can act as a healthy check on political abuse and as a channel for reform of archaic personnel policies.

The CSRA provides only limited support for the bargaining rights of federal employees. It includes an open shop policy and limits employee input to consultation. The open shop policy has created a weak union system that is designed to fail. Unions that win representation in an agency are required to represent all workers in the bargaining unit, but workers do not have to join the union. Financially weak, these locals are in no position to mount a strong campaign to protect employee rights or even to adequately handle grievances and arbitration. A closed shop system is necessary to adequately protect employee rights and strengthen unions.

In addition, union bargaining rights are seriously limited by the management rights clause in Title VII of the CSRA. Negotiations over work organization, personnel rules, budgets, and wages are not allowed. Unions can bargain over procedures for implementing new policies that may have an adverse effect on federal workers. Within strict limitations, unions can also negotiate with management over grievance and arbitration rights. Any items not covered by already published personnel rules (which are extensive and excessively detailed) are also negotiable. Further, federal workers are prohibited from striking. These restrictions confuse the public interest with strict limitations on the rights of federal workers. While agency budgets are considered the domain of Congress, a matter of public deliberation, the organization of work and personnel rules that affect individuals' lives are not.

Unions have a legitimate role in the workplace. To deny them strength is to deny the integrity of the workers themselves. Strong unions, through collective bargaining and a role in participative management, can help improve rather than hinder agency work. Public sector unions have a purpose beyond the protection of employment rights. They can help implement a more open management system in the federal workplace.

It is widely understood that top-down management stifles creativity and innovative problem-solving. The federal sector requires professional, creative, and innovative individuals with good problem-solving and interdisciplinary skills. Work in federal agencies is accomplished by groups or teams (rather than individuals) of multi-skilled and interdisciplinary employees. Cooperation, rather than competition, among workers is essential. The recent increased emphasis on managerial control has made the federal workplace unpleasant for many of the types of employees most needed to make agency programs work. Merit-pay systems and performance appraisals which stress competition among federal workers, rewarding and punishing them as individuals rather than as part of a team, have increased the frustration. These types of policies must be eliminated from personnel practice.

Participative management policies would greatly improve morale among federal workers and allow for innovative solutions to chronic organizational problems. Pilot programs, such as those attempted in the Department of Commerce during the Carter administration, could test different strategies for democratic decisionmaking in the federal sector. Contrary to some fears, a more democratic approach to federal work will not threaten public accountability or usurp the power of Congress to set agency budgets or of political appointees to set broad policy goals. Participative management would simplify organizational structure, flatten rigid hierarchies, and hold managers and workers accountable to one another. Because political circumstances and public debate can easily thwart even the best planned program, and decisionmaking is subject to public review, work in the federal government requires flexibility and a strong sense of professional judgment. Rigid organizational practices are unworkable in this type of environment and may be a cause of policy failures in the federal system. For instance, in regulatory agencies such as the EPA, where policy decisions rely on professional judgments of scientists and where science itself has become highly politicized, less rigid and more participative organizational structures encourage open scientific debate. This is essential in fields such as environmental and cancer policy where scientific uncertainty is inevitable, making independent professional judgment crucial for policy decisions.

Participative management systems would also enhance the quality of work life. Reforms like flexible work arrangements that accommodate both the personal and professional needs of employees are needed. Some scattered attempts have been made to introduce flexible work schedules into federal agencies, and parental leave legislation for the civil service is pending, but a piecemeal process will not achieve what is most important to all federal workers: a comprehensive program that recognizes the need for individual professional growth as well as

the varied demands on employees to meet family responsibilities. Innovative personnel rules for job-sharing, leave, childcare, and flexible
work hours are essential to good management. Educational opportunities for lower-graded employees (women and minorities comprise
the bulk of the lower grade levels) to retrain and become professional
workers will improve the work environment as well.

In summary, a cadre of federal workers dedicated to the public
interest will emerge only when the civil service becomes a work environment that encourages innovation, participation, and creativity; that
stresses the importance of independent professional judgment; that
creates a flexible work situation allowing for both individual development and family commitments.

Currently, federal agencies are held accountable to the public
through various reporting requirements, information policies, and administrative rules. Laws such as the Administrative Procedures Act, the
Freedom of Information Act, and the Advisory Committee Act ensure
citizen access to agency decisionmaking. These laws are a foundation,
but they are not enough. Other avenues of public access and input
must be opened. Citizen participation can flourish only if citizens are
actively engaged in identifying problems for public policies to address
and in designing strategies to implement these policies. Current laws
may provide citizens with information and allow comment during the
final stages of decisionmaking, but they also keep citizens on the fringe
of government and continue to insulate federal bureaucracies from the
public. How can we solve this problem?

One important area needing attention is the isolation of federal
workers from citizen perspectives on policy and implementation
problems. In many agencies, federal workers are aware of citizen attitudes and concerns primarily through second-hand information.
Research which investigates new questions or attempts to provide in-
sights into old social problems is very limited and usually contracted
out to profit-making research firms. Professional federal workers are
vital to the information-gathering necessary for policy formation, yet
they are seriously alienated from the public. Generally attuned to the
viewpoints of the noisier interests in their policy fields (often the same
lobbying groups that influence Congress), federal workers hear little
from local communities, ordinary workers in the private sector, and
minority groups. This can be corrected to some extent by involving
federal workers in social research rather than contracting it out, involving workers in implementing federal programs (also too often contracted out), and initiating agency hearings in local communities on
major policy decisions (something rarely done).

More important would be instituting worker-citizen advisory
councils throughout the federal system. Their purpose would be to
allow citizens and federal workers to study, discuss, and recommend
policy alternatives in major areas of concern to each agency. The Administrative Procedures Act provides formal access to agency decisions

well after they have been formulated internally. Worker-citizen councils would provide opportunities for public debate during the earlier stages. Some might argue that this opens bureaucracies to more political pressure and compromises the independence of the civil service. However, it is more likely that citizen insight and experience will aid federal workers and provide an alternative perspective to established lobbies. In addition, citizens are unaware of the policy process, and local community leaders would benefit through involvement on these councils. One successful effort that brought Department of Agriculture meat inspectors together with citizen groups has had an important effect on new inspection procedures in the meat industry. Interestingly, the American Federation of Government Employees bargaining unit in the USDA played a major role in this alliance.

Worker-citizen advisory councils should be funded to conduct local public hearings and empowered to gather and publicize information through reports to Congress and the agency. Councils might be organized to address major policy areas (e.g., automotive safety) or to handle short-term implementation problems (e.g., methods for achieving the best community outreach strategy for AIDS). Congress, through its oversight function and use of the General Accounting Office, often identifies major problems in agency programs. Citizens and federal workers knowledgeable about the shortcomings of many federal programs could play an advisory role in developing solutions. Currently, decisions are made and advice given without the benefit of worker or citizen insight. This is a cost of top-down management and elaborate hierarchies that we cannot afford.

Citizen participation is a top priority for government reform. A strengthened federal union movement and programs that institutionalize citizen-worker collaboration in solving tough policy problems can make major strides in this direction.

Resources

Recommended Appointees for a New Adminstration

- Robert G. Vaughn, Professor of Law, American University, has written extensively on civil service law and open government policies.

- Representative Patricia Schroeder (D-CO), as chair of the House Subcommittee on the Civil Service, is active on Hatch Act reform and family-oriented work policies.

- Michael Maccoby, Director, Project on Technology, Work, and Character, has consulted extensively on work organization reform with private industry and the federal government.

- Kenneth Blaylock, National President, American Federation of Government Employees (a progressive public-sector union), has detailed ideas for civil service reform.

Organizations

- Federal Government Services Task Force, House Annex 2, Room H-2301, Washington, DC 20515-6822; (202) 226-2494
- Project on Work, Technology, and Character, 1636 Connecticut Ave. NW, Washington, DC 20009; (202) 462-3003
- Government Accountability Project, 25 E St. NW, Suite 700, Washington, DC 20001; (202) 347-0460
- American Federation of Government Employees, 80 F St. NW, Washington, DC 20001; (202) 737-8700
- National Treasury Employees Union, 1730 K St. NW, Suite 1100, Washington, DC 20006; (202) 785-4411
- Coalition of Labor Union Women, 15 Union Sq., New York, NY 10003; (212) 242-0700

Further Reading

- Patricia Ingraham and Carolyn Ban, eds., *Legislating Bureaucratic Change: The Civil Service Reform Act of 1978*, State University of New York Press, 1984.
- "Proposed Federal Employees' Political Activities Legislation," *Congressional Digest*, Vol. 67, No. 1, Congressional Digest Corporation, January 1988.
- Michael Maccoby, *Why Work: Leading the New Generation*, Simon and Schuster, 1988.
- Carol MacLennan, "The Democratic Administration of Government," in Marc V. Levine *et al.*, *The State and Democracy: Revitalizing America's Government*, Routledge & Kegan Paul, 1988.

Carol A. MacLennan is an Associate Professor of Anthropology in the Science, Technology, and Society Program at Michigan Technological University. She was a civil servant in the Department of Transportation during the Carter and Reagan administrations and was active as a local officer in the American Federation of Government Employees. She is co-author of *The State and Democracy: Revitalizing America's Government* and has published articles on the automotive industry, health and safety regulation, and government administration.

William B. Cannon

A Constitutional and Strong Presidency*

Platform

The president of the United States is the central character in catalyzing our nation to the identification and resolution of our common public problems. The president's task is that of preparing a workable program which can be carried out in the nation within the context of our laws and the Constitution.

- That task requires that the president see far, and know that the common good for the nation is yielded by protecting the rights of the people, and by creating and sustaining programs which assume that citizenship includes economic, educational, social, political, cultural, and participatory rights and opportunities.

- The president must take care that the common defense is understood in its broadest meaning, namely: to assure peace for the American people; to establish and strengthen international institutions to serve peace.

- The president must recognize both the centrality of Congress and the need to increase citizen participation in the governing process.

- The president, while recognizing the importance of foreign policy, must be aware that intended social reconstruction is necessary and that task requires clearly defined budgetary priorities.

---

* Marcus Raskin contributed to parts of this article, and participated in its formulation.

High levels of citizen participation and a strong executive are mutually reinforcing political phenomena. We may be coming into a period of great political change; to the end of a political era and culture which have been characterized by a weak and ignoble executive, a dominant but turbulent Congress responsive to special interests, a Supreme Court with a rigid commitment to a corporate market economy and erratic in its positions on equality and liberty. The key to change can be the presidency, not just through turnover of office, but through restoring the office to its constitutional position of independent national leadership, rather than maintaining it simply as a glamorous (or unglamorous) chairmanship of a Joint Governmental Powers Committee.

The great constitutional scholar Edward Corwin pointed out that the "Constitution reflects the struggle between two conceptions of executive power: that it ought always to be subordinate to the supreme legislative power, and that it ought to be, within generous limits, autonomous and self-directing: or, in other terms, the idea that the people are represented in the legislature versus the idea that they are embodied in the executive."

There is a third view, based on the experience of post-World War II history. The presidency has motivated the increased possibility of representation for those hitherto unrepresented or underrepresented. It would be a mistake to believe that modern civil rights legislation would have emerged from Congress without leadership by a president. The 1950s and 1960s civil rights legislation was a direct outgrowth of presidential sensitivity to massive public demonstrations and involvement, subsequently legitimated through the judiciary. So it is the case with other pieces of social legislation spearheaded through Congress by executive involvement. Comprehensive education acts, the idea of maximum feasible participation of the poor, and women's rights legislation were all mechanisms to increase participation in the democratic process beyond those offered by a Congress which, until recently, has been dominated by a rotten-borough system of one-party districts, the blandishments of lobbying funds, and a supine willingness to accept those aspects of executive power which asserted "expansionist responsibility" in the national security realm, thus satisfying defense contractors and others who benefited from the Cold War expansionist stance.

Because of the quality and character of recent American presidents, it is conventional wisdom to distrust the executive branch of government. Indeed, the Vietnam War fortified that view; it was common currency to call that quagmire "Johnson's war," thus exculpating Congress's responsibility. But the actual workings of the separation of powers between Congress and the president are simple neither in conception nor in execution. In many cases, powerful chairs of congressional committees have had far more influence on government departments than did their respective cabinet secretaries. This usually occurs during periods of weak presidential leadership, where the agenda is set by lobbies and Congress. Such was the case, for example, under Carter, Ford, and Eisenhower and Reagan in their last six years of office.

But a cursory analysis of American history suggests that the presidency can play a central role in fulfilling those great purposes of the people as outlined in the Constitution's preamble. He or she can catalyze the government in fulfilling the rights of citizenship as guaranteed in the Constitution. One should not forget that the fundamental outcome of the Civil War, the end of slavery, was effected through the actions of a federal government whose entire character, purpose, and role changed with the leadership of President Lincoln. Mass action and presidential leadership came together to form the basis for a new kind of responsive federal government seeking to fulfill the constitutional mandate of equality, social freedom, and justice. In times of crisis, Congress turns to a strong president precisely because Congress speaks with so many local voices. It was for this reason that, at the beginning of the New Deal, through national emergency legislation, Congress ceded enormous powers to the president in order to stabilize the economy. Indeed, the labor movement in the United States was given much of its impetus through a strong president who recognized its importance.

The genius of the American system of government, when it is allowed to work, is that where any particular branch slackens its commitment to meet popular needs, an alert citizenry can use one of the other branches to be heard, and positive change can occur. At this juncture in American history, the president, if committed to equity, dignity, disarmament, and the reallocation of our national priorities, can work with the citizenry to bring about change toward a constitutional democracy, using democratic procedures. The Franklin Roosevelt presidency, for example, was predicated on obvious, felt, popular needs during its first two terms. The same needs exist today. While much can be done at the grassroots level, it is clear that presidential authority (as well as congressional legislation) will have to be invoked to end the arms race, control and redirect capital, stop the decay of our cities and our industries, and the deskilling of our youth. All branches of government are required to actively reach out to the citizenry so that the formal government remains in touch with the citizenry as a whole, using and applying its talents for the common good.

Every Republican president—whether an Eisenhower, Nixon, Ford, or Reagan—has been a weak president in this constitutional and responsive sense, reflecting the history, tradition, and permanent structure of the Republican Party and its belief in the desirability of legislative supremacy. Of course, an individual president can appear strong, and in a television era it is understandable that appearances may substitute for reality. The Democratic Party structure and tradition is conversely that of a strong presidency, although in fact a weak president may not be able to make the structure function. A strong presidency (such as the one FDR created), which gives priority to increased participation on the part of the oppressed groups, is historically the only one which can resist the pull of Congress toward using the government primarily for the benefit of the middle and upper classes. The consequences of congressional dominance in domestic affairs and a weak presidency governed by reactionary myths and imperial hubris have been severe and harmful since they began following World War II: two violent military conflicts; McCarthyism, which permanently crippled political thought and action; oppression of the poor, and political domination by the middle class in an American political life increasingly organized on a class basis; and above all, the weakening of the presidency—the essential element of the American constitutional arrangement—exemplified by Congress's destruction of the Carter administration's capacity to govern after only one term in office.

The era of congressional dominance has been characterized by certain major policies and approaches.

Uncoordinated and at times chaotic national economic policy and programs have led to periods of massively high unemployment, extraordinary inflation, and low productivity, alternating with periods of selectively impacting prosperity which insulate the middle and upper class from excessive damage while penalizing the rest of the nation.

Excessive defense spending has been characteristic of every government since World War II (with the exception of parts of the Nixon and Carter administrations). Contrary to popular wisdom, it is impossible for Congress to keep defense spending down, because of the belief that defense spending regulates the economy, because of Congress's need to dispense patronage, and because of its position on foreign affairs, which leaves it free, if the executive is not strong, for all kinds of expensive and harmful military adventures. Inequalities in public defense service, such as the Vietnam draft and the present volunteer service, abound in eras of congressional dominance. The executive, beleaguered by a bellicose Congress, has resorted to extraordinary measures, such as Truman's impounding of funds which Congress had voted for an excessive number of Air Force Groups (an action which Congress subsequently made illegal under the 1972 Impoundment Act). Budgets have been unbalanced and Congress has controlled them. The Reagan administration shows the lowest income-to-expenditures ratio of any administration for the past thirty years. This is the mark of a weak administration and a weak president, since deficits primarily fund defense spending and class patronage, rather than economic management and justice, social harmony, morale, or improvement.

Congressional legislation on the budget during the 1970s and 1980s reflected the weakness of the executive. Various pieces of legislation which controlled presidential appropriation acts (probably in conflict with constitutional provisions for presidential execution of the law) have established a new congressional budget process, new congressional committees and bureaucratic staff, and a trend away from a fifty-year policy of the executive branch budgeting in a way that transcends narrow interests. The institution of a congressional budget is a notorious practice which conceals Congress's accountability for its main function—substantive programming—which means legislating on a total basis and not simply on a financial one.

Taxes have been reduced and made more regressive. Eras of congressional dominance are marked by a diminished and deformed tax base. The erosion results directly from pressure from well-to-do constituents, and from members of Congress themselves, to increase their disposable income. It should be noted that the Congress went even further than the executive in gutting progressivity. Debt has been excessive. The enormous growth of the national debt over the past twenty years is a clear mark of a weak executive; a strong executive concerned with the common good would never permit the permanent national interest, including that of the future, to be so mortgaged, nor would such an executive accept the false depreciation of the debt burden, i.e., expressing it as a proportion of some economic measure and potential such as GNP or historical economic trends. Excessive debt is a clear mark of an undisciplined government, and an undisciplined government is particularly harmful to the poor and disadvantaged. On the other hand, it is favorable to investors and borrowers, both in general and as a means of reducing the costs of government to such buyers of government debt.

Unnecessary subsidies have been given to the middle class. Distorted congressional representation inevitably leads Congress to provide unnecessary subsidies for its most powerful constituencies. An executive infused with the strength of wide-ranging grassroots participation, on the other hand, is far better able to represent all classes. Social Security and health care programs, financed through regressive taxation and in the absence of a sufficient means test, disproportionately benefit the middle class. Poor people have been disregarded and saddled with junk programs in the name of "welfare reform." We have run through the Nixon-Moynihan Family Assistance Plan, the Carter-Califano Program for Better Jobs and Income, Stockman abolitionism, and now another Moynihan children's crusade is wandering through the Congress. Welfare reform has been a code word for the congressional effort to regulate the poor, using the bureaucratic apparatus as social control policy. Funds, too, have been cut as the history of reducing support for Aid to Families with Dependent Children over the past seven years proves. Pending and earlier welfare reform programs have been give-and-take programs; on the net, either the poor have lost out absolutely, or increased inputs to them were financed off the backs of the poor themselves through patronage work programs, making the poor twice as unblessed, having already financed (by taxes) government programs disproportionately to the benefits they receive. Congressional programs often have a confused objective, too often meant to assuage middle-class guilt rather than resolve the intended problem.

Public service jobs programs, negative income tax, and tax credit programs are another sign of congressional government at work. They are usually actualized as patronage handouts, or as pressure release valves for minorities. The aim, like so much of congressional action, is to appear to be doing something for the poor, but in a way that will not cost the middle class, usually by having the poor themselves finance the program costs, through work and concealed taxation. Public service work has been and still is the special favorite, despite its high cost and low cost/benefit ratios, because it puts more patronage into congressional and local political hands. Only in periods of a strong executive has congressional disregard been pushed aside, as during the brief heyday of the Great Society.

Attack on the ideas and practices of a national government—the executive being the main target—has risen. The federal system of the United States is a structure very vulnerable to non-cooperation and antagonism by the state governmental element. When false federalism increases, one may be sure the presidency is weak, as is indicated by President Reagan's accommodating response to Congress in augmenting state powers and independence. The Civil War, which began the attack of the states on the national government, is not over. It continues to this day with great social and political costs, particularly in terms of reduced political participation and often marginalized local populations.

Congress has interfered with executive departments. The weakened executive, itself an impetus to the national security state but captured by it in day-to-day operations, has been unable to carry out its constitutional duties effectively or directly, and has resorted to devious, extralegal methods of running the executive departments, with inefficient and frequently immoral results (e.g., the National Security Council). Yet the basic problem rests more fundamentally with Congress. It is necessary to restore balance by equipping the executive with more accountably powerful instruments for managing the government. With strong policy instruments and through greater participation of grassroots citizens' groups in early formulation, oversight, and implementation, the president can truly be a democratic representative of national intent.

In foreign affairs, Congress has courted national disaster by allowing, indeed encouraging, secrecy, which in turn allows runaway groups to undertake military frolics on their own initiative. Congress must reclaim its constitutional authority in foreign affairs. The historic notion of the Senate acting as a Foreign Policy Council to advise and restrain the executive and its foreign affairs departments should be refashioned, because it is clear from the events of the past several years that the oversight committee process does not work. Moreover, the Senate's overall responsibility was present but largely concealed in both the Korean conflict and the Vietnam War, where the blame was totally—and to a considerable extent wrongly—placed on the executive.

The Senate as a Foreign Policy Council, given the particularistic and local nature of the Congress, may tend to de-internationalize U.S. foreign policy and constrain U.S. action to its own territory. The executive, captured as it is by pretension and an outmoded national security bureaucracy, has the tradition and inclination to expand the U.S. to imperial dimensions.

The trends outlined above set the boundaries and objectives for a program to strengthen the executive. The general goal is to equip the executive with new or modified planning, budgeting, and management instruments which will prevent, or at least balance, the problems listed above, arising from a government out of balance and overcontrolled by one of its principal institutions. The aim is to reform both the executive and the Congress, by enabling the executive to operate efficiently and accountably, while enabling Congress to return to its position of a controlled, rather than controlling power. This change will, in turn, serve the common good rather than an aggregate of localized interests.

Strengthening the Executive: General Planning and Budgeting Measures

A presidential program aims to build on existing institutions by providing a deep analysis of programs the country needs. Such a program should include the development and issuance of an annual Presidential Program Planning and Budgeting document. This document would pull together and integrate the outputs and processes of the Office of Management and Budget, the Council of Economic Advisors, the Science Advisor, sections of the Labor Department involved in labor planning, the Bureau of the Census, and the planning units and processes of all of the executive department agencies and independent agencies, including the Federal Reserve. The existing separate planning and programming documents, such as the Budget and the Annual Economic Report, would be integrated, not just folded into, the presidential document. Yet coordinated executive planning cannot be limited to economics. The basic organization of an executive planning process should be quadrilateral: (1) basic public goals separated into those directly related to governmental action and to the action of major "public corporations" (such as the states or the automobile industry); (2) an analysis of governmental goals into specific, detailed, time-scheduled objectives, together with planned governmental actions to achieve them; (3) a statement by the government, drawing on data from the Federal Reserve, Departments of Education and Commerce, etc., of desirable objectives for major public corporations, together with such data and analyses as the government can supply to assist the public corporations in the planning process; and (4) similar analyses in the case of mixed areas where public corporations and government are already in or necessarily must be in joint cooperation.

The major topical areas of the plan for both the government and other public corporations could be the major functions used by the government in the federal budget, although other categories may have to be added. The categories of the plan, as well as its actual content, should give preference to those most in use. This means a special commitment and program for the non-middle class in order to redress the growing imbalance in governmental and social programming that has developed over the past twenty years. The functional category of, for example, "Agriculture" or "Commerce and Housing Credit" should have major subcategories specifically addressed to problems of poverty and hidden class differentiation, such as education.

In general, for at least the next five years, the central priority of the planning document must be that of overcoming the dangerous and threatening imbalance in social programming which government has encouraged or permitted over the past seven years. Closely related to this point is that a coordinated planning process should eschew, deliberately, the congressional programming mode, namely, the development of national or all-inclusive programs as purportedly the only mode of achieving programming favorable to the poor, often using the poor as the stalking horse for other classes. If daycare, for example, is considered to be a desirable program for the working poor, the executive's coordinated plan should develop a program specifically for that group. To do otherwise, to follow the congressional mode of programming benefits to the non-poor, is inevitably to go the way of excessive costs and huge budget deficits. Rooted electorally and otherwise in the nation directly, the executive, as Congress cannot, is in a position to designate as national selective needs.

The new executive planning structure could be a composition of agencies from the current Executive Office, augmented with a special project team drawn from the executive departments and the independent agencies. It would consist of the following agencies which are now in the Executive Office of the President: the Offices of Management and Budget and Science and Technology, the Council of Economic Advisors, and the National Security Council. The project team would be drawn from every department and agency and would include extra participation from the analytic and statistical agencies (e.g., the Census Bureau, Bureau of Labor Statistics, National Center for Educational Statistics). Such a planning structure would preside over an annual planning process, yielding a rolling three-year plan. It is clear that this structure and process will much more tightly organize and focus the executive function of government—as well as bring much fuller public disclosure from the government itself and those corporate entities which have profound effect on our social and economic life. It can produce a plan which in and of itself will be a major device for coordinating governmental activities. But above all even such a beginning planning structure, process, and document as delineated above can make a major contribution toward the objective of generating responsible government.

It is to be emphasized that coordinated planning requires inclusion of planning of activities of certain independent agencies— federal land banks, federal home loan banks, and above all the federal Reserve System (agencies which have either statutory and/or customary status independent of the executive branch). Such agencies are not now fully integrated even into the formal annual budget process but obviously have major implications for any coordinated executive plan, and must therefore be treated on a parity with the executive agencies so far as the planning structures, processes and documents are concerned. Independent agencies —e.g., the Federal Trade Commission, the Interstate Commerce Commission—are also to be fully integrated into the plan, as are all government corporations, sponsored enterprises, and the like. Balancing the budget is possible. It depends on correlating taxes with expenditures and an appropriate allocation of resources among programs and on strengthening the existing budgeting process. A step toward that end would be to borrow the practice of the British government and combine into the president's annual budget request both the tax and expenditure programs, so that these items would be looked at together, and the need for reconciling divergences made apparent. More important than this technical modification is the renewal and purification of the budget process, particularly at the level of the Office of Management and Budget (OMB). Over the past seven years, budgetary discussions have been overly centralized in the political leadership of OMB and the White House staff. This has not only reduced the role and influence of the budget examiner as a watchdog of the Treasury, but has made a major component of budgetary decisions to be that of ignorance. This is probably as much responsible for the unbalanced budget as any other intellectual or analytic factor. One way of strengthening the OMB is to give it much greater entree to and control over such matters as defense budgets.

Furthermore, the Tax Act of 1986 must be amended to restore the progressivity of the income tax system. The massive reduction in tax progressivity in 1986, effectively to two brackets, 28 percent and 15 percent, means that tax payments and government benefits are inequitably distributed. In short, the tax program as it stands, even in the face of heroic expenditure reductions, is in good times an invitation to an unbalanced budget, and in bad times to economic disaster.

The Federal Reserve System has a major effect on national planning, programming, and budgeting, and so should be incorporated into an executive planning department. In the past twenty years, the Federal Reserve has come to take a much more direct and active substantive role, pushing out the limits of its central banking function to that of attempting to manage the economy as a whole or its various sectors, such as the stock market (which the Federal Reserve has inflated at the same time as it has deflated other sectors). Looked at over the past eight years, it is now clear that the Federal Reserve System program can be and is used as an alternate or supplement to the government budget—and as an alternate which favors well-to-do social groups and not the less well-off. It has been used to obtain a necessary expansion of government expenditures without comparably expanding expenditures to the less well-off. As the growth rate of government budget expenditures has been slowed over the past three years, the economic effects of that slowdown have been deliberately compensated for by increased Federal Reserve expenditures; without them, the country would have been in a recession in the fall of 1987. The Federal Reserve and the government are two closely related and principal parts of the government's total financing program and should be treated as a unit. The Federal Reserve should be required to join the budget process and compete for budget allocations on the basis of analytic and political judgments. They should compete in terms of the adequacy of their respective programs for the provision of low-income housing, for example. Combining them will provide a much more straightforward and systematic method for developing and comparing the effectiveness and efficiency of alternative ways of managing inflation, recessions, and the like, now fragmented between independent and little-cooperating institutions. It will bring into explicit balance the relationships between fiscal and monetary policy, and give the executive the power needed for planning and operating the government as a whole, and for guiding Congress effectively. It is known already that the Federal Reserve System can be used to make significant reductions in the budget deficit through reducing budget expenditures for budget borrowing by enabling the government to borrow from the Federal Reserve at low rates of interest. The potentialities for skimming off Federal Reserve System income (its profits) or creating low- or no-cost income for the general budget would seem to be very great. In this context, the issue of budget balancing takes on a new form.

Budgetary redefinition is just one aspect of a strong new presidential program. Except for brief flares of action, since the early 1950s the organization and management of government has been an unattended subject of near derision. Yet it was not always so. The transcendent importance of the underlying structures for human affairs was clearly recognized by the Democratic Party and the president in the New Deal era. President Roosevelt developed (via such study groups as the president's Committee on Administrative Management of 1937) organization and management as a basic approach to policymaking and executive responsibility. In other words, FDR used structural modifications as a way of shaping and controlling policymaking and its implementation on the behalf of the executive.

Confrontation with Congress and the Supreme Court were of course not without struggle. The New Deal experience says that the reform of governmental policy and changes of structural process are feasible ways of obtaining innovative and effective executive programming and operation of government. It says that structural change is an area in which the executive has great political advantage, since it is not feasible for 535 independent individuals, either alone or in committee, to run a government. From such experience alone it would behoove a new executive to consider as a top priority reorganization of government agencies and processes as a politically feasible and administratively efficient way to create a powerful executive program and provide leadership to the country. The establishment of an executive department of planning, furthermore, is part of a larger objective of modernizing a government structure which has had little intelligent attention for fifty years, and which, by virtue of special claims and interests filtered through Congress, is verging on decrepitude. Such modernization would include restoration of the honor of government employment as public service, creating conditions in which, from the lowest- to the highest-paid positions, acts of public worthiness are encouraged and rewarded.

A New 'New Federalism'

Federalism should be seen as an ongoing conflict between states and the central government, sometimes pitched, as in the Civil War, sometimes tame, as in the New Deal and Great Society eras, and recurring periodically during times of a weak executive such as the Reagan era. A responsible executive structure must be based on a federalist structure which will recognize and control this continuous tension. To create such a structure is the first order of business for a new administration, and requires three lines of action: a new theory and policy for separating the spheres of government powers; a mechanism to protect the federal bureaucracy from "invasion" by state and local governments; and the creation of an executive federalism to establish and maintain direct executive connections with local communities (as was developed initially by the Community Action Program of the 1960s, which encouraged the "voiceless" to speak and participate in government). Local community action must fill this gap in public life, and is an essential complement of the strong presidency idea proposed here, informing the formal governments of true realities and with an independent status.

For example, the spheres of federalism separate the federal and local governments. Thus, instead of sharing AFDC clients between the central and state governments, clients would become the total responsibility of the national government. In general, the long-standing policy of grants to the states would be dissolved, and all functions would be assigned to the level of government best equipped to handle them. The "new federalism" would limit state and local government activity to the narrow, constitutional realms of public health, safety, and justice. Economic development and other functions would fall to the federal government. The main beneficiaries of this divestiture would be the people at the grassroots, since they would participate in and control public safety, health, and other direct services. Business interests would be required to accept greater economic guidance from the coordinated executive planning department, so that their national effects could be controlled. An essential component of this federalism is expansion of the network of community action agencies, which would ensure executive responsiveness to community needs. It is at the community level that all spheres would integrate, so that programs such as education could be truly community-based, drawing on a variety of community inputs as well as local and federal government support. To this end, local representation at the federal level must be increased, with direct lines from communities to the executive, as well as to Congress. This heightened community power would redress the imbalance of special group interests which now dominate Congress and control its members.

The notion of a strong executive will be received with skepticism by those who say the presidency is already too strong. It will be objected, too, that historically, a strong executive has been an invitation to tyranny. Executive domination, however, is illusory, and tyranny can be understood as a result of class-bound legislative assemblies. The strong executive proposed here is embedded in our own Constitution and could usher in a new era of progressive and efficient government management that redresses some of the inequalities and excesses which Congress has created by accepting some of the assumptions of the national security state, while simultaneously averting its gaze from it.

Congressional dominance, the main factor of government since World War II, except for brief periods, has not provided us with good policies. Good policies that are truly democratic, especially for the below-middle class and poor elements of society, can come most effectively from a strong, decent presidency. For a president to be morally and politically exemplary and strong, there has to be a disposition within the party structure towards that objective. A Republican president will not find attractive the idea of strength or the institutional changes proposed above. A strong Republican president in conjunction with either a Republican or Democratic Congress is therefore not to be expected. At best, with a Democratic Congress and a Republican president, institutions could be played off of one another, as they have been since the 1982 elections, in order to achieve some of the desired, progressive effects, especially with regard to the poor.

The attempts on the part of President Jimmy Carter to present a moderate liberalizing program were quickly destroyed in 1977-79 by his own congressional party, which proclaimed him to be weak and out of touch. This mistaken project by leaders such as Speaker O'Neill need not be repeated in the future if the Democratic Party is clear on its own purposes. The party must move away from those Cold War and reactionary policies which gave the president the illusion of power, but which in fact demonstrated the reverse in the face of pressing domestic problems in every aspect of our lives, whether it be education, production, security, health insurance, or shared dignity.

There is fear in the land of strong leadership. But the nature of leadership described in this essay is of the catalytic kind which seeks participation of all groups, not those who have the arrogance to think they were born to govern, or who have enough leisure time to think that their leisure should be taken up with controlling the public space. Instead, the leadership spoken of here recognizes needs and problems, showing the way and challenging the people to unify in their solution.

The hydraheaded nature of the three-branch system of government, now masked by the national security state, where activities are coordinated but not subject to public awareness, scrutiny, or participation, requires that each branch relate its purpose to the common good. That branch which has the initiating, catalyzing, and implementing capacity is the executive. Having said this, if the presidency continues to be in the hands of the few, it will have to be Congress and the courts that reach out with the citizenry to seize the initiative of social reconstruction. And if the president becomes a fool or a tyrant, Congress must not be afraid to impeach. In our time the impeachment clause of the Constitution must be more than a scarecrow, just as the president must be more than an actor who reads other people's lines, or indeed, does not even know when lines are being read in his name.

Resources

Further Reading

- Marcus Raskin, ed., *The Federal Budget and Social Reconstruction*, Institute for Policy Studies, 1978.
- Edward Corwin, *The President: Office and Powers 1787-1957*, New York University Press, 1957.
- Rexford Guy Tugwell, *The Enlargement of the Presidency*, Doubleday, 1960.
- Bernard Schwartz, *The Constitutional Law: The Powers of Government*, Vol.II, Matthew Bender, 1983

William B. Cannon is a Professor in the School of Social Service Administration at the University of Chicago. He has served as Dean of the Lyndon B. Johnson School of Public Affairs at the University of Texas, and as Deputy Chairman of the National Endowment for the Arts. He was Assistant Director of the Bureau of the Budget (Office of Management and Budget), and participated in the planning and drafting of the War on Poverty program. He served as Executive Secretary to the President's Task Force on Education in 1964 and again in 1967. He is the author of, among other works, *New Class Politics*.

Restoring Regulatory Policy to Serve the Public Interest

Platform

- Direct all regulatory agencies to base their decisions on the standards established by the underlying regulatory statutes, rather than on the economic preferences of the regulated community or the new administration.

- Replace the regulatory review process established by Executive Orders 12291 and 12498 with a new system in which the reviewing agency's mission is not to veto or delay regulatory initiatives, but rather to ensure that the regulatory agencies are performing their required functions expeditiously and efficiently.

- Transform the annual regulatory planning process into a management tool for ensuring that regulatory agencies are provided with adequate resources to perform their regulatory duties in timely fashion.

- Restore the technical expertise of the federal regulatory agencies by providing them with the necessary resources for data gathering, analysis, and monitoring.

- Implement new disclosure policies that permit the public to monitor the progress of all regulatory initiatives and that require regulatory review to be conducted on the public record.

- Direct executive agencies to write regulations in a manner that will facilitate enforcement and to respect decisions by state and local governments affording citizens additional protection beyond federally-prescribed minimum standards.

Attitudes toward economic regulation vary dramatically, but there is wide agreement that social regulations—those designed to protect public health, safety, and the environment—are necessary and desirable. Even free-market advocates recognize the need for government intervention to correct market failures and to provide safety, a clean environment, and protection of public health. Although economic deregulation, which was initiated prior to the Reagan presidency, may sometimes benefit consumers, the Reagan administration's assault on social regulations has been harmful.

Private industry resists regulation because it inevitably increases the costs of doing business. Yet regulation can benefit society by requiring regulated industries to bear the true social costs of their activities, thus ensuring that resources are used most efficiently. Government regulation plays a vital role in protecting public health, safety, and the environment, as required by law.

The Reagan administration espoused regulatory "reform" as one of its top priorities upon assuming office, but it soon demonstrated that its overriding objective was regulatory "relief" for big business. The administration's Task Force on Regulatory Relief, chaired by Vice President Bush, canvassed business leaders to develop a "hit list" of regulations to repeal. On February 17, 1981, President Reagan promulgated Executive Order 12291, which suspended pending regulatory actions and created a regulatory review process centralized in the Office of Management and Budget.

Although the executive order described OMB's role as advisory and consultative, it gave OMB effective veto power over agency actions by prohibiting issuance of proposed or final regulations without OMB approval. Detailed cost-benefit analyses were required for all major regulatory actions, and agencies were directed to refrain from acting unless benefits outweighed costs. A subsequent Executive Order (12498) expanded OMB's role by requiring that regulatory initiatives be approved by OMB up to a year in advance and incorporated in an annual report, *The Regulatory Program of the United States.*

Not surprisingly, the Reagan administration used the new review process to block regulations opposed by its big business constituency. The administration's central concern was not to maximize net benefits to society, but rather to reduce costs borne by industry. Many significant initiatives to control threats to public health and the environment were vetoed by OMB or blocked until agencies agreed to weaken them.

The most pernicious part of the administration's anti-regulatory strategy was an assault on the technical expertise of the regulatory agencies. OMB slashed the budgets of the regulatory agencies even as it demanded costlier and more complicated analyses from them. Agencies were prohibited from proposing major new regulations until detailed cost-benefit analyses were performed, but major regulations could be repealed (as the administration tried to do with the extraordinarily beneficial limits on lead in gasoline) without any analysis at all.

OMB cloaked its actions in extreme secrecy to avoid disclosure of instances when they were not consistent with statutory requirements or were products of *ex parte* contacts with affected industries.

Despite its anti-regulatory fervor, the Reagan administration has had remarkably little success in changing the basic structure of federal health, safety, and environmental laws. Perhaps the most lasting legacy of the administration's policies will be to undermine the prospects for genuine regulatory reform, which was discredited by the administration's biased program.

Despite the Reagan administration's abuse of the regulatory review process, the next administration should resist the temptation to abolish regulatory review entirely. A modified regulatory review and planning process could be a significant tool for revitalizing regulatory policy. The review process could be transformed into a positive tool for ensuring that regulatory policy operates more efficiently, expeditiously, and equitably. These changes can be accomplished by replacing Executive Orders 12291 and 12498 with a restructured regulatory review process and by implementing new regulatory and disclosure policies.

First, the new administration should direct all regulatory agencies to base their decisions on the standards established by the underlying regulatory statutes, rather than on the economic preferences of the regulated community or the new administration.

The Reagan administration made little effort to seek statutory change to accomplish its anti-regulatory goals. Instead, it often attempted to "repeal" regulatory statutes indirectly by forcing executive agencies to base their decisions on factors not permissible under the statutes. This raises serious legal concerns, because our constitutional system of government charges the executive with making sure that laws are faithfully executed.

The new administration must recognize the importance of statutory directives, even those the president may disagree with. If the administration wishes to change the law to implement new regulatory policies, it should ask Congress to do so. Otherwise, it must ensure that the regulatory decisions made by executive agencies conform to statutory requirements.

Second, the new administration should replace the regulatory review process established by Executive Order 12291 with a new system in which the reviewing agency's mission is not to veto or delay regulatory initiatives, but rather to ensure that the regulatory agencies are performing their required functions expeditiously and efficiently.

Regulatory review and planning must be used to expedite the regulatory process while opening regulatory decisionmaking to full public scrutiny. The reviewing agency should not be allowed to displace agency decisionmaking or to put an indefinite hold on agency actions.

The new administration should transform the annual regulatory planning process into a management tool for ensuring that regulatory agencies are provided with adequate resources to perform their regulatory duties in a timely fashion.

Even before the Reagan administration, the glacial pace of the regulatory process was a chronic problem. The administration's actions aggravated this problem by building further institutional delays into the process. These delays are evident to anyone who has examined the progress of agencies in meeting their own deadlines for regulatory action, as reported in the agencies' semi-annual *Regulatory Agendas* and the annual *Regulatory Program of the United States.*

The new regulatory review process should be used to monitor the progress of agency initiatives. Budgetary authorities should ensure that adequate resources are allocated in advance for agencies to perform their anticipated regulatory functions. Regulatory review should be used to expedite the regulatory process by alerting program managers to important issues at an early stage, rather than to generate indefinite delay at the final stage of the process.

The new administration must make a concerted effort to restore the technical capacity of the federal regulatory agencies by increasing the resources available to them for data-gathering, analysis, and monitoring. Such investments will pay great dividends because the impact of regulatory decisions is so enormous.

The new administration should establish a disclosure policy that permits the public to monitor the progress of all regulatory initiatives and that requires regulatory review to be conducted on the public record.

Secrecy has been essential to the Reagan administration's anti-regulatory efforts. Unable to convince Congress to change the regulatory statutes, the administration resorted to extra-legal behavior to accomplish its ends. It abused the so-called "deliberative process" privilege in order to shield improper behavior from public scrutiny.

To ensure fairness in the regulatory process, regulatory review must be conducted on the public record. Significant comments by any reviewing agency should be submitted in writing and placed in public rulemaking dockets at the time the comments are made. Contacts by agency personnel with outside parties should be logged and placed in rulemaking dockets. The public record also should reflect any changes in regulatory proposals that occur in response to comments by reviewing agencies. This can be accomplished by requiring that drafts of all regulatory proposals submitted to other agencies for review be included in the docket. Concern that disclosure of deliberative information may have a chilling effect is misplaced; it will deter only comments that urge consideration of inappropriate factors.

The new administration should also disclose, upon request, the status of any pending regulatory proposal even if such disclosure is not required by the Freedom of Information Act). This will facilitate public monitoring of regulatory initiatives, enhancing public participation and pressure for expeditious action. Conducting regulatory review on the public record also will help ensure that agency decisions conform to statutory requirements.

The new administration should direct executive agencies to write enforceable regulations. A credible threat of enforcement is essential to achieving voluntary compliance with regulatory standards. Yet regulatory standards often are developed without adequate consideration of their enforcement implications. Too many regulations are written in a manner that makes enforcement difficult. The result is a kind of "Victorian compromise," in which very ambitious sounding standards are on the books, but often ignored in practice.

The Reagan administration aggravated this problem by reducing monitoring and enforcement resources. This policy shift was particularly dramatic in the early years of the Reagan administration at the Environmental Protection Agency (EPA), the Occupational Safety and Health Administration (OSHA), and the Department of Interior.

The new administration should expand the resources devoted to monitoring and enforcement while giving enforcement authorities greater input into the design of regulatory standards. Regulatory strategies based on economic incentives that afford regulated industries more flexibility will be successful only if they are enforceable. Expanded use of alternative dispute resolution techniques and other enforcement innovations will be effective if coupled with measures to expand the credibility of traditional enforcement techniques.

The new administration should direct executive agencies to respect decisions by state and local governments to afford their citizens additional protection beyond federally prescribed minimum standards. Despite its rhetoric, the Reagan administration applied its "federalism" selectively and inconsistently. While invoking federalism to justify weakening nationally applicable social regulations, it did not hesitate to preempt occasional state efforts to afford citizens greater protections. For example, after opposing OSHA's efforts to issue a national hazard communication standard, the Reagan administration abruptly shifted gears and acted to preempt state regulation after certain states enacted tough standards.

The new administration should recognize that minimum national standards are important to prevent economic competition among states from undermining health and environmental protection. But when states and localities choose to afford their citizens a higher level of protection (and to bear the costs of doing so), that choice should be respected by federal authorities.

The new administration will face a formidable task in restoring regulatory policy to serve the public interest. This can be accomplished by transforming the regulatory review and planning process into a positive tool for improving the speed, efficiency, and fairness of the process.

Resources

Recommended Appointees for a New Administration

- William J. Baer, Partner, Arnold & Porter, Federal Trade Commission official in the Carter administration, expert on regulatory policy issues

- William Drayton, Director of Environmental Safety, MacArthur Fellow, former Assistant Administrator for Planning and Management, Environmental Protection Agency

- George C. Eads, former Dean of the University of Maryland School of Public Affairs, member of President Carter's Council of Economic Advisors and chairman of Regulatory Analysis Review Group, currently Vice President and Chief Economist for General Motors

- Michael Fix, Senior Research Associate and attorney at the Urban Institute, who has written extensively on regulatory review and regulatory policy issues

- Alfred Kahn, former CAB Chairman and anti-inflation czar in the Carter administration, currently Professor of Economics at Cornell University, has written extensively on regulatory policy

- Richard Morgenstern, Director, Office of Policy Analysis, Environmental Protection Agency, who coordinated EPA regulatory policy in the face of OMB opposition

- Alan Morrison, Director, Public Citizen Litigation Group, who has brought much of the most important litigation on regulatory policy issues

- Robert Pitofsky, Dean of the Georgetown University Law Center, former member of the Federal Trade Commission, expert on antitrust and regulatory policy

- Robert Reich, former Federal Trade Commission official, has written extensively on regulation and the interface between business and government, now at Harvard's John F. Kennedy School of Government

- Cass R. Sunstein, Professor at the University of Chicago Law School, has written brilliantly and extensively on administrative law and the regulatory policy process

- Susan J. Tolchin, Professor of Public Administration at George Washington University, an expert on the regulatory policy process, co-authored *Dismantling America: The Rush to Deregulate* (1983)

Organizations

- Advocacy Institute, 1730 M St. NW, Washington, DC 20036; (202) 659-8475
- Alliance for Justice, 600 New Jersey Ave. NW, Washington, DC 20001; (202) 624-8390
- Oversight and Investigations Subcommittee, House Energy and Commerce Committee, 2323 Rayburn HOB, Washington, DC 20515; (202) 225-4441
- OMB Watch, 2001 O St. NW, Washington, DC 20036; (202) 659-1711
- Public Citizen Litigation Group, 2000 P St. NW, Washington, DC 20036; (202) 785-3704

Further Reading

- Christopher Demuth and Douglas Ginsburg, "White House Review of Agency Rulemaking," 99 *Harvard Law Review*, 1975, 1986.
- George C. Eads and Michael Fix, *Relief or Reform? Reagan's Regulatory Dilemma*, Urban Institute Press, 1984.
- Michael Fix and George C. Eads, "The Prospects for Regulatory Reform: The Legacy of Reagan's First Term," 2 *Yale Journal on Regulation*, 293, 1985.
- John M. Mendelhoff, *The Dilemma of Toxic Substance Regulation, 1988*.
- Lester B. Lave, *The Strategy of Social Regulation: Decision Frameworks for Policy*, Brookings Institution, 1981.
- Alan Morrison, "OMB Interference with Agency Rulemaking: The Wrong Way to Write a Regulation," 99 *Harvard Law Review*, 1059, 1986.
- Erik D. Olson, "The Quiet Shift of Power: Office of Management and Budget Supervision of Environmental Protection Agency Rulemaking under Executive Order 12291," 4 *Virginia Journal of Natural Resources Law*, 1, 1984.
- OMB Watch, *OMB Control of Rulemaking: The End of Public Access*, August 1985.
- Robert V. Percival, "Rediscovering the Limits of the Regulatory Review Authority of the Office of Management and Budget," 17 *Environmental Law Reporter*, 10017, 1987.
- Morton Rosenberg, "Beyond the Limits of Executive Power: Presidential Control of Agency Rulemaking under Executive Order 12291," 80 *Michigan Law Review*, 193, 1981.
- Peter L. Strauss and Cass R. Sunstein, "The Role of the President and OMB in Informal Rulemaking," 38 *Administrative Law Review*, 181, 1986.

- Subcommittee on Intergovernmental Relations, Senate Committee on Governmental Affairs, 99th Cong., 2nd Sess., *Oversight of the Office of Management and Budget Regulatory Review and Planning Process,* 1986.

- Subcommittee on Oversight and Investigations, House Committee on Energy and Commerce, 99th Cong., 1st Sess., *EPA's Asbestos Regulations: Report on a Case Study of OMB Interference in Agency Rulemaking,* 1985.

- Subcommittee on Oversight and Investigations, House Committee on Energy and Commerce, 99th Cong., 2nd Sess., *OMB Review of EPA Regulations,* 1986.

- Susan J. Tolchin and Martin Tolchin, *Dismantling America: The Rush to Deregulate,* Houghton Mifflin, 1983.

Robert V. Percival is an Assistant Professor at the University of Maryland Law School. Prior to joining the Maryland faculty, Percival was a senior attorney with the Environmental Defense Fund, where he served as lead counsel in *EDF v. Thomas,* the first successful legal challenge to OMB's use of regulatory review to delay promulgation of regulations subject to statutory deadlines. He has written and testified frequently on regulatory review and policy issues.

Communications Policy
in the 21st Century

Platform

- The purposes and principles of the First Amendment should guide communications policy choices.
- Separation of content and conduit should be maintained in the mainstream communications channels.
- There should be legally enforceable rights of entry and access to mainstream communications channels.
- The Fairness Doctrine should be reaffirmed and reinstated.
- In the absence of rights of entry and access, stringent ownership standards should be imposed upon media monopolies and conglomerates.
- The costs of modernizing telecommunications services should be born by large institutional, rather than residential, users.
- Widespread literacy and educational programs are essential to maximize the social and economic return on the information age.
- Communications policies should strive to narrow the gap between the information-rich and the information-poor.

We have passed from the agricultural age through the industrial age into the information age with such tornado-like speed that policymakers have yet completely to identify, let alone address and resolve, the new possibilities and perils.

One half of our GNP and workforce is involved with the "information economy," my shorthand for a number of common labels:

telecommunications, computers, the media, electronics, and what the military calls C3I (command, control, communications, and intelligence). So defined, virtually every chapter of this book involves subjects that will continue to be addressed by communications policy. Communications is: the driving force in the self-governing of our democracy; the biggest share of the defense budget; the hope for an improved balance of trade and better international relations; integral to much education; the lifeline to rural America; the source of perceptions of women and minorities; an alternative to transportation and other energy consumption; a central element in health care delivery; a tool in high-tech crime; the cause of increasing disparity between the information-poor and the information-rich; and the instrumentality for much loss of privacy.

Moreover, a major consequence of the technological innovations in communications is that the old conceptual categories no longer work. The Federal Communications Commission used to have a "Common Carrier Bureau" and a "Broadcast Bureau," the first named for a legal concept (for telephone and telegraph companies), and the other for a technology (over-the-air broadcasting). Today, IBM, the computer company, is in the telephone business; AT&T sells computers; television and FM radio stations distribute textual information displayed on home and business screens; newspapers are broadcast via communications satellites to remote printing plants for national distribution, and many even come over the telephone line to a desktop computer.

Conventional television stations, once considered to be in competition with movie theaters, now find themselves competing with alternative delivery mechanisms (such as cable and pay cable, subscription television, home satellite dishes, and multi-channel multipoint microwave distribution systems). Rapidly substituting for electronic delivery is the home videocassette recorder (VCR), using tapes that were purchased, rented, or previously taped from an over-the-air station, cable system, or satellite. With a video camera, the tapes may even be one's own creation. The home movie theater is just one of the consequences of rapidly declining prices. Used to dealing with sale prices of 20-50 percent off, we now confront the "99.9 percent off sale": a $3 million computer that sells for $3,000; the $2 million satellite dish that is discounted to $2,000; the $250,000 video tape recorder on sale for $250. In such a tornado of social, economic, legal, political, and technological change, one searches for a Polaris by which to navigate. What are the principles by which we can judge our purpose and destination?

It is useful to start not only with the First Amendment ("Congress shall make no law abridging the freedom of speech") but the Supreme Court's view of it in the *Red Lion* case: "It is the right of the viewers and listeners, not the right of the broadcasters, which is paramount." In short, First Amendment values exist to benefit the entire society, not just the gate-keepers sitting astride our arteries of communication. Ad-

mittedly, *Red Lion* was based, in part, upon the scarcity of available frequencies; but the underlying philosophy is applicable to other communications media as well, and is the interpretation most consistent
with the purposes of the First Amendment.

What are those purposes? Why do we want a First Amendment?
Why is life in America different because of it? From its legislative history and a body of judicial and academic analyses the following reasons
emerge:

- Self-governance. Free speech is necessary for a self-governing people
  to have access to the information it needs to produce an informed
  public opinion. The Supreme Court, in *Garrison v. Louisiana*, called
  it "the essence of self-government."

- Self-expression. Thinking, speaking, and writing are central to what
  it means to be human, a basic quality of "liberty," central to self-
  realization or self-actualization, and the biological basis for the First
  Amendment.

- Search for truth. The conclusions which emerge from a marketplace
  of ideas are as good a definition of political truth as any, and more
  useful to a free society than those handed down by edict.

- Safety valve. People excluded from the media may turn to terrorism
  or hostage-taking.

- Checking value. Free speech can provide a check on the excesses of
  government, corporations, and other large institutions. The process
  becomes, in effect, a fourth or fifth branch of government.

From these purposes come the standards I would apply in formulating or reviewing proposed communications policies for the information age.

Cable Access and Fairness

Cable television operators would like to do away with public access channels and, in general, reserve a legally enforceable personal
right to censor all 54, or 107, communications conduits into a
community's homes on the grounds that cable systems are more like
newspapers than television stations. Should they be permitted to do so?
The answer is found by asking whether that policy will hinder or advance: self-governing, self-expression, the search for truth, the safety
valve to violence, and the check on institutional abuse. In this instance,
these goals are better served by providing a legally enforceable right
of entry for cable program providers than by leaving an absolute power
of censorship in the hands of cable operators. By "right of entry," I
mean the legally enforceable ability to enter the mainstreams of mass
media with one's message, notwithstanding the owner's desire to censor the content.

There were many economic and political objections to the pre-1980 power of AT&T. But, at a time when it had a hammerlock control of all 150 million channels of telephonic communication, no one ever thought to complain of its monopolistic control over the content of telephone conversations. The reason? The groundrules, law, custom, and expectation were that anyone who wanted a phone and a line could get one, and having done so, could communicate whatever ideas he or she chose.

That control of content is exactly what we have given to monopoly newspapers, radio and television stations, and cable companies. The media have the time or space for sale, the customer has the money, but entry is conditioned upon the media's acceptance, or censorship, of the copy. And therein lies the difference.

One cable company could control 54 or 107 channels, or even all of the nation's cable systems, just as it made no difference that the phone company controlled 150 million. The presence or absence of "scarcity" (in the sense of total number of outlets) is a phony issue. What is relevant is not the single company control of most channels, or the total number of channels available, but the groundrules for legally enforceable entry. Without the right of entry, the control of two outlets in the same community may be too much; with it, one company can control every channel in the land.

Phony issues are similarly being used to debate the propriety of the First Amendment implications of "the Fairness Doctrine." This congressional (Section 315) and Commission-created standard (repealed by Reagan's FCC and under reconsideration by Congress) requires, first, that broadcast stations cannot be merely juke boxes or movie houses with commercials. They must deal with controversial issues of public importance. And, second, in doing so, they cannot be unrelieved instruments of one-sided propaganda. The Fairness Doctrine does not require that specific issues or persons be aired and equal time be granted. Nor does it mandate any specific formats. It simply requires some reasonable range of viewpoints.

The argument is made that such a modest requirement, one a professional journalist would find it virtually impossible not to meet, somehow violates the broadcasters' freedom of speech. But it should be noted that there are no limitations whatsoever on what the broadcaster can say or show. There are even express provisions permitting a station's personal attacks on public and private individuals. The only real issue here is the broadcaster's ability to censor other people's speech. Whatever sophistry a lawyer may be able to fashion from court opinions interpreting the language of the First Amendment, its purposes are clearly better served by enforcing the Fairness Doctrine.

Note that what we are talking about are procedures for content, not the substance of the content. The government is not telling the broadcaster what words may or may not be broadcast. These procedures enhance rather than abridge the freedom of speech for all Americans.

Ownership and Content Regulation

There is an often ignored relationship between ownership standards and content procedures. Just as the monopoly position and abuses of the railroads and grain elevators created concern (and early demands for their common carrier status), so does the increasingly powerful position of today's media giants, and the perceptions of their abuses, lead to concern about their power.

Such media power is not inevitable. It could be otherwise but for the overwhelming opposition to change by virtually every media owner. We could, for example, limit the ownership of media outlets to human beings, rather than conglomerate corporations, while placing severe restrictions upon concentration. We could limit the power and antenna height of radio and television stations to service areas with no more than a population of, say, a congressional district. We could require that licensees share a station's ownership, subdividing the time until everyone who wants a piece of a station has one. We could require that all media be operated as common carriers, with virtually unlimited right of entry. We could tolerate a little more interference, and let anyone who wants to operate a broadcasting station do so without any licensing at all. Licenses could be returned to the FCC after one term if anyone were waiting in line. Stations could be operated by viewers' associations receiving the most votes (as in the Netherlands).

It is highly unlikely that any of these things will occur. And perhaps some shouldn't, even in a utopian society. They are mentioned, however, to make a point. Those who profess to be advocates of "deregulation" or "marketplace competition" have a curious attraction to that aspect of the status quo creating the medallion value of FCC licenses. They like the idea of government-created and -protected monopolies on given frequencies. They like being able to send unlicensed competitors to Leavenworth. They have not the slightest interest in creating genuine competition through the kinds of mechanisms just mentioned. But it is that very lack of competition which produces the demand, and need, for some form of content procedures.

Deregulation advocates shouldn't be allowed to have it both ways, because such a position is inconsistent with the purposes of the First Amendment. Those purposes could conceivably be served by a total absence of content procedures for a media open to all, with stringent limits on monopolies. Or they could be served with oligopolistic and conglomerate corporate media subject to content procedures. What are absolutely intolerable in our democratic society are powerful, oligopolistic media, protected by the government, and operated without the check of content procedures.

Content and Conduit

The purposes of the First Amendment are as ill-served by censorship driven by competitive as by ideological motivations. For example, there are cable companies jointly owned with pay program distributors. When such companies use their own pay services on their own cable systems, excluding those of their competitors, the anti-competitive consequences befall viewers as well as the marketplace.

In this example, the pay cable programming service may be thought of as "content," while the communications satellite service and the cable distributor may be thought of "conduit." The conflict is obvious. If conduit and content can be jointly owned, the owner has a very real incentive to keep competing content out of the conduit. This conflict was recognized by the Justice Department and Supreme Court in the *Paramount* case ban on movie producers owning movie theaters. It was even recognized by the FCC in limiting networks' control of syndication and foreign distribution rights for programming. Because such conflicts are difficult to spot or prove, the easiest solution is simply to prohibit content-conduit combinations in the first place. This would mean that a cable operator would be operating either as a common carrier or program supplier, but not both. Networks could distribute others' programs, but could own neither programs nor stations. And, of course, phone companies would continue to be barred from selling information.

Information-Poor and Information-Rich

To the extent that we accept the purposes of the First Amendment as our guide and find them equally valid for all Americans, we must confront the disparity between the information-poor and the information-rich. There are a number of programs already in place designed to reduce the gap. Thomas Jefferson saw the need for public education and public libraries. There is a "lifeline" telephone service (a reduced-rate, unlimited-calls-in, limited-calls-out service), and advertiser-supported ("free") over-the-air television. Some cities have required free basic cable service, while the FCC used to require licensees to broadcast, for free, "public service announcements."

If those who can afford it do not have legally enforceable rights of paid entry and access to media and information sources (as is the case today), clearly the poor will not either. Because the media's denial of paid access or entry is the more difficult for them to justify, establishing rights of paid entry is the most politically sensible first step. But it should be taken in ways that are consistent with, and do not preclude, future realizations of some measure of the same opportunities for the poor.

It is tempting to urge federal, or common carrier, funding of "free" telephone networks with broad band capacity. But it does not necessarily follow that this is the most logical, feasible, or desirable solution.

There would be enormous costs to providing such service for all citizens.

What is happening today, in the view of many, is that the phone companies and major corporations are absolutely committed to installing such optic fiber, ISDN capacity for two-way video and access to electronic libraries or mammoth computing systems. It is they, not the average citizen, who will be the major beneficiaries of high data transfer rates and other communications capacities. But the "access fee," and rising local telephone rates, enables them to shift the cost to the small consumer. Perhaps the public interest lies more in the opposite direction: giving consumers the option of not having, and paying for, electronics equipment, services, and capacity they have no prospect of using.

There are many restrictions on the availability of information other than economics and technology. Would more high-tech have enabled citizens to find out what Oliver North was up to, when at least some believe that even President Reagan did not know? Information is kept out of circulation through motives of fear, selfishness, competitiveness, and other reasons beyond the reach of conventional reform.

One may dream of the day when every citizen can get immediate access to any book, film, or recording. But that is possible today, through inter-library loan, if the patron is willing to wait. Our libraries are crammed with unused information of enormous potential benefit to citizens in every aspect of their lives. Those with cable can watch C-SPAN or CNN twenty-four hours a day. Ratings indicate they are tuned elsewhere. Newspaper and magazine subscriptions can bring any of tens of thousands of sources to our homes or libraries, yet millions prefer to pick up *The National Enquirer* or *TV Guide* in their neighborhood supermarket. This is not to suggest that increasing the potential supply of available information is not a good thing, only that there is no magical technological fix. We should give, if not more, at least equal attention to universal literacy rates and basic education in the "information society."

If citizens will not use the libraries that now exist, there is even less likelihood that they will make good or frequent use of large-scale computing facilities. Building telecommunications connections from 90 million homes to thousands of mainframe computers raises another problem. One of the consequences of rapidly changing technology is that today's great idea can become tomorrow's folly. We are rapidly reaching the point where stand-alone computers with access to compact laser disks containing encyclopedias of information (CD ROM), or comparable storage, will make much more sense (for purposes other than communication) than paying telecommunication charges. Whatever may be today's economic answer to that one, the example makes the point: there are enormous hazards in massive national investments in evolving technologies.

Nor need we return to the old days of "regulation." There are, in some contexts and for some purposes, benefits from "deregulation." But the Polaris of First Amendment purposes can best guide our hand in drawing these lines: self-government, self-expression, search for truth, safety valve, and a check on other institutions. These purposes are as applicable today as in the late 18th century. They suggest the value of maximizing the diversity and distribution of the national dialogue. They can be a benchmark for judging proposals for private censorship, ownership standards, and the operation of telecommunications in "the public interest."

Resources

Recommended Appointees for a New Adminstration

Robert Entman and Michael Goldhaber have included on their lists many of the individuals I also would recommend. Given the breadth of the subject and range of its impact, the potential lists are, of course, endless.

- To Robert Entman's mention of former UCLA Communication Law Program Director Charles Firestone I would add two other former directors: Geoffrey Cowan and Tracy Westen

- There are a number of lawyers in Washington with FCC or other communications experience, who have a demonstrated public interest orientation, including: Geoff Aronow (former FCC), Kenneth Cox (MCI, former FCC Commissioner), Albert Kramer (former FTC and founder of the Citizens Communications Center), Simon Lazarus (former FCC and White House), Frank Lloyd (former FCC), Nicholas P. Miller (former Senate Communications Subcommittee Counsel), Robert Stein (former FCC), and Robert Thorpe (former FCC)

- Communications studies experts include Timothy Haight, Santa Cruz, CA and Karen Possner, Washington, DC

- Walter Baer, Times-Mirror Corporation, Los Angeles, physicist with communications experience in both government and industry

- Anne Branscomb, Armonk, NY, lawyer and policy analyst

- Robert Chartrand, follows information policy issues for the Library of Congress, worked with the White House Conference on Libraries and Information Service

- Harlan Cleveland, author of *The Knowledge Executive*, immediate past director of the Hubert Humphrey Institute, Minneapolis, MN

- Dr. John Craven, engineer, lawyer in Honolulu

- Dr. William Melody, former FCC economist, currently director of the London-based Program on Information and Communication Technology

- Anthony Oettinger, Director of the Harvard University Program on Information Technologies
- Fruitful general sources of names would be those who have participated in the annual Telecommunications Policy Research Conference at Airlie House, staff of the House or Senate Communications Subcommittees, NTIA, OTA, or Ralph Nader.

Organizations

- Audience Network, Box 19367, Washington, DC 20036; (202) 387-8030
- Citizens Communications Center, 25 E St. NW, Third Floor, Washington, DC 20001; (202) 662-9535
- Communications Consortium, 1333 H St. NW, Washington, DC 20005; (202) 682-0940
- Consumer Federation of America, 1424 16th St. NW, Washington, DC 20036; (202) 387-6121
- Media Access Project, 1609 Connecticut Ave. NW, Washington, DC 20009; (202) 232-4300
- National Black Media Coalition, 38 New York Ave. NW, Washington, DC 20002; (202) 387-8155
- National Communications Citizens Lobby, Box 1876, Iowa City, IA 52244; (319) 337-5555
- Telecommunications Consumer Coalition, Office of Communication, United Church of Christ, 105 Madison Ave., New York, NY 10016; (212) 683-5656

Nicholas Johnson, a writer and public lecturer currently teaching at the University of Iowa College of Law, served as Commissioner of the Federal Communications Commission and Presidential Advisor to the White House Conference on Libraries and Information Sciences. He is the author of *How to Talk Back to Your Television Set.*

Jane E. Kirtley

Openness in Government and Freedom of Information

Platform

Because secrecy in government precludes the possibility of democratic participation, accountability, or intelligent decisionmaking, the U.S. government must operate in an atmosphere of openness and accessibility to information.

- The government must conduct its activities in the open, with honesty and candor, subject to public scrutiny and review. Accordingly, domestic "disinformation" and COINTELPRO-type campaigns should be abolished; covert operations should be strictly limited and held to close congressional oversight; the government should ensure members of the civilian press full and timely access to all military operations as they occur.

- Classification of government documents on the grounds of "national security" is only rarely justified. Accordingly, Executive Order No. 12,256 should be abolished, and a new order issued establishing a classification system where secrecy is the exception, rather than the rule; the requirement that government employees with security clearances take lifetime secrecy oaths should be abolished. Modified secrecy oaths should be required only from those few employees with the highest level of clearance, and should be as limited in scope and as short in duration as possible.

- The Freedom of Information Act (FOIA) must be enforced and strengthened. Accordingly, oversight of FOIA enforcement should either be shifted out of the Department of Justice and into an independent, depoliticized agency which would act as "ombudsperson" between agencies and requesters, or the Justice Department FOI Office should be completely depoliticized and reorganized, with specific instructions to facilitate, rather than obstruct, the flow of information to the public.

- The free exchange of ideas, both from within the United States and from abroad, encourages uninhibited, open, and robust debate. Accordingly, exclusion of aliens on ideological grounds should be abolished; attempts to suppress unpopular opinions and ideas, including those pertaining to sexually explicit materials, through legislation, regulation, intimidation, or other censorship techniques, must be ended.

Restrictions on Press Coverage

Press freedom means that the news media and the public may disseminate and receive information without government interference. During the Reagan administration, however, the government has carried out a campaign to manipulate the news media and also to restrain it from gathering information. Curtailment of the number of presidential press conferences and photo opportunities is only the tip of the iceberg.

Manipulation of the press is hardly a new tactic, but it has been attempted by the Reagan administration to a truly unprecedented degree. Perhaps the most striking example was the disinformation program aimed against Libya's Muammar Kadhafi, revealed in a memorandum prepared by Admiral John Poindexter, which included lying to the American news media. President Reagan told a press conference that such conduct was acceptable if it made Kadhafi "go to bed at night wondering what we might do."

A General Accounting Office report also found that the administration used a special office in the State Department to conduct "prohibited, covert propaganda activities" designed to influence the news media and sway public opinion in favor of the administration's Latin American policies—activities which, it said, violated a congressional ban on the use of taxpayer money for unauthorized publicity or propaganda purposes. The operation apparently included underwriting the preparation of opinion columns by outside publication consultants to be placed in major American newspapers under the names of *contra* leaders.

Military activities similarly offer vast opportunities for disinformation. The Reagan administration engaged in the ultimate disinformation campaign—the total ban on unbiased, objective reporting—when it excluded U.S. journalists from the invasion of Grenada. It also dispatched its own Defense Department news service to provide favorable coverage of the invasion, detained three U.S. reporters who were already on the island during the invasion, and threatened to shoot at any reporters who tried to reach the island on their own. Secretary of Defense Caspar Weinberger later told reporters that the government had the right to exclude the news media from future military operations if it should wish to do so.

As a result of the outcry from the press over the exclusion, the Sidle Commission issued a report recommending the creation of emergency press pools to guarantee initial access to military operations until full coverage becomes feasible. After many false starts—including an abortive attempt to operate a press pool during a mock invasion, while military officials claimed a pool member had leaked information to organizations not involved, and journalists complained that communications equipment was defective and that news dispatches were not delivered for two days—the press pools began to operate in earnest covering U.S. escort operations in the Persian Gulf.

Contrary to the Sidle Commission guidelines, the pools continued to be the only way reporters could obtain official access to the operation months after it began. Access to specific operations was denied arbitrarily. And a memo from Pentagon spokesman Robert B. Sims to Secretary Weinberger said that some Pentagon officials advocated terminating on-scene press coverage altogether.

While some restrictions on combat coverage are generally accepted as necessary to prevent the loss of lives during wartime, the military have their own reasons for limiting press coverage, many of which are unrelated to the security of operations. They have found a soulmate in the Reagan administration.

A new administration must commit itself to a policy of truth-telling. Disinformation and false and misleading domestic propaganda programs have no place in a democratic society. Prudent statesmanship may dictate that, at times, all information may not be made immediately available. But any information that is disseminated by the government to the American people must be truthful.

National Security, Classification of Government Documents

In 1982, President Reagan signed Executive Order No. 12,256 to provide a "uniform system for classifying, declassifying, and safeguarding national security information." Perhaps the most telling statement in the order appears in Sec. 1.1(c):

> If there is reasonable doubt about the need to classify information, it shall be safeguarded as if it were classified pending a determination by an original classification authority...If there is reasonable doubt about the appropriate level of classification, it shall be safeguarded at the higher level of classification pending a determination by an original classification authority.

In other words, when in doubt, classify—a significant departure from earlier Executive Order No. 12,065 which directed that doubts concerning classification were to be resolved by classifying at a lower level—if at all.

As a result, the Reagan administration has become obsessed with secrecy. Employees with security clearances in the Defense and State Departments have been required to sign lifetime secrecy oaths and submit to polygraph testing; news organizations have been threatened with criminal prosecution under the federal espionage statutes for publishing certain types of classified information; the administration has attempted to close espionage trials to the press and public, and to remove from library shelves books and documents which, having been declassified, were subsequently reclassified by the National Security Agency; the government in an unprecedented action prosecuted a government employee for espionage for leaking classified information to a British publication; covert intelligence operations have been conducted abroad.

Although the Reagan administration can boast relatively few court victories to date, the claim of dire consequences resulting from release of information allegedly pertaining to the national security is powerful and, on its face, compelling. The administration has successfully employed intimidation to coerce compliance with its directives to suppress stories, especially in those cases where court actions probably would not succeed.

In May 1986, then CIA Director William Casey advocated the prosecution of NBC News for broadcasting a report that included the code name "Ivy Bells" for what the network described as a program involving eavesdropping by U.S. submarines in Soviet harbors. The story aired prior to the espionage trial of former NSA analyst Ronald Pelton. Casey also considered seeking prosection of *The Washington Post* for publishing articles including information on Pelton's activities, much of which was available from court records.

While the cases were being reviewed by the Justice Department, several members of the administration, including President Reagan, contacted *The Washington Post*, urging the newspaper to refrain from publishing information which they said would damage national security.

This smoothly orchestrated campaign was designed to achieve through intimidation what the administration probably knew it could never achieve through court order: a prior restraint on publication. From the administration's perspective, the goal of secrecy was obtained in the best possible way. No court or other independent authority was asked to evaluate the evidence of potential damage to national security, or to force the government to overcome the heavy presumption that prior restraints are unconstitutional, as the Supreme Court has recognized in *Near v. Minnesota* and in the Pentagon Papers case.

Instead, these officials decided that the people could not have access to information, much of which was already in Soviet hands or had previously been made public. They did so without consideration for the First Amendment rights of the news media to publish and of the public to know.

As recent events in the United Kingdom under Margaret Thatcher's administration have demonstrated, a government with authority to classify any information on national security grounds will go to absurd lengths to preserve governmental secrecy—even when the information is no longer secret. Banning books, requiring prepublication clearance of manuscripts written by former government employees, attempting to restrain the news media in various ways have all been an integral part of the Thatcher intimidation campaign.

Perhaps the most notorious example revolves around the *Spycatcher* case, in which a former MI5 agent published his memoirs, which included embarrassing allegations about covert activities by Great Britain's domestic intelligence service. In addition to banning the book in Britain, the Thatcher government also sought and won preliminary injunctions against British newspapers, preventing them from republishing the agent's allegations. The dissenting opinion of Lord Bridge of Harwich is particularly instructive. He wrote, "Freedom of speech is always the first casualty under a totalitarian regime...Censorship is the indispensable tool to regulate what the public may and what they may not know."

Freedom of Information

The Freedom of Information Act (FOIA) was enacted in 1966 to ensure that the public would have the right to obtain information about the government's operations and activities. Prior to that time, in order to obtain government documents, members of the press and public had to rely on Section 3 of the Administrative Procedure Act which permitted federal agencies to withhold records if doing so was "in the public interest" or "for good cause," and to deliver the documents only if the requester was found by the agency to be "properly and directly concerned" with the documents sought.

The FOIA was amended in 1974 and several times subsequently, and, at least on its face, affirmatively empowers the public to obtain government information. However, federal agencies have often been reluctant to comply with requests for information. As the law enforcement arm of the federal government, the Justice Department is charged with seeing that the laws of the nation are carried out. But its treatment of the FOIA represents an odd divergence from purpose.

No visible effort is made by the Justice Department to enforce this law. Justice officials speak of successful efforts to bar release of information as "wins," court decisions requiring disclosure as "losses."

The Justice Department has litigated enthusiastically to expand the parameters of secrecy in government. By devoting its energies to the defense of questionable denials, prohibitive fee levies, and refusals to waive fees, the Justice Department has, during the Reagan administration, simply abandoned the role it once assumed of enforcing the FOIA. One recent example illustrates this.

In the last days of the 99th Congress, Republican members of the U.S. Senate, led by Sen. Orrin Hatch (R-UT), slipped amendments to the FOIA into a comprehensive drug control bill. Among other things, the amendments broadened the FOIA's exemption for law enforcement investigatory records. However, as a result of negotiations with Sen. Patrick Leahy (D-VT) and representatives of public interest and media groups, the amendments also established, as a compromise, a new structure for fees and fee waivers.

Representatives of the news media and educational and scientific institutions could be charged only duplication fees for FOIA requests generating responses exceeding 100 pages. All other non-commercial requesters would pay only search and duplication charges (with two free hours of search time and 100 pages supplied free). Commercial requesters would pay customary search and duplication charges, plus a new fee to cover time spent by agency personnel reviewing documents.

The FOI Reform Act of 1986 states that waivers or reductions are to be granted if disclosure is "in the public interest because it contributes significantly to public understanding of the operations or activities of the government and is not primarily in the commercial interest of the requester." Hailed as a major reform intended to encourage the free flow of information to the public at large, the ink was barely dry on the act before the Office of Management and Budget and the Justice Department set to work to circumscribe it.

Under the act, Congress entrusted agency oversight on fee waivers to the OMB, whose guidelines reiterated the statutory language of the new, reformed, public interest fee waiver standard without imposing restrictions on its use. But it also defined preferred categories of requesters more narrowly than Congress had intended: for example, defining "representative of the news media" as one who gathers "news," which in turn is defined as only that information which is "about current events" or "of current interest to the public."

Most agencies simply parroted this language in their proposed fee waiver regulations. The practical result was that a government agency, itself the target of a press inquiry, and with no discernible expertise in news judgment, would decide whether the information sought was of current interest. One journalist has already been denied a fee waiver for information on an emerging political party on the grounds that such information was not "news."

Frustrating as the OMB guidelines were, the Justice Department's twelve pages of guidance to agencies were even worse. They included a multi-factor test requesters must meet to qualify for fee waivers, which demands that the information be about government itself, be "meaningful," would enhance public understanding significantly, and that the requester will distribute the information to the public at large.

The guidelines, adopted virtually wholesale by most agencies, conclude that the new standard will result in fewer rather than more public interest fee waivers. Thus, reform legislation specifically intended to overcome high fee levies on information of public interest was manipulated by the Department of Justice and opportunistic agencies to create new hurdles for FOIA requesters. Scarcely surprising, when it was engineered by the Reagan Justice Department.

Absent affirmative executive oversight, policy, and regulatory review, agencies enjoy wide latitude in disregarding the FOIA provisions. For example, they routinely ignore the mandated 10-day limit to respond to requests. Release is delayed because fee issues are not settled, search requirements are narrowly interpreted, and because routine backlogs in processing, exacerbated by budget cuts, grow into months and years. In practice, many agencies fail to treat the FOIA as law.

A possible solution to the problem would be creation of an independent ombudsperson agency charged with affirmative enforcement of the FOIA. The office should provide administrative education and guidance to agencies so that FOI specialists and officers within the government can fulfill the mandates of the FOIA and follow court decisions. By challenging agency abuses of the FOIA, it would ensure that citizens receive the government information to which they are entitled.

What such an agency must not do is attempt to balance the interests of enforcement versus non-enforcement of the FOIA. That is clearly the responsibility of Congress, not the executive branch. Any administrative procedures adopted by the agency must not further encumber the FOI process. Finally, the agency must exist in addition to, not in lieu of, the option of full judicial review of denials.

What is critical is that oversight of the FOIA be shifted to an entity that will vigorously enforce openness. Executive agencies exist to carry out or enforce laws. Almost every statute finds a home in an agency which dedicates energy to its enforcement. If the FOIA is not currently a homeless child, with no agency responsible for its nurture, it is an abused one, regularly thrashed by its guardian.

Free Trade in Ideas

The free flow of ideas from every ideological sphere is essential to ensure that the electorate is well informed about the United States and the world at large. Yet the Reagan administration has consistently attempted to restrict the flow of opinion both inside and outside our borders.

The methods employed range from delaying delivery to U.S. citizens of books from Cuba to detaining or excluding foreign journalists at points of entry into the United States under the McCarran-Walter Act, either because they are carrying documents or have written books suspected of espousing "communist doctrine" or have links with political groups opposed to the Reagan administration.

Corrective legislation modifying for one year the exclusion and deportation provisions of the McCarran-Walter Act was signed into law in December 1987. The change prevents denial of visas, restrictions on visas, or deportation on the basis of a person's beliefs or associations, as long as the person would be protected under the Constitution. However, exclusion and deportation of aliens on foreign policy grounds, as well as on grounds of membership in terrorist groups, the PLO, or former membership in the Nazi Party, would still be permitted. Changes still must be made not only to remove ideological grounds for exclusion and deportation, but grounds as well relating to mental health and sexual orientation.

The Justice Department has labeled films produced by foreign entities, such as three films on acid rain and nuclear war produced by the National Film Board of Canada, as "political propaganda," which designation also requires the agent distributing the films in the United States to file a report with the Attorney General indicating where and when the materials were disseminated, as well as an estimate of the number of people who received them.

Outside the realm of political thought, the Reagan administration has also been active policing morality. The Federal Communications Commission issued vague guidelines governing the broadcast of "indecent" materials on the nation's airwaves and promised swift retribution against broadcast outlets daring to violate them. The Commission on Pornography established by Attorney General Edwin Meese engaged in an extensive study of the supposed effects of pornography and on efforts to control its production and distribution. In addition to issuing a 2,000-page report recommending ways in which legislatures, law enforcement agencies, and citizens' groups could prevent dissemination of sexually explicit material, the commission also wrote to retailers of *Playboy*, *Penthouse*, and similar magazines, threatening to list them in the report as "distributors of pornography." A federal judge in Washington, DC ordered the commission to retract the letter.

Any new administration must be committed to a policy that will encourage free flow of ideas, both inside and outside the United States. The right to air dissenting or unpopular points of view must never be abridged. And the right of adults to read and view whatever material they choose should not be subject to divestiture by the government of the day. Freedom of thought and expression are essential to a free society.

Resources

Organizations

- Advocacy Institute, 1730 M St. NW, Washington, DC 20036; (202) 659-8475

- American Newspaper Publishers Association, The Newspaper Center, P.O. Box 17407 Dulles International Airport, Washington, DC 20041; (703) 648-1000

- American Society of Access Professionals, 2001 S St. NW, Washington, DC 20009; (202) 462-8888

- American Society of Newspaper Editors, P.O. Box 17004, Washington, DC 20041; (703) 620-6087

- Associated Press Managing Editors Association, 50 Rockefeller Plaza, New York, NY 10020; (212) 621-1552

- Coalition on Government Information, c/o American Library Association Washington Office, 110 Maryland Ave. NE, Washington, DC 20002; (202) 547-4440

- FOIA Inc., 145 W. 4th St., New York, NY 10012; (212) 477-3188

- Gannett Center for Media Studies, Columbia University, 2950 Broadway, New York, NY 10027; (212) 280-8392

- Government Accountability Project, 25 E St. NW, Washington, DC 20002; (202) 347-0460

- Institute for Freedom of Communication/Freedom of Expression Foundation, 414 S. Capitol St. SE, Washington, DC 20003; (202) 546-1917

- Inter-American Press Association, 2911 NW 39th St., Miami, FL 33142; (305) 634-2466

- Investigative Reporters & Editors, P.O. Box 838, Columbia, MO 65205; (314) 882-2042

- Lawyers Committee for Human Rights, 36 W. 44th St., New York, NY 10036; (212) 921-2160

- National Association of Broadcasters, 1771 N St. NW, Washington, DC 20036; (202) 429-5350

- National Federation of Press Women, 1105 Main, P.O. Box 99, Blue Springs, MO 64015; (816) 229-1666

- National Lawyers Guild, 55 Avenue of the Americas, New York, NY 10013; (212) 966-5000

- National Newspaper Association, 1627 K St. NW, Washington, DC 20006; (202) 466-7200

- National Security Archives, 1755 Massachusetts Ave. NW, Washington, DC 20036; (202) 797-0882

- Radio Television News Directors Association, 1717 K St. NW, Washington, DC 20006; (202) 659-6510
- Reporters Committee for Freedom of the Press, Suite 300, 800 18th St. NW, Washington, DC 20006; (202) 466-6313
- Society of Professional Journalists, Sigma Delta Chi, 53 W. Jackson Blvd., Chicago, IL 60604; (312) 933-7242
- Women in Communications, Inc., P.O. Box 9561, Austin, TX 78766; (512) 346-9875
- Writers Watch, 421 New Jersey Ave. SE, Washington, DC 20003; (202) 547-5000

Further Reading

- Melville B. Nimmer, *On Freedom of Speech*, Matthew Bender, 1984.

- Steven L. Katz, *Government Secrecy: Decisions Without Democracy*, People for the American Way, 1987.

Jane E. Kirtley is Executive Director of The Reporters Committee for Freedom of the Press, an association of reporters and editors dedicated to protecting the First Amendment interests of the news media. In addition to overseeing the Reporters Committee's legal defense and research activities, she is editor of the quarterly magazine, *The NEWS Media & The LAW*. She has prepared numerous *amicus* briefs on behalf of the Reporters Committee, and writes and speaks frequently on First Amendment issues. She is a former newspaper reporter, and practiced law in Rochester, New York and Washington, DC before joining the Reporters Committee in 1984.

Don Adams and Arlene Goldbard

Cultural Democracy: A New Cultural Policy for the United States

Platform

- Establish a national policy of cultural democracy.
- Promote cultural diversity by supporting minority cultural enterprises and multicultural education.
- Undertake a coordinated approach to the electronic media to assure democratic control, encourage media literacy, and stimulate independent voices.
- Encourage community cultural participation by redirecting public resources to provide the means for cultural creation: facilities, equipment, instruction, and services.
- Deploy thousands of creative workers in community cultural projects through a new public service employment program.
- Re-enter global cultural dialogue by rejoining UNESCO, developing new cultural exchange programs, and opening U.S. borders to visiting artists and scholars from abroad, without political restriction.
- Establish a cabinet-level Department of Cultural Development to oversee federal involvement in cultural affairs.

Federal policy helps answer many questions about our national cultural identity: how the arts are supported, who decides what is broadcast, what will be built, what pastimes will be encouraged, when certain languages can be spoken or customs practiced, how we educate our children and treat our elders, how we relate to our diversity as a nation and to the rest of the world.

Whether or not cultural policy is made explicit, government has massive cultural impact. From Indian removal to urban renewal, from importing human beings as slaves to excluding others through immigration quotas, U.S. cultural policy has been conceived and implemented by every arm of government. Though cultural policymaking in the United States is fragmented, haphazard, and frequently *sub rosa*, government intervenes in cultural life at many points.

The next administration needs to acknowledge the federal government's enormous cultural impact, bring it under democratic control, and turn it toward cultural democracy. Many new initiatives must be taken to encourage pluralism, participation, and equity in our national cultural life.

This chapter concentrates on the most critical aspects of public policy: elements of culture with broad social impact, such as the mass media; and initiatives with great democratizing potential, such as public service employment for creative workers. These emphases go against the grain of current policy, which treats certain cultural issues with obsessive attention—for instance, the level of public subsidy for such prestigious arts institutions as the major opera and ballet companies, museums, and symphony orchestras. This narrow focus would end under a democratic cultural policy, which would offer major institutions new roles to play in implementing programs like those outlined below.

Nurturing Cultural Diversity

The new democratic cultural agenda should promote diversity where government, market forces, and other powerful interests have discouraged it.

The United States has a long history of suppressing minority cultures. We now need a full-scale campaign acknowledging diversity as the source of our cultural vitality. Support must be directed to minority cultural enterprises so that they attain economic parity with their counterparts in the dominant culture. There must be truly equal opportunity for women and people of color throughout the cultural industries and allied government agencies.

Educational policy is key. Teaching must reflect the history and contributions of women, of people of color, of all of the cultures that enrich our society. The federal government will have to provide financing for teacher training, experimental curricula, and textbooks. The Reagan administration has been shamefully short-sighted and jingoistic in opposing bilingual education. The next administration should consider the U.S. role in the world and our own changing population and declare universal bilingualism and cross-cultural understanding to be national educational goals.

It is easy to deduce current cultural values from grants made by the National Endowments for the Arts and the Humanities, two of the leading agencies: in effect, they say that what is most worth preserving and extending in our culture has been contributed by men of privilege and European heritage. This pattern of subsidy will have to change. Instead of mimicking private philanthropy, public funding should be invested in communities, institutions, and organizations working to advance cultural democracy and support diversity.

The electronic media's great potential to foster diversity has instead been used to stifle it. Reagan administration deregulation has diminished democratic control of broadcasting and cable franchising and accelerated consolidation of power within the cultural industries. Meager support for independent media has declined even further. A policy of cultural democracy would require a shift in government's entire stance toward the great interlocking complex of film, radio, television, publishing, and recording.

Current policy incorporates a clumsy and arbitrary division between commercial cultural enterprises (allowed to do pretty much as they please) and nonprofit cultural institutions (where government grants help to fill the gap between aspiration and income). The new democratic policy must address the cultural industries as a whole because there is an intrinsic relationship between commercial culture and the nonprofit realm. Hollywood corporations may be able to make almost anything, but they cannot manufacture one ingredient vital to their existence: creative imagination. Independent artists and arts' groups constitute a huge, vibrant, and largely uncompensated research and development wing of the cultural industries. Ideas originate at the grassroots, spring up in the streets, pass from galleries to museums and from clubs to concert halls, then return to the streets via radio, television, and movies.

The most effective public role is to nourish the roots of this massive system. By financing independent production and setting up alternative distribution systems and retail outlets that escape the stranglehold of the majors, public action can help introduce independent voices into a system dominated by a chorus of cash registers.

Many countries have discovered ways to harness economic success at the top of the cultural industries to provide sustenance for the grassroots. Developing nations swamped by "I Love Lucy" reruns have levied tariffs on imported programs to generate support for domestic production. Independent media in the United States can be seen as an underdeveloped nation in the shadow of a rich, fat commercial realm. A full-scale development program is needed. The advertising revenues of commercial broadcasters could be taxed to finance independent production. A fee could be assessed on transfers of commercial broadcast licenses, to provide funds for public radio and television. A substantial annual percentage of public broadcasting budgets could be earmarked for independent projects. These would be decent first steps, but much more is needed to redress the imbalance in the nation's airwaves.

These initiatives must be backed up by a long-term national commitment to media literacy. We all know the critical importance of written literacy to a democratic society; people who are unable to read and write are at the mercy of those who can. The same applies to mastery of electronic media. Too many of us see television as a fixture of the natural world, something that just happens. We are at the mercy of those who understand that electronic media are products and tools of human agency.

The next administration should make media literacy a national educational priority. Every high school graduate should have basic knowledge of audio, video, and film production as well as the psychological, physiological, and social dimensions of the media's influence. Every citizen should understand how the media have developed, who owns and controls them, how public policy affects these developments, and how to be a critical consumer of media. As media literacy grows, so will the pool of talent and initiative that can diversify and democratize the media.

Encouraging Public Participation

There is no democracy in a land of couch potatoes. Vibrant culture continuously multiplies opportunities for participation. One of the main goals of the new democratic cultural policy should be to stimulate active participation in community life in all its forms, including political life. This would be a radical redirection. Key federal agencies now channel the lion's share of their budgets to selected end-products—works of scholarship or art—rather than the means for cultural creation. The resulting need to decide which ends are most worthy has led to a baroque, exclusive fascination in the public sector with questions of taste, and a national policy that looks more toward developing markets for symphony and ballet tickets than to an active, engaged citizenry.

Access is fundamental to democratic cultural life. Free and low-cost facilities for amateur sports, exhibitions, studio work, performances and rehearsals, and community broadcasting should be available to everyone. Expensive tools such as darkroom equipment, light and sound systems, film and video cameras, kilns, and printing presses should be available for public use in community centers. Government should finance needed services such as classes and workshops, graphic design assistance, and pools of scripts, costumes, props, and scenery. Underused public buildings—for instance, schools and government offices after hours—should have second lives as community cultural centers.

To enliven political life, every arena should be made available for debate: schools and public halls thrown open for town meetings, theaters presenting relevant work, exhibition spaces featuring visual contributions to the dialogue, multitudes of publications giving voice to every stripe of opinion. Community animation projects should be supported, making artists and organizers available as public resources, helping their neighbors use cultural tools to articulate their own concerns and aspirations.

Livelihood for Creative Workers

As we strive to remedy chronic unemployment, we must broaden our definition of work to include occupations having social value but lacking commercial markets. Our workforce includes many thousands with training in cultural fields but unable to find jobs that put their skills to good use. The centerpiece of the next administration's cultural policy should be a contemporary version of the 1930s' "Federal One," the constellation of Works Progress Administration projects in the visual arts, theater, music, writing, history, and other areas of cultural development.

Unlike today's public policymakers, who play follow-the-leader with the private sector, the architects of Federal One sensibly decided that public intervention should be focused where private initiative had failed. Where theaters had gone under because audiences lacked money for tickets, the government created a new Federal Theatre, putting performers, writers, and technicians to work throughout the nation, making theater an affordable entertainment and a critical arena for social dialogue. Where private wealth was unable or unwilling to preserve our history, government workers produced such invaluable materials as the slave narratives recorded by the Federal Writers' Project.

More recent experience hints at the impact such a cultural employment program could have today. In the mid-1970s, at the height of the CETA (Comprehensive Employment and Training Act) jobs program, thousands of artists were employed in public service. When the first eighty-five CETA arts jobs in San Francisco were advertised, 3,000 artists showed up to apply. Across the country, CETA workers formed performing troupes to work with school children, at senior centers, and in the summertime streets. CETA jobs fueled dozens of murals, new publications, documentaries, community gardens, workshop programs, and neighborhood beautification projects.

A new Federal One could pick up where these earlier initiatives left off—or more precisely, were cut off by reaction in Congress or the White House. A new WPA could provide staffing for the publicly-subsidized community facilities that democratic cultural life demands. Artists employed in public service could operate media literacy campaigns, set up distribution networks for independent media, and work on community animation projects.

Smaller public initiatives can also help create economic opportunity for artists and cultural workers. Potential lies in one of the great ironies of the post-industrial age: the rising cost of energy is reversing some of the economic advantages of centralized mass production and distribution. Planners discovered this during the redevelopment of Washington's Pennsylvania Avenue: they learned that a wrought iron grille to protect the soil around a tree could be designed and fabricated by a local sculptor for less than the cost of buying it ready-made from a foundry and paying hefty shipping charges. It has become economically viable to commission local artisans to create street furniture, interior furnishings, implements, artifacts, and decorative embellishments.

The next administration should adopt a two-pronged program for reviving artisanship in the United States: helping establish networks to put local artisans in touch with businesses and public agencies that could use their services, and offering tax incentives for employing local artisans rather than purchasing mass-produced items. This is just one example of how the next administration could encourage the development of local cultural life by opening economic niches for creative workers.

Under the present system of public support for artists, need is not a criterion. In fact, it is sometimes considered a debit. With public policy modelled on private patronage, the safest grant is one given to an artist who has already been proven worthy by attracting private money. This silly supposition—that if you need the money, you probably don't deserve it—should be overturned by the next administration.

International Cultural Relations

Under the Reagan administration, the United States has become more than ever estranged from international cultural discourse. Reagan's withdrawal from UNESCO was the most striking indication of his indifference to global cultural problems.

One of the next administration's first actions should be to re-enter UNESCO as an expression of commitment to the UN Universal Declaration of Human Rights, which incorporates the right to culture. Within UNESCO, the United States should take an active stance in favor of cultural democracy. Instead of being guided by special interests—for instance, the Motion Picture Export Association's campaign against foreign restrictions on film imports from the United States—our government should work with developing nations, helping them to build their indigenous cultural production and preservation capabilities.

Existing cultural exchange programs affect very few people outside prestigious institutions. This is a pity because we have a great deal to learn from other nations. The next administration should launch an intensive cultural exchange program with three components. First, the federal government should finance exchanges between U.S. ethnic communities and their heritage cultures abroad, expanding on the Smithsonian's similar work as part of the American Folklife Festival. This 1976 Bicentennial program enabled Swedish-American fiddlers from Seattle and Minneapolis, for example, to meet and work with their counterparts in Sweden and perform in different parts of this country. Second, to educate creative workers in the United States for roles in implementing the new democratic cultural policy, there should be a substantial international exchange program aimed at widening our repertoire of methods and approaches. Third, the next administration should open our doors to artists and scholars from around the world, without political restriction. U.S. cultural missions abroad should function as satellite centers of cultural democracy, with libraries, visiting artists and groups, readings, and screenings of material which may not be freely available in host countries.

Department of Cultural Development

To make all of this possible, the federal cultural apparatus has to change. The United States needs a cabinet-level department to create and implement a responsive policy of cultural democracy. The overall aim of this new department should be to stimulate cultural vitality and diversity, always increasing access and participation, multiplying forms and styles, encouraging creativity, invention, and artistic freedom.

The new Department of Cultural Development would oversee a coordinated federal policy that enables the greatest possible degree of structural decentralization. Its direct authority should be restricted to those aspects of public cultural responsibility best accomplished at the national level: protecting cultural rights; nationwide research; training; information exchange; skills-sharing; distribution; financing national or regional projects; and acting as a funder of last resort for projects too experimental or controversial to attract local funding. Everything else— including most of what is taken on by existing federal agencies—should be devolved to more responsive local authorities. Lasting commitment to decentralizing authority and encouraging public participation in policymaking must extend to every corner of the new federal apparatus.

The purview of this new department would encompass the arts and humanities, recreation and sports, the electronic media, libraries, museums, minority cultural affairs, key aspects of public education, and international exchange. This would lend coherence to the extensive array of atomized agencies and programs now scattered throughout the federal structure, including: the National Endowments for the Arts and the Humanities, the Federal Communications Commission, the Public Broadcasting Service, the Corporation for Public Broadcasting, National Public Radio, the Library of Congress, the Institute for Museum Services, and programs within such agencies as the Bureau of Indian Affairs and the Departments of the Interior, Housing and Urban Development, Commerce, State, Labor, and Education.

Monitoring Cultural Impact

A democratic policy requires that government be held accountable for its cultural impact. No single department should have the task of monitoring cultural impact; a Big Brother is the last thing we need. Responsibility should be shared by numerous agencies and representative bodies, each assessing cultural impact within its own purview, preventing or ameliorating harm, and showing us where remedial actions are needed.

A cultural impact report should be part of every government process to design legislation, plan programs, or regulate public and private
initiatives. When a developer proposes to tear down an old neighborhood to make way for a new shopping center or factory, the residents'
cultural rights must be given standing alongside economic, environmental, health, and legal considerations. When a corporation applies
for the franchise to lay cable in a community and offer subscription
television, the requirements of local cultural development must be
brought into the negotiations from the start.

The United States badly needs an administration which can mobilize the same kind of creative imagination in the social arena that artists
bring to conceiving works of art. These proposals are only a beginning.
To those who suggest we cannot afford to undertake a national campaign for cultural democracy, we reply that we cannot afford not to.

Our cultural values as a nation are symbolized by the way we
have been squandering our national wealth—as a stockpiler and mer-
chant of arms, with no apparent higher priority than manufacturing
death. The next administration can begin to renew this country's cultural vitality by turning toward cultural democracy: pluralism, participation, and equity in a democratic society.

Resources

Cultural policies emerge from more than a dozen federal agencies. More than 100 presidential appointments are involved. Instead of
proposing a half-dozen candidates, we want to suggest a few of the
many networks from which the next president should draw. Many of
the national and regional groups listed below can refer readers to local
organizations.

Organizations

- Action for Children's Television works to encourage diversity and
  eliminate commercial abuses from children's television and publishes
  a magazine, *re:act.* ACT, 46 Austin St., Newtonville, MA 02160; (617)
  527-7870
- The Alliance for Cultural Democracy is an association of community-
  based arts programs and activist artists committed to political,
  economic, and cultural democracy. ACD publishes an occasional
  newsletter, *Cultural Democracy*, and sponsors an annual conference.
  ACD, c/o Neil Sieling, 217 North Cedar Lake Road, Minneapolis, MN
  55405; (612) 377-8524
- Alternate ROOTS (Regional Organization of Theatres South) is an alliance of performing artists in the Southeast creating original, com-

munity-oriented work. ROOTS has been a progressive voice in advocating equity for the region, particularly for groups working in rural and minority communities. ROOTS, 1083 Austin Ave. NE, Atlanta, GA 30307; (404) 577-1079

- The Association of American Cultures seeks to promote equity within the present system for artists and administrators of color. TAAC publishes a bimonthly newsletter, *Open Dialogue*, and sponsors an annual symposium. TAAC, Suite 210, 1377 K St. NW, Washington, DC 20005; (202) 724-5613

- The Association of Independent Video and Filmmakers (and its nonprofit Foundation for Independent Video and Film) promotes the interests of independent media people. FIVF publishes *The Independent*, a magazine appearing ten times a year. AIVF monitors public policy, lobbies in support of independent media, carries out research, and publishes technical assistance information. AIVF/FIVF, 625 Broadway, 9th Floor, New York, NY 10012; (212) 473-3400

- The Institute for Cultural Democracy, a new organization founded by Adams & Goldbard and other cultural democracy supporters, is a think tank and education center for artists, administrators, teachers, and policymakers. ICD, 618-A Walnut Ave., Ukiah, CA 95482; (707) 462-0169

- National Federation of Community Broadcasters provides programs, services, and national leadership for the growing number of community radio stations, and publishes the *NFCB Newsletter*. NFCB, 1314 14th St. NW, Washington, DC 20005; (202) 797-8911

- PEN American Center is a writers' organization active on such public policy issues as censorship and restrictions on freedom of travel. PEN, 568 Broadway, Room 401, New York, NY 10012; (212) 334-1660

- Union for Democratic Communications, a group primarily composed of academics and researchers, is devoted to the critical study of communications issues and policies and the development of democratic communications systems. UDC publishes *The Democratic Communique* and sponsors an annual conference and regional meetings. UDC, c/o Karen Paulsell, 5338 College #C, Oakland, CA 94618; (415) 655-0818

Further Reading

- The Cultural Correspondence Library is a collection of periodicals and articles, many inspired by cultural democracy. Write for a free catalog of reprints. CC, 505 West End Ave., New York, NY 10024; (212) 787-1784

- Augustin Girard and Genevieve Gentil. *Cultural development: experiences and policies*, Second edition. Paris: UNESCO, 1983.

- *Heresies, a feminist publication on art and politics.* P.O. Box 1306, Canal St. Station, New York, NY 10013; (212) 227-2108
- Owen Kelly, *Community, Art and The State: Storming the Citadels*, London: Comedia Publishing Group, 1984.
- Kwesi Owusu, *The Struggle for Black Arts in Britain*, London: Comedia, 1986.
- *UPFRONT* is the occasional magazine of Political Art Documentation/Distribution, a progressive artists' resource and networking organization. Publication is being suspended with the Winter 1988 issue, but many back issues are available. PADD also maintains an international archive of art of social concern. PADD, 339 Lafayette St., New York, NY 10012

Don Adams and Arlene Goldbard have, since 1978, been partners in Adams & Goldbard, a consulting firm now based in Ukiah, California. Their clients include arts organizations, media groups, and public agencies throughout the United States and abroad. They have written and spoken widely on cultural politics, including keynote speeches at both the U.S. and British national conferences of cultural democrats in 1986. Their first book, *Cultural Democracy*, awaits publication.

Establish Justice...

Civil Rights: The Continuing Agenda

Platform

The great effort to eliminate the scar of racism from our national life and remove the burden of race from millions of our citizens must continue in the form of government programs of the highest priority for the next president and administration.

- *civil rights enforcement:* The damage done by the Reagan administration to civil rights enforcement agencies in the federal government such as the Equal Employment Opportunity Commission, the Civil Rights Division and the Community Relations Service in the Department of Justice, the Office of Federal Contracts Compliance in the Department of Labor, the Office of Civil Rights in the Department of Education, the United States Commission on Civil Rights, and the civil rights enforcement units in all the departments and agencies across the government must be repaired and those agencies must be staffed by highly motivated and effective people.

- *full employment:* Jobs for every person who wants to work must be a priority of the first order for the next administration and must be pursued by a variety of public and private strategies, including use of the whole range of economic and fiscal policy tools available to the federal government together with joint public and private planning efforts, targeted investments, and public jobs programs at all levels of government.

- *social welfare programs:* Improved and expanded federal efforts in such critical areas as health, housing, community self-help and development, welfare, crime prevention, and inner-city education must be mounted, with sustained and vigorous care taken to ensure that programs intended for minorities and the poorest of the poor actually benefit them for as long as the programs are in existence.

The following are recommendations for initiatives to be undertaken by the new president.

- Race-specific civil rights remedies, like affirmative action, are still required. In part, they empower and develop middle-class black leadership—a process slowed to a crawl recently because of the injury done to these remedies. Contrary to conservative doctrine, empowerment of middle-class blacks also helps poor blacks because middle-class blacks are more likely to act as their advocates in places of power than will middle-class people in general.

- Government jobs programs to help achieve full employment are necessary for the black poor, who either do not have jobs at all or who do not have jobs that pay enough to get them out of poverty. No investments—whether encouragement of the private sector to create jobs for people who need them or government expenditures as employer of last resort—would pay more direct dividends in improving our human capital and our urban ecology. They would be bonuses above and beyond the justice payoff.

- A decent national welfare benefit floor must be established. Benefits in the richest states have been eroded in the last few years and those paid in some of the poorer states are shameful.

- Improvements in inner-city schools must be urgently sought at the same time we pursue the continued desegregation of all our schools.

- The stock of decent and affordable housing must be expanded.

- Federal grant assistance to local law enforcement programs should be reinstated and efforts to diminish both the demand and the supply of illegal drugs in this country should be redoubled.

- Urgent efforts need to be made to improve the system of health care for the poor.

- While most of the foregoing programs are cross-race in application, serious and sustained efforts must be made to target a substantial share of the resources appropriated for efforts aimed at the population in greatest need, the black poor.

———

In matters of race, acts of leadership are crucial. The new president must establish early on and regularly thereafter that the executive office is both a symbol of racial justice and a means to achieve it.

The president has the power of the "bully pulpit" and it should be used to change the nature of racial thought and the content of racial etiquette in the country. President Reagan used it to turn the message of racial justice upside down and helped create an ugly racial climate. Another power consists of the laws and regulations already in place and the administrative agencies which have been set up to enforce them. The new president must use those agencies to change the racist behavior which the laws and regulations were intended to outlaw. Reagan used his power to weaken both the enforcement mechanisms and the strength of laws and regulations. A third power is the power to propose new laws and regulations as conditions demonstrate that existing measures need strengthening and that other areas not yet reached by government activity must be addressed if justice is to be achieved. Reagan vetoed one major civil rights bill and had his Justice Department attempt to water down another. Partly because of Reagan's negative uses of these powers, our racial problems are still so severe that all three powers must be exercised vigorously during the term of a president who understands that our still unresolved racial problems disable our country in a number of critical ways.

America's racial problems are more critical today than at any time in the twenty years since the murder of the Reverend Dr. Martin Luther King, Jr. In 1968, blacks who rioted and risked death by forces attempting to restore order expected some political response to their acts. Although they had seen Congress respond to the civil rights movement by passing the Civil Rights Act of 1964, the Voting Rights Act of 1965, and the Economic Opportunity Act of 1964, they had felt no changes in their own lives. The riots demanded—incoherently perhaps—that the nation invent political solutions to the host of problems afflicting the poorest people in black America.

In those riots, after property and people were destroyed, the nation did finally act. Today, in isolated black ghettoes all over the country, blacks are still being destroyed in alarming numbers. The gun epidemic is murdering hundreds each year. The drug epidemic is bringing an untimely death to thousands each year. Black infant mortality rates—third world rates, which shame this first world nation—are death sentences for thousands more. Second-tier medical care, which exacerbates such poverty-related maladies as malnutrition, AIDS from intravenous drug usage, high rates of cancer, stress, and homelessness, all lead to gradual deterioration and early deaths of untold tens of thousands of others.

But people who suffer from such futurelessness do not expect the political system to respond to them. Many do not believe the economic system is relevant to them. They persist in behavior that mainstream sociologists and psychologists call self-destructive and which the 1988 Commission on the Cities, which reviewed racial conditions twenty years after the Kerner Report, called, with some real insight, "quiet riots." This time around, there is little inclination to respond to the steady destruction that is occurring in poor black communities.

By and large, the insight of the ghetto dwellers is quite right. The Reagan administration has repeatedly and convincingly demonstrated its hostility to their interests and its unwillingness to do anything significant about their plight. The great majority of powerful politicians in America, either because of a belief that Reagan has reformulated American politics, a fear of the deficit, or because of their own bigotry, have been willing to finesse issues of race and poverty and largely to ignore what the Reagan era has done to blacks and the poor.

Throughout these past seven years, mainstream blacks have almost been rendered politically impotent. Despite repeated requests, the Congressional Black Caucus has been denied any meeting with the president since a perfunctory introductory session during the first year of his first term. The views of those black leaders and others who have real constituencies in the black community have been continually discounted and derided by such high administration officials as Edwin Meese, III and William Bradford Reynolds. As a result of relaxed—some would say comatose—enforcement of civil rights requirements such as affirmative action, the positions of many middle-class blacks in white institutions have become precarious and a good number of them have lost their jobs. Others have seen low ceilings erected over their aspirations.

Whether middle-class blacks have been in public service or private life, Reagan's policies have severely limited their abilities to help that portion of the black population Reagan has really injured, the poor and the vulnerable. The black unemployment rate, which seemed fixed—prior to the Reagan years—at twice the white rate, has now risen to two and one-half times the white rate. The respected Center on Budget and Policy Priorities reported two years ago that during the Reagan presidency blacks in all five income quintiles had less disposable income than they had in the final year of the Carter presidency. It also reported that the income gap between the top fifth of the population and the bottom fifth was larger than at any time since 1947, when the Census Bureau first started keeping such statistics.

Finally, a number of studies, most notably those of Dr. William Julius Wilson of the University of Chicago, have documented the fact that the black poor are severely isolated. They are isolated from whites by their lack of money and by the absence of any other levers by which they might manage their way out of the ghettoes. They have also been left behind by those blacks in a position to take advantage of openings created by the civil rights movement to move up economically and away geographically. The ghettoes are barren places now, lacking the service organizations, businesses, social groups, and successful role models that were found in black neighborhoods in abundance when segregation forced all blacks to live together. They are also bereft of the informal network of news and information that exists among job holders about where job openings are occurring and new possibilities lie.

Moreover, those old black neighborhoods had fire and passion—though some of it was surely violent and degraded and though segregation itself was a massive assault on the dignity of all who were forced to endure it. But at least there was color and life. Many of today's urban ghettoes are pictures of desolation, abandonment, and pervasive drug-induced criminality. Youngsters growing up in such circumstances are having the actual experience of their civilization disintegrating around them and their nation abandoning them.

The Reagan years have spawned at least three approaches to all of this. The first is the approach of the Reagan administration and philosophers of the right. That is essentially to do nothing more, on the ground either that we've pretty much solved our racial problems or that anything we try injures the character of black people. I dismiss those out of hand as either absurd or as fig leaves for raw racism. The second approach is to look at that portion of the black population—a little more than one-third—that has achieved middle-class status and to conclude that the problems of the black poor—again, about one-third of all blacks—is a matter of class, not race. The final approach is to suggest that self-help and entrepreneurial efforts are the only answers to the problems blacks now face.

The "it's class, not race" diagnosis fits too nicely into the normal American way of dealing with racism—denial. Racism is deeply embedded in American culture. Even the Los Angeles Raiders declined the opportunity to hire the first black coach in the National Football League. American journalists with their endless psychobabble put-downs of the Rev. Jesse Jackson have surely demonstrated that racism is not limited to the intellectual domain of jock-following septuagenarians like Al Campanis and Jimmy "The Greek" Snyder. In very few American institutions do successful blacks have real power. If racism still limits the possibilities and injures the spirits of successful blacks, how can it be absent from the factors that so damage the lives of poor blacks?

Race affects all blacks. I have often observed that class accounts for most of my success and that race accounts for the limitations on my possibilities and a lot of my pain. The balance between the two has a great deal to do with the racial history of individual families. All blacks did not start the race at the same starting line. Some of our ancestors were luckier than others. Some slaveowners were kinder than others (and most slaveowners were kinder to some slaves than they were to others). Some slaves learned to read before they were freed. Some slaves were free long before Emancipation. Other blacks were held in semi-slavery generations after the Civil War ended. In 1965, for example, Martin Luther King, Jr. was shocked to find some black sharecroppers on an Alabama plantation near Selma who had never seen U.S. currency.

Thus, when the great rural to urban migrations took place in this century, some blacks came to the cities with more skills and more self-esteem than others. The blacks who came late carried enormous burdens of generations of racial oppression. That is what defined their class position. Moreover, as Professor Wilson pointed out in his landmark work, *The Declining Significance of Race*, in American economic arrangements, which are configured to benefit whites, blacks are an afterthought. That in itself is a racial burden, which all blacks share, but which, in a period when high technology jobs are increasing and those requiring limited skills in manufacturing are disappearing or moving abroad, is devastating to the black poor.

Thus, it seems clear to me that those who clutch at the conclusion that the problem is not race but class are engaging in the classic American racial tactic of denial (much like the southern whites who would regularly produce an Uncle Tom to assure visiting whites that blacks were happy and satisfied in segregation). If the problem is not race, America no longer has a moral obligation to do anything about it. And if it is class, then perhaps the problem reflects character defects in all of the afflicted, regardless of race, and the country has no obligation to them beyond the tender mercies of the "invisible hand."

It is true that a number of cross-class remedies are required to attack the problems of the black poor adequately and that such remedies are easier to sell in the political arena than are race-specific remedies. On the other hand, we know from our experience with general revenue-sharing and other non-race-specific efforts that programs originally intended to benefit the poor—when unaccompanied by strong and enforceable targeting requirements—are often dissipated among powerful non-needy segments of the polity.

The argument—advanced by some black conservatives during the Reagan years—that self-help and entrepreneurial efforts alone are the answer to blacks' problems is too absurd for serious treatment. Blacks have always relied on self-help, but they have always sought and welcomed outside help as well. Both self-help and massive governmental action are required to deal with the enormous problems facing black Americans—particularly the poor. Double-digit jobless rates, disastrous inner-city education, horrific drug and crime problems, decaying housing, and abysmal health care are such large-scale problems that government involvement at all levels is imperative if solutions are seriously sought.

But it is also true that new modes of self-help are urgently required. The growing isolation of the black poor poses awful problems for them and for those who would help them. Isolation and futurelessness breed adaptive habits, which, though perhaps useful for survival in the conditions and locations which receive the ultimate hostility of this society, work against participation in the larger society. The isolation also means that institutions and systems designed to serve ghetto areas become weaker and the political urgency of dealing with them as part of our national community disintegrates.

It ought to be clear that breaking down the isolation and helping to moderate some of the most destructive survival habits now being learned in the ghettoes of our nation is the business of everybody who cares about the health of our society. But, unfortunately, it is also clear to even the most casual observers of American life that most white people don't care enough about the black poor to even make the feeblest effort to understand their plight, much less to do anything about it. Therefore, if non-governmental help from outside the ghetto—help which is surely needed in conjunction with massive governmental efforts—is to be forthcoming, blacks, at least initially, will have to take the lead in providing it.

Voluntarism by newly empowered segments of the black community would make fortunate blacks partners with ghetto residents already at work on these problems and would place them in perfect positions both to learn from their new partners and to make a new politics with them. The skills that fortunate blacks had developed in the wider world and their connections to it would make the new politics visible and would supply the fuse needed to develop a national will to pass the legislation required to mount serious attacks on the afflictions of the black poor. The model I have in mind here as the engine for a new politics is the explosive force that blacks developed with the Montgomery bus boycott. The fuse lit there led directly, over the course of ten years, to the great legislative victories of the mid-1960s.

The Reagan-sponsored notion that those pieces of civil rights legislation and a few years of experimentation with Great Society programs could rectify the destructive impacts of two centuries of slavery and another century of legalized racial oppression after that is clearly ludicrous. The process of making blacks, as a people, whole is still a multi-generational project in which massive societal assistance is required in conjunction with sustained and creative rebuilding and reconstructive community efforts developed and carried out by black people. Neither can succeed without the other. It is the task of the national administration to reignite the energies for racial justice in this society and to provide for them powerful and unwavering leadership.

Resources

Recommended Appointees for a New Adminstration

For Attorney General
- A. Leon Higgenbotham, currently a judge on the U.S. Court of Appeals for the Third Circuit

- Damon Keith, currently a judge on the U.S. Court of Appeals for the Sixth Circuit

- Nathaniel Jones, currently a judge on the U.S. Court of Appeals for the Sixth Circuit

- William L. Taylor, a private lawyer, who served as Staff Director of the United States Commission on Civil Rights in the Johnson administration

- Drew Days III, currently professor at Yale Law School, Assistant Attorney General for Civil Rights in the Carter administration

For Secretary of Education

- Mary F. Berry, professor of history at the University of Pennsylvania, Assistant Secretary for Education in HEW in the Carter administration

For Secretary of Health and Human Services
- Marian Wright Edelman, president of the Children's Defense Fund, Washington, DC

For Secretary of Labor
- Harry Edwards, currently a judge on the U.S. Court of Appeals for the District of Columbia Circuit

For Sub-cabinet Presidential Appointments in Civil Rights and Closely Related Fields
- David Tatel, a lawyer who served as Director of the Office for Civil Rights in the Department of Health, Education, and Welfare in the Carter administration

- Elaine Jones, currently Deputy Director of the NAACP Legal Defense and Education Fund

- Lani Guiniere, a staff lawyer at the NAACP Legal Defense and Education Fund who served in the Civil Rights Division of the Department of Justice in the Carter administration

- Lynn Walker, a Ford Foundation officer, who served as Deputy Assistant Attorney General for Civil Rights in the Carter administration

- Christopher Edley, Jr., Professor at Harvard Law School, who served in the White House and at HEW in the Carter administration

Organizations

- Joint Center for Political Studies, 1301 Pennsylvania Ave. NW, Washington, DC 20001; (202) 626-3500. The Committee on Policy for Racial Justice (see list of readings below) can be contacted through the Joint Center for Political Studies

- Children's Defense Fund, 122 C St. NW, Washington, DC 20001; (202) 628-8787

- National Urban Coalition, 1120 G St. NW, Washington, DC; (202) 628-2990

- NAACP Legal Defense and Education Fund, 99 Hudson St., New York, NY 10013; (212) 219-1900

- National Urban League, 500 E. 62nd St., New York, NY 10021; (212) 310-9000

- Center on Budget and Policy Priorities, 236 Massachusetts Ave. NE, Suite 305, Washington, DC 20002; (202) 544-0591

Further Reading

- William Julius Wilson, *The Declining Significance of Race*, 2nd edition, University of Chicago Press, 1980.

- William Julius Wilson, *The Truly Disadvantaged*, University of Chicago Press, 1988.
- Derrick Bell, *And We Are Not Saved*, Basic Books, 1987.
- *A Children's Defense Budget*, Children's Defense Fund, 1987.
- *The State of Black America*, National Urban League, 1988.
- *A Policy Framework for Racial Justice*, Committee on Policy for Racial Justice, 1983.
- *Black Initiatives and Governmental Responsibility*, Committee on Policy for Racial Justice, 1987.
- Fred R. Harris and Roger W. Wilkins, eds., *Quiet Riots: Race and Poverty in the United States*, Pantheon, forthcoming.

Roger Wilkins is a Senior Fellow at the Institute for Policy Studies. He is also a Robinson Professor of History at George Mason University and on the steering committee for the Free South Africa Movement. He shared a 1972 Pulitzer Prize for his Watergate editorials, and served as Assistant Attorney General from 1966-1969. His most recent book is *A Man's Life*.

Achieving Economic Equity for Women

Platform

- Public policy concerning women should be geared toward the achievement of economic equity for women, through establishment of a Council of Advisors on Women's Issues, whose Chair would have cabinet rank, and through the specific policy proposals that follow.

- Improve women's labor market status through: strengthening and broadening enforcement efforts by the Equal Employment Opportunity Commission (EEOC); ensuring that federal programs in job training and contract procurement require the employment of women in nontraditional jobs; making the federal government a leader in promoting pay equity, in its own civil service, among federal contractors, and—through guidelines from the EEOC—among all employers; amending federal labor laws to support collective bargaining and encourage unionization, provide temporary and part-time workers with pro-rated benefits, and raise the minimum wage; improving job security through full employment policies, job creation when necessary, and the regulation of closings, layoffs, and subcontracting.

- Enable women and men to meet work and family responsibilities and broaden the social responsibility for children through: establishing the 30-hour work week and the six-hour day as the new norm through amendment of the Fair Labor Standards Act; providing universal, publicly-funded childcare and after-school programs; enforcing child support payments by absent parents through automatic payroll deductions and standardized awards; providing job-protected dependent care and illness leaves through new federal legislation; providing public insurance for the care of disabled children; developing publicly-supported elder care programs.

- Build community infrastructure and provide social services through: developing a national public health care system; providing federal

95

assistance for improved transportation, the encouragement of private and public enterprises, and the construction and operation of multi-purpose community service centers, particularly in economically depressed communities; encouraging the construction of private and public housing that meets women's needs (with communal facilities for childcare and meals), and prohibiting housing discrimination against families with children.

- Provide adequate support for individuals, and families, when not employed, through: increasing, at a minimum, current Aid to Families with Dependent Children (AFDC) benefit levels to the poverty level; replacing AFDC with a more universal income support program based on, first, broadening the unemployment system to include new labor market entrants and those re-entering after a period of family care, and, second, providing small cash allowances to all individuals (replacing the current standard dependents allowances in the federal income tax system); reforming the Social Security system to improve equity between women and men.

- Guarantee women's basic rights through strengthened rights to control their own reproductive capacity and through passage of the Equal Rights Amendment.

The past two decades have seen increased economic equity for women. The growth of the service sector has provided jobs for women; women have increased their participation in the labor market; the pay gap between women and men has been reduced somewhat; women have entered a wider range of jobs; and women's share of higher-paying jobs has increased. Women's educational attainment is now almost equal to men's. Yet, despite their progress, women are still significantly disadvantaged relative to men. Women who support children on their own are disproportionately poor and women make up a disproportionate share of the poor elderly. Women of color experience more poverty and unemployment, lower wages, and a narrower range of job possibilities than white women. Women thus have many urgent needs to be addressed by public policy, particularly because of the general neglect of issues important to women during the Reagan administration.

The central goal of public policy should be to ensure that women have full access to economic resources, that they be as capable of supporting themselves and their dependents as are men, and that they not be economically dependent on individual men. These changes would further restructure economic relations between women and men, and likely change social and intimate relations as well, perhaps dramatically.

Economic equity for women is a matter of basic fairness, and economic justice for all people is a central feature of democracy. Women's full social and political participation is not possible until their economic status is enhanced. For women to achieve economic independence, what is required is not only a substantial jump in their wage earning capacity but also societal support for the functions generally performed by women on an unpaid basis—childcare, elder care, and community building. Societal support on the order required would also redistribute income from the haves to the have-nots and the have-less.

Women must have access to better jobs in the labor market. This requires a three-fold approach: women must get more access to the better jobs that already exist; the female-dominated jobs that women do now must have improved wages and working conditions; and jobs must be created in periods and areas of high unemployment. Second, responsibility for care of children and other dependents must be shared more broadly, and workers must be enabled to meet both their home and work responsibilities. Key components here are publicly-supported, universally available childcare and the 30-hour work week. Third, social infrastructure that builds communities, supports family life, and meets human needs must be developed. A national health care system is critical. Fourth, the income support system for those who are not employed must be improved and unified, so that women and men generally enjoy adequate levels and similar kinds of income maintenance. For example, unemployment insurance could be broadened to cover the needs of new entrants, re-entrants who have been out of the labor market for a period of family care, and others who have not been working but can be expected to develop attachment to the labor market.

These policy initiatives would help women become more economically independent and secure because they would improve women's income-earning capacity and help them combine income-earning and family care; help men combine work and family tasks and encourage a more equitable distribution of family and household work; and help all families care for dependents and achieve economic security. These policies also recognize the mutual dependence of women, men, and children, and indeed of all people.

A general policy consensus on appropriate roles for women and men—and government—in family life should be actively sought and developed:

> Women and men are equally responsible for financial support of themselves and family members, the care of family members, and the maintenance of the home. Government policies and programs should reflect these equal obligations, assist families and individuals with basic human needs—such as health care and housing—and support families and individuals financially when needed. Government policies must recognize all family types as equally valid and support the right of homosexual women and men to form families as they wish.

To accomplish these policy goals, a Council of Advisors on Women's Issues should be established within the Executive Office of the President. The Chair of the Council, like the Chair of the Council of Economic Advisors, would have cabinet rank. The central goal of the Council would be to advise the president on how equality for women could best be achieved and monitor the executive agencies to ensure that programs and policies were contributing to equality for women. The Council should be charged with maintaining communication with public commissions on women throughout the nation and should be empowered to hold hearings as needed to illuminate women's concerns and develop policy alternatives.

Women's labor market status could be raised by improving equal employment opportunity. Equal employment opportunity enforcement needs to be strengthened and broadened at the EEOC, which should reinstate class actions and systemic discrimination cases against large employers and increase the use of affirmative remedies such as goals and timetables. The EEOC should also initiate a thorough campaign against sexual harassment; the list of prohibited activities in Title VII of the Civil Rights Act should be amended to include discrimination on account of sexual orientation; consideration should be given to amendments designed to streamline current legal procedures, for example, by providing the EEOC with power to mandate remedies.

Government programs should vigorously encourage the employment of women and people of color in jobs where they are underrepresented, including in job training programs (such as the Job Training Partnership Act and any new programs) and among employers with government contracts (the Federal Contract Compliance Program). The sanction of removal of contracts should be used much more frequently; goals and timetables must be established and compliance monitored, possibly by on-site auditors for large employers.

Women's labor and market status could also be improved through improving wages and working conditions: the federal government must support and initiate pay equity strategies, both in its own civil service and throughout the labor market. The government, through the EEOC, should issue wage guidelines for typical jobs—such as secretarial—that place their wage rates relative to other typical jobs that are not female-dominated. Federal contractors should be required to abide by these guidelines. Federal labor law should be reformed as necessary to support collective bargaining and encourage unionization; employers should be legally required to provide temporary and part-time workers with the same hourly wages, fringe benefits (pro-rated), and job rights as full-time workers; the Fair Labor Standards Act should be amended to raise the minimum wage to $4.65 in stages and then index it so that it remains approximately half the average hourly wage of nonsupervisory employees, as currently proposed in the Congress.

Women's labor market status must also be improved by increasing employment security. At a minimum, unemployment benefit formulas should be revised so that women's labor market patterns are not discriminated against (unemployment insurance currently benefits the typical male worker more than the typical female worker, because it is based on a model of cyclical layoffs for full-time workers). Unemployment should be reduced by a commitment to full employment, including job creation when and where necessary. Job creation for women entails creating jobs in occupations in which women already work in large numbers, such as childcare and social work, and hiring them in jobs in which they are underrepresented, such as construction. Layoffs should be preceded by substantial advance notice; business closings that would result in worker displacement should be regulated; subcontracting that would result in job loss, lower wages, or worse working conditions should be prohibited. Training and retraining programs for displaced workers should be established, and women's special needs, such as for childcare and transportation, should be provided for; the emphasis in training and retraining programs should be to train women and people of color for higher-paying jobs than they traditionally hold.

Women and men must be able to meet work and family responsibilities, and the social responsibility for children and other dependents must be broadened. In order to support this goal, the 30-hour work week must be made the new norm, through amendment of the Fair Labor Standards Act to require overtime premiums after a 30-hour week or a 6-hour day. At a minimum, proposed family and medical leave legislation in Congress should be passed, including its provisions for job protection in the event of illness or childbearing, parental care for newly born or adopted children, and care for elderly parents or ill children; a further step would be to require all employers to carry temporary disability insurance, as five states now do, which provides for some wage replacement for pregnancy and other disabilities. An insurance system for paid dependent care leave should be developed, perhaps as part of an expanded unemployment insurance system. Universally available, publicly-funded childcare services and afterschool programs must be developed by local, state, and federal government working together. Automatic payroll deduction (with the federal income tax withholding system as a possible back-up) should be used to collect child support payments from absent parents (usually fathers), and levels of child support payments should be standardized according to the absent parent's income and the number of children. Furthermore, a national publicly sponsored insurance plan for the care of disabled children and improved facilities for disabled children must be developed; currently the added burden of caring for disabled children falls on the parents, and disproportionately on the mother. Public programs to assist families and individuals with elder care should be developed.

The needed infrastructure for social services and community rebuilding must be created through the development of a publicly-supported national health care system, with emphasis on prevention; patient participation, empowerment, and adequate facilities in under-served neighborhoods and regions should have high priority. Other community support systems should be developed with federal assistance, such as improved transportation systems and community centers that can provide daytime elder care, youth programs, or childcare services, as well as neighborhood meeting places. Public and private enterprise in depressed communities should be facilitated by federal subsidies, and women's participation in these ventures should be encouraged.

Adequate housing that meets women's needs must be provided; public housing authorities and private developers can be encouraged to provide housing with communal facilities for childcare, meals, etc. Housing discrimination against families with children should be prohibited by law.

Adequate support for unemployed individuals and their families must be provided. At a minimum, benefit levels in the current AFDC program must be increased to the poverty level. Ideally, AFDC would be replaced with a more universal income support program that might include small cash allowances (these would replace the current standard dependents' allowances in the federal income tax system) to all individuals (including children), and an expanded unemployment insurance system that would provide assistance to those newly entering the labor market or reentering after a period of family care as well as to the more traditionally unemployed. The Social Security system needs to be reformed from the point of view of improving equity between women and men.

Women's basic rights must be guaranteed. Women's right to control their own reproductive capacity must be established beyond a doubt; this includes the right to abortion services and the right not to be forcibly sterilized. The government should not withhold abortion services from government workers or poor women. The passage of an Equal Rights Amendment that guarantees women and men equal rights under the law should have especially high priority.

In addition to the above policy initiatives, public policy must be scrutinized for the ways in which it contributes to inequities for women. The proposed Council of Advisors on Women's Issues should review major legislation, such as the income tax code, for its inherent assumptions about women's roles and specific provisions that encourage outmoded life and work patterns. It should also review the enforcement of existing legislation where it appears to be inadequate. For example, vocational education that receives federal funding must by law promote sex equity, but far too often vocational education continues to teach boys to learn skills that will pay well and girls skills that will not. In areas such as these, the Reagan administration's actions have been sorely inadequate.

Despite the negative policies of the Reagan administration, however, women's economic status continued to improve, on average, because many of the recent changes in women's lives are not directly dependent on public policy. Economic and cultural forces have drawn women into the labor market, increasing women's incomes and economic autonomy. Indeed, we are in the midst of a major transformation in how women expect to and do lead their lives. Women are now less dependent on men and marriage for economic survival. Women increasingly spend more of their adult lives outside marriage and in the labor market. More women can now maintain households on their own above poverty. More women have children without men. Women also marry later, have fewer children, and do less housework. For many of them, the economic shift has proven beneficial. Other women, displaced homemakers for example, find themselves less able to negotiate the transformation. For these women, the costs of autonomy are too high.

The goal of public policy should be to maximize the benefits of these changes for women and to minimize the costs. Women will make even greater progress toward economic equity and full social and political participation, and poverty will be substantially reduced, if public policy assists women as wageearners and distributes the burden of family care more equitably.

The policies discussed above that directly affect the hiring, earnings, and promotion of women are critically important, and the rationale behind them is relatively well known. Less well known and justified are policies that seek to redistribute family care. Universally available, free, publicly-provided childcare and the 30-hour work week are essential if we are to maximize the benefits from the transformation in social life that is now occurring.

The standard work week has not been reduced by federal law in over fifty years, when it was set at forty hours in the Fair Labor Standards Act. The struggle to achieve the eight-hour day was waged by workers for decades and was not won until the Depression made shortening the work week appear to be a useful job creation policy. Today, those economists not predicting an imminent severe recession point to likely labor shortages between now and the year 2000, and indeed beyond. The baby boom generation is aging and is not repeating the high fertility of its parents' generation. The economic situation is far different from what it was in the 1930s.

Today's families are probably supplying more adult labor to the wage economy than ever before. But families are still largely responsible for the care of children and other family members. The forty-hour week was based on the wife's economic dependence on the husband. He could work forty, or more, hours per week *because* she took care of the household and him. True, not all families had this arrangement (many poor and working-class women worked, whether married or not), but it was more common in 1950 than it is in the 1980s, and, because it was a middle-class norm, it was the established cultural ideal. In today's two-parent family, both parents are more likely to be working in the labor market, and no one is available to maintain the family full-time. Even with children in childcare or school, too many family functions fall by the wayside. Women still do the vast majority of this work, but they necessarily do less than they used to.

Many observers view the two-income family as the result of "capitalist speed-up" of the family, forcing it to work harder than before. What we must realize is that, if it is a speed-up, it is one based on preconditions that no longer exist. Families cannot be "sped up" to this extent; they must reclaim time to maintain themselves. The best way to do this is to mandate a six-hour day as the normal working day and the 30-hour week as the standard work week. This schedule would correspond well with school hours for children. It would allow both men and women time for family concerns, so that the burden could be shared more equally between them. Shortening the work week is preferable to simply encouraging flex-time and part-time work, options which are likely to be used more by women than men, perpetuating inequality based on gender, and doing nothing toward reclaiming time for families. Establishing a standard day that would be shared by women and men is critical because research shows that when men use flex-time plans, they generally "batch" work time and use the resulting extended free time for leisure pursuits. Women still end up with a disproportionate amount of the family care. The goal of social policy should be to make leisure equally available to women and men. This requires that men take on more housework.

With both parents in two-parent families likely to be in the labor market, and with an increasing number of children being raised by single parents, childcare is an obvious need. Support for the public provision of childcare is growing. Childcare has been seen, up to now, as a personal problem for which individuals who have made individual choices seek individual solutions. As more families need childcare, it is increasingly seen as a social problem requiring a collective solution.

To replace the "free" labor of women at home is expensive. Employers, who are increasingly called upon to help provide childcare, recognize that they can rarely provide it on a cost-effective basis. Like education, childcare can best be provided by the public sector, because it can rarely be offered at a profit to the provider and because providing it serves a social as well as private purpose. Like Social Security, publicly provided childcare can be viewed as an insurance program to help people with one phase of their life cycle. Childbearing and rearing is becoming more common and more similar. Childbearing has actually become more universal, with most women having one or two children, probably closer together. Proportionally fewer women are having no children, and fewer women are having more than two children. Compared to the past, the period of life when parents need assistance with childcare is more limited, and everyone can expect to need about the same amount of assistance. This is an ideal situation in which support for public provision can grow.

To determine the best form of public provision, further discussion and experimentation should occur. Clearly, public schools, particularly in inner cities, have not always been effective; parents are concerned that public provision of childcare work better. The Headstart program clearly indicates the public sector can provide good childcare, and parents probably have more trust in the government than they would in for-profit providers. Some form of voucher system, redeemable only at nonprofit agencies, including the public schools, may work best. It would provide choice, but keep public subsidies from becoming private profits. Public bonds might provide the needed capital investment. The cost of such a program would be less than for the Social Security system or for public education; it could be paid for by a payroll tax system, to which both workers and employers contribute, but it should be a system that is not regressive.

Social invention on a grand scale took place in the 1930s in the face of grave economic crises. Today's crises are in some ways no less severe. The strain on women and men who are transforming family life without social supports is telling, and the social programs that once seemed daring and revolutionary—unemployment insurance and AFDC—are no longer adequate. New policies must recognize women's new economic and social role and enhance their full integration into the economy. At the same time, provision must be made for the care of children and other individuals in need. The central barrier to reorganizing our social priorities and fully accepting economic equity for women is that women have performed a vast amount of unpaid labor at home. That history of unpaid work has led to the devaluation of women's work when it is paid and the expectation by some that women should remain in unpaid work. Most women, however, are no longer willing or able to do this. They are not willing to bear the costs, as individuals, of social reproduction work that benefits everyone. It is time for us to invent new social forms fitting to our time and place.

Resources

Recommended Appointees for a New Adminstration

- Barbara Bergmann, Department of Economics, University of Maryland, noted economist, author of *The Economic Emergence of Women* and articles on economic policy issues

- Barbara Ehrenreich, Fellow, Institute for Policy Studies, co-chair, Democratic Socialists of America, noted speaker and author on women's and economic issues

- Myra Strober, Professor, Stanford University School of Education, economist with knowledge of women's employment problems, childcare, and education issues
- Isabel Sawhill, Senior Fellow, Urban Institute, reviewed the economic policy record of the Reagan administration, currently working on urban poverty issues
- Bella Abzug, former Congresswoman from New York, served as chair of a national commission on women under President Carter
- Alexis Herman, President, Herman and Associates, Chairperson of the National Commission on Working Women, Vice Chair of the National Council of Negro Women, former Director of the Women's Bureau, U.S. Department of Labor in the Carter administration
- Johnetta Cole, President of Spellman College, has written extensively on women, race, and class
- Vikki Gregory, Gregory Resource Associates, Wheaton, Maryland, attorney and policy analyst
- Eleanor Holmes Norton, Professor, Georgetown Law Center, former Chairperson, Equal Employment Opportunity Commission
- Teresa Amott, Professor, Department of Economics, University of Massachusetts, Boston, specializing in women's economic justice issues
- Mary Berry, Professor of History and Education, University of Pennsylvania and Howard University, Commissioner, U.S. Commission on Civil Rights
- Julianne Malveaux, economist, works on employment and related issues, especially for black women
- Lourdes Beneria, economist, Department of Urban and Regional Planning, Cornell University, knowledgeable about women's employment issues in the United States and abroad

Organizations

- Women's Equity Action League (WEAL), 1250 I St. NW, Washington, DC 20005; (202) 898-1588
- Women's Economic Agenda Project, 518 Seventeenth St., Suite 200, Oakland, CA 94612; (415) 451-7379
- Women's State Wide Legislative Network, 34 1/2 Beacon St., Boston, MA 02108; (617) 367-6669
- Wider Opportunities for Women (WOW), National Commission on Working Women (NCWW), 1325 G St., NW, Lower Level, Washington, DC 20005; (202) 638-3143
- 9 to 5, National Association of Women Office Workers, 614 Superior Ave. NW, Cleveland, OH 44113; (216) 566-9308

- National Institute for Women of Color, 1400 20th St. NW, Suite 104, Washington, DC 20036; (202) 828-0735
- Women's Legal Defense Fund, 2000 P St. NW, Suite 400, Washington, DC 20036; (202) 887-0364
- National Center for Policy Alternatives, 2000 Florida Ave. NW, Washington, DC 20009; (202) 387-6030
- National Coalition on Women, Work, and Welfare Reform, c/o WOW, 1325 G St., NW, Lower Level, Washington, DC 20005; (202) 638-3173
- Institute for Women's Policy Research, 1400 20th St. NW, Suite 104, Washington, DC 20036; (202) 785-5100
- Women's Initiative, American Association of Retired Persons (AARP), 1909 K St. NW, Washington, DC 20049; (202) 872-4700
- Children's Defense Fund, 122 C St. NW, 4th Floor, Washington, DC 20001; (202) 628-8787
- Child Care Action Campaign, 99 Hudson St., Room 1233, New York, NY 10013; (212) 334-9595
- National Committee on Pay Equity, 1201 Sixteenth St. NW, Suite 420, Washington, DC 20036; (202) 822-7304
- Council of Presidents, c/o National Women's Political Caucus, 1275 K St. NW, Suite 750, Washington, DC 20005; (202) 898-1100

Further Reading

- Barbara Bergmann, *The Economic Emergence of Women*, Basic Books, 1985.
- Family Policy Panel of the Economic Policy Council of the United Nations Association of the United States of America, *Work and Family in the United States: A Policy Initiative*, UNA-USA, December 1985.
- Sheila B. Kamerman, "Women, Children, and Poverty: Female-Headed Families in Industrialized Countries," *SIGNS: Journal of Women in Culture and Society*, 10:2, 1984, pp. 249-272.
- Diana Pearce, "Toil and Trouble: Women Workers and Unemployment Compensation," *SIGNS: Journal of Women in Culture and Society*, 10:3, 1985, pp. 439-459.
- Women's Economic Agenda Working Group, *Towards Economic Justice for Women: A National Agenda for Change*, Institute for Policy Studies, 1985.
- Working Seminar on Employment, Welfare, and Poverty, *Women, Families, and Poverty: An Alternative Policy Agenda for the Nineties*, Institute for Policy Studies, 1987.

Heidi Hartmann is the Director of the Washington-based Institute for Women's Policy Research and Director of Women's Studies and Professor of Sociology at Rutgers University. She edited the National Academy of Sciences report on pay equity, *Women, Work, and Wages,* as well as reports on sex segregation in the labor market and the impact of new technologies on office work. She writes and lectures frequently on economic issues affecting women.

John Conyers

Toward Democratic Justice

Platform

- Revise laws relating to the national security apparatus to provide criminal penalties for violations of congressional and other legal mandates.

- Fight the nation's drug epidemic with: financial and technological assistance to drug-exporting countries to develop alternative crops, and by conditioning economic aid on cooperation with plans to limit export of drugs; an increased budget for enforcement of drug laws; appointment of a national "drug czar" to coordinate the anti-drug efforts of the DEA, FBI, Coast Guard, Justice Department, and financial institution regulatory agencies; and establishment of an Institute on Drug Use within NIH, to consider the cultural, psychological, and economic aspects of drug use in our society.

- Pass federal legislation banning the sale, purchase, importation, manufacture, transfer, and transport of handguns.

- Direct the Department of Justice to collect and publish statistics annually on "hate crimes."

- Combat "white-collar" crime via: revision of insider trading laws to clarify what constitutes criminal conduct; strengthening the civil portions of the Racketeer Influenced Corrupt Organizations Act (RICO) to create a strong consumer protection and fraud deterrent tool; creating stronger criminal sanctions under the Occupational Safety and Health Administration Act, and allowing states to pass more stringent laws in this area; establishing a new section within the Department of Justice to deal with defense contracting abuses.

- Outlaw capital punishment.

- Allocate funds to provide for greater use of alternatives to incarceration.

- Restore the federal grand jury system to its historical role as a people's watchdog against overzealous prosecutors and government corruption.

———

When historians seek examples of how ideology and politics can affect the administration of law, they will surely look to the Reagan administration's Department of Justice. Never have we known an administration that has so politicized the enforcement and administration of law, and never has the price been so high.

From the very beginning, the administration made evident that its understanding of law was a radical one, devoted to changing fundamental precepts and judicial precedent, enforcing statutes only when convenient, proposing constitutional doctrine widely at variance with the federal courts, and advocating a legislative agenda to promote a conservative world view rather than public safety and accountability.

Because of this bias, the Reagan Department of Justice has failed to have a measurable impact on crime, either in the streets or in the suites. It has failed, for instance, on narcotics, using drugs as a political football, demogogically asking the American people to "just say no to drugs," while it said "no" to the war on drugs by cutting funds for enforcement from the Coast Guard and Drug Enforcement Administration, treating international drug traffickers who supported administration policy in Panama and Nicaragua as friends, and failing to implement real, albeit undramatic, solutions abroad, such as alternative crop programs for drug-exporting countries. It chose not to prosecute defense contractors who bilked the Treasury of millions and pharmaceutical manufacturers who knowingly marketed products with lethal defects.

Too often, the Reagan Justice Department has ignored the problem of race, refusing to enforce critical civil rights laws while attempting to overturn the most modest of them in the courts. It openly challenged the legitimacy of Supreme Court decisions in the areas of civil rights and criminal law; it suggested that decisions on affirmative action and desegregation were neither clear nor binding; it has repeatedly challenged the long-accepted "doctrine of incorporation," the principle that the Bill of Rights applies to the states; it even questioned, in a congressional hearing, the cherished legal ideal that a person is presumed innocent until proven guilty.

The chief legal officer of the United States, Attorney General Edwin Meese, like more than 100 of his administration colleagues, has personified the "just us" concept of justice, which includes an arrogant disregard for accountability. He has been subject to repeated charges of ethical impropriety and conflict of interest which have prompted calls for his resignation from conservatives, mass resignations of high-ranking Department of Justice officials, and chuckles from Democrats who consider such charges beneficial in an election year. As Reagan's most controversial Attorney General, Meese has been the subject of not one independent counsel investigation, but three.

The Reagan Justice Department has advocated solutions to violent crime that make no difference: the death penalty, for instance. At the same time, it lobbied for relaxation of guns laws, while reports of over 10,000 gun-related homicides—a figure that on a per capita basis exceeds the rate of homicides in other western democracies by 1,000 percent—continue to show us the obvious: that gun control is the single most important method of reducing the murder epidemic.

With some important exceptions, the Reagan Justice Department has failed to acknowledge and take action on the growing phenomenon of "racial hate crimes"—such as the Howard Beach case. Instead, it has squandered scarce resources to investigate the peaceful activities of organizations—like CISPES—and individuals opposing administration policy in Central America.

The Meese Department of Justice has bred a new cynicism, creating the widespread and highly destructive perception that law and legal standards apply only when their enforcers want them to apply. The guarantee of legal neutrality has been severely damaged as a result.

The Department of Justice is one of the key agencies of government. It is responsible for a wide range of legal and legislative policy decisions: which civil and criminal cases the government will investigate and prosecute; who will be nominated to interpret federal and constitutional law as federal judges; how overall law enforcement policy will be developed in such matters as drugs, organized crime, including white-collar crime, racial violence, enforcement of voting rights, and civil rights. It enforces tax law and environmental law, securities law and laws on corruption. Its actions indicate how serious a $200 billion annual fraud problem is, and how serious racial divisions are. The Department of Justice sets national priorities.

More than any other department, Justice must have integrity and consistency, even-handedness and accountability. The important issues that define our constitutional and democratic rights fall under its jurisdiction. Its officials guide the entire government to the highest standards of law.

The Iran-*contra* affair gave a clear indication of the administration view of accountability, constitutional separation of powers, and the law. In 1984, after public revelations that the CIA was mining Nicaraguan harbors and distributing assassination manuals, Congress reacted by controlling *contra* aid dollars, a power the Constitution vests entirely in that body. The Boland Amendment first restricted and then prohibited the use of any federal funds for *contra* support efforts.

After the president and his administration signed that law prohibiting aid, federal agencies assisted the *contras* anyway, helping private *contra* support efforts and interfering with the few criminal investigations into these schemes. The administration then claimed that the law and the investigations were unconstitutional because the only body that could investigate corruption within an administration was that administration itself.

With the exception of the pioneering work of Senator John Kerry (D-MA), whose monthly reports chronicled evidence of drug links to the *contras* and administration support for them when it was prohibited, Congress averted its eyes amid repeated news reports of *contra* support efforts and interrupted government investigations. Congressional inaction may have been as important as anything in understanding the climate that led to the most dramatic and zealous of the *contra* supply activities, the Iran-*contra* affair. In some measure it was the silence of Congress that gave the zealots the cover they needed. The Justice Department clearly would not prosecute violations of law involved in supporting the *contras*, and Congress refused to exercise its oversight. That failure, and the general quiescence of Congress in foreign affairs, sent a message to the White House that it was unaccountable.

What was most startling about the congressional Iran-*contra* report was the detailing of systematic violations of law by White House officials. Laws requiring presidential findings and congressional notification had been defiled; Congress' most basic check on executive power—the control of public monies for programs—had been ignored; a secret war had been conducted in violation of the Boland Amendment and international treaties.

The report charges that in trading arms for hostages to Iran and in illegally supplying weapons to the Nicaraguan *contras*, the Reagan administration disregarded "fundamental processes of government" and subverted "the rule of law." The report places ultimate responsibility for wrongdoing on President Reagan himself.

Drugs

If the United States were to declare war, the administration would understand that any serious attempt to win that war would require a strategy to identify resources and manpower needed to achieve certain results. It would then require that we commit the resources to execute that strategy. One fundamental concern would have to be studied as part of any overall strategy: why do so many people use drugs? Are their lives so empty, so stressful, so without hope, that they feel they have little choice? Are pushers in it for the money, and if gigantic profits were not part of the sale, would they leave the criminal enterprise? These are questions which need asking and answering.

A comprehensive strategy has been absent in our approach to the entire drug question. The administration has asked Americans to "say no to drugs." At the same time, after passage by Congress of major anti-drug legislation, it proposed a recision of $1 billion in a $3.7 billion drug enforcement effort.

Undeniable facts show that the Reagan administration's war on drugs has failed. Cocaine use tripled between 1982 and 1985 and increases every year. More than one-third of Americans have used illegal drugs and nearly one-fifth use them regularly. Drug use in high schools has increased rapidly; nearly one-third of high school students now use drugs. The illegal drug industry in the United States, with an income of over $130 billion, is currently the largest tax-free industry in the world.

Drugs destroy communities, lives, and futures. Their links to crime, organized and on the street, are well known. In some localities drugs account for 85 percent of crimes. Drug operators have even become enmeshed in our foreign policy: generals in Panama trafficked large amounts of drugs into the United States, with the knowledge of the Reagan administration; the Nicaraguan *contras'* links were widely reported by news organizations and in congressional hearings.

We are losing the drug war not because we do not know how to fight it; we do. We are losing the war because of a lack of leadership. A new administration's strategy should include the following:

- The United States must support, with financial resources and technology, a program for alternative crops for drug-exporting countries, which are generally poor and depend on export crops. Our policies must make it economically beneficial for exporting countries to export agricultural products we need, rather than drugs.

- The narcotics business should be seen for what it is: one of the greatest national security threats we face. The drug enforcement budget should be increased substantially. President Reagan's most recent budget proposals virtually ignored funding requirements for local police departments and public prosecutors. As a result, many police departments are being forced to lay off officers who could have been used to raid crack houses. Similarly, lawyers who could have been prosecuting drug peddlers will be working in private practice.

- A "drug czar" with responsibility for overseeing the many agencies—the Drug Enforcement Administration, FBI, Coast Guard, Department of Justice—in their interdiction and enforcement efforts. This effort should be coordinated with the Comptroller of Currency and other federal banking officials to track funds from federal and other banks.

- Foreign aid packages, most favored nation status, and approval of International Monetary Fund and World Bank loans should all be conditioned on cooperation from recipient countries in stemming their drug exports and converting to other cash crops. (Bipartisan legislation is now pending in Congress to do that.)

- Establishment of an Institute on Drug Use as part of the National Institutes of Health, which will consider all aspects of drug use in American society.

Street Crime and Guns

Street and violent crime, with some important exceptions, falls under the jurisdiction of state and local governments. The federal government and the Department of Justice, however, play important policymaking and legislative roles in matters that have simultaneous federal jurisdiction. The federal government can substantially stem the murder epidemic and cut street crime by banning the sale, purchase, importation, manufacture, transfer, and transport of handguns.

The facts and figures are there for everybody to see. In an average year, more than 10,000 Americans will be murdered with a handgun. The nearly 200,000 Americans killed with handguns in the United States over the last ten years amounts to four times the number killed in the Vietnam War. Yet, despite the fact that this country is confronted with a handgun murder crisis, Congress has managed to pass only the weakest form of gun control laws. Strong gun control laws are not the complete answer to murders. However, they make clear society's values. Just as the fifty-five mile-per-hour speed limit does not eliminate all speeding, it has saved thousands of lives.

Hate Crimes

During the past few years, the number of physical and psychological attacks on persons who were targeted solely because of their race, religion, sexual orientation, or ethnic origin has increased alarmingly. According to a report by the Atlanta-based Center for Democratic Renewal, there was more violent crime by hate groups from 1983 to 1986 than there had been over the previous two decades. These crimes ranged from murder to the desecration of religious property.

Participants in the "Brotherhood March" in Forsyth County, Georgia, on January 17, 1987, were attacked by white-hooded Ku Klux Klansmen hurling rocks, bottles, and racial slurs. This incident brought home to many the fact that, despite a decline in membership, the Klan is still a visible and active organization. The extent of the problem, however, is still not always publicly realized. In recent years, a number of new, more sinister, and more militant extremist groups, such as the Aryan Nations and The Order, have surfaced and engaged in robbery, assaults, bombings, and murder to advance their white-supremacist agenda. Though its leadership has been decimated by arrests and successful prosecutions, the "Christian Identity" movement is thriving, with up to 30,000 members, and continues to sow the seeds of racial hatred throughout the country.

Dramatic incidents like the death of Michael Griffith in the Howard Beach neighborhood of Queens, New York, or the bombing death in Santa Ana, California of American Arab Anti-Discrimination Committee official Alex Odeh, capture the attention of the public and remind us that hate crimes are still a reality. But few across the nation will ever know about a cross being burned in front of a rural black family's home unless such information is collected and publicized in the type of report called for in H.R. 3193, the "Hate Crime Statistics Act." One of the first steps that must be taken is for the Justice Department to collect and publish annual statistics on hate crimes. There are at present no comprehensive, accurate, up-to-date statistics kept on the national incidence of hate crimes. Keeping statistics about these offenses would be very useful, for they can provide the basis for cooperative state and federal law enforcement efforts. Currently, most police departments are left to speculate about the frequency, location, and possible perpetrators of hate crimes. The Department of Justice has the ability to do this job through its Uniform Crime Report system.

The Department asserts that collection of statistics on the number of bias-motivated crimes is too burdensome a task. This contention, however, is baseless. With proper training and clearly drawn criteria for evaluating the circumstances of a crime, the job can easily be done. Further, the value of what will be produced is well worth the investment of time and resources. The public's awareness of hate crimes should be increased in order to improve human relations in this country. Hate crimes are aimed at discouraging the free exercise of a person's civil and constitutional rights. They are intended not just to scare or injure a particular victim, but to intimidate a group of people. Hate crimes are a danger to the entire community.

The Justice Department has frequently abdicated its position as our nation's protector of civil rights and left the investigation and prosecution of hate crimes up to the states and localities. A more vigorous and even-handed prosecutorial effort is needed in the future if we are to successfully deter those who would commit such crimes.

White-Collar Crime

Crime in the suites is a major and serious problem which costs dearly. The Department of Justice's conservative estimates of white-collar crime put the price tag at the top of the crime charts—$200 billion annually.

Insider trading—access to and trading of securities information not available to the public—is one of those costly crimes. It gives an elite group of greedy securities investors and their accomplices the opportunity to make gigantic profits. The loser is the average investor, who must make investment decisions without the benefit of inside information, and who ends up being manipulated by insiders and their accomplices. If the integrity of, and public confidence in, the stock market is to be maintained, there must be tough federal criminal laws against insider trading. One of the lessons we learned from Black Monday—October 19, 1987, when the stock market declined over 500 points—is that confidence in Wall Street is critical at times of financial crisis and instability. The confidence wasn't there, and investors suffered.

We are now moving away from the concept of self-regulation and into the era of criminal prosecutions for insider trading. The Securities and Exchange Act of 1934, the primary law used to prosecute insider trading, is basically a civil statute, and was never intended to be used for criminal prosecutions. Consequently, the federal government has been forced to create novel legal theories in order to reach conduct which all would consider criminal. However, the three leading Supreme Court cases in this area, *United States v. McNally*, *Chiarella v. United States*, and *Dirks v. SEC*, have severely limited the types of conduct which can be prosecuted under the Securities and Exchange Act, and have returned the law on insider trading back to where it was in 1909. We need a law specifically aimed at criminal conduct if we are to prosecute the sophisticated illegal securities schemes now being practiced. Current insider trading law requires proof of a direct or indirect personal gain to the insider. This law creates too much difficulty for prosecutors and should either be eliminated or clarified. Making criminal liability under insider trading law clear is not only fair, but will produce market efficiency by eliminating confusion about what conduct will be considered criminal. We also need more prosecutors: U.S. Attorney Rudolph Guiliani of New York said that he could double his criminal staff and still not make a dent in the insider trading problem.

Recent revelations about insider trading not only underscore the seriousness and scope of white-collar crime and fraud, but also demonstrate the need for a strong *civil* Racketeer Influenced Corrupt Organizations Act (RICO). The RICO statute makes it a federal crime to use income derived from a pattern of racketeering activity in order to acquire control of, or an interest in, an enterprise. RICO also contains a civil remedy that enables someone whose business or property has been damaged by a pattern of racketeering activity to recover three times the value of the damage plus attorney's fees from the wrongdoer.

Civil RICO is among the most important pro-consumer protection and fraud deterrents in the law today. Congress created it in 1970, giving consumers a private attorney general function, because public prosecutors lacked adequate resources to combat a serious and growing white-collar crime problem. It was recognized as an important deterrent to cheats and crooks and as a tool for restitution for crime victims.

Today, some financial interests have asked Congress for weaker anti-fraud and RICO laws. They claim the law is too expansive and that consumers should not be entitled to automatic treble damages. Those arguments are unconvincing, and a RICO rollback should be seen as a soft-on-crime, anti-consumer posture in American law.

The issue of concealed dangers—toxic, carcinogenic, and acute hazards—in consumer products, workplaces, and the environment have been the single most repeated theme in recent major public health catastrophes such as asbestos, dioxin, Agent Orange, and Depo Provera. Conscious corporate decisions to conceal workplace hazards and unsafe products have killed hundreds of thousands of Americans.

Federal criminal law should be amended to criminalize such anti-social conduct. A criminal sanction would hold corporate officials accountable. Since our goal should be to create optimum incentives for worker and product safety, the best way to achieve that deterrent effect would be to impose personal criminal sanctions on the corporate officials who are creating these risks.

Presently, the Occupational Safety and Health Administration Act (OSHA) provides criminal penalties only for employers who *willfully* fail to furnish employees a place of employment free from recognized hazards, and where that failure results in the *death* of an employee. Recent changes in the criminal fine levels have raised the fine to $250,000, as well as a six-month prison term, if the defendant is an individual, and $500,000 if the defendant is an organization. Six months of imprisonment has little deterrent effect and the period should be increased. In cases involving no death, but involving serious bodily injury, there are currently no criminal penalties under the Act; this must be amended. Criminal penalties apply only to willful conduct by the employer. Thus, lower-level supervisors often are insulated from prosecution by arguing that they were simply following orders. Finally, the Act appears to permit criminal fines to be paid out of company proceeds. This reduces them to a cost of doing business and thus has little deterrent effect on corporate misconduct.

Flaws in OSHA have been compounded by the lack of aggressive enforcement by the Justice Department. The National Safe Workplace Institute reports that since the passage of the Act in 1970, the Justice Department has failed to have a single employer serve any jail time for violations of OSHA.

State prosecutors are also experiencing a serious problem with preemption of state law by OSHA. For example, in November 1987, a Brooklyn jury convicted the owners of a thermometer factory of assault for exposing workers to unsafe levels of mercury fumes, and a judge immediately set aside the verdict, saying that OSHA preempts the state's jurisdiction. That case is on appeal. In the Chicago Magnet Wire case, a trial and appellate court have recently dismissed murder charges against corporate officials for the death of an employee, arguing similarly that the state law is preempted by OSHA.

Legislation before the House of Representatives, H.R. 2664, provides that business managers who, after discovering a serious concealed danger, fail to inform their employees and the appropriate federal agency within fifteen days, shall be fined not more than $250,000 or imprisoned not more than ten years, or both. The bill also provides that any fine imposed on an individual business manager under this section cannot be paid by businesses on behalf of that manager. H.R. 2664 also contains a so-called "whistle blower" provision, protecting individuals who disclose product or manufacturing dangers from retaliation by business officials.

The Reagan administration has viewed such ideas as unnecessary government intervention into the marketplace. The facts suggest otherwise.

We have all heard stories of defense contractors charging $600 for a toilet seat and $45 for a hammer, but we have rarely heard about the Justice Department prosecuting these sham-artists and making them pay for cheating taxpayers out of millions of dollars. In the 100th Congress, Congress began joint hearings on the Justice Department's management of several major defense procurement fraud cases. No accurate figures exist on the cost to the taxpayer of defense procurement fraud. However, it is safe to say that defense contractors illegally charge hundreds of millions of dollars annually to the federal government, making this one of the most serious white-collar crime issues confronting this nation.

At last count, the Inspector General of the Department of Defense had 60 of the top 100 major defense contractors under criminal investigation. Over the past two years 200 individuals and 55 corporations have been convicted of defense fraud on a wide range of charges, including kickbacks, overcharging, and false claims. Recently, the Justice Department has either declined to prosecute or dismissed several major defense procurement fraud cases (e.g., General Dynamics Electric Boat Division, General Dynamics Pomona, and Pratt & Whitney Aircraft Group) after extensive investigations. In view of the enormous expenditure of time and money used to investigate these cases, as well as the damage done to the Department's credibility in this area, these cases represent a major blow to the fight against defense procurement fraud. Special attention should be paid by the next administration to defense contracting: specifically, a new section of the criminal division of the Justice Department should be established for this purpose.

Victims of Crime

The Victims of Crime Act, as amended, establishes a $110 million Crime Victims Fund. The money in the Fund comes from fines, special penalty assessments, and forfeited bail bonds from convicted federal defendants. This year the Fund took in $77.7 million, the highest level since its creation.

The Act needs reauthorization, and more money. The administration sought to limit the Fund and has indicated an intention to cap it at $35 million, and it has also deferred the expenditure of funds earmarked for the federal victims' program.

Capital Punishment

Presently, there are thirteen bills pending in Congress, including one drafted by the president, calling for reactivation of the federal death penalty. Although the 1972 Supreme Court decision in *Furman v. Geor-*

gia nullified the federal death penalty, the proposed laws have been introduced to reverse that decision.

Fifteen years after the Supreme Court, in *Furman,* found Georgia's death penalty statute unconstitutional because it was "arbitrary" and "freakish" in its application, the Court found itself once again examining that state's capital sentencing system in *McCleskey v. Kemp.* Racial disparity was a factor in both cases. However, its presence did not compel the Court to remedy the situation in *McCleskey.*

There is abundant evidence that in Georgia, black defendants who are convicted of killing white victims are more likely to be sentenced to death and executed than white defendants who kill white or black victims. Culpability of black defendants and the circumstances of their crimes are less of a factor in determining the sentence imposed than is the victim's race.

Evidence shows that the inherent racial bias found in Georgia's capital punishment system is not limited to that state. Other studies have shown that racial discrimination is pervasive in capital sentencing across the nation. For example, a 1984 study by Samuel Gross and David Mauro used the FBI's Supplemental Homicide Reports to examine sentencing patterns in eight states (Arkansas, Florida, Georgia, Illinois, Mississippi, North Carolina, Oklahoma, and Virginia) and found "remarkably stable and consistent" discrimination based on the victim's race in all the states, even when several other factors which might affect sentencing decisions were statistically controlled.

It is against this backdrop of clear evidence of racial discrimination in capital punishment that McCleskey petitioned the Supreme Court to examine the pattern in which the Georgia death penalty was imposed and find if there was a risk of inherent discrimination which clearly violated his constitutional rights. Rather than invalidating McCleskey's death sentence, the Court held that McCleskey was required to prove that he himself had been a direct victim of intentional acts of discrimination. For the Court to conclude that racial discrimination in the imposition of the death penalty is an inevitable part of the judicial process is unconscionable. For it to assert that the defendant must show intentional acts of discrimination in his particular case is tantamount to depriving him of equal access to justice.

Considering the vast evidence of both fallibility and racial discrimination inherent in the use of the death penalty, it appears that we can no longer look to the Supreme Court to protect the civil and constitutional rights of capital defendants. It is up to a new administration and Congress to ensure that equal justice under the law remains the cornerstone of our nation's criminal justice system. A new administration must provide the leadership in asserting a forthright anti-capital punishment posture for our society, developing and disseminating the religious, moral, ethical, and constitutional values that argue against this extreme and irrevocable sanction by the state.

Incarceration Alternatives

Building more prisons and giving defendants longer prison sentences are not crime prevention measures. Prisons should not be thought of as black holes into which convicts can be made to disappear.

Community-based programs which provide alternatives to incarceration are better able to assist offenders in developing the motivation and skills necessary to avoid recidivism. A variety of models exist, such as halfway houses, third-party custody, community service, and restitution. They are being tried in some jurisdictions and ignored in others. If these programs were more widely utilized, they, along with traditional and intensive probation, could make possible the release of many thousands of offenders from overcrowded prisons without any significant risk to public safety. With the nation's prison population now at a record level, unconstitutionally overcrowded by 50 percent in many prisons, according to federal courts, it is imperative that funds be allocated to provide for the greater use of alternatives to incarceration.

Federal Grand Juries

The Fifth Amendment to the Constitution provides that, "No person shall be held to answer for a capital, or otherwise infamous crime, unless on a presentment or indictment of a Grand Jury." Historically, the grand jury has served a dual function. It determines whether there is probable cause to believe that a crime has been committed, and it protects persons against unfounded criminal prosecutions.

The traditional role of the grand jury as an independent and impartial fact-finder has been eroded. It now serves as a virtual rubber-stamp for prosecutors. The unchecked power of examination by prosecutors has been used to pry into the beliefs and associations of unpopular groups, invading First Amendment rights to free speech, free press, and association. The time is long overdue for reformation of the federal grand jury. A new administration, working with a sympathetic Congress, could return the federal grand jury to its historical role as a peoples' watchdog against overzealous prosecutors and government corruption.

In the last eight years, the Department of Justice has declined in stature because the law and justice have not been adequately administered. New laws necessary for a modern, multiracial, and pluralistic society have not been championed, while class- and race-biased administration of justice, especially in the criminal law sphere, has been pervasive.

The law can be a tool for justice or a tool for bias, even criminal behavior. History will judge the Reagan administration harshly in this regard. It will judge future administrations just as harshly if the obvious and necessary changes are not made.

Resources

Recommended Appointees for a New Administration

- Eleanor Holmes Norton, Professor of Law, Georgetown Law Center, former Chair of Equal Employment Opportunity Commission
- Mary Frances Berry, member, U.S. Civil Rights Commission, professor of history at the University of Pennsylvania, Assistant Secretary for Education in the Carter administration HEW
- Drew Days, Professor, Yale Law School, former Deputy Solicitor of the United States
- Laurence Tribe, Professor, Harvard Law School
- Aryeh Neier, Vice Chair of Americas Watch, former Executive Director of American Civil Liberties Union
- Vernon Jordan, civil rights lawyer, former Executive Director, National Urban League
- Morris Dees, Director, Southern Poverty Law Center
- Charles Ogletree, Professor, Harvard Law School
- Steven Sachs, former Maryland Attorney General
- Ralph Nader, consumer advocate, author
- Nic Littlefield, Professor, Harvard Law School

Organizations

- American Civil Liberties Union, 132 W. 43rd St., New York, NY 10036; (212) 944-9800
- Lawyers Committee for Civil Rights Under Law, 1400 I St. NW, Washington, DC 20005; (202) 371-1212
- Center for Constitutional Rights, 853 Broadway, New York, NY 10003; (212) 674-3303
- American Bar Association, 1800 M St. NW, Washington, DC 20036; (202) 331-2200
- United States Public Interest Research Group, 215 Pennsylvania Ave. SE, Washington, DC 20003; (202) 546-9707
- Public Citizen, 2000 P St. NW, Washington, DC 20036; (202) 293-9142
- People for the American Way, 1424 16th St. NW, Washington, DC; (202) 467-4999
- Amnesty International, 608 Massachusetts Ave. NE, Washington, DC 20002; (202) 544-0200
- Center for Science in the Public Interest, 1501 16th St. NW, Washington, DC 20036; (202) 332-9110

- Center for the Study of Responsive Law, 1530 P St. NW, Washington, DC 20036; (202) 387-8030
- Association of Trial Lawyers of America, 1050 31st St. NW Washington, DC 20007; (202) 965-3500
- Leadership Conference on Civil Rights, 2027 Massachusetts Ave. NW, Washington, DC 20036; (202) 667-1780
- NAACP Legal Defense and Education Fund, 99 Hudson St., New York, NY 10013; (212) 219-1900
- National Urban League, 500 E. 62nd St., New York, NY 10021; (212) 310-9000
- National Lawyers Guild, 55 Avenue of the Americas, New York, NY 10003; (212) 966-5000

Further Reading

- Russell Mokhiber, *Corporate Crime and Violence*, Sierra Club Books, 1985.
- Dan Moldea, *Dark Victory*, Penguin, 1985.
- Anthony Lewis, *Gideon's Trumpet,* Vintage Books, 1986.
- Edwin Sutherland, *White Collar Crime*, Yale University Press, 1983.
- Francis Wormuth and Edwin Firmage, *To Chain the Dogs of War*, Southern Methodist University Press, 1983.
- Hugo Adam Bedau, ed., *The Death Penalty in America, 1983.*
- Ralph Nader and William Taylor, *The Big Boys*, Pantheon, 1986.
- James Stark and Howard Goldstein, *The Rights of Crime Victims*, Bantam Books, 1985.
- Charles Silberman, *Criminal Violence, Criminal Justice*, Random House, 1978.
- Elliot Currie, *Confronting Crime*, Pantheon, 1985.
- Joan Peter Silia, *Racial Disparity in the Criminal Justice System*, Rand Corporation, 1983.
- David Bazelon, *Questioning Authority*, Knopf, 1988.

Representative John Conyers (D-MI) chairs the House Subcommittee on Criminal Justice. A senior member of Congress, he also serves as ranking member of the House Government Operations Committee.

Nan Aron

Toward a More Just Federal Judiciary

Platform

To address the underrepresentation of minorities and women on the federal bench and to base judicial selection on merit rather than ideology:

- The new president should establish, as President Carter did, a Circuit Judge Nominating Commission to set forth standards in selecting judges to the Courts of Appeals. The commission shall be composed of thirteen panels, each to serve a geographic area.

- The new president should establish nonpartisan, broadly representative judicial selection committees to help Senators in advising the president to fill District Court vacancies.

- The aforementioned District Court and circuit-wide committees should conduct a search outside the regular channels of recruitment to reach lawyers, particularly minorities and women, who may not have achieved success within the hierarchy of the organized bar. Both committees should undertake statewide searches and suggest several candidates to fill vacancies occurring in the District Court and the Court of Appeals.

- Selection standards for federal judges should emphasize a demonstrated commitment to equal justice under the law.

- The Senate Judiciary Committee should reject and return to the home state Senator any list of nominees he or she has proposed which includes only white males. Senators should document outreach efforts made to identify prospective nominees.

- The Senate Judiciary Committee should not consider any nomination from a state until nominees for all vacancies to the District Court and Court of Appeals in that state have been submitted. The overall composition of the federal court should be taken into account, not simply the merits of each individual.

- The Justice Department should resume consultation with civil and women's rights groups about each prospective judicial nominee.

To strengthen the confirmation process:
- The Senate Judiciary Committee should prepare written, substantive reports on nominations for all federal judgeships, providing background information and explaining why the committee approved the nominees.
- The Senate should establish a timetable for proper scrutiny of nominees and adequate deliberation by the Senate.
- Senators' votes should be recorded in committee on all nominees for federal judgeships.
- The Senate should establish standards for confirmation and make findings that presidential nominees are affirmatively qualified to serve in the positions to which they have been appointed.

To encourage wider public participation:
- The ABA should solicit information from a wide variety of sources such as public interest, legal aid, ACLU, and civil rights attorneys.
- The ABA should place more importance on factors such as fairness and commitment to equal justice rather than relying so heavily on professional competence as the basis for its ratings.
- The ABA should notify the Senate Judiciary Committee, home state Senators, and national minority and women's bar associations each time it receives a nominee's name.

To allow for increased access to the courts.
- Congress should liberalize the rules on who has "standing" to bring a case into court. Limitations on standing to sue and other technical bars that unnecessarily thwart the resolution of disputes should be reformed. Class actions and other procedural devices to facilitate dispute resolution should be simplified and made more available.
- Government support for the Legal Services Corporation should be dramatically increased to assure that poor people are adequately represented.
- The private bar, government, individuals, and foundations should increase their support for public interest legal services.
- Congress should reaffirm its support for the proposition that fees in public interest cases be comparable to fees in other federal cases.

The federal courts hold a unique position in our constitutional system, ensuring that minorities and other citizens without political power are heard. The judiciary protects against violations of civil and constitutional rights, and is often the only avenue for citizens to assert their claims to decent housing, a job, health care, and freedom from discrimination on the basis of race, sex, or national origin. While state and local courts provide another important forum, plaintiffs generally prefer the federal courts because their decisions often carry more authority than those rendered in state courts and federal judges are more likely to be sensitive to and knowledgeable about federal rights.

During the 1960s and 1970s, the courts became the vehicle through which citizens pursued their struggle to achieve social and economic justice. The courts struck down racial segregation and school prayer, upheld the rights of the accused, and provided broad remedial relief to victims of discrimination. Courts also rendered decisions making access to the courts more available to those who felt they had just claims.

During this period, Congress enacted scores of statutes directing governmental and private entities to protect the environment, safeguard consumer rights, and provide equal opportunities for women and minorities. The public turned to the courts to interpret and clarify these new laws and ensure that they were effectively enforced. The public interest bar joined with the federal government in securing, in the courts, the rights guaranteed by these laws.

However, as the role of the judiciary became more prominent and visible, concerns were raised from several sources—the business community, state and local officials, and the Right —about the judiciary's involvement in public interest law issues. Some critics, such as Chief Justice Warren Burger, railed against an "explosion of litigation." Others complained that the courts were siding with plaintiffs in too many instances.

Those seeking to reverse the advances made by the courts in civil rights and liberties and environmental protection gained momentum when Ronald Reagan was elected in 1980. In the forefront of this drive was Edwin Meese, a long-time colleague of President Reagan, who, as White House Counsel and later as Attorney General, guided the administration's legal policies. Dedicated to implementing an ultra-conservative agenda for the nation, Meese lobbied hard against reauthorization of the Voting Rights Act, filed legal briefs arguing against affirmative action and abortion rights, and persuaded Congress to pass a tough anti-crime bill. He has also been the administration's crusader for adoption of the "original intent" theory, which holds that the Constitution should reflect the views of the men who drafted it, not necessarily the views of the judges who are interpreting it today.

The Reagan administration also sharply restricted the power of the judiciary by making the courts unavailable and inhospitable to public interest causes and claimants. For instance, the president substantially trimmed the budget of the Legal Services Corporation and sought to eliminate many of its key support and training programs, steps that excluded the poor from the legal system. The Department of

Justice, a chief enforcer of civil rights, brought few cases to court under Reagan's tenure and attacked legal theories and remedies used by lawyers for decades to correct discrimination against women and minorities.

Conservatives have also tried to make it more financially onerous for public interest lawyers to represent environmental, consumer, and civil rights interests in the legal system. One legislative proposal would have eliminated court-awarded legal fees when public interest organizations successfully sue the government for violations of statutory or constitutional rights. Other bills would have removed from court jurisdiction cases involving school prayer, abortion, and affirmative action.

Despite intense lobbying campaigns, the administration has encountered widespread opposition in implementing its agenda. The Supreme Court upheld affirmative action programs and Congress rebuffed Reagan's efforts to enact court-stripping bills and strengthened the Voting Rights Act in 1982. Public opinion polls showed that a strong consensus exists among the American people for the civil rights gains of the past decades. Reagan needed a new strategy. He adopted a court-packing plan to appoint judges who adhered to his conservative political and judicial philosophy. Reshaping the federal bench is potentially the most serious and far-reaching threat to our constitutional structure and the American justice system.

Commentators and policymakers agree that the most enduring legacy of the Reagan era will be the nearly 400 judges, almost a majority of the federal judiciary, whom the president will have appointed by the end of his second term—more than any other president in history. In addition, President Reagan has appointed the Chief Justice of the United States and three associate justices of the Supreme Court.

In fact, during President Reagan's second term, federal judgeships have sparked the most intense debate of any issue on the administration's social policy agenda. The Senate's proceedings and vote on the nomination of Robert Bork involved a highly publicized discussion of constitutional issues, the meaning of the Bill of Rights, and the role of the courts. With Judge Bork's defeat, President Reagan lost not only one of the most powerful trademarks of his presidency, but the opportunity to radically alter the composition and future direction of the Supreme Court.

The Bork nomination, however, was not the only one which generated national attention and media coverage. A number of organizations, including the Alliance for Justice, People for the American Way, the NAACP Legal Defense and Education Fund, and the AFL-CIO, have mounted major campaigns against other controversial nominees, such as Jefferson Sessions, Daniel Manion, and William Rehnquist. President Reagan himself made judicial candidates an issue by vigorously defending them and attacking their opponents.

From its inception, the administration sought the appointment of judges who share its desire to overturn landmark rulings in the areas of civil rights and liberties and its hostility to such social issues as abortion, school busing, and affirmative action. The 1980 Republican Party platform pledged the appointment of judges who "respect traditional family values and the sanctity of innocent human life…and who share our commitment to judicial restraint."

The right wing's crusade to reshape the bench has not been limited to the federal judiciary. In California, conservative and business groups waged a multimillion-dollar campaign to oust Chief Justice Rose Bird and two other justices whose views, particularly on the death penalty, were considered too liberal. The three were the first justices to be denied re-confirmation in California.

The 1984 Republican Party platform ensured that this litmus test would continue to be applied during President Reagan's second term. In addition to the approximately fifty vacancies which arise on the federal bench each year, his efforts received a boost by passage of the Bankruptcy Act in 1984, which created eighty-five new seats.

From day one, a small group that has included Attorney General Meese, his aides, the White House Counsel, and the president's assistant for legislative affairs has met regularly to choose judicial nominees. Professor Sheldon Goldman of the University of Massachusetts, an expert on the judicial selection process, asserts it is almost unprecedented for the senior White House staff to play such an active role.

The administration conducts extensive interviews of each candidate, designed to elicit his, and rarely, her views on a wide range of social issues. Computer data banks are also consulted to research writings, speeches, and biographic data of nominees. Senators' choices for District Court seats have often been rejected by the White House as not meeting its selection criteria. According to Stephen J. Markman, the Assistant Attorney General who oversees the judicial selection process, the administration has in place what is probably the most thorough and comprehensive system for recruiting and screening federal judicial candidates of any administration ever.

In looking for what it considers to be a "new breed" of federal judges, the administration has appointed unusually young, ideologically conservative males to the courts. Alex Kozinski, whose nomination to the Ninth Circuit Court was bitterly opposed by public interest groups, was thirty-four at the time. Frank Easterbrook, thirty-seven, and Richard Posner, forty-four, both free-market economic theorists, were placed on the Seventh Circuit. Kenneth Starr, who was an assistant to former Attorney General William French Smith, was thirty-six when named to the U.S. Court of Appeals for the District of Columbia. Senators also have placed a premium on seeking out youthful judges. Phil Gramm (R-TX) proposed Sidney Fitzwater, only thirty-one, as a Federal District Court judge, specifically citing his age as an advantage. Speaking of Fitzwater, Gramm said, "The added bonus...is that he will be making rulings when I'm dead."

Every president since Lyndon Johnson has appointed a higher percentage of blacks to the federal District Courts than has Reagan, an especially significant fact in light of the larger pool of minorities from which Reagan can choose. Johnson appointed five out of 122, or 4.1 percent; Nixon appointed six out of 179, or 3.4 percent; Ford appointed three out of fifty-two, or 5.8 percent; and Carter appointed twenty-eight out of 202, or 13.9 percent, to the District Courts. In his two terms, Reagan has appointed only five blacks, or 1.9 percent. In oversight hearings, Attorney General Meese defended this record with the feeble rationalization that few blacks are members of the Republican Party.

President Reagan's record of appointing women to the federal bench lags far behind President Carter. Thirty-one, or 8.4 percent, have been women, in contrast to forty, or 15.5 percent, appointed by Carter. Reagan's record is even starker in light of the statistics that 13 percent of the nation's lawyers are women. The number of women with law degrees rose from 44,000 in 1980 to 86,000 in 1985.

There has been a distinct drop in the quality of nominees for the Court of Appeals in the Reagan administration's second term, which may be a result of the increasingly ideological selection process. One indication of this phenomenon are the ratings given by the ABA's Standing Committee on the Federal Judiciary. Almost one-third of President Reagan's nominees to the appellate courts in the beginning of his second term were given the lowest passing grade by the ABA and were considered unqualified by some committee members. Sheldon Goldman, writing in the April-May, 1987 *Judicature*, noted, "None of the other four previous administrations had such a high proportion with this rating."

No Democrat has received an appointment to the Court of Appeals during the Reagan administration. Not since the administration of Warren Harding has a president appointed only members of the same political party to the Appeals Court. (A president has a freer hand in choosing Court of Appeals judges than he has with District Court nominees, whose names are put forward by Aenators.) The record of partisanship in President Reagan's Appeals Court appointments demonstrates the systematic efforts in screening judicial candidates.

Judgeships have always been the object of partisan struggles and patronage. Franklin Roosevelt's court-packing plan earned him much notoriety and was eventually defeated. Presidents Eisenhower and Nixon gave great weight to ideology and party affiliation. The Carter administration brought about historic changes in the process when it aggressively sought to recruit women, blacks, and other minorities for judgeships. It created nominating commissions for Circuit Courts and issued guidelines for Senators to follow in making recommendations for District Court positions. The panels' emphasis was on merit selection and affirmative action. While Carter appointed judges who agreed with him philosophically, the panels were instrumental in opening the process to more participants, invited greater public scrutiny, and focused the selection process on professional qualifications. Carter encouraged wide public participation by sharing the names of nominees with the National Bar Association, an organization of black attorneys, and women's groups, as well as with the American Bar Association.

The Reagan administration abandoned these reforms. The current procedure omits participation by any groups other than the ABA's fourteen-member Standing Committee on the Federal Judiciary. Since 1952, all prospective judicial nominees have been evaluated and rated by this committee, which has come under increasing criticism from both liberals and conservatives. Liberal groups claim the committee bowed to Justice Department pressure in finding qualified controversial candidates such as Jefferson Sessions, Daniel Manion, and Bernard Siegan. Conservatives are unhappy with the committee's split ratings on Robert Bork and charge that it forced certain candidates, such as William Harvey, former Chairman of the Legal Services Corporation, to withdraw from consideration. In the past, the committee has been attacked for bias toward corporate lawyers, which meant that women and blacks had a more difficult time obtaining a qualified rating. Nevertheless, the committee has been credited with excluding the most unqualified individuals.

In 1988, President Reagan has the opportunity to make between fifty and seventy-five new judgeship appointments. His desire to fill those seats with people who share his ideological philosophy underscores the importance of the Senate's role.

During Reagan's first six years, the Senate Judiciary Committee, under the chairmanship of Strom Thurmond, routinely confirmed the vast majority of judicial nominees. Most had *pro forma* hearings and were voted out of committee without debate. Daniel Manion, one of the most controversial of Reagan's nominees, was reported out of committee without a recommendation. Alex Kozinski and Sidney Fitzwater, the objects of fierce confirmation battles, easily gained committee approval. The only nominee defeated in committee was Jefferson Sessions, because of his anti-civil rights record.

In the vast majority of cases, the committee did not file a report or even have a transcript of the hearing available at the time of the confirmation vote. For example, in the Fitzwater confirmation, Senator Paul Sarbanes (D-MD) blasted the committee's laxity:

> Far be it from me really to intrude into the procedures of the Judiciary Committee, but it does seem to me that if we are going to have controversial nominations on the floor of the Senate—and this obviously is such a nomination, with a fairly close closure vote, and I assume a fairly close vote on confirmation—we ought to have a report, or at a minimum that the hearings of the committee should be printed so that the Members of the Senate can have the opportunity to at least have the printed hearing record before them and be in a position to review it.

Ever since the Democrats regained control of the Senate in 1986, and Joseph Biden took over as Chairman of the Judiciary Committee, nominees have been investigated more thoroughly, and adequate time has been allotted to evaluate their qualifications. While the committee has been accused by the Republicans of "holding up" the process, its hearings on the Bork nomination were commended by both Republican and Democratic Senators for their fairness, comprehensiveness, and substantive focus. Nevertheless, even under the Democrats' leadership, the sheer number of nominees has meant that some are still being considered without the benefit of a full public record or thorough scrutiny.

Recent studies substantiate the claim made by both liberal and conservative groups that the Reagan judiciary has lived up to expectations. A study by political scientists from the University of Kansas demonstrates a dramatic difference between Reagan and Carter appointees on civil rights. It shows that Carter appointees are twice as likely as Reagan appointees to support a civil rights claim. A *Columbia Law Review* study concludes that in non-unanimous cases in 1985-86, appellate judges named by President Reagan voted considerably more conservatively than did Carter appointees and those of previous Democratic presidents. By far the largest measure of President Reagan's impact, however, lies with the Supreme Court. His four appointments, including the pivotal seat formerly held by Lewis Powell and now filled by Anthony Kennedy, will undoubtedly tilt the balance in favor of the administration's point of view.

Expectations that politics and ideology will be eliminated from judicial selection are unrealistic. Each new administration generally chooses candidates identified with its political party who share its philosophy. However, the issue of how we select judges, and who is selected, is too important to be entrusted to the far right, or any one political party, for that matter.

The proposals outlined above contain a number of reforms that would open the process to greater scrutiny, involve interested segments of the population, and make the judiciary more representative. They suggest measures for the Senate Judiciary Committee to adopt that would help to guarantee a more rigorous and informed Senate confirmation process. They also call for a tougher, more constructive role for the ABA.

In addition, the proposals suggest possible legislative solutions that would remove some of the barriers which limit access to the courts. Reopening the federal courts for the vindication of federal statutory and constitutional rights is of critical importance to thousands of poor clients, minorities, and other powerless citizens.

Throughout our history, the courts have been called upon to resolve difficult and controversial social issues. To perform this crucial function effectively, the judiciary must merit the respect of all citizens. That confidence can be earned only if the public believes that judges are fair, open-minded, independent, and committed to equal justice.

Resources

Recommended Appointees for a New Administration

Attorney General and top-level Justice Department positions
- Eleanor Holmes Norton, currently professor at Georgetown University Law Center and formerly a member of the EEOC

- Anthony Amsterdam, professor at New York University School of Law

- Al Meyerhoff, Senior Staff Attorney, Natural Resources Defense Council

- Elaine Jones, Assistant Counsel, NAACP Legal Defense and Education Fund

- Marsha Greenberger, Managing Attorney, National Women's Law Center

- Mark Silbergeld, Director, Washington, DC office of Consumers Union

- Norman Rosenberg, Executive Director, Mental Health Law Project

- Frances Dubrowski, former Senior Staff Attorney, Natural Resources Defense Council, now in private practice

Supreme Court or Court of Appeals
- Nathaniel Jones, for the Supreme Court, currently serving on U.S. Court of Appeals for Sixth Circuit

- Patricia Wald, for the Supreme Court, currently serving on Court of Appeals for the District of Columbia

- Jack Greenberg, for the Court of Appeals or Supreme Court, currently Vice-Dean and professor at Columbia Law School and formerly executive director of the NAACP Legal Defense and Education Fund

- William Coleman, for the Court of Appeals or Supreme Court, currently practicing law in Washington, DC and board member of the NAACP Legal Defense and Education Fund

---

Organizations

- Mexican American Legal Defense and Education Fund, 1430 K St. NW, Washington, DC 20005; (202) 628-4074

- AFL-CIO, 815 16th St. NW, Washington, DC 20006; (202) 637-5000

- Alliance for Justice, 600 New Jersey Ave. NW, Washington, DC 20001; (202) 662-9548

- People for the American Way, 2000 M St. NW, Washington, DC 20036; (202) 467-4999

- National Abortion Rights Action League, 1101 14th St. NW, Washington, DC 20005; (202) 371-0779

- Planned Parenthood, 2010 Massachusetts Ave. NW, Washington, DC 20036; (202) 785-3351
- Federation of Women Lawyers, 2000 P St. NW, Suite 610, Washington, DC 20036; (202) 822-6644
- Leadership Conference on Civil Rights, 2027 Massachusetts Ave. NW, Washington, DC 20036; (202) 667-1780
- NAACP, 1025 Vermont Ave. NW, Washington, DC 20005; (202) 638-2269
- NAACP Legal Defense and Education Fund, 806 15th St. NW, Suite 940, Washington, DC 20005; (202) 638-3278
- National Lawyers Guild, 55 Avenue of the Americas, New York, NY 10013; (212) 966-5000
- Women's Legal Defense Fund, 2000 P St. NW, Suite 400, Washington, DC 20036; (202) 887-0364

Further Reading

- Lawrence H. Tribe, *God Save This Honorable Court: How the Choice of Supreme Court Justices Shapes Our History*, Random House, 1985.
- Herman Schwartz, *The Burger Years: Rights and Wrongs in the Supreme Court, 1969-1986*, Penguin, 1988.
- Sheldon Goldman, "Reagan's Second Term Judicial Appointments: The Battle at Midway," *Judicature*, Vol. 70, April/May, 1987, pp. 324-29.
- David O'Brien, *Judicial Roulette: Report of the Twentieth Century Fund*, Priority Press Public, 1988.
- Herman Schwartz, *Packing the Courts*, Charles Scribner's Sons, 1988.

Nan Aron founded the Alliance for Justice, a national organization of public interest legal organizations, in 1980 and has served as its Executive Director since then. Her previous experience includes employment with the National Prison Project of the ACLU and the Office of General Counsel of the Equal Employment Opportunity Commission. She has been an adjunct law professor at Georgetown University Law Center since 1979 and at George Washington Law School since 1977.

Robert S. McIntyre

Tax Policy After Reagan*

Platform

- Reject calls for a regressive new national sales tax (or increased federal excise taxes) and instead focus on further income tax reforms such as the following:

- Close or narrow some of the most egregious loopholes left over after the 1986 tax reform act. These include excessive accelerated depreciation writeoffs, tax-free bonds, tax breaks that encourage multinational corporations to move plants overseas, and oil and gas loopholes. Curb tax incentives for corporate mergers and acquisitions and for tax shelter farming, which rob the Treasury of revenue and damage the economy. Business writeoffs for meals and entertainment should be scaled back, and the remaining tax concessions to defense contractors should be eliminated. Foreign investors should once again be required to pay U.S. tax on the interest they earn in this country.

- Strengthen the "alternative minimum tax" on profitable corporations and wealthy individuals. Corporations should pay the minimum tax, if applicable, on all the profits they report to their shareholders, not on half those profits, as under current law. Loopholes that allow *Forbes* 400 real estate moguls to escape paying the minimum tax should be closed. And the minimum tax rate on big companies and rich people should be increased to 25 percent, from the current 20 percent corporate and 21 percent individual rates.

---

* This chapter was prepared with help from Jonathan Crystal, a Policy Analyst at Citizens for Tax Justice (CTJ), and Margaret Marr, Policy Director at CTJ.

- Increase the top personal tax rate on the wealthiest 1 percent of the population. The super-rich should pay a higher marginal tax rate than the near-rich, rather than the lower rate they enjoy under current law.
- Future tax policy should aspire to cut the deficit, pay for needed new spending initiatives, and restore the role of the federal tax system in making the distribution of income in America more just. Only by focusing on the income tax and building on the foundation laid in the 1986 tax reform act can all these goals be accomplished.

What should be done about federal taxes after Ronald Reagan returns to his California ranch in January 1989? Whoever becomes our next president is likely to be stymied in accomplishing goals in other areas unless he faces the tax issue squarely. Reagan leaves behind a federal tax system that fails to raise enough money to support the cost of government spending and that is far less progressive than it used to be. The two problems are inexorably linked. In fact, the decline in income taxes on corporations and wealthy people explains virtually the entire increase in the federal deficit over the past ten years.

If Ronald Reagan's successor is going to deal with the overwhelming fiscal dilemma that Reaganomics has created, not to mention find the funds to address the many other problems confronting our nation, then increased revenues clearly must be a central part of the solution. If that were all there were to it, however, Walter Mondale might have won the 1984 election.

Simply to call for higher taxes is both bad politics and bad policy. The cause of our huge budget deficits is not that taxes on average Americans are too low. To the contrary, most families are paying higher federal income and Social Security taxes than they did ten years ago. The real source of the deficit problem is the shift in tax burdens away from those most able to pay—the ongoing legacy of Reagan's 1981 supply-side tax program. The solution to the problem should be to reverse that shift.

Indeed, ever since 1981, Congress has been doing penance for the excesses of that year. The overhaul of the income tax in 1986, in particular, took major steps toward restoring fairness. The critical issue for the future is whether tax policy will continue in the spirit of the 1986 reform act, or whether it will revert to the supply-side, soak-the-poor policies of 1981.

The roots of our current tax problems go back to the 1970s. As inflation constantly pushed most people into higher tax brackets, frequent adjustments to the tax code were needed to keep tax burdens under control. To be sure, Congress passed numerous so-called "tax cuts"—but only a portion of those "cuts" went toward keeping middle- and low-income people even with inflation. A large share of the

Treasury's inflation windfall was diverted to provide new tax breaks for favored industries, campaign contributors, or pet projects.

As a result, average families found themselves paying more and more of their earnings in taxes, while getting no additional government services in return. Most voters felt that the government was no longer delivering full value for their tax dollars. But no one in Washington was willing to admit the truth to the people: that they were paying the taxes avoided by the politically powerful.

Instead, in 1980, candidate Ronald Reagan offered an alternative explanation for the public's discontent. The government, he asserted, was wasting a great deal of taxpayers' money. Reagan pledged to be so diligent in rooting out "waste, fraud, and abuse" in government that he would be able to cut taxes, increase defense spending, and balance the budget all at the same time.

To ordinary taxpayers, who saw only what they were paying in taxes, not what others were *not*, Reagan's prescription seemed plausible. The voters had to choose between continuing a tax policy they sensed was unfair or electing Reagan and supposedly lowering everyone's taxes. They chose Reagan.

Having misdiagnosed the problem, President Reagan moved quickly after his inauguration to exacerbate it. An old idea, "trickle-down," was repackaged as supply-side economics. As explained by Andrew Mellon, Treasury Secretary under Calvin Coolidge and Herbert Hoover, the theory holds that "the welfare of the lower and middle classes is dependent upon the good fortune and low taxes of the rich." Knowing that the public would be suspicious of a tax and economic program that showered benefits on the well-to-do, Reagan offered a description of his program that diverged wildly from what it actually entailed. "Across-the-board" tax cuts turned out to mean reductions targeted to the affluent; "business incentives" translated into virtual abolition of the corporate income tax; and "free-market economics" meant a complex web of large tax subsidies for powerful interests.

Although the 1981 act reduced personal income tax rates, it did not (until 1985, when indexing was instituted) stop inflation from continuing to whittle away the value of the standard deduction, the personal exemption, and the earned-income credit for the working poor. It pushed most people into ever higher tax brackets. Increases in Social Security taxes that took effect in 1981 and 1982 further reduced the paychecks of wage-earners.

According to the Congressional Joint Committee on Taxation, after offsetting the tax increases from inflation and higher Social Security taxes, only people making more than $75,000 a year actually ended up paying a lower share of their income in taxes after the 1981 law went into effect. The rest of us paid considerably more. While the very rich enjoyed huge tax cuts as a result of the 1981 tax act, working poor families watched their taxes skyrocket. In 1979, a couple with two kids and one spouse working 46 hours a week at minimum wage had a gross annual income (including overtime pay) of $7,412—exactly the poverty line. Its total federal tax burden was $133, or 1.8 percent of its earnings. By 1985, a family living on the same income (after inflation) made $10,989, but they paid $1,150 in taxes. That's an effective tax rate of 10.5 percent, almost a six-fold increase over 1979.

Although the individual tax changes received most of the media attention, the 1981 act's reduction in corporate income taxes was its most dramatic aspect. Under the guise of "depreciation reform" and "incentives," the 1981 act, as Roger Altman, a former assistant Treasury secretary, told the *Washington Post,* "virtually phased out the corporate tax in America."

By 1983, corporate taxes had fallen to only 6 percent of federal revenues, down from 15 percent in 1970s and 25 percent in the 1960s. A survey of 250 of the nation's biggest and most profitable corporations by Citizens for Tax Justice found that 130 of them paid absolutely nothing in federal income taxes—and in many cases, actually received tax rebates—in at least one year between 1981 and 1985. Forty-two of these giant companies, including such familiar names as AT&T, Dupont, Boeing, General Dynamics, Pepsico, General Mills, Transamerica, and Texaco, managed to avoid federal income taxes entirely from 1982 to 1985. In fact, despite $59.1 billion in pre-tax domestic profits during these years, those forty-two companies received net tax *rebates* totalling $2.1 billion.

The policy of throwing huge sums of money at large corporations and wealthy people was central to supply-side theory. Supposedly, corporations would take their cash bonanza and invest in new machines and factories, thereby increasing worker productivity and creating new jobs. Lower tax rates on the wealthy and new incentives such as expanded Individual Retirement Accounts would lead to added savings. Altogether, the supply-side policy was to produce a balanced federal budget by 1984.

But things didn't exactly work out that way. Instead of skyrocketing, business investment stagnated. From 1981 to 1984, capital spending grew at less than half the rate of the previous four years. And the types of investment that the 1981 "incentives" were supposed to stimulate did not grow at all.

In early 1986, Citizens for Tax Justice looked closely at the 1981-84 annual reports of 259 of America's top nonfinancial companies to see if there was any correlation between tax "incentives" and increased capital spending or job creation. Our report, *Money for Nothing,* found that, in fact, the exact opposite of what the supply-siders promised occurred. The forty-four companies in our survey that paid no taxes at all (despite $53.6 billion in pretax domestic profits) reduced their aggregate capital spending by 4 percent, and cut their total number of employees by 6 percent. (Meanwhile, the highest-taxed companies examined, which paid $18.2 billion in federal income taxes on their $49 billion in pretax profits—for an average tax rate of 37.3 percent—boosted their capital spending by 21 percent and added 4 percent more workers to their payrolls.)

Where did all the money go? Presented with this unparalleled largess from the nation's taxpayers, America's tax-subsidized corporations spent their tax savings on virtually everything but new plants and equipment. The forty-four no-tax companies, while cutting investment and employment, increased their dividend payouts by 22 percent. They also lined the pockets of their chief executive officers with pay hikes averaging 54 percent. And from 1980 to 1985, the amount of money spent on corporate mergers more than tripled (in constant dollars), to an estimated $200 billion in 1985.

Contrary to the supply-side assertions, tax "incentives" explain little or nothing about increases or declines in a company's total investment or employment. What really matters are factors such as whether or not the company already has more machines or buildings than it can efficiently use, the rate of technological advances in the production process, the level of interest rates, the commitment of top management to long-term growth, and, most important, the level of demand for a company's product.

Meanwhile, the predicted supply-side boom in personal savings also failed to materialize. Instead, the personal savings rate fell after 1981. And the budget deficit, rather than disappearing, ballooned to unprecedented levels.

As the unfairness and economic wrong-headedness of the 1981 tax act became painfully obvious, Congress turned tax policy in the opposite direction. In 1982 and then again in 1984, Congress, with the president's reluctant acquiescence, enacted tax legislation that corrected some of the worst excesses of the 1981 bill, and scaled back the regressive tax cuts by tens of billions of dollars a year in the process. The process culminated in the 1986 overhaul of the tax code, which put hundreds of corporations and wealthy individuals back on the tax rolls, rolled back some of the previous tax increases on poor and middle-income families, and went a long way toward restoring a measure of fairness to the federal tax code.

Under the 1986 tax reform act, tax "incentives" that had made widespread corporate and upper-income tax avoidance possible—such as the investment tax credit, accelerated depreciation, special accounting rules for defense contractors, and so forth—were repealed or scaled back. These reforms were backed up with a new corporate and personal minimum tax, which makes it hard for rich people and corporations to avoid taxes entirely. In particular, big companies generally must pay taxes equal to at least 10 percent of the profits they report to their shareholders.

Altogether, the 1986 act closed loopholes that otherwise would have cost $500 billion between 1987 and 1991. Some of the money raised from reform was used to cut the corporate tax rate to only 34 percent—the lowest rate in any major developed country. But even though this means considerably lower taxes for the minority of large companies that were paying high tax rates under the old tax system, the tax reform act increased overall corporate taxes substantially from the depths they had reached in the Reagan heyday. Indeed, it was the partial rollback in the Reagan corporate tax cuts that paid for the tax relief enjoyed by most American families.

The expansion of the standard deduction (from $3,540 in 1985 to $5,000 in 1988 on joint returns), the almost doubling of the personal exemption (from $1,040 in 1985 to $2,000 in 1989), and the expansion in the earned-income tax credit took more than six million poor families off the income tax rolls. The combination of lower rates, larger personal exemptions, and the increased standard deduction also left the vast majority of middle-income taxpayers better off, even though some deductions and credits used by middle-income families were curtailed.

Some people argue that the 1986 reform act was a blow to progressivity because of the sharp reduction in the top personal income tax rate—from 50 percent to only 28 percent. Certainly, the 1986 act did cut taxes for many wealthy people; indeed, half of those making more than $200,000 a year got tax cuts averaging $50,000 each. But the other half of this elite group, whose members had been paying a lower share of their incomes in taxes than families at the poverty line, saw their taxes increase by an average of $50,000 each. The truth is that the switch from a largely avoided 50 percent top rate to a 28 percent rate with teeth means that the rich now pay a somewhat higher share of the personal income tax burden than before the change. Taking account of both the personal and corporate income tax changes, a 1987 Congressional Budget Office report found that the 1986 reform act scaled back the tax cuts previously granted the richest 5 percent of the population by about one-fifth.

Reaganomics and the Federal Budget Deficit

Despite deficit-reducing tax reform acts in 1982 and 1984 (and the small tax changes made as part of the 1987 "budget compromise"), almost 30 percent of non-Social Security federal spending today is paid for by borrowing—up from just 5 percent in the 1960s. The clear connection between the sharp decline in taxes on those most able to pay and the federal deficit has been obscured by a lot of misleading rhetoric about "out of control" federal spending. These spending critics point to growth in "entitlements"—a code word for Social Security—as the main source of our deficit problem. But to blame Social Security for the deficit is ludicrous. Certainly, Social Security benefits have risen over the years, but so have Social Security taxes. In fact, Social Security now is building up huge reserves to pay for future benefits—with additions amounting to an estimated 1.3 percent of the GNP in FY1988 alone. Because those reserves are invested in government bonds, Social Security actually is loaning money to the rest of the federal government to finance part of the deficit.

Putting aside Social Security reveals a quite different picture:

Spending

The cost of non-Social Security federal programs as a share of the GNP is now lower than it was in the 1960s, 1970s, or early 1980s. To be sure, defense spending has grown—from 5 percent of the GNP in 1980 to an estimated 6.2 percent of the GNP this year. But over the same period, the cost of non-defense programs (excluding Social Security and interest) fell from 10.3 percent of the GNP to an estimated 8.1 percent of GNP.

Taxes

In contrast, non-Social Security federal taxes have declined markedly as a share of the GNP—from 15.5 percent in the 1960s, to 13.8 percent in the 1970s, to only 12.6 percent currently. And the sources of that decline are clear: reduced income taxes on corporations and wealthy people.

Over the past ten years, the non-Social Security budget deficit has more than doubled, from 2.5 percent of the GNP in 1978 to 5.2 percent in 1988. The drop in income taxes on corporations (down by 0.7 percent of the GNP) and on the richest 1 percent of individuals (down by 0.4 percent of the GNP), plus the rise in interest payments on the national debt (up by 1.9 percent of the GNP), more than explain the problem. Of course, the added interest outlays reflect the increased federal debt incurred due to corporate and upper-income tax reductions in the past. Thus, lower taxes on corporations and the wealthy ultimately offer a complete explanation of the hugely increased federal budget deficit we now confront.

Future Federal Tax Policy

How to raise needed revenues while continuing the 1986 reform act's progress towards fairer taxes? It is precisely by focusing on the right way to raise taxes that presidential candidates can avoid the notorious and feared "Mondale mistake." When Walter Mondale told the Democratic convention in August of 1984 that he planned to increase taxes if elected, most Americans assumed he meant their taxes. Not surprisingly, in light of the fact that the typical family already was paying 10 percent more of its income in federal income taxes due to the "supply-side" policies of the previous several years (in addition to a 17 percent jump in Social Security taxes), Mondale's message did not go over very well with the voters.

Mondale's real mistake was not in calling for higher revenues, but in rejecting tax reform as the way to achieve his goal. Had Mondale called for a reversal of the Reagan tax shift, had he demanded an end to widespread corporate tax avoidance and the proliferation of upper-income tax shelters, his proposal to increase taxes would have found far more receptive ears among the public.

In the first half of 1987, Congress was considering a $19 billion increase in excise taxes on gasoline, beer, wine, cigarettes, and telephone service to help meet its deficit reduction targets. Had these excise tax hikes been enacted, they would have more than wiped out the tax relief that middle- and lower-income families gained from the 1986 tax act, while leaving wealthy people virtually unscathed. In fact, the proposed excise tax increases would have taken twenty-five times as large a share of the income of the poor as from the rich.

Enactment of a national sales tax, or "value-added tax," would be similarly regressive. Because those with lower incomes spend a greater share of their earnings, sales taxes take a much greater percentage out of poor and middle-income people's earnings than from the rich. And despite the claims of some sales tax advocates, there is no way that this problem can be solved.

Defending his plan to raise $40-50 billion a year through a 5 percent national sales tax, former presidential candidate Bruce Babbitt (quoting economist Lester Thurow) argued that "you can make it as progressive as you want to." Toward that end, Babbitt proposed to exempt food, medicine, housing, and clothing from the tax, while providing income tax credits or larger standard deductions for the less well-off. "It would be simple and fair," he asserted, "with no loopholes and no special breaks."

Yet despite exemptions for necessities, average families would pay almost two-and-one half times as much of their income in sales tax as would the richest people. Poor families would pay three-and-one half times more of their income than the rich. Schemes to offer income-tax credits to the poor run afoul of the fact that most poor people don't have to file federal income tax returns and don't have any income taxes to offset. And, in any event, no one has a solution to the heavy burden a national sales tax would impose on middle-income families compared to the wealthy.

The regressive arithmetic of a national sales tax is so apparent that it is difficult to believe sales tax supporters do not fully understand it. The argument is that by discouraging consumer spending, a new sales tax supposedly would lead to increased savings, which, it is argued, would be good for the economy. But the contention that higher taxes on spending will produce economic miracles is simply the flip side of supply-side rationalizations. Just as decreased corporate taxes and tax "incentives" for personal saving did not lead to added savings and investment, so increased taxes on spending are not likely to accomplish those results either.

After the sad experience of the 1980s, policymakers ought to have learned that tax incentives (and disincentives) rarely, if ever, achieve their putative goals. Rather than revisiting supply-side follies, the focus of future tax policy should be on raising sufficient revenues fairly.

For starters, carrying on the spirit of the 1986 reforms means going after those unfair loopholes that remain in the law—and there still are some costly ones. According the Congressional Joint Committee on Taxation, corporate tax breaks will cost the Treasury $37 billion in FY1989 alone. That's a big drop from the $120 billion a year that the loopholes cost before the 1986 reform act, but it shows how much more reform remains to be accomplished. Those same business tax breaks save upper-income individuals more than $35 billion a year.

What are the biggest remaining loopholes? Accelerated depreciation, which was hardly touched by the tax reform act, is expected to cost $22 billion in fiscal 1989, and a total of $127 billion over the next five years. Tax-free bonds will produce a revenue loss of $20 billion next year, and $106 billion from 1989 through 1993, with virtually all the tax savings going to financial institutions and the richest 1 percent of individual taxpayers. Tax breaks for multinational companies, which can give companies an incentive to move factories and jobs overseas, will amount to more than $7 billion next year, and $44 billion over five years. Loopholes for oil and gas and other natural resources will total more than $13 billion over the next half decade. The remaining tax concessions to defense contractors, breaks for corporate mergers and acquisitions, and incentives for tax-shelter farming rob the Treasury of billions annually, in addition to the economic damage they often cause. Cutting business writeoffs for meals and entertainment to half the cost (instead of 80 percent under present law) would recapture $2.5 billion a year. Reinstating a tax on U.S. interest earned by foreign investors (repealed under Reagan) could raise several billion dollars a year, even at only a 5 percent rate.

Next, the alternative minimum tax enacted in 1986 should be strengthened. On the corporate side, that provision was touted as assuring that big, profitable corporations would have to pay at least 20 percent of their earnings in federal income taxes. But currently, the 20 percent minimum rate applies to only half the profits companies report to their shareholders. In other words, the supposed 20 percent minimum tax in practice is a 10 percent tax. The rules should be changed to make corporations pay the minimum tax on *all* the profits they report to their stockholders and the Securities and Exchange Commission.

The minimum tax on wealthy individuals needs improvement, too. Right now, it appears that many of the extremely rich real estate developers who make it to the *Forbes* 400 list of the wealthiest Americans may be able to continue to pay little or nothing in federal income taxes despite the minimum tax. To correct this problem, several changes are needed. First, no deduction should be allowed for real estate "depreciation" for purposes of computing the minimum tax. After all, in most cases the combined value of buildings and land goes up in value over time, not down. Second, "loss carryforwards" that real estate developers have accumulated from even more dubious "depreciation" deductions under the old tax law should not be allowed to reduce minimum taxable income either. Finally, something needs to be done about a huge loophole that now allows developers to tap their unrealized capital gains without paying any income tax—by borrowing against the increased value of their holdings. When someone refinances property for more than the original purchase price, it's clear beyond doubt that the property has gone up in value. Such refinancing should be treated as realized capital gains under the minimum tax. If, in addition, the minimum tax rate on corporations and wealthy people were raised to 25 percent, the total additional revenue raised from minimum tax changes could exceed $11 billion a year.

The vastly broadened tax base from the 1986 tax act and the reforms outlined above mean that tax rate increases can be shared more fairly, rather than being stuck on those who have not been able to find ways to shelter their incomes. But personal income tax rates ought to be more progressive. Currently, the tax rates include a strange "backward bend." The highest rate is 33 percent, but for those at the very top of the income scale—making more than $240,000 a year—the rate drops back to 28 percent. Simply extending the 33 percent tax rate to the richest taxpayers could raise $10 billion a year. Reinstating the 1987 top rate of 38.5 percent on the wealthy would raise twice that amount. And either change would reverse an unnecessary result of the 1986 bill whereby half of the nation's richest taxpayers received tax reductions averaging $50,000 a year.

The kinds of income tax changes suggested here could easily raise more than $50 billion a year and close to $80 billion a year by 1992. They also would go a long way toward restoring the tax system's time-honored role of making the distribution of income less inequitable. But is calling for more tax reform a dangerous political strategy? Quite the contrary. A 1987 poll conducted by Opinion Research Corporation for Senator Carl Levin (D-MI) found that three-quarters of those responding favored keeping the top personal tax rate on the wealthy at 38.5 percent, rather than 28 percent. Other surveys show similarly overwhelming public support for closing corporate loopholes and strengthening the minimum tax. In contrast, 76 percent of the people responding to the Levin poll opposed increasing regressive federal excise taxes.

Improving tax fairness and addressing the deficit problem can and should go hand in hand. Both require continuing the recent progress toward reversing the sharp decline in corporate income taxes and personal income taxes on the rich that are the legacy of the 1981 Reagan tax shift program.

Resources

Recommended Appointees for a New Administration

- Jerome Kurtz of Paul Weiss Rifkin & Garrison, Commissioner of Internal Revenue 1977-1980, Treasury staff member in the 1960s

- Gina Desprey, legal counsellor to Senator Bill Bradley (D-NJ), expert on finance, defense, and Soviet issues, worked extensively on the 1986 tax bill

- David Brockway of Dewey Ballantine Bushby Palmer & Wood, former Chief of Staff, Joint Committee on Taxation

- Michael J. McIntyre, Professor of Law, Wayne State University

- Michael Graetz, Professor, Yale Law School

- James Wetzler of Bear Sterns & Co., former Chief Economist, Joint Committee on Taxation

Organizations

- AFL-CIO, 815 16th St. NW, Washington, DC 20006; (202) 637-5000

- Center on Budget and Policy Priorities, 236 Massachusetts Ave. NE, Washington, DC 20006; (202) 544-0591

- Citizens for Tax Justice, 1311 L St. NW, Washington, DC 20005; (202) 626-3780

Further Reading

- Congressional Budget Office, *The Changing Distribution of Federal Taxes, 1975-1990*, October 1987.

- Joint Committee on Taxation, *Description of Possible Options to Increase Revenues*, prepared for the Committee on Ways and Means (JCS-17-87), June 25, 1987.

- Michael Kinsley, *The Curse of the Giant Muffins*, Simon and Schuster, 1987.

- Michael Kinsley, "Neither Low, Nor Simple, Nor Fair," *The New Republic, July 11, 1983*.

- Robert S. McIntyre, "The Populist Tax Act of 1989," *The Nation*, April 2, 1988.

- Robert S. McIntyre, "Tax the Forbes 400!" *The New Republic*, August 31, 1987.

- "VAT Is A Bad Idea," *The Atlantic*, January 1987.

- Robert S. McIntyre and Jeff Spinner, *130 Reasons Why We Need Tax Reform*, Citizens for Tax Justice, 1986.

- Robert S. McIntyre and David Wilhelm, *Money for Nothing: The Failure of Corporate Tax Incentives, 1981-1984*, Citizens for Tax Justice, 1986.

- Robert S. McIntyre and Jeff Spinner, "Voodoo Incentives," *The New Republic*, February 25, 1985.

- Robert S. McIntyre and Jeff Spinner, "Just Taxes, and Other Options" in *Less Taxing Alternatives*, Democracy Project, 1984.

- Robert S. McIntyre and Dean Tipps, *Inequity and Decline: How the Reagan Tax Policies Are Affecting the American Taxpayer and the Economy*, Center on Budget and Policy Priorities, 1983.

- Joseph A. Pechman, "Tax Policies for the 1980s," *Tax Notes*, December 1980.

- Stanley S. Surrey, "Our Troubled Tax Policy: False Routes and Proper Paths to Change," *Tax Notes*, 1981.

- U.S. Department of the Treasury, *Tax Reform for Fairness, Simplicity, and Economic Growth, Volume 3: Value-Added Tax*, November 1984.

Robert S. McIntyre has been the Director of Citizens for Tax Justice since 1987. CTJ is a coalition of labor, public interest, and citizens groups, fighting for fairer taxes at the federal, state, and local levels. Prior to joining CTJ in 1980, McIntyre was Director of Public Citizen's Tax Reform Research Group. His writings on taxes over the past decade include articles in *The New Republic, The Atlantic, The New York Times, The Washington Post, The Los Angeles Times, Tax Notes, Boston College Law Review* and *University of Pennsylvania Law Reviews*. His recent publications include *The Sorry State of State Taxes, 130 Reasons Why We Need Tax Reform, Corporate Taxpayers and Corporate Freeloaders,* and *Money for Nothing: The Failure of Corporate Tax Incentives, 1981-84.*

Insure Domestic Tranquility...

Workers' Rights:
The Key to Real Workplace Democracy

Platform

the right to organize

- Government must guarantee for all working people the right to organize and to bargain collectively with their employer. This right, which has been severely eroded during the Reagan years, should be protected through measures such as the following:

- Providing workers immediate legal recognition of their union when a majority requests that recognition in writing, eliminating the current, more complicated system under which employers can often refuse to recognize unions for years.

- Ensuring that workers are free from discipline or discrimination for union activity. When workers charge that they have been punished for union activity, their job and conditions of employment should be maintained until the charges are resolved, as opposed to the present system in which workers may be out of work for two years or more while waiting for a final ruling.

- Imposing strong penalties on employers who violate the legal right to organize. Under the current system, the only penalty normally imposed on employers who punish workers for union activity or refuse to bargain with a union in good faith is that they are ordered not to commit future violations! Those employers should have to pay extra damages so that violating the law becomes more costly than dealing with the union in good faith would have been. Violators also should be barred from bidding on government contracts, and individual executives should be liable for criminal penalties for repeated or willful violations.

144

the right to information

- Even if organized, workers cannot participate in democratic decision-making without knowing everything the employer knows about current operations, short-term and long-term plans, finances, relationships with customers or clients, and similar subjects.

- Under current law, workers have to know what information to ask for, employers can refuse to provide it on grounds that it is not relevant to the union or involves trade secrets, and the government imposes no penalty even in the rare cases in which it finds an employer in violation of its duty to provide information. Employers should be required to share with workers all information about their enterprise as soon as that information becomes available, with stiff penalties for failure to do so.

the right to independent education and training

- A requirement for workplace democracy is that workers have the time, training, and resources to analyze information from the employer and develop their own positions and proposals.

- Employers should be required to provide a certain amount of paid time off so every worker can take part in union-sponsored education and training programs, with additional time provided for more intensive training of workers' committees and elected representatives. A payroll tax or other broad-based tax on employers should be used to finance the development and presentation of those programs under workers' control.

the right to democratic decisionmaking

- Under our economic system, even organized, informed, and trained workers cannot play a meaningful role in decisionmaking unless government protects the following rights:

- The right to exercise collective power. Management—whose primary responsibility is not to improve conditions for workers—is more likely to listen to the concerns of workers if they have the power to impose costs when the employer will not negotiate fairly. Yet laws and court decisions issued since the great period of labor militancy in the 1930s have systematically taken away much of that power. For example, most workers no longer have the right to strike over disputes, except during negotiations on a new contract. Workers who turn to other kinds of tactics do not have the clear legal right to publicize management failures or ask supporters to put economic pressure on an employer's financial backers. When contract negotiations reach an impasse, employers can lock out and replace workers, while strikers who want to protect their jobs normally are limited by courts to using two or three pickets to reach hundreds or thousands of people. Millions of workers, including most public employees, do not have the legal right to strike at all. Government must restore workers' inherent democratic rights to speak and assemble freely and to withhold their labor.

- The right to veto certain management decisions. Current law requires employers to confer with organized workers about wages, hours, and working conditions, but there is no obligation to reach agreement. There are many areas in which workers should have the final decisionmaking power. Examples include workplace changes that affect health and safety, the investment of pension funds, and measures needed to insure that technological change is used to benefit workers as well as management.

- A more far-reaching reform would require employers to prepare short-term and long-term Worker and Community Impact Statements, which would spell out employer plans and their likely effects and would have to be ratified by the workers before employers could change the *status quo*. Such a procedure would force employers to reach agreement with workers on such fundamental issues as staffing, workloads, training, scheduling, and compensation—issues on which management now has a free hand once it goes through the motions of conferring with the union—as well as on issues such as investment plans, which are now totally outside the bargaining arena.

---

the right to equal protection

- Rights that U.S. workers now enjoy often depend on which state they live in, which sector they work in, and whether they have a strong union. The principle that the federal government should guarantee some universal rights has been recognized with the enactment of programs such as Social Security, the minimum wage, and federal standards for occupational health and safety and equal employment opportunity. Current standards should be strongly enforced, and greatly expanded standards should be established by the government to cover such areas as protection from unfair firings, minimum health care benefits, equal pay for work of comparable worth, uniform benefits for workers' compensation and unemployment compensation, and protection from invasions of privacy through drug testing, polygraph tests, and secret monitoring.

The quality of life for working people has been devastated in the Reagan years.
- Real average earnings fell 10.5 percent between 1979 and 1987.

- The number of full-time workers with incomes below the poverty line doubled during the same period.

- The average pay for jobs permanently lost since 1979 was $444 per week, while the average pay for new jobs created was $272 per week.

- Nearly half the new jobs created pay less than $7,400 per year.

- At least 37 million people have no health insurance coverage.

- Despite passage of the Occupational Safety and Health Act in 1970, each year five million workers suffer serious injuries on the job, and uncounted millions suffer job-related health problems.

- Millions of older workers have been laid off and forced to start over after a lifetime of service.

- Young workers have less chance of obtaining a well-paying job and being able to afford a home than young people did fifteen years ago.

- Women and minorities who had begun to obtain better paying jobs have seen millions of those jobs disappear.

These changes have come about largely as a result of management decisions about investment, mergers, buyouts, and corporate restructuring; employer demands for rollbacks in union-negotiated pay and benefits; and deregulation won through employer lobbying. In many cases, profitable operations have been closed down or moved because employers believed they could make even greater profits by investing elsewhere.

With workers clinging defensively to the jobs that remain, employers in both private and public sectors have been able to attack workers' rights on the job. Millions of workers are required to work overtime at the employer's whim, with the result that hours worked now average closer to nine hours per day than eight. Many employers have imposed two-tier pay systems, so that new workers are paid up to 50 percent less for doing the same work as other employees. Even unionized workers have been forced to accept greatly reduced health insurance coverage for their families.

The basic economic decisions undermining workers' living standards and working conditions have been made in a completely undemocratic manner by executives who are not accountable to the great majority of Americans.

Yet government regulation alone will not bring increased democracy. There are more than five million workplaces in this country. Even if we had the most stringent employment standards imaginable, there could never be enough government inspectors, accountants, economists, lawyers, or other enforcement agents to monitor compliance at all of them. Even if there were, those government representatives would not necessarily be familiar with or responsive to workers' particular concerns.

Instead, increased workplace democracy depends on giving workers some federally-mandated standards to fall back on and the rights to enforce and build on those standards.

Before exploring the idea of workplace democracy further, it is important to discuss what it does *not* mean, because the term often has been appropriated in recent years by people who are not talking about worker empowerment at all.

In the wake of the social upheaval of the 1960s, employers began experimenting with new programs to respond to workers' increased demands for job satisfaction and respect for their dignity. These programs have gone by many names, such as "Quality of Work Life," "Employee Involvement," "Workers' Participation," "Team Concept," and "Quality Circles."

Almost without exception, these programs have been initiated by management, not by workers. Employers have seen these schemes as a way to keep nonunion workers from organizing and to weaken unions where they exist.

When they are introduced, these supposed experiments in workplace democracy are usually popular with most workers. After all, who wouldn't be happy to hear management say it wants to listen more carefully to workers' ideas, eliminate an "us-and-them" atmosphere in the workplace, and make everyone feel part of a team?

Eventually, however, the initial enthusiasm dies because workers discover that they do not have increased democratic *rights*. Management will gladly take workers' ideas for how to get more productivity but balks when it comes to sharing power over decisions that involve significant costs and potential loss of management control. Labor activists often describe this phenomenon by saying that, "When they talk about 'labor-management cooperation,' they mean that the employer should do the managing while labor does the cooperating."

Similarly, many employers in the private sector—and many politicians claiming to have "new ideas"—have been pushing workers to accept compensation in the form of profit-sharing or stock ownership instead of more traditional wages, benefits, and paid time off. These schemes also give the appearance of greater employee involvement, but do not give workers any more control over decisions management makes. In fact, they can make workers even more vulnerable to financial losses resulting from management failures or other factors outside their control.

"Workplace democracy," then, does not mean programs to make workers feel better about their powerlessness. Instead, it means establishing rights that will give them more power.

As our mainstream politicians are fond of saying about countries like Poland, the right to organize is fundamental to all other freedoms. Effective exercise of democratic rights in the workplace requires that workers be able to pool their bargaining power.

Yet from 1957 to 1987, the percentage of nonfarm workers protected by unions dropped from 33 percent to less than 20 percent. One can point to many possible contributing factors in this decline, including some which are the fault of unions themselves. But anyone who has direct experience with workers' attempts to organize in recent years knows that the overriding problem is the failure of the government to protect the supposed legal right to organize.

One key employer tactic tolerated by the government is delay. Before passage of the Taft-Hartley Act in 1947, workers could establish legal recognition of a union simply by getting a majority at a particular workplace to sign cards or a petition supporting the union. That system still is in use in Canada, where about twice the proportion of workers belong to unions.

Under U.S. law, however, workers have been forced to go through a long procedure that revolves around an election supervised by the National Labor Relations Board (NLRB). Employers can insist on drawn-out NLRB and court hearings both before and after the election so that the entire process may take several years.

During that time, management officials often fire key union supporters, make barely veiled threats to shut down operations, and distribute misinformation about the union.

To get a fired union supporter reinstated requires proving to often hostile NLRB officials that opposition to union activity was an employer motive. That process also may take several years, during which time the worker must find other means of financial support. If the worker is vindicated, the employer pays no penalty other than the back pay it would have owed the worker anyway.

Under the Reagan administration, an already ineffective NLRB has officially decided to no longer classify most employer threats, promises, and outright lies as violations of the law.

Faced with these unrestricted abuses of management power, the wonder is not that unions lose about half the representation elections held but that they win any at all!

The reforms outlined in the preceding platform proposals would not by themselves guarantee the right to organize. No matter what protections government provides, workers will always bear the primary responsibility for building their own organizations. But those reforms would be a start toward recreating a framework in which workers could organize to exercise democratic rights.

The National Labor Relations Act supposedly requires employers to provide information to organized workers, on request, that unions need in order to negotiate over wages, hours, and working conditions. In the real world, however,

- Unions can't request information they do not know exists in the first place. If a company is secretly planning to shift investment from one operation to another, how would the union know to ask about those plans?

- Employers have great discretion in determining what requested information the union is entitled to receive. If asked about investment plans, for example, management could legally respond that it is not required even to discuss those plans—only to ask the union's opinion about the implementation of the decision once it is made.

- Enforcement of the narrow rights workers do have depends on the NLRB, which again means long potential delays and no penalty for an employer violation other than being told to comply with the law.

The federal government ought to require employers to keep workers as informed as top management itself about every aspect of the employer's operations, with stiff penalties for employers who fail to do so. Protection of legitimate trade secrets could be handled by legal limits on the way workers and their representatives could use the information provided to them.

To exercise democratic rights, workers must be trained by their own organizations both on the technical aspects of subjects such as health and safety, technological change, or employer finances and on how to use their workplace rights.

Using employer financial resources and paid work time, management can train its own officials to deal with workers, while most worker groups must pay out of their own pockets for training concerning exercise of their rights and must conduct classes outside their normal work day.

One model for providing workers with the training they need is the Work Environment Fund in Sweden. Paid for by a national payroll tax on all employers, the Fund is guided by a union-controlled board. It pays for the development of training programs which workers have a right to take during paid working hours. The "study circle" method is used, in which workers are trained to lead study groups and identify collective strategies for improving working conditions. Through this method, financial resources are used primarily to involve workers and not to create a huge new bureaucracy.

A similar program could be established in the United States with the flexibility for groups of workers to arrange education and training on the subjects most important to them. For example, worker education funds could be used for literacy programs and other services for recent immigrants, health and safety, ways to make technological change benefit workers, economics, equality for women and minorities, or the situation of workers in other countries to which multinational corporations have shifted investment.

The question of how to give workers more power over decisions that affect them is most difficult under our economic system, with its basic premise that only management should have that power.

In theory, workers affect decisions through collective bargaining. In practice, employers have no legal obligation to do more than *listen* to workers' ideas. Workers' means of forcing employers to negotiate in good faith—strikes, slowdowns, boycotts, and so on—have been so severely limited by laws and court decisions that few unions can mount a successful pressure campaign.

The employers with whom workers must negotiate today often are multinational corporations whose overall economic position is not affected by a strike at one location or even in one division or subsidiary. Yet it generally is illegal for workers involved in a dispute with the corporation at one location to ask workers at other locations to put economic pressure on management through a strike or other means; nor do workers have the clear legal right to ask consumers not to buy products from the multinational's other subsidiaries.

If employers are to have any incentive to truly bargain in good faith, as the law requires, then the government must allow workers to impose significant costs on employers who fail to do so.

In addition, in a democratic workplace workers would have the right to veto certain management decisions. Under Swedish law, for example, employers cannot implement workplace changes that would affect safety and health without approval from workers' elected representatives.

Workplace democracy legislation might give workers such rights as the following:

- to shut down unsafe or unhealthful operations until a workers' health and safety committee determines that hazards have been corrected

- to veto plans to contract out work that could be performed within the workplace

- to reject staffing plans which provide unnecessary layers of supervision or unrealistic workloads

- to rearrange work schedules when it is possible to provide greater flexibility and shorter hours for workers while still maintaining salaries and getting the job done

- to invest pension funds so that they both provide a good return and advance the interests of working people

- to adjust plans for introducing new technology to ensure that workers—and not just management—benefit.

To effectively address job security and other fundamental issues, workplace democracy ultimately must mean that workers have the right to review and approve employers' short-term and long-term plans. Since workers realize that it is in their interest for their employer to succeed, their goal in using that power would be to identify plans which would both meet workers' needs and the needs of the enterprise as a whole.

In a genuine democracy, everyone has the same rights. Equal rights are particularly important to workers, because without them employers can play off one group against another. Jobs can be moved to states or plants or offices where workers have fewer rights, and the threat of doing so can discourage workers from asserting the rights they have.

Examples of unequal protection that should be corrected by the federal government include the following:

- Although unions are required by federal law to provide equal representation for all workers in units they cover, so-called "right to work" laws in twenty states prohibit unions from negotiating agreements with employers to require all workers to pay for that representation. These laws dilute workers' organized strength in the same way that public programs would be weakened if citizens were told that they could receive the same government services as their neighbors but not pay any taxes.

- Although nearly all unionized workers cannot be fired without a ruling by a neutral arbitrator that the employer had "just cause," most workers can be fired legally without the employer giving any reason at all. Federal legislation should protect every worker's right to due process before he or she can be discharged.

- Federal law prohibits paying women or minorities less for the same work, but currently allows employers to discriminate against those groups by paying them less for work of equal value. For example, many employers pay female secretaries less than male employees with jobs which require fewer skills and are no more important to the operation.

- A worker whose leg is cut off in a workplace accident in one state may receive in compensation only a small fraction of what he or she would have received in another state. The same is true of unemployment benefits.

- Although some workers are protected by union contracts or state laws from invasions of privacy through random drug-testing, polygraph tests, or secret electronic monitoring such as video cameras in break rooms, most workers are not protected from those abuses.

- Most public employees do not have the basic rights that private sector employees are supposed to enjoy, including the right to bargain collectively with management and to strike if necessary to win a fair agreement.

- Farm laborers, who are among the most oppressed workers in the country, are not covered by federal labor laws and have either no legal right to organize or only the rights they can win through state legislation.

In the past, the federal government has set some national employment standards, such as a minimum wage and a ban on child labor, and has established certain workers' rights in areas such as collective bargaining, health and safety, and equal opportunity. In each case, employers claimed that such requirements would put many of them out of business, and no doubt the same arguments will be raised against any proposed steps toward real workplace democracy. But because those past reforms applied to all, predictions of economic havoc proved false. Those reforms were part of our continuing effort to make our nation more just and more democratic. Now, new workers' rights are needed to further that process.

Resources

Recommended Appointees for a New Administration

Secretary of Labor
- Susan Bianchi Sand. Currently president of Association of Flight Attendants, AFL-CIO. She was rank-and-file flight attendant, elected member of negotiating team at United Airlines, then national Vice President in charge of organizing, flight safety, education and training, and other union activities. Strong expertise on issues related to women in the workforce and the expanding service sector. Heads one of nation's most democratic unions.

Chair of the National Labor Relations Board
- Joseph A. "Chip" Yablonski. Attorney in private practice. Served as co-counsel to his father, Jock Yablonski, who led the reform movement which eventually ousted corrupt union president Tony Boyle from the United Mine Workers. (Jock Yablonski and his wife and daughter were murdered under orders from Boyle.) Served as general counsel at the United Mine Workers when the reform administration completely rewrote the union constitution to insure rank-and-file democracy and launched an active new organizing campaign. Has since represented workers attempting to exercise democratic rights in other unions.

Organizations

The nation's labor unions, as the official representatives of organized workers, obviously should be a key source of information about the needs and concerns of workers. In addition, many of the nation's universities have labor education programs which work closely with local unions. A number of independent groups also provide publications, training, and assistance to those interested in furthering genuine workplace democracy.
- American Labor Education Center, 1835 Kilbourne Pl. NW, Washington, DC 20010; (202) 387-6780. Publishes newsletter and labor education guide, *American Labor*.

- Association for Union Democracy, YWCA, 30 Third Ave., Room 619, Brooklyn, NY 11217; (718) 855-6650. Publishes a newsletter, *Union Democracy Review*, and books on workers' rights.

- Labor Education and Research Project, 7435 Michigan Ave., Detroit, MI 48220; (313) 842-6262. Publishes newsletter on developments in labor movement, *Labor Notes*, and has produced books on so-called quality of work life (*Inside the Circle*, South End Press) and team concept experiments (*Choosing Sides*, South End Press, fall 1988).
- Labor Research Association, 80 E. 11th St., New York, NY 10003; (212) 473-1042. Publishes newsletter on economic developments and labor's response, *Economic Notes*.
- Midwest Center for Labor Research, 3411 W. Diversey, No. 14, Chicago, IL 60647; (312) 278-5418. Publishes an in-depth journal, *Labor Research Review*.

Further Reading

- Harley Shaiken, *Work Transformed: Automation & Labor in the Computer Age*, Holt, Rinehart, and Winston, 1984.
- Richard Kazis and Richard Grossman, *Fear At Work: Job Blackmail, Labor, and the Environment*, Pilgrim, 1982.
- Richard Freeman and James Medoff, *What Do Unions Do?* , Basic, 1984.
- Donald Wells, *Empty Promises: Quality of Working Life Programs and the Labor Movement*, Monthly Review Press, 1987.
- Juliet Shor and Daniel Cantor, *Tunnel Vision: Labor, the World Economy, and Central America*, South End Press, 1987.
- Barry Bluestone and Bennett Harrison, *The Deindustrialization of America*, Basic, 1982.
- Staughton Lynd, *The Fight Against Shutdowns*, Singlejack, 1982.

Matt Witt has worked in the labor movement for sixteen years as an educator, organizer, and journalist. He is director of the American Labor Education Center in Washington, DC and editor of *American Labor*.

An Economic Policy for the 1990s

Platform

- If we are not in a recession in 1989, reduce the federal deficit by (a) cutting military spending by $50 billion, down to a $250 billion level; (b) cutting farm subsidies, which now go mainly to large corporations; (c) raising revenue through restoring the 1987 marginal tax rate on high incomes, increased excise taxes on alcohol and cigarettes, and an oil import tax.

- Invest in human capital—education, health care and physical fitness, low-cost, quality childcare—to raise productivity and increase the social wage of low- and middle-income people.

- Increase employee participation in profits through enterprise profit-sharing plans and through national mutual funds. Increase decision-making at the level of individual enterprises.

- Redistribute national income gradually from the rich to the middle class and the poor in three ways: through fuller employment (which would also promote a shift from part-time to full-time employment); through a higher marginal tax rate on higher incomes without expanding loopholes; and through a shift in government spending from military to education, health care, childcare for low- and middle-income families, subsidies to low-income earners to buy housing, and improving the environment (improvement in the quality of life), including the workplace environment.

- Increase cooperation between federal and state governments in assisting local traditional industries in modernizing their production of goods and services and training local labor forces for such modernized production.

- Increase exports, not through destabilizing dollar devaluations, but rather through: increased competitiveness of U.S. industry; more rapid growth in Latin America, one of the most important purchasers of U.S. products; more aggressive export promotion policies, such as greater facilities for exports and trade fairs for American products; continued pressure on Japan to open its domestic market to U.S. companies and products.

———

Give credit where credit is due. The Reagan administration got inflation down and kept it down. We are in the midst of a long economic expansion (more than seventy months at the moment). The labor force has continued to grow but much more slowly than in the 1970s (1.5 percent in 1980-87 versus 2.5 percent in the 1970s), and not quickly enough to absorb the 6 percent still unemployed. Profits after taxes were higher in the 1980s than in the 1970s, corporate America prospered, and, at least until October 1987, Wall Street rode a spectacular expansion.

Behind these apparent successes, however, is an economic monster. The Reagan economic model staked its legitimacy on increasing consumption power even at the cost of unequal distribution. But economic growth in the 1980s was much lower than expected. Worse, having produced a low 2.4 percent growth rate in 1981-87—far below the average (recessions and all) 3.5 percent growth of 1947-79 (even the four best Reagan years, 1983-86, were not much better than that) and lower than the 3.0 percent growth during the "disastrous" Carter years—the Reagan administration has gambled away America's economic future.

The federal budget deficit since 1982 has averaged almost 5 percent of GNP. Rather than declining in growth years, the deficit has risen. Reaganomics has borrowed heavily against the future to produce low growth rates now. Interest on the debt now absorbs almost 20 percent of the federal budget, up from 8.8 percent in 1980. Should any downturn occur in the next few years, future governments will be that much less able to use fiscal policy effectively to combat recession and unemployment.

The Reagan administration could have used the federal deficit to invest in future jobs and in a more equitable society: in improved education for all citizens, research and development of high-tech commercial applications, incentives for modernizing and even bringing back traditional industries from abroad, retraining of displaced workers, improved health care and preventive medicine, better and more extensive childcare, particularly for single parents. But it did not. Instead, most of the deficit represents inefficient spending on weaponry. The defense purchases component of GNP rose at 6.6 percent annually in the 1981-86 period, almost three times the growth rate of GNP. Reduced research and development spending was oriented toward military objectives. Putting the same money directly into commercial applications or social programs would have much greater impact on our future economic competitiveness and on economic opportunity.

Since 1980, real average weekly earnings are down. In 1980, the average nonagricultural worker earned $172.74 a week (in 1977 dollars); in 1986, he/she earned $171.07. Although the difference is small, it means that the Reagan expansion has left the average person behind. Even in manufacturing, where real weekly earnings have risen since 1980 ($222.22 versus $212.06, in 1977 dollars), the increase represents less than 0.8 percent growth rate per year. This tiny increase has been bought at the cost of manufacturing jobs, which have not increased since 1980. There is also evidence that a high percentage of the jobs that have been created since 1980 are dead-end and low-wage.

The Reagan administration's main argument in selling the 1981 tax-spending package to Congress was that reduced taxes and reduced social spending would increase work effort, personal savings, and business investment.

None of this has occurred. The Reagan tax plan shifted billions of dollars to the rich and to business at the expense of the middle class and the poor. At least 50 of America's 500 largest corporations did not even pay taxes in 1981-85. In return for this windfall, and despite much higher profit rates after taxes, businesses and individuals slowed down their investments, reducing them far below gross domestic private investment (GDPI) increases during the Carter administration. Even during the best Reagan years (1983-86), GDPI in non-residential structures and equipment grew at about one-half the rate during the good Carter years (1977-79). Nor is business saving more than in the past. Business saving is about the same as in the Carter years.

One of the costliest of the unintended effects is that personal savings as a percentage of GNP have dropped steadily after an initial rise in 1981. The 2.8 percent figure for 1986 is the lowest in history. This has drastically shifted reliance for capital from American savers to foreign (primarily European, some Canadian, Latin American, and now Japanese) governments and private investors.

Real personal consumption did increase more rapidly under Reagan than under Carter, and almost as quickly as in 1947-79 (3.5 percent annually). But there is an important difference between rising consumption in the past and during the past five years. Between 1960 and 1979, real median family income (in 1985 dollars) rose from $20,400 to $29,000 (mostly between 1960 and 1973), or about 2 percent annually. According to the *President's Economic Report*, during the Reagan years, real individual wages and average family income did not rise at all (median family income in 1985 dollars stayed at about $27,500).

There is widespread agreement that income inequality both before and after taxes/social benefits has increased sharply under Reagan's economic policies. Although this continues the trend that began in the mid-1970s, inequality after 1981 increased for four major reasons: wages in professional jobs rose more rapidly than wages in low-income jobs, and the number of two-professional families rose; the number of families headed by women (whose real wages have risen slowly, if at all) rose; the real value of welfare benefits (mainly to low-income recipients) dropped; and average unemployment rates in the 1980s, particularly for the young and poorly educated, rose.

The average family may be consuming more, but purchases are coming out of savings and borrowing. Consumer debt as a percentage of personal disposable income is at an all-time high, and personal savings are at an all-time low. So consumers are doing exactly the opposite of what the Reagan administration predicted. Instead of saving more, they are borrowing more (and at record real interest rates).

Foreign investment in the United States has also increased (about 25 percent in government paper; foreign direct investment in the United States is also increasing rapidly: it more than doubled between 1980 and 1985). This investment, and the surpluses accumulating in the states (also invested in federal government paper), are covering the huge increases in federal debt.

In a nutshell, instead of making the economy less dependent on government spending, the Reagan administration has merely shifted this dependence from social spending to military spending. It has also made the economy dependent on foreign investment.

People have lower federal taxes, but higher state and local taxes, than in 1981. States pass these higher taxes along to the federal government by buying its debt, but even that is not enough. Reagan has also depended on bringing foreign holdings of dollars back to the United States to buy debt. About 10 percent of the trillion dollars in new debt created by Reagan was bought by foreigners.

There is nothing wrong with shifting things around if it builds the basis for a new round of growth or a higher quality life in the future for all Americans. But it has not. Instead, we are left to deal with an enormous debt that will constrain future fiscal policy. Wages are kept low and savings reduced, which means that people are living more precariously than seven years ago, despite reduced inflation. We have had an orgy of military spending instead of effective diplomacy and wise investments in future skills. Inequality in U.S. society has increased. The rich are richer but they do not invest as much as they did in the past. There are millions of new poor.

The Reagan years have taught us an important lesson: economic growth is a means to an end, not an end in itself. It matters greatly how growth is produced, what is produced, and how its benefits are distributed. We do not really need (nor will we get) higher economic growth in the future than in the past few years, but we do need a system of production and distribution that "works," not just for those who are wealthy now, but for everyone and for future generations.

The next administration has a giant task; it must undo eight years of misguided, costly economic policy that has left the United States in a disadvantaged international economic position, made U.S. income distribution more unequal than in 1980, and severely reduced domestic economic policy flexibility. Whereas the Reagan administration produced economic growth with greater domestic economic inequality and poorer international performance, the new administration will be charged with the difficult goal of simultaneously maintaining present growth, improving international competitiveness, and increasing income equality and economic opportunity for the disadvantaged.

Some specific economic policies to implement the general policy guidelines outlined in the platform include the following:

The Federal Deficit

The next administration has little choice on deficit policy. If we want to regain some independence in our own economic policymaking from foreign investment and other countries' interest rates, the deficit has to be reduced by rapidly cutting the military budget and farm subsidies and by finding new ways to collect revenue. Even as we reduce the deficit, there is still room to invest more in education and retraining, set up a more efficient, wider-coverage health care system, improve our environment, make better self-owned housing available to low-income earners, and develop local childcare centers. It means shifting federal money from high-cost weaponry to low-cost, innovative programs that will bring the U.S. economy into the 21st century international economy in a just and equitable fashion.

Foreign Economic Policy and Foreign Trade

Huge domestic deficits plus low domestic personal savings growth has created a new kind of fallout: the need to attract foreign capital with high domestic interest rates. The Reagan administration was successful in this strategy, but at the price of a high dollar exchange rate, falling exports, and increasing imports.

To correct a large foreign trade deficit caused in part by the overvalued dollar and in part by Japanese and European protection, the United States Treasury has pushed hard and successfully for devaluing the dollar. The dollar has already fallen about 75 percent against the yen and 100 percent against the mark, from the highs of three years ago. One of the problems in using dollar devaluation to reduce our foreign trade deficit is that several countries, such as Hong Kong, South Korea, and Taiwan, peg their currencies to the dollar, so that devaluation has had no effect on the price of their exports to us. Some of the biggest buyers of our imports, such as Canada and Latin America, also have their currencies closely tied to the dollar, so our exports are not becoming cheaper to them. Oil is one of our most important imports and its price is also set in dollars. Another problem is that Japanese and European exporters have kept price increases in the U.S. market at a minimum, preferring to take profit reductions rather than lose market share. Many U.S. companies—such as the Big Three auto producers—

have made this easier for them by raising prices rather than fighting for an increased market share. Most important, devaluation—which is seen by most U.S. transnationals as a temporary measure—is not inducing those firms to reorganize their present international structure of production. It is not moving them to restore domestic production of goods that are no longer produced in the United States (for example, television sets and VCRs).

Nevertheless, the present devaluation is helping reduce the foreign trade deficit. It has taken some time for its effect to be felt, but manufacturing output is up, and increases in exports have become an important component of growth. Yet the negative impact on the U.S. economy of the latest reductions in the value of the dollar through upward pressure on interest rates, may be greater than the positive impact, through lowering the foreign trade deficit.

In the last analysis, dollar devaluation is a form of protectionism. It unfortunately does not solve the underlying problem of declining U.S. competitiveness. Although it may make U.S. business temporarily more competitive against Japanese and European companies, those countries could take steps to improve efficiency while U.S. producers sit back behind a lower-valued dollar.

The next administration should therefore do more to stimulate exports in a more "permanent" and internationally stabilizing way. One important step would be to get Latin American economies growing again, and to do that we have to reduce their debt payment burden. When Latin America grows, our exports increase rapidly. Another step is to increase the competitiveness of U.S. industry. A third step is to come to an agreement with the other major actors in the increasingly internationalized economy on a more coordinated world development strategy, one in which the United States, Japan, and Germany manage their domestic economies in a coordinated fashion, and the Group of Seven coordinate a policy of stimulating development in the third world. This will require a cooperative approach to the international economy—an approach in which the new administration, on the one hand, admits that it no longer has the same hegemonic control it did in the 1950s and 1960s, and Japan and Europe (especially Germany), on the other hand, begin to take a more internationally responsible position vis-à-vis their own domestic economic policies.

Unemployment

Average unemployment during the Reagan years has been higher than at any time since the Great Depression in the 1930s. Even after four years of economic growth, unemployment is still hanging around 6 percent. The easiest way for the next administration to reduce unemployment is to increase the rate of growth. Our growth rate since 1981 has averaged only 2.4 percent, which is what it has been in the last two years. If we could get the growth rate up to 3-4 percent a year, unemployment would fall into the 5 percent range. However, the danger in pushing up growth rates is increased inflationary pressures, higher interest rates, and the risk of recession.

The next administration has to find ways to combat inflation while it simultaneously increases growth and reduces unemployment. The simplest way is to expand training and retraining programs so that employers can find all the skilled workers they need. Good, dependable, low-cost childcare will also increase the availability of skilled women workers, even as it provides jobs. We also have to reduce the federal deficit so that we reduce pressure on interest rates.

In addition to lowering the general level of unemployment, the next administration must do more to reduce unemployment rates in target groups. As long as we have 30 percent school dropout rates among minority youth, it is going to be tough to bring that group into decent jobs—or any jobs. A shift from military to social spending would have a positive effect on minorities' and women's employment opportunities, but employment programs for minority youth will also have to be developed at the community level. Although these programs would be state-run, they should have federal support and be connected to regional modernization programs.

We have skilled, capable, productive workers who have lost their jobs and cannot find new ones because they have committed the sin of being over forty. A good retraining and job placement program should make sure that we do not waste these valuable resources. Many states have already begun retraining programs. The federal government should help beef them up, a prime example of a relatively low-cost federal program that could have very high payoffs. Since our economy is going to be changing rapidly in the future, we should begin now to make retraining a permanent feature of adult working life, where going back to school to learn new skills is a choice available to every person.

Competitiveness

There is no secret to increasing competitiveness: you have to come up with more products that people want to buy, and you have to produce them cheaply and well. We Americans are great at coming up with the new products, and people all over the world want what we produce. But we seem to be falling behind in producing our goods and services more efficiently than other countries. A big part of the problem is that productivity has risen less than 6 percent in the past ten years, and two-thirds of that increase occurred in 1983-84. We are doing much better in manufacturing, where productivity has been going up at about 3 percent annually for the past four years (but at the cost of employment stagnation), than in the rest of the economy, where productivity is stagnant but employment has increased.

Getting productivity to rise again means, above all, better management and a more motivated work force. We need management that is more interested in what makes better workers. For the past ten years, U.S. enterprise has spent too much time trying to lower wages rather than trying to increase productivity. All too often, it has been looking for the fast buck instead of building for the longer term. If there is anything we can learn from the Japanese, it is how to motivate workers to produce more and produce it better. That means greater attention to what workers think about what they are doing, better training, and clearer communication. Workers are smart; if they can have a say in how things are done and management listens to them, productivity will increase.

The federal government can help raise productivity through incentives to firms to develop real worker participation, both in decision-making and profits. It can send a message to employers that health and safety standards will be enforced and that firms should work with employees to make workplaces safer and cleaner. The government can also help with health care and fitness programs that keep employees healthy and on the job, which will also lower insurance costs for private enterprise.

Education

The new administration must put greater emphasis on education as part of its economic policy. It should support the states' reform initiatives of the past few years, which have been aimed primarily at middle-class children, and complement them with federal legislation and leadership that increases the number and quality of teachers, especially teachers with high levels of specific subject knowledge. Such measures have consistently been opposed by the Reagan administration.

At the same time, the new administration should press for equal educational opportunity for all children. We know how to achieve equal opportunity: during the 1970s, we eliminated 40 percent of the gap in reading achievement between black and white children. In 1976, 36 percent of all whites, 34 percent of all blacks, and 36 percent of all Hispanics who were eighteen to twenty-four years old and had graduated high school went to college. This percentage declined for all groups during the Carter years. But with the cuts in compensatory education programs, and by giving clear signals to minorities and the poor that poverty and equal opportunity were no longer national issues, the Reagan administration pushed enrollment rates still lower among minority groups even as rates recovered among whites. By 1985, black college enrollment among 18-24 year old high school graduates had dropped to 26 percent (from 28 percent in 1980) and to 27 percent among Hispanics (from 30 percent in 1980), whereas the white rate rose to 37 percent (from 33 percent in 1980).

Republican efforts to cut compensatory education programs are bad economics. The quality of our labor force is crucial to improving our competitive economic position in the future. An increasing proportion of the labor force is minority workers, who are already filling the ranks of semi-skilled and low-skilled jobs. In California, for example, approximately 40 percent of the pupils now in public schools are Hispanic or black; by the year 2000, that figure will be closer to 50 percent. Inadequate education at all levels for these groups not only reduces our future economic potential, but also ensures future inequality and mocks this country's commitment to democracy.

The Environment

The Reagan administration has tried to ignore environmental concerns in its economic growth policies. The new administration should do precisely the opposite; it should make environmental improvement part of its economic platform, because improving the quality of life creates more jobs than it destroys, and improved environmental quality (including health and safety on the job) is part and parcel of sound economic development. What is the value of greater material consumption if consumers' health is imperiled and the "free" goods in society, such as clean air, unpolluted oceans and rivers, and the natural wilderness, are disappearing?

Environmental concerns are national and international. Acid rain and the Chernobyl accident make dramatically clear that one country's environmental errors are other countries' problems. The new administration must take the lead in dealing with international aspects of the environment after eight years of neglect by the Reagan administration.

Environmental concerns and arms control are also intimately connected, because personal security is eroded by the arms race, and, of course, the ultimate environmental disaster would be a nuclear war.

By bringing environmental concerns into a mainstream national economic and social development program and into foreign policy, the next administration can put the environment where it belongs—at the center of an alternative vision.

The new administration is going to face severe economic problems. Much of its work will be undoing the damage caused by Reaganomics and developing the basis for a new economy, structured for the next century. The new economics has to be built on the "human factor"—on the quality of work, of workers and management, and of our children and the environment in which we raise them. All this has to be carried out in the context of more equal income distribution, gradual deficit reduction, and a shift from military to "human factor" spending. It also has to be carried out in the context of federal-state-local cooperation to modernize U.S. industry for improved competitiveness and much greater international cooperation for domestic economic policy coordination among the major industrial countries—a coordination that takes much more seriously the needs of the third world.

Resources

Recommended Appointees for a New Administration

- Myra Strober, Associate Professor, School of Education, Stanford University
- Claire Brown, Professor, Department of Economics, University of California, Berkeley
- David Smith, Staff Economist, Senate Joint Economic Committee
- Michael Reich, Department of Economics, University of California, Berkeley
- Juliet Schor, Department of Economics, Harvard University
- David Gordon, Department of Economics, New School for Social Research, head of the Center for Democratic Alternatives, New York, NY
- Lester Thurow, Dean, Sloane School of Management, Massachusetts Institute of Technology
- Albert Fishlow, Department of Economics, University of California, Berkeley
- Theresa Amott, Department of Economics, University of Massachusetts, Boston, member of the editorial collective of *Dollars and Sense*
- Derek Shearer, Director of Public Policy, Occidental College
- Steven Quick, Senior Economist, Senate Joint Economic Committee
- Laura Tyson, Department of Economics, University of California, Berkeley
- Samuel Bowles, Department of Economics, University of Massachusetts, Amherst
- John Gurley, Department of Economics, Stanford University
- Everett Ehrlich, budget analyst, Congressional Budget Office
- Herbert Gintis, Department of Economics, University of Massachusetts, Amherst
- Jamie Galbraith, Associate Professor, Lyndon B. Johnson School of Public Affairs, University of Texas at Austin, former Executive Director of the Senate Joint Economic Committee
- Richard Feinberg, Vice President, Overseas Development Council, Washington, DC
- Henry Levin, Professor, School of Education, Stanford University

Organizations

- Overseas Development Council, 1717 Massachusetts Ave. NW, Washington, DC 20036; (202) 234-8701

- Council on Economic Priorities, 30 Irving Pl., New York, NY 10003; (212) 420-1133

- Union for Radical Political Economics, 155 W. 23rd St., New York, NY 10011; (212) 691-5722

- Economic Policy Institute, 1730 Rhode Island Ave. NW, Washington, DC 20036; (202) 775-8810

- Center on Budget and Policy Priorities, 236 Massachusetts Ave. NW, Washington, DC 20002; (202) 544-0591

- Council on International and Public Affairs, 777 UN Plaza, New York, NY 10017; (212) 972-9877

Further Reading

- Gar Alperovitz and Jeff Faux, *Rebuilding America*, Pantheon, 1983.

- Gar Alperovitz and Roger Skurski, *American Economic Policy*. Notre Dame Press, 1984.

- Barry Bluestone and Bennett Harrison, *The Great U-Turn*. Basic Books, forthcoming, 1988.

- Samuel Bowles, David Gordon, and Thomas Weiskopf, *Beyond the Wasteland*. Doubleday, 1983.

- Martin Carnoy and Derek Shearer, *Economic Democracy*. M.E. Sharpe, 1980.

- Martin Carnoy, Derek Shearer, and Russell Rumberger, *A New Social Contract*, Harper and Row, 1983.

- Martin Carnoy and Manuel Castells, "After the Crisis," *World Policy Journal*, Spring 1984.

- *Workplace Democracy* (magazine published in Amherst, Massachusetts).

Martin Carnoy is Professor of Education and Economics at Stanford University. In 1984, he was the Democratic candidate for Congress in California's 12th District. He is the author of *Economic Democracy* (with Derek Shearer), *A New Social Contract* (with Derek Shearer and Russell Rumberger), *The State and Political Theory*, and *Schooling and Work in the Democratic State* (with Henry Levin).

A New Family and Children's Policy for America: Real Welfare Reform

Platform

Employment and Income

- Job creation and preservation
- Increase minimum wage, with regular cost-of-living adjustments
- Pro-rated benefits to part-time workers
- Pay equity/comparable worth
- Reduction of work hours without salary reductions
- Parental leave, at least partly paid
- Flex-time and personal leave for children's needs
- Enforceable child support from absent parents
- Basic family allowance replacing AFDC available to all one- and two-parent families

Childcare

- Universal, federally-funded childcare: utilization of payroll tax for financing; local program development, involving parents

Health Care

- Universal, comprehensive, accessible health care
- Expansion of home health care and hospice services

Education and Training

- Rigorous, quality, basic education
- Training for specialized occupations and new technologies

- Equal access for women
- Elimination of sex stereotyping
- Restoration and expansion of college loans and grants to single parents, displaced housewives, children of poor and working-class families

Reproductive Rights

- Availability of family planning and full spectrum of choices
- Right of abortion, covered through health benefits; right not to be sterilized

Legal Rights

- Right of gay and lesbian couples to marry
- Right of gay men and lesbians to adopt children

Housing

- Adequate, low-cost housing

Social Services

- Review and overhaul of foster care: small, decentralized group care facilities; adequately trained and paid personnel
- System of funded shelters for battered women and women's centers
- Counseling, referral, linkage, and advocacy services to humanize education, training, and employment programs
- Decentralized, accessible services, emphasizing advocacy
- Expansion of daycare and respite care for infirm, elderly, and mentally and physically disabled adults to enable them to remain at home without overburdening family caretakers

———

Families in the United States today are under stress. The need for quality childcare is a universal issue, important to rural and urban, black and white, poor and middle-class families. Women in families are particularly burdened by the double or triple bind of maintaining their traditional roles as primary child caretaker and housekeeper and, increasingly, by their new role as wageearner as well. As women approach middle age, they are also expected to provide care for aging parents.

The changing U.S. economy, reflected in increasing deindustrialization, longer and deeper recessions, tenacious structural unemployment, particularly in the midsector of the country, creates stress and pressures on families. Increases in unemployment have been directly linked to increases in family violence, alcoholism, mental illness, and suicide. In the last recession, in the early 1980s, it was the two-parent, male-headed family that experienced the greatest downward mobility. A number of recent studies have exposed the disappearance of the middle class and the concomitant increase in poverty among this sector of the population.

Nevertheless, it is mothers raising their children alone who are most likely to be poor, especially if they are black or Hispanic. Thirty-four percent of all female-headed families live below the official poverty line—over 25 percent of all white and over 50 percent of all black and Hispanic female-headed families do as well. In 1985, the median income for all female-headed families was $13,660—less than half of that for all families ($27,740); for black and Hispanic female-headed families it was about $9,000.

Female-headed families are poor not only because there is one earner instead of two, but because women's wages are lower than men's and women are still largely confined to traditionally female, lower-paid jobs. Moreover, without adequate childcare or transportation, they often must work part-time, at minimum wage, and without benefits. One-third to one-half of absent fathers are either not paying any child support or are paying less than what is stipulated in their court orders. Only about half of all such families even have a support order. For those receiving payments, the average annual support paid in 1983 was less than $1,500.

Increasingly, mothers and their children are among the homeless in cities, suburbs, and rural areas. Real estate inflation, gentrification, and condominium conversion, coupled with the Reagan administration's abandonment of new construction of subsidized housing, make this a growing family problem.

Health care is another gnawing issue for families. For those previously middle-class families whose primary wageearner is unemployed or underemployed, employer-provided health benefits are no longer available. Nor is such health care available to the millions in part-time jobs. Medicaid to the working poor has been cut back or eliminated in most states, as has coverage for abortions. For women raising their children alone, welfare has often been the only way they could provide health care (through Medicaid eligibility) for themselves and their children.

Recommendations for policies concerning families must recognize the economic, political, social, and cultural environments effecting families and their individual members. Unfortunately, most family policies have been developed in a vacuum without taking cognizance of these factors.

The definition of family will vary according to different ideologies. There was considerable controversy during the Carter administration, for example, as to whether to use the term "the family" or "families" for their White House Conference. The first implied that there was one acceptable family—a married couple with children; the second implied that there were many types of families, including not only married couples but single parents, foster families, homosexual couples with children, and adults, whether or not related or married, living together in a supportive relationship without children.

In order to understand what a family is, it may be more useful to ask what it is that a family does, or should do, rather than to define a family based on its composition. Over time and across cultures, families have served primarily as small groups where children are raised and cared for and where the norms and values of a culture are transmitted intergenerationally. Families have often functioned as an economic unit and have been described as units of production and reproduction. Although U.S. families no longer tend to operate as a unit of economic production, they have become the prime unit of economic consumption. Finally, families serve to provide physical and emotional sustenance to their members.

At one end of the spectrum of what may be considered a family would be any group of people living together and providing emotional support to one another. In fact people living together not merely as roommates sharing expenses but in communes or collectives with common values and shared responsibilities to the group and to one another, often refer to their group as a family. At the other end of the spectrum would be the traditional married couple raising their children. Raising children is a major task of families, but a family does not cease to be one once its children are raised. Despite the fact that extended families seldom live under one roof any longer in this society, the extended family still maintains some responsibility for care of its elderly or troubled members. How much responsibility the family has, what type of care should or can be given, and what the larger society's role is in the care of both children and the elderly are key issues in family policy today.

A functional definition of family is not concerned with the marital status or number of its members, what gender they are, or whether or not children are present. Rather, if it provides emotional support and care for its members and functions as an economic unit, it is a family.

Who defines the family and determines whether it is "good" or "healthy"? In considering the needs of families, too often the traditional male-headed family has been reified and the needs of individual family members, particularly women, have not been considered. Despite women's entry into the labor force in unparalleled numbers in the last two decades, they are still seen primarily as the childrearers and nurturers in the society.

Social control of the family is an extra-familial as well as intra-familial issue. In the past, child welfare workers have removed children from families whose cultures and norms were different from those of the majority. On the other hand, a prevailing social norm has been that the family is sacrosanct and society should not be allowed to interfere—even when it seeks to protect children and spouses from physical or sexual abuse.

In addition to the apparent conflicts between the individual and the family, women and the traditional family, and society and the family, another less obvious conflict is that between corporations or the larger economic sector and the family. It is usually assumed that the needs of the workplace take precedence over the needs of the family. Childcare must be organized around the eight-hour day, rather than the workplace organized around children's developmental needs. The economic pressures requiring two parents to be employed in order for a family to achieve middle-class status, or often in order to simply get by, forces parents to choose between supporting and caring for their children. Neither the workplace nor the government has taken responsibility to provide substitute childcare.

Families frequently are just completing the task of rearing their children when they are faced with the task of caring for their ailing parents. The responsibility often falls upon the daughter or daughter-in-law. Women are assigned the role of caretaker in our society and are expected to put the needs of other family members before their own.

As schools assume mothers are home to chauffeur children to after-school events or attend parent-teacher conferences during school hours, so hospitals assume these same women are available to care for an ailing parent (or husband). Nursing homes are expensive (or force the spouse to become pauperized before the patient can become eligible for Medicaid payments), inaccessible, or inadequate. Often they would not be needed if home health care were available. With so many women in the labor force, even if they want to assume the caretaker role, economic necessity requires them to be out of the home.

Until the New Deal, the federal government did not acknowledge any obligation to establish policies or provide services to families. Under an earlier constitutional interpretation (dating back to the mid-19th century when Dorothea Dix unsuccessfully attempted to establish mental hospitals on federal land), social welfare was deemed to be "reserved to the states and the people" (which would include local or non-governmental authorities), based on the Tenth Amendment.

During the Depression, it became obvious that these entities did not have the resources to provide, as they had in the past, through Widows' Pensions, "friendly visiting," or baskets of food at Christmas. Because these provisions at the local level were inadequate and unevenly available, the federal government enacted the Social Security Act. This was primarily established to provide for elderly workers and their spouses in their retirement, or for their families, should they die sooner (Old Age Survivors and Disability Insurance), and for the families of workers who lost their jobs (Unemployment Insurance) or were injured on the job. (Workers' Compensation, which was originally entitled Workmen's Compensation, reflecting the fact that it was male workers and their non-employed wives who were the object of the legislation.)

One title of the Act, Aid to Dependent Children (the title changed to Aid to Families with Dependent Children (AFDC) only in the 1950s when benefits were added for the mother as well as her children) was seen as a short-term, residual benefit for the families of widows who were not yet eligible to receive Social Security benefits. It was envisioned as a subsidy to white, middle-class mothers, enabling them to care for children in their own home rather than removing the children to orphanages or foster care after the father's death because of the mother's inability to provide both income and childcare. (Poor and minority mothers had already been in the workforce either supplementing a husband's income or as sole provider for their family.) Although it was a national program, eligibility standards and benefit levels were set by each state, which also administered the program. This led to enormous disparities in who received welfare and how much they were entitled to.

Of course, this program did not wither away but grew larger as the recipient population shifted from widows to mothers who were divorced, separated, abandoned, or never-married. Moreover, in the 1950s, as the composition of recipients shifted ethnically (although, contrary to popular belief, the majority of recipients continued to be white), the program became more stigmatized and an easy target for political expedience. The 1962 Social Security amendments for the first time included provisions for services in addition to financial payments. These included services for both adults and children, especially for foster care, adoption, and daycare.

During the 1960s War on Poverty more families were apprised of their eligibility, and, despite generally favorable economic conditions, the welfare ranks soared. Moreover, welfare rights organizations conducted campaigns to increase benefits and mobilize welfare recipients.

Ironically, it was President Nixon who sought to address the "welfare problem" by proposing a guaranteed income to replace state-administered welfare programs. Liberals split over whether to support this initiative. Some felt it was too little ($2,400 was being proposed for a family of four at a time when the poverty level was more than double this figure). They argued that such an inadequate payment level would further exacerbate the problem because Congress would believe the issue had been addressed, making further real reform more difficult. Supporters, on the other hand, saw this initiative as an important symbolic breakthrough—establishment of the principle of entitlement; a minimum income as a right for every family. Although they acknowledged the level was too low, they believed that once established, benefits could be increased incrementally. The debate was overshadowed by the events of Watergate, however.

For almost a decade the problems of poor families in the United States were ignored. Then, President Reagan was elected and his first budget slashed human services programs by 25 percent. Even more significantly, a whole range of categorical services to children and families, built up incrementally since the New Deal, were summarily wiped out and replaced by block grants to the states, which could then choose whether or not to implement the programs.

The Reagan administration also introduced the concept of "workfare," which was at complete variance with the original intention of AFDC to guarantee the ability of a single mother to care for her children at home. Under workfare, introduced initially as an "experiment" that individual states or subdivisions could opt for, recipients would work off their grants at the minimum wage rate, but without any employee benefits. Refusal could mean losing their grant.

In his 1986 State of the Union message, President Reagan called for a major overhaul of the welfare system. This unleashed a number of studies and reports. Welfare reform was once again "in." This is not the place to review all the proposals, but in general they argue that the society has changed and that at a time when over 50 percent of mothers with preschoolers are employed, a federal program that pays poor women to stay home with their children is no longer viable. Instead, most proposals call for universal education, training, and employment for single mothers with children over the age of three. The welfare reform bills introduced in the 100th session of Congress by Representative Thomas Downey (D-NY) and Senator Daniel Patrick Moynihan (D-NY) also call for extension of benefits and work provisions for two-parent families. Currently, coverage for two-parent families is optional, with only about half the states choosing such coverage. The concept of a "contract" is proposed: parents have an obligation to support their children and the government has the obligation to provide job training, childcare, and other supports to enable them to fulfill their obligation.

Again, liberals and progressives are divided as to whether to support or oppose such a program. On the one hand, it may offer some opportunity to mothers who would otherwise be locked into inadequate and demeaning welfare benefits with no job skills, no education, and no hope of escaping the welfare rolls. On the other hand, it may force mothers to leave their children and work at jobs which, even if available, are so low-paid that it would insure their families would remain poor. The basic problem with the approach of these bills, like the many proposed solutions in the past, is that the focus of the problem is the government's responsibility in caring for the needy, rather than the larger problem of eliminating poverty and enhancing families.

What is needed is a new family policy that will benefit a large segment of the population, the near-poor and working poor as well as those on welfare. The bottom 40 percent of households are often just a step above the poverty level, even though both parents are employed.

They, as well as the "official" poor, need support. One in four U.S. families is likely to be poor for at least one year out of eight. Most AFDC recipients remain on the rolls less than five years, about half that for less than two years. Focussing only on "welfare reform" does not address the real problem. To make a difference, a new family policy must also address larger and long-term structural and preventive measures in addition to concrete financial, educational, and social supports for families currently in need.

Employment Policies

For female-headed families, employment provides the major source of income, as it does for families in poverty. Programs to strengthen long-term employment opportunities and increase wages would, therefore, help all groups of workers.

Addressing the deindustrialization problem by developing new jobs at salaries that will support families is essential to any overall family policy. Not only job creation, but job preservation, is essential. Penalties for corporations leaving the country, opportunities for worker buyouts, and other provisions are needed.

But jobs are not a solution unless work can raise families out of poverty. The minimum wage needs to be increased and adjusted regularly, based on cost-of-living increases. Part-time workers should receive the same (pro-rated) health, retirement, vacation, and other benefits received by full-time workers. Pay equity for women must be implemented so that women are paid in accordance with their level of education, preparation, skill, and work conditions rather than by arbitrary assumptions about the lesser value of "women's work." A decrease in the work week or work year, without salary decreases, would simultaneously create more jobs, reduce the need for childcare, provide more time for parents to be with their children, and possibly raise the rate of productivity.

Parental leave for either parent must be made available. Unless some part of that is paid, however, it will not be utilized by single parents, who cannot afford to take the time. Flex-time and personal leave time to care for sick children, attend school functions, and fulfill other parental obligations need to be extended.

In female-headed families it should not be the mother who bears the sole burden of both care and financial support. A number of proposals are currently afloat to ensure that fathers, whether or not they live with their families, provide financial support. Automatic payroll deductions from the earnings of the non-custodial parent at a fixed percentage of income is one proposal receiving considerable attention. Such a plan would do much to assure child support payments, but other mechanisms would need to be devised to assure payments from the self-employed.

Childcare

Because of the dramatic increase in labor force participation by mothers of young children, broad support exists for universal, federally-funded childcare. This needs to cover before and after school as well as preschool and infant care. Utilizing the payroll tax, paid by both employers and employees, would not add much to current Social Security taxes and would be a popular way to provide a service needed by a large part of the population, although for a relatively brief time for each family. Mechanisms for local program development, assuring involvement of parents and choices in types of care, would need to be developed.

Health Care

Universal, comprehensive, accessible health care is another integral part of a broad family policy. Not only would such care address the short-term problems of mothers who now stay on welfare in order to be eligible for Medicaid, but it would alleviate the more pervasive problems of chronic poor health, lack of adequate nutrition, low birth weight, and other factors that keep people poor and unemployable. Many families currently receiving aid will not benefit from the proposed new welfare reforms, because their physical or mental disabilities, or those of their children, will prevent them from steady, full-time employment.

Education and Training

Most of the current welfare proposals call for job training. A necessary first step is basic education. Numerous reports have attested to the inadequacy of our educational system, especially in, but not limited to, inner-city schools. Even the corporate sector is now expressing concern that the new generation of workers will not be prepared for employment in an increasingly sophisticated service sector economy. At least half of all AFDC recipients have not completed high school. Many who have are functionally illiterate.

A rigorous, quality, basic education will eliminate the need, in the long run, for remedial training programs. Where training for specific specialized occupations or new technologies is required, equal opportunities for women, and elimination of sex stereotyping and sexual harassment must be vigorously promoted and enforced. Restoration and expansion of college loans and grants for single parents, workers with obsolescent skills, displaced housewives, and the children of poor and working-class families are also necessary to prevent further stratification of our society.

Universal Family Allowance

Because not every parent will be able to work, a basic family allowance is necessary. Replacing the inadequate, uneven, stigmatizing, state-run AFDC programs, the basic allowance would operate like a negative income tax and be available to all families—in or out of the labor force, female-headed, male-headed, or two-parent-headed. This would be a modest payment, which could be funded by eliminating personal tax deductions and replacing them with cash payments, thus providing a basic income floor for all families. Although we are addressing family policy here, such a plan need not be limited to families, but also could be made available to single individuals or couples not eligible for Supplemental Security Income (SSI).

Reproductive Rights

The right to decide if, when, and how many children to have must be preserved and enhanced in a new family policy. Family planning, providing a full spectrum of choices, including abortion, must be made available, regardless of income. Reproductive rights protect not only the right to have an abortion, without harassment, but also the right against forced sterilization.

Housing

Adequate, low-cost housing is a basic necessity for preserving and enhancing family life. Shelters for homeless families are a stop-gap measure rather than a solution. Life for the homeless in shelters, hotels, and motels is disruptive and destructive to families.

Social Services

A number of issues affecting families are included here, ranging from domestic violence, child abuse and neglect to foster care, adoption, counseling, and advocacy. While the frequency of domestic violence and the need for child protection and removal of children to foster homes will be substantially reduced by enactment of the policies proposed here, some services still will be needed. The entire concept of foster care needs to be reviewed and perhaps overhauled in light of changing societal conditions—it is no longer the case that many women are home to be caretakers for foster children. Many more small, decentralized group care facilities with adequately trained and paid personnel are needed, especially for adolescents. Additional shelters for battered women and women's centers where women can gain or recover their self-respect and self-confidence should also be developed. Policies need to be introduced so that the battering spouse is removed from the home.

Additionally, in order to humanize and individualize the education, training, and employment programs currently being proposed, counseling, referral, linkage to other community resources, and advocacy are needed. Without such services, the best conceived program will deteriorate into a bureaucratic nightmare. Recipients must be treated with dignity and respect for individual differences. Each family has a different set of problems, needs, and hopes which must be addressed. Decentralized, accessible services which provide advocacy on behalf of families and help empower them to make their own decisions must be the foundation for the array of all other programs provided. They can be empowered both as individuals and as members of groups with common concerns, through such programs as women's centers, voter registration projects, welfare rights organizations, and labor unions.

A number of these proposals have been heard before; some have even been tried in limited ways. What is needed is a *holistic* and *developmental* approach to families—addressing one component without the others is doomed to fail. Moreover, commitment to fund these programs adequately, not for a year or two, but for the long run, is essential. We are currently the only western industrialized nation without a national system of childcare, health care, or parental leave. Rather than focusing on problems alone, we must dedicate ourselves to the strengthening of families by providing the supportive environment in which they can best care for their children.

Many will argue that these programs are too expensive. The price of *not* investing in the future of our families, however, is much higher than the cost of not providing for them today.

Resources

Recommended Appointees for a New Administration

- Heidi Hartmann, Director, Rutgers University Women's Studies Program and Institute for Women's Policy Research, Washington, DC
- Sheila Kamerman, Professor at Columbia University School of Social Work
- Rosemary Sarri, Professor, University of Michigan School of Social Work
- Harriett McAdoo, Professor, Howard University School of Social Work
- Marion Wright Edelman, Executive Director of the Children's Defense Fund
- Diana Pearce, Director of the Women and Poverty Project, and Associate at the Institute for Women's Policy Research
- Greg Duncan, University of Michigan Institute for Social Research
- Ann Rosewater, Chief of Staff, House Select Committee on Children, Youth, and Families

Organizations

- Institute for Policy Studies, 1601 Connecticut Ave. NW, Washington, DC 20009; (202) 234-9382
- Institute for Women's Policy Research, 1400 20th St. NW, Washington, DC 20036; (202) 785-5100
- National Organization for Women, 1401 New York Ave. NW, Washington, DC 20005; (202) 347-2279

- Women's Equity Action League, 1250 I St. NW, Washington, DC 20005; (202) 898-1588
- National Association of Social Workers, 7981 Eastern Ave., Silver Spring, MD 20910; (202) 565-0333
- American Civil Liberties Union, 122 Maryland Ave. NE, Washington, DC 20002; (202) 544-1681
- Children's Defense Fund, 122 C St. NW, Washington, DC 20001; (202) 628-8787
- Villers Foundation, 1334 G St. NW, Washington, DC 20005; (202) 628-3030
- National Abortion Rights Action League (NARAL), 1101 14th St. NW, Washington, DC 20005; (202) 371-0779

Further Reading

- Mimi Abramovitz, *Regulating the Lives of Women: Social Welfare Politics from Colonial Times to the Present*, South End Press, 1988.
- Ruth Brandwein, Carol Brown, and Elizabeth Fox, "Women and Children Last: The Social Situation of Divorced Mothers and Their Families," *Journal of Marriage and the Family* (August 1974), pp. 498-514.
- Ruth Brandwein, *et al., Women, Families and Poverty: An Alternative Policy Agenda for the Nineties*, Institute for Policy Studies, March 1987.
- Linda Burnham, "Has Poverty Been Feminized in Black America?," *The Black Scholar*, 1985, Vol. XVI, No. 2, pp. 14-24.
- Center on Budget and Policy Priorities, *Smaller Pieces of the Pie: the Growing Economic Vulnerability of Poor and Moderate Income Americans*, November 1985.
- Children's Defense Fund, *A Children's Defense Budget: An Analysis of the FY1987 Federal Budget and Children*, 1986.
- Greg Duncan, *Years of Poverty, Years of Plenty: The Changing Economic Fortunes of American Workers and Families*, Institute for Social Research, University of Michigan, 1984.
- Barbara Ehrenreich and Frances Fox Piven, "The Feminization of Poverty," *Dissent* #31 (Spring 1984), pp. 162-170.
- Diana Pearce, "The Feminization of Poverty: Women, Work and Welfare," *Urban and Social Change Review*, February 1978.
- Diana Pearce and Harriet McAdoo, *Women and Children: Alone and in Poverty*, Center for National Policy Review, 1981.
- Ruth Sidel, *Women and Children Last: The Plight of Poor Women in Affluent America*, Viking Press, 1986.
- Karin Stallard, Barbara Ehrenreich, and Holly Sklar, *Poverty in the American Dream: Women and Children First*, South End Press, 1983.

Ruth Brandwein is Dean of the School of Social Welfare at the State University of New York at Stony Brook, where she oversees both graduate and undergraduate programs stressing issues of social change and empowerment, particularly for groups historically devalued in our society. She has written and taught in the areas of family policy, single-parent families, homelessness, organizational and social change, community organization, and social welfare administration. She has also written about and practiced feminist models of administration. She has been Director of the School of Social Work at the University of Iowa, chair of community organization at the Boston University School of Social Work, and Executive Director of the Central Seattle Community Council, a grassroots community organization.

Justice for America's Elders

Platform

Income Security Needs

- Make substantial improvements in the Supplemental Security Income program, to assist elderly and disabled Americans most in need.
- Maintain Social Security benefit levels, including full protection against inflation, for current and future beneficiaries.
- Avoid spending Social Security trust funds on new benefits for relatively well-off elders.

Health Care Needs

- Establish a long-term care program, with universal access for all ages to a full range of services, progressively financed through a range of sources.
- Out-of-pocket cost burdens under Medicare should be eased for the elderly poor and economically vulnerable.
- Reform Medicare's payments to physicians, to protect elders against excessive charges and to better compensate physicians for providing primary care.
- Establish a cost control system—for Medicare and other payers—that would rein in skyrocketing health care costs and provide access to care for the 37 million younger Americans with no health coverage at all.

Other Needs

- Help meet the shelter needs of older Americans by revitalizing federally-assisted housing and restoring assistance in meeting home energy costs.

- Promote greater participation in society by elders, through expanded volunteer opportunities.

If we believe what we read and hear, the elderly have moved from being poor, hopeless, helpless—and deserving of public generosity—to being a rich, greedy, self-serving group that neither needs nor deserves governmental largess.

Unquestionably, there have been important changes in the economics of old age in this country. Within the relatively short span of a quarter-century, much progress has been made in the struggle against poverty and the fear of economic insecurity, an achievement that should make us proud.

Largely because older people have such a high degree of homeownership (only about one-fourth rent), they have also accumulated more assets than other age groups. In 1984, the $60,000 median net worth of elderly households was almost twice the national average. But many older Americans have no reason to rejoice. Millions remain poor or economically vulnerable. For these among our elders, increasing age means increasing need. Health deteriorates. Spouses die. Pensions shrink in value.

Enlightened intervention by government has clearly fallen short. According to the Census Bureau, some 3.5 million elderly people (men and women aged 65 or older), 12.4 percent of the aged population, had incomes below the elderly poverty line in 1986. While this represents a dramatic improvement from the 1959 elderly poverty rate of 35.2 percent, this statistic understates the income insecurity of many millions of seniors. Here's why.

First, the official poverty line for the elderly is lower than it is for all other age groups. In effect, the Census Bureau assumes that an adult 65 years of age or older can escape poverty on less income—8 to 11 percent less—than an adult aged 64 or younger. If the same poverty standard were applied to the elderly as for other age groups, the poverty rate for the aged would increase from 12.4 percent to 15 percent.

Second, poverty among the elderly is more widespread than in any other adult age group. Only among children—whose poverty rates rose dramatically in the past decade—is the incidence of poverty higher than it is among elders. For persons aged 45-54, for example, the 1986 poverty rate was 8.2 percent.

Third, the poverty rates among significant segments of the elderly—most notably women, minorities, and persons living alone—are extraordinary. The poverty rate for older women is nearly twice the rate experienced by older men. Poverty rates for older blacks and Hispanics in 1986 were 31 and 22.5 percent, respectively—compared to 10.7 percent for aged whites. For elderly black women living alone—persons in "quadruple jeopardy"—the poverty rate was an astonishing 59.4 percent.

Fourth, the elderly poor stay poor longer than any other age group. According to the chief researcher on chronic poverty, Greg Duncan of the University of Michigan, escaping from long-term poverty is generally possible only by "acquiring a job with decent pay or marrying someone who has one." For most of the elderly poor, these are not options. Thus, the aged account for one out of every three persons in the nation experiencing chronic poverty.

Fifth, and perhaps least understood, there are incredible numbers of economically vulnerable aged persons subsisting barely above the poverty line. About eight million elderly Americans live above the official poverty line but remain poor with incomes ranging from $101-202 a week in 1986. In total, there are 11.5 million older Americans who are either poor or economically vulnerable. This constitutes 41 percent of the total elderly population—more than two out of every five—a rate substantially above the general population's and, ironically, the same rate as for children.

Income Security

The most direct and targeted solution to these income gaps is to improve the federal-state program that serves low-income elders, as well as low-income blind and disabled Americans. That program is Supplemental Security Income (SSI).

The SSI program began in 1974 to guarantee a minimum cash income to elderly and disabled persons. But in 1988, this benefit provides just under $82 a week for individuals—only about 74 percent of the poverty line. About half the states choose to supplement the federal benefit, but the median supplement is $8 a week.

An elderly person cannot qualify for SSI benefits unless he or she has extremely low "countable assets": not more than $1,900 for an individual and $2,850 for a couple in 1988. Inflation since 1974 has eroded more than half the real level of those limits. That erosion alone has squeezed almost a quarter million persons out of the SSI-eligible ranks, on the grounds that they have "too many resources."

The next administration should move quickly to increase the federal benefit standard to the poverty line, and restore the resource limits at least to their 1974 real levels. That would translate, in 1988 terms, to individual benefits of about $480 a month and a resource limit of about $3,500.

About 4.2 million persons—half of them age 65 or over—receive benefits from the SSI program each month. Yet about half of the potentially eligible population does not participate—in large part because of a lack of information about the program. If SSI is to fulfill its promise, a major outreach program must be launched. Such an effort needs the active assistance and planning of the Social Security Administration, the involvement of state and area agencies on aging, and the leadership of community groups that potential applicants can trust.

A further needed change is to eliminate the one-third reduction in benefits when a recipient lives in another's home. In theory, this reflects the value of food and shelter received; in practice, it remains a major penalty for families or friends who help care for vulnerable elderly or disabled persons. Another modest change would encourage states to supplement federal SSI benefits by sharing the cost with them. Not only must a state now bear the entire cost of any increase to its beneficiaries, but almost one-third of the increase is immediately offset by a reduction in federally-financed food stamp benefits. Thus, a state must spend over $1.40 of its funds to provide $1 in financial relief to its poor.

Many of these recommended steps would, in addition to increasing benefits for those already receiving SSI, extend eligibility to many new elderly and disabled poor persons. In most states that would in turn make them automatically eligible for Medicaid, to help with out-of-pocket health costs not covered by Medicare.

Some people think that Social Security benefits can be trimmed in a time of budget constraints because it is mainly a middle-class entitlement. The most visible target over the years has been the cost-of-living adjustment (COLA), that keeps benefits constant over time in the face of inflation.

The fact is, the lower the elderly household's income, the more dependent it is on Social Security. For 93 percent of the poor elderly, Social Security brings in most of the family's income. For half of the elderly poor, it constitutes 90 percent or more of their income. Across-the-board cuts in COLAs hurt low-income beneficiaries the most. Even more complicated COLA cut proposals—e.g., a flat amount for all recipients or a COLA only on the first $400 of benefits—neglect the fact that people with relatively high incomes may have very low Social Security benefits because of their work histories, and *vice-versa*. There is no good way to cut COLAs without hurting the economically vulnerable elderly. Proposals to restrict Social Security COLAs, therefore, should be opposed.

If any benefit improvements are to be made in Social Security, they should be closely targeted to the need for more income. This is not only because progressivity needs reinforcing at every possible stage, but also because the cash benefits trust funds are in extremely close actuarial balance over the 75-year period for which projections are made.

Two such proposals should be rejected on these grounds. For one, the Social Security "earnings test," which partially reduces benefits for those age 65-69 with earnings over $8,400, should *not* be abolished. Such a change would give a multibillion dollar windfall to high-income elders who choose to continue working and receive high salaries. For another, no additional benefits should be given to the so-called "notch babies." These persons, born between 1917 and 1921, receive less in benefits than those born just before them—but only because those older people were inadvertently awarded too much. Once again, this is a multibillion dollar solution to a not-very-pressing problem.

Health Care

When Lyndon Johnson signed Medicare into law in 1965, he hailed the dawn of a new era: "No longer will illness crush and destroy the savings that [older Americans] have so carefully put away over a lifetime..." Despite a quarter century of operation, and the expenditure of $88 billion this year, Medicare's promise remains only partly fulfilled. Astoundingly, older people currently spend a higher proportion of their incomes on health care than when Medicare and Medicaid were enacted. There are two fundamental reasons for this. First, Medicare fails to cover a wide array of health care needs: prescription drugs, dental care, preventive services, eyeglasses and hearing aids, and, most notably, long-term care. Second, the services that are covered by Medicare require elders to share costs, and these out-of-pocket costs have risen dramatically in recent years. As might be expected, increases fall most heavily on those with low and moderate incomes.

Through Medicare itself, and through a catastrophic acute care insurance plan expected soon to be law, most older Americans can be reasonably protected from financial devastation due to health care costs. For some, gaping holes remain to be plugged in Medicare's coverage. But the most burdensome risk of financial devastation for most elders comes from the lack of long-term care coverage. Nursing home stays account for over 80 percent of the expenses incurred by older persons who experience very high out-of-pocket health care costs. Struggling to avoid those stays—and suffering through them—places wrenching emotional and financial burdens on all members of the families affected.

Moreover, there is a demographic "time bomb" already ticking. Americans over the age of 85—those most likely to need long-term care—will grow in number from about three million today to more than seven million in just thirty years. The 85-and-over age group will grow twice as fast as the population aged 65-85, and eight times as fast as the under-65 population.

Private, long-term care insurance cannot meet this vast and growing need. Current and planned policies suffer from fatal flaws: they are too expensive for most elders; leave too many risks uncovered; fail to provide protection against future, inflated long-term care costs; and completely ignore the needs of younger people.

What is needed—and what Americans in public opinion polls clearly favor—is a long-term care plan with the following features:

• universal participation

• eligibility depending on how severely impaired the persons's capacity to function is

- a full range of in-home, community-based, and institutional services
- no co-payments or deductibles paid for through Medicaid for Americans with incomes below twice the official poverty line

This proposal can be financed fully and progressively from a variety of sources, including a tightening of gift and estate taxes for the well-off, raising the $45,000 ceiling on earnings subjected to payroll taxes, and fuller taxation of Social Security benefits for the most affluent retirees. But it must be underscored that, whatever the nominal price tag for putting a coherent long-term care system in place, most of the cost does not involve raising new funds. Rather, it would redirect money now being spent on long-term care—federal and state Medicaid dollars, as well as out-of-pocket expenditures by families—and redistribute those costs in a more equitable manner, through a social insurance program that would prevent bankruptcy for those with long-term care needs.

A large number of the medical bills of senior citizens are not covered by Medicare. Beneficiaries are subject to various "cost-sharing" requirements, including the Part B (physicians' services) monthly premium, the Part A (hospital) deductible, an annual Part B deductible, and co-insurance on the amount of doctors' bills not covered by Medicare.

These costs have escalated dramatically during this decade. As a result of these and other increases, cost-sharing requirements frequently add up to nearly one-quarter of the annual income of poor beneficiaries living alone. Unfortunately, only one-third of poor seniors are protected by Medicaid, so the overwhelming majority receive no help in paying the health care costs that Medicare fails to cover.

Two years ago, Congress passed legislation permitting, but not requiring, states to use Medicaid funds to pay the Medicare premiums, deductibles, and co-insurance for low-income seniors. Only the District of Columbia, Florida, New Jersey, and Rhode Island have exercised this option. Therefore, what is needed is the following:

- mandate Medicaid coverage of all Medicare-related cost-sharing for poor beneficiaries; and
- offer that same Medicaid coverage to economically vulnerable beneficiaries—those with incomes between the poverty line and twice that figure—with a sliding-scale premium

The cost of doctors' services under Medicare Part B has been skyrocketing, up 17 percent a year since 1979. Because beneficiaries pay a monthly premium pegged to cover 25 percent of total program costs, those premiums have also skyrocketed: more than 38 percent in 1988 thus far. Moreover, unlike under the Medicaid program, doctors are free to charge Medicare patients more than the amount Medicare determines to be fair. Those overcharges amounted to more than $3 billion in 1987. Medicare will pay none of that, so it comes almost exclusively out of beneficiaries' pockets.

At the same time, there is general agreement that Medicare reimbursements, which reflect physicians' previous charges, overcompensate surgical procedures while shortchanging primary care. A series of changes should address these shortcomings:

- limit physicians' power to charge patients in excess of what Medicare determines to be reasonable

- limit increases in the Part B premium to the same percentage as the increase in Social Security benefits

- put in place a "relative value scale" for physician services that redresses the imbalances in fees between primary care and surgical procedures

It should be obvious that, for both direct and indirect reasons, elders have a stake in seeing that the 37 million Americans with no health protection at all gain access to basic care. First, many older people would benefit directly; dislocated older workers and those forced to retire early often find themselves losing employer-related insurance long before becoming eligible for Medicare at age 65. Less obviously, extending universal access is certain to be coupled with better controls on staggering cost increases in health care. That can only help the troubled Medicare Hospital Insurance Trust Fund.

Besides addressing the basic income and health problems facing low- and moderate-income elders, the next administration should also take aim at two other areas of concern: the crisis in meeting the shelter needs of older Americans and the chance for elders to contribute more fully to the communities in which they live.

Housing

Older Americans have a great stake in the outcome of the debate over the state of this country's housing policies. Older people occupy almost half of all federally-assisted housing units in the country. The program aimed exclusively at lower-income elders and disabled persons, the "Section 202" program, is a proven success limited only by the resources committed to it. As residents of those units grow older—as the tenants "age in place"—the need for greater emphasis on linking housing units to services for the residents of those units becomes even clearer. The Congregate Housing Services Program (CHSP), for example, has already demonstrated how to bring support services and housing together to prevent unnecessary institutionalization.

A basic plan of action should include:

- a substantial increase in the number of assisted housing units in both urban and rural areas

- expansion of the CHSP program, which links the service availability to the housing units in advance, so that developers can plan on a sounder economic footing

- extension of CHSP beyond Section 202 and public housing, to rural rental units financed through the Farmers Home Administration Section 515 program, and to units assisted through state housing finance agencies

- mandating closer coordination between housing programs and programs to provide services to tenants with special needs, such as those under the Older Americans Act

Energy costs, especially home energy costs, are a major burden for low-income people. In 1984, the average household spent three percent of its income on home energy; the average elderly household had to spend another two-thirds as much, about 5 percent. By contrast, the 5.8 million elderly low-income households spent on average 17 percent of their incomes on home energy. Once it has paid for housing, food, and home energy, the average low-income elderly household has about $9 a week in "discretionary" income to spend on everything else: clothing, transportation, medical care, etc.

Two points are key to a rational federal energy policy toward low-income older Americans. The first involves the Low-Income Home Energy Assistance Program (LIHEAP), which helps low-income families with home energy bills. The elderly, given their susceptibility to hypothermia and heat stress, are especially targeted by LIHEAP, but the program reaches only one-third of those eligible for assistance. Funds appropriated for LIHEAP have fallen precipitously, from the $2.1 billion in 1985, to $1.5 billion in 1988. At a minimum, LIHEAP funds should be restored, in real terms, to their 1985 levels.

The second major area of concern involves efforts to reduce federal deficits. Increasingly, suggestions are made to impose an oil import fee, a gasoline tax, or some other energy consumption tax, as a way to lower deficits, promote conservation, and lessen our dependence on foreign energy sources. Whatever their merits, energy taxes could be calamitous for the poor, especially the elderly poor, who have never recovered from the price increase shocks of a decade ago. Any policymaker sensitive to the needs of vulnerable older Americans must assure that new energy taxes don't deliver a final knockout blow.

Voluntarism

Administered through the ACTION agency are three Older American Volunteer programs: the Retired Senior Volunteer Program (RSVP), the Foster Grandparent Program (FGP), and the Senior Companion Program (SCP). All three provide opportunities for persons 60 and older to volunteer part-time in a variety of community service activities. The fact that these programs continue to generate additional funding at the state and local levels and are a cost-effective means of providing community services has made them enormously popular with both Congress and the administration. For FY1988, the combined budget for the programs was $111 million.

In 1987, 383,000 RSVP volunteers served in projects around the country in such areas as youth counseling, literacy enhancement, long-term care, crime prevention, refugee assistance, and housing rehabilitation. These volunteers receive reimbursement for out-of-pocket expenses, but no stipends. In 1987, 17,500 FGP volunteers provided supportive services to children with physical, mental, emotional, or social disabilities; 7,000 SCP volunteers provided assistance to homebound, chronically disabled older persons. Each Foster Grandparent and Senior Companion (all must be low-income to participate) receives an hourly stipend of $2.20, transportation assistance, an annual physical examination, and meals during volunteer hours.

There would be support in Congress and among senior citizens for increasing the number of Older American Volunteer program slots. By focusing the increase on the Foster Grandparent Program and the Senior Companion Program, the next administration would make it possible for increased numbers of low-income and minority elders to participate in meaningful volunteer service. Older people are eager to serve their communities, and those communities are in desperate need of their service. Beyond the intrinsic value of service itself, such a major increase would reaffirm the continuing positive role of elders in our society.

Financing

Simply advocating greater federal spending to meet the needs of vulnerable older Americans fails the most basic test of political reality. Virtually all of the steps outlined in this chapter would benefit less well-off elders, but not exclusively. Objections will be voiced—not without merit—that poor children's needs deserve priority attention over those of the "newly rich" older class.

There is no denying the increased affluence of a good part of our older population. Overall, age is no longer necessarily a good predictor of need. Better-off elders, like the better-off of other ages, should be expected to bear the heavier burden in financing these improvements. Here are a number of suggestions for raising revenues, which, while not painless, are rooted in fairness.

- "Uncap" the Hospital Insurance (HI) part of the payroll tax. For Medicare-based benefits, part of the financing should come from requiring that the Medicare portion of the payroll tax—currently 1.45 percentage points of the total of 7.51 percent paid by both employer and employee—be paid on total earnings, rather than simply those below the ceiling ($45,000 in 1988). Nineteen of twenty Americans have wages below the ceiling, and thus pay the HI tax on their entire earnings. It is progressive and not burdensome for the most affluent 5 percent to do likewise.

- Cover all state and local employees under Medicare. Some 30 percent of state and local employees do not participate in Social Security or Medicare, yet 90 percent of them are eventually covered by it, either through a spouse or through other employment. Those 90 percent are, in effect, getting a free ride at the expense of Medicare contributors. The others truly need the coverage and don't get it. Newly hired employees have come under the system beginning in 1986. By covering those hired before then, revenue would be raised and equity served.

- Reduce estate tax windfalls to the wealthy. In 1981, federal estate taxes were virtually repealed, creating enormous tax breaks for the wealthiest Americans. The 1981 changes alone will cost the federal treasury more than $10 billion in 1989. Significant amounts of that loss could be recovered by keeping current rates in effect (rather than allowing them to fall, as under current law) and lowering the current $600,000 threshold below which no estate tax whatever is levied.

- Tax Social Security benefits more fully. Currently about 10 percent of the elderly—those with adjusted gross incomes above $25,000 ($32,000 for couples)—pay income taxes on half of their Social Security benefits. If those benefits were taxed to the same extent as most other retirement income, about 85 percent of the benefit amount would be taxable. This change would raise increasing amounts of revenue in future years, and would do so in a manner consistent with the taxation of other comparable retiree income.

Resources

Organizations

- National Council of Senior Citizens, 925 15th St., NW, Washington, D.C 20005; (202) 347-8800

- National Association of Older American Volunteer Program Directors, 11481 Bingham Terrace, Reston, VA 22091; (703) 860-9570

- National Caucus and Center on the Black Aged, 1424 K St. NW, Suite 500, Washington, DC 20005; (202) 637-8400

- National Senior Citizens Law Center, 2025 M St. NW, Suite 400, Washington, DC 20036; (202) 887-5280

- Older Women's League, 730 11th St. NW, Suite 300, Washington, DC 20005; (202) 783-6686

- Center for the Study of Social Policy, 1250 I St. NW, Suite 503, Washington, DC 20005; (202) 371-1565

Further Reading

- Stephen Crystal, *America's Old Age Crisis: Public Policy and the Two Worlds of Aging*, Basic Books, 1982.

- *On the Other Side of Easy Street: Myths and Facts about the Economics of Old Age*, Villers Foundation, 1987.

- Eric Kingson, Barbara Hirschorn, and John Cornman, *Ties That Bind: The Interdependence of Generations*, Seven Locks Press, 1986.

- Greg Duncan, *Years of Poverty, Years of Plenty: The Changing Economic Fortunes of American Workers and Families*, Institute for Social Research, University of Michigan, 1984.

Ronald F. Pollack is Executive Director of the Villers Foundation in Washington, DC. He is the former Dean of Antioch Law School and founder and Director of the Food Research and Action Center (FRAC). He is the author of "If We Had Ham We Could Have Ham and Eggs...If We Could Have Eggs: A Study of the National School Breakfast Program" and "Out to Lunch: A Study of USDA's Daycare and Summer Feeding Programs."

Edward F. Howard is Public Policy Coordinator for the Villers Foundation and former general counsel to the House Committee on Aging (chaired by Congressman Claude Pepper) and to the National Council on the Aging.

Decent, Affordable Housing for All*

Platform

- Proclaim decent, affordable housing as a *right* for all Americans, with a detailed timetable and action plan for attaining this entitlement.

- Create a strong, expanded "social housing" sector, capable of developing, rehabilitating, and managing large numbers of housing units at the local, neighborhood level.

- Provide outright capital grants for new construction and rehabilitation, to replace loans, with capital costs assumed by the government and not borne by occupants as part of their monthly payments.

- Transfer significant amounts of the existing housing stock, both owned and rented units, to the social sector, using government funds for permanent debt retirement.

- Provide subsidies (in the form of additional operating monies or housing allowances) to all occupants of social sector housing with incomes too low to afford operating costs (excluding repayment of capital).

- Create effective programs to retain and strengthen the existing stock of subsidized housing.

---

* This chapter draws on "A Progressive Housing Program for America," the July 1987 document produced by the Institute for Policy Studies' Working Group on Housing. The full program is available from IPS, 1601 Connecticut Ave. NW, Washington, DC 20009.

The goal of decent, affordable housing for all Americans is becoming more and more elusive. Nearly four decades ago, in the Preamble to the 1949 Housing Act, Congress set a National Housing Goal of "a decent home and suitable living environment for every American family." The obvious question is why have our society and economy been unable to achieve this basic goal in forty years? Why are we falling behind? Quite simply, the private housing market is unable and unwilling to solve the problem, and government interventions and subsidies have been wholly inadequate. If the goal of decent, affordable housing is ever to become a reality in the United States, a fundamental restructuring of the system by which housing is produced, financed, owned, and managed will be required that places housing rights above property rights and profit.

Congress did not specifically mention affordability in 1949, in large part because the central issue in that era was the prevalence of slum conditions. The principal innovation of the 1949 Act was the "slum clearance" program called urban renewal, which wound up displacing hundreds of thousands of low-income, mostly minority families, almost always to more expensive and all too often equally slummy quarters. Then as now, the concept of decent housing presumably meant that households would not have to pay so large a proportion of their income for housing as to make it impossible to obtain decent food, medical care, clothing, and other basic necessities.

Today the central housing issue is affordability (which is not to ignore or downplay the fact that millions of people, in rural as well as urban areas, are still forced to live in physical conditions far below what the society regards as acceptable, as embodied in building, housing, and health codes). As of the 1983 American Housing Survey, there were 6.5 million renter households paying half or more of their income for housing. (That we do not have more recent data—which doubtless would show a far higher number—is shocking, the result of a Reagan administration switch from annual to bi-annual national housing surveys and the failure of the Census Bureau to publish the 1985 survey results as of mid-1988.)

Lower-income and minority households experience this growing affordability crisis most severely. A 1986 General Accounting Office study showed that among renter households with incomes 80 percent or less of the area median the number of households paying more than 30 percent of their income for rent (the percentage HUD uses as a benchmark for an affordable rent burden for lower-income households) rose from 7.8 million in 1975 (54 percent of all such households) to 11.9 million in 1983 (64 percent of all such households). Looking at the very lowest income category—renters with incomes 50 percent or less of the area median—the number of households with rent burdens in excess of half their income rose from 3.6 million in 1975 (38 percent of all such households) to 6.0 million in 1983 (49 percent of all such households). Among black and Hispanic renters of all income levels, a staggering 20-22 percent were paying 60 percent or more of their income for housing.

Similar data for homeowners are both more recent and less meaningful because monthly mortgage expenses are significantly determined by the proportion of the original housing cost (and subsequent improvement costs) represented, respectively, by downpayment and mortgage loans. Even so, large numbers of homeowners are also devoting an increasing portion of their income to housing and are facing severe affordability problems, which frequently result in mortgage delinquency and foreclosure. The nation's homeownership rate dipped during the 1980s from its historic high point in 1980 (65.8 percent) to its current rate of less than 64 percent, reversing a historic trend toward increasing homeownership.

But housing cost:income ratios are not the sole manifestation of housing affordability problems. Increasingly, households are doubling up with friends or relatives in order to reduce housing costs or simply to find a place to live. Generally this is a temporary solution and often leads, after a few weeks or months of stressful living, to "eviction" and possible homelessness. Systemic data on this phenomenon are inherently difficult to come by because people who fear alerting immigration officers, welfare workers, or code enforcement officials will not readily admit to living in overcrowded conditions. The New York City Housing Authority estimates that 50,000 of the 174,000 public housing apartments it manages are illegally occupied by more than one family, a figure up from the 17,000 estimate of just a few years ago.

Beyond inadequate income and support services, the housing stock that lower-income households formerly relied on—low-rent apartments, single room occupancy (SRO) hotels, rooming houses—is being drastically reduced via gentrification as well as landlord neglect and abandonment, and virtually no new additions to that stock are being provided.

Outright homelessness, of course, is an extreme manifestation of the absence of affordable, available, suitable housing. While there is considerable dispute over what the actual number of homeless persons is, there is consensus that the number is growing and that more and more of the homeless are families rather than individuals. The vast majority of homeless people in city shelters are children and their parents, even though individuals with alcoholism or drug dependency problems or those who suffer from mental illness are more visible to the public. The latter lack decent, affordable housing, in addition to their other needs for support and services.

At the root of the housing affordability problem is the growing gap between people's incomes and the market cost of providing housing. Exacerbating that squeeze is the Reagan administration's sharp retreat from federal housing subsidies, particularly those that add to the stock of decent, affordable housing through rehabilitation and new construction. If we are ever to reach the National Housing Goal, programs must deal directly with this structural problem,

In theory, the gap can be covered in one of two ways, or some combination of the two. Incomes could be raised so that everyone could afford the market cost of decent housing, or housing costs could be lowered. But with decent housing beginning in the $300-$400 per month range in most areas (well above that in high-cost cities), and housing sales running $50-60,000 and up (except in isolated, depressed pockets where employment opportunities are scant), the magnitude of income transfer required for the first solution would be staggering and would inevitably produce severe inflation in the housing market, requiring even greater income redistribution.

A substantial lowering of housing costs is feasible, but not via industry-promulgated proposals such as lowering zoning and code standards and further industrializing the construction process. These reforms would at best produce relatively small cost savings, in some cases at the price of reduced environmental and housing standards, deterioration of work conditions and wage levels for construction workers, and other negative effects. Dramatic reduction in the cost of providing housing can be achieved only via restructuring the system by which housing is produced, financed, owned, and managed, and moving housing away from the notion of a profit-making commodity. Profit maximization and speculation in land and buildings benefit a very small, identifiable class of wealthy people; the average resident, even one who sells his or her home for far more than the original purchase price, is also a housing consumer and thus faces paying rents or prices in the same inflated market in which he or she acted as a profit-maximizer.

A radically restructured housing system, designed to produce the lowest cost for a given product, would have two central elements: elimination of the central element of housing costs, the repayment, with interest, of the money borrowed for construction or purchase; and development, ownership, and operation of housing by nonspeculative, nonprofit entities.

For single-family homeowners with mortgages—the only group for which such data are available but the largest single residential category—roughly two out of every three housing dollars go toward mortgage repayment; for renters, who pay such costs indirectly, the proportion likely is higher, as owners of multifamily structures tend to have second and third mortgages, refinance wherever possible in order to extract cash from their properties, and pay higher interest rates for the loans they get. Repayment of the debt burden is virtually a permanent cost attached to the occupancy of housing, since most mortgage loans are never retired, and new and larger debt burdens are incurred when mortgage-free homes are sold to new owners. Elimination of the cost of repaying borrowed capital would cut ongoing housing expenditures by two-thirds. The way to do this is to provide one-time capital grants for construction and rehabilitation costs and to retire existing debt permanently, with housing becoming, in effect, social infrastructure; occupants would be obligated to pay only ongoing maintenance expenses (utilities, insurance, taxes, repairs, etc.)

Such a system, of course, is costly at first, but the long-term benefits of making housing permanently affordable for millions of Americans who otherwise are priced out of the market are enormous. (For those with incomes insufficient to pay even this sharply reduced cost, a gap payment—in the form of an operating subsidy or rent voucher—would be made available.) Providing housing capital in this form would not be a totally new idea in the United States: substantial portions of the military's family housing is provided in this way, via Congressional appropriations as part of the Department of Defense budget; some Farmers Home Administration programs embody this same principle; and recent Housing and Urban Development (HUD) and other programs partially embrace the concept of small capital grants to write down the ultimate cost of housing to the occupant.

In most cities, a range of non-profit entities that develop, own, and operate housing now exist. These include religious groups, trade unions, community development corporations, resident cooperatives, and one or more public agencies such as a local housing authority. (Many housing authorities are far from model landlords, to be sure; financial weaknesses structured into the public housing program nationally and the use of agency jobs as political patronage have led to poor operations in several cities. But there are also some excellent local housing authorities in cities and towns—New York City being perhaps the outstanding example—that run exemplary programs, given severe financial, locational, design, and social impediments. A revitalized social housing program would do much to restore the sense of mission and dedication that characterized the early public housing movement of the 1930s and 1940s. These agencies and other nonprofit groups exist to serve the housing needs of particular sub-populations, providing housing at the lowest costs in the most user-responsive fashion. With additional technical assistance, the number and capacity of such groups could expand dramatically, into a plethora of "social housing entities," the basic delivery mechanism for nonspeculative housing of all types.

Let me briefly outline how such a system might work, with respect to existing stock, and then with respect to new construction and rehabilitation.

Substantial portions of the existing housing stock could be transferred to social ownership and permanently relieved of debt burden by the following methods:

- Any lower- or moderate-income homeowner facing mortgage or property tax foreclosure could opt to deed his or her home and mortgage to a social housing entity. Rather than facing eviction and possible homelessness, the family would continue living there, with security of tenure, paying an affordable monthly cost graded according to income. The social housing entity would then receive government funds to cure the delinquency and retire the mortgage over time (with additional funds to cover operating costs if the affordable "rent" was insufficient to meet that set of expenditures). Once the mortgage was paid, the home would no longer bear a debt burden. Thus, the cost of maintaining it would be permanently lowered by about two-thirds, and it would be made available to other households whenever the current occupant chose to move. Periodic improvements and major repairs would be covered via government capital grants to the social owner, as described below.

- Any lower- or moderate-income homeowner could be given the same option: trading the right to sell one's home for a dramatic and permanent lowering of the monthly housing cost, while retaining (even enhancing) security of continued occupancy. In this and other assignment situations, provision might be made to compensate the owner for all or part of the equity buildup.

- Elderly lower- or moderate-income homeowners living in valuable homes but cash-poor could make the same deed assignment (and mortgage assignment, if a mortgage existed) in exchange for a lifetime annuity large enough to permit them to live decently. In this and the other assignment situations, provision might be made to give heirs and relatives preference in moving into the former owner's home, once it was available for reoccupancy.

- Lower- and moderate-income homeowners faced with the need to make major repairs they cannot afford would be offered direct rehabilitation grants in exchange for an agreement to deed their properties to a social housing entity upon termination of occupancy.

- Rental housing could also be transferred to the debt-free social sector in cases of property tax or mortgage foreclosure, abandonment, or serious noncompliance with housing codes. Unlike the homeowner programs outlined above, which would be voluntary, use of public powers might be necessary to force rental properties out of the hands of landlords who have demonstrated an inability to provide decent housing conditions while meeting their financial obligations. There simply is no reason to allow some misguided notion of sanctified property rights to outweigh the society's interest in providing everyone with safe and decent housing, especially with regard to the country's shrinking and seemingly irreplaceable supply of lower-rent housing. Procedures currently exist (e.g., receivership, eminent domain) in most localities for removing properties from their owners in such situations as property tax delinquency, abandonment, and noncompliance with codes; these should be expanded and joined to a program that facilitates title transfer to social housing entities, with adequate subsidies to rehabilitate these properties (where necessary), retire the existing debt, and provide operating subsidies where needed. Regulations and incentives should also be provided to accomplish similar transfers in the case of mortgage foreclosure. Enactment of local or state right-of-first-refusal laws would permit social housing entities to purchase rental properties on the open market when they come up for sale, plugging these into the federally-funded debt retirement/subsidy program.

New housing and substantial rehabilitation would follow the same basic principles. Capital grants rather than loans would be given to social housing entities to plan and build new units and remodel sub-standard or obsolescent buildings. Upper limits on costs and amenities, as well as controlled "rent" levels, would inhibit any tendencies for non-profits to create housing beyond generally agreed upon standards or to charge occupants more than what is needed to cover operating costs. (Higher standards and additional amenities might be allowed, so long as people were willing to allocate their discretionary income for this purpose.) Allocation of federal funds would be governed and facilitated by the development of metropolitan and regional housing assistance plans that set targets for achieving the National Housing Goal within a set time period, crafted according to the particular needs of the area's current and projected future population and its existing housing supply. A wide range of locations, housing types, and sizes—replicating the variety and choice now available in the private market for those fortunate enough to have the resources to take advantage of them—would be produced. Social control over the cost and use of land must accompany a program of this sort, so as not to allow land speculation and local exclusionary practices to undermine its financial feasibility or goals.

A special focus of attention must be the existing subsidized housing stock of some 3.4 million units, built under a variety of HUD and Farmers Home Administration (FmHA) programs. This multi-billion dollar capital investment, backed by the federal government, is a national resource that, once lost, would be far more costly to replace, apart from the time and difficulties involved. Threats to this stock come from several sources, principally the undermaintenance, abandonment, demolition, and sale of public housing units by local housing authorities in response to financial constraints on maintenance and modernization, and, in some cases, to conscious local and federal policy. Local influences include recent gentrification pressures on projects placed decades ago in unappealing locations; federal obstacles include an ideological commitment on the part of the Reagan administration to reduce the supply of government-owned housing. In some cases, however, the local housing authorities are just incompetent.

Another major threat affects not public housing but various programs whereby private developers (both for-profit and nonprofit) use low-interest government loans and other subsidies to construct moderate-income rental housing with occupancy and rent controls mandated for a limited period of time. After that period, usually twenty years, owners are permitted to prepay the remaining mortgage amount and convert their housing to purely private status, thereby losing that housing to lower-income use. It is essential that federal programs be instituted immediately to save all such housing, to ensure that it is maintained in or restored to decent condition, and that those occupying such housing not be forced to pay rent in excess of what they can afford. An arsenal of aids will be required: full operating subsidies, mortgage writedowns for projects owned by nonprofits, renovation grants, conversion of developments owned by profit-oriented entities to social ownership, including tenant cooperatives.

(Details of these specific programs, plus complementary programs and the overall analytic framework underlying this approach, are laid out in the document cited in the note to the chapter title.)

What will all this cost? The answers are, "Plenty, compared with what we now spend on housing subsidies," and "It all depends on the level at which the program is implemented." Tackling America's housing crisis seriously requires coming to grips with the fact that it will not be done cheaply: there's too much catching up to do. Administrations prior to that of Ronald Reagan, although for the most part considerably better, were no models of housing reform or program appropriations either. The programs outlined skeletally above have been projected at three levels. The "lower cost" version calls for 150,000 new and rehabilitated units annually; conversion of 200,000 privately-owned units to social ownership annually; extensive modernization and conversion of existing subsidized developments; and operating subsidies for 5 million units of social housing. It totals just under $30 billion a year. The "higher cost" version produces 1.1 million new and rehabilitated units annually; converts 400,000 units annually to the social sector; modernizes and converts about one-third more existing subsidized developments; and provides operating subsidies for 8 million households living in social housing. It totals $88 billion a year. A "medium cost" option comes in slightly less than midway in terms of results, with a cost representing just about the amount the tax system currently provides in subsidies, via regressive deductions from taxable income for homeowners and housing developers/investors of various sorts. (This was the figure before the 1986 tax reform legislation, which, by reducing tax rates, also will reduce the value of all such deductions.)

The "medium cost" program represents about four times what the federal government now spends in direct housing subsidies. It is a quantum leap in expenditures and commitment, but one which the society clearly can afford if it so chooses. It is about one-fifth the nation's military budget. The question boils down to the political issue of how seriously we want to take the National Housing Goal. Beyond that, how effectively and efficiently can housing funds be spent?

Any program that merely covers the gap between what the market charges for housing and what people can afford (for example, the various Section 8 and housing allowance/voucher programs that have been the principal federal tools for the past fifteen years), without either imposing serious market controls or demanding wholesale revision in the housing system, is simply stupid and wasteful. The programs proposed here are ways of spending large sums of tax money in order to effect a drastic and permanent decrease in housing costs for vast numbers of lower- and moderate-income people, the impact of which will spread throughout the full range of the housing market. A further benefit would be steady and guaranteed construction demand, which will be attractive to companies that build housing efficiently and construction workers who all too often are the victims of erratic construction cycles and uncertain and inadequate annual incomes.

Finally, let me turn briefly to issues beyond decent housing conditions and affordable costs with respect to the individual living unit. "A suitable living environment," it should be remembered, is one of the two elements of the National Housing Goal, although there have been no attempts to define the exact meaning of that vague phrase. It is clear, from Census data, polls, and other sources, that there is large and growing dissatisfaction with many aspects of neighborhood life and municipal services: crime, litter, noise, schools, public transportation, and recreational facilities. Adequate government funding for services and facilities and community control over their provision are both needed. An essential element of any good housing program is resident control. The more control and security people feel, and the less people feel ripped off and vulnerable in their housing conditions and costs, the more capable they are of dealing effectively with environmental conditions and creating safe, liveable communities. Effective planning for the full range of neighborhood environmental issues and secure funding to implement service programs must begin with the basic building block of control over the individual living unit. The program outlined above contains the seed out of which true and rapid achievement of this now forty-year-old goal—"a decent home and suitable living environment"—can finally come into being.

Resources

Recommended Appointees for a New Administration

- Emily Achtenberg, Boston housing consultant, principally around tenant ownership and control of housing developments.
- Bonnie Brower, Association of Neighborhood Housing Developers, New York, NY, and leader of New York's "Housing Justice Campaign."
- Gordon Cavanaugh, attorney, Washington, DC (Roisman, Reno and Cavanaugh); FmHA administrator in the Carter administration.

- Cushing Dolbeare, founder and chair of the National Low Income Housing Coalition, Washington, DC

- Peter Dreier, Director of Housing, Boston Redevelopment Authority; former Housing Advisor to Boston Mayor Raymond Flynn.

- Robert Hayes, Counsel, National Coalition for the Homeless, New York, NY.

- Chuck Matthei, Institute for Community Economics, Greenfield, MA; leader in the community land trust movement.

- Florence Roisman, attorney, Washington, DC (National Housing Law Project), one of the nation's leading tenants' rights attorneys.

- Joel Rubenzahl, Community Economics, Inc., Oakland, CA; specialist in housing cooperatives and community-based development.

- Ann Schnare, ICF, Inc., Fairfax, VA; specialist in the relation of welfare assistance to housing programs.

- David Schwartz, National Housing Institute, Orange, NJ; New Jersey State assemblyman

- Ron Shiffman, Director, Pratt Center for Community and Environmental Development, Brooklyn, NY.

- Michael Stone, College of Public and Community Service, University of Massachusetts-Boston; originator of "shelter poverty" concept, relating proper amount to spend for housing to what is needed for other basic necessities.

- Barry Zigas, President of the National Low Income Housing Coalition, Washington, DC

Organizations

- Institute for Community Economics, 151 Montague City Rd., Greenfield, MA 01301; (413) 774-5933

- National Coalition for the Homeless, 105 E. 22nd St., New York, NY 10010; (212) 460-8110 and 1439 Rhode Island Ave. NW, Washington, DC 20006; (202) 659-3310

- National Housing Institute, 439 Main St., Orange, NJ; (201) 678-3110

- National Housing Law Project, 1950 Addison St., Berkeley, CA 94704; (415) 548-9400

- National Low Income Housing Coalition, 1012 14th St. NW, #1006, Washington, DC 20002; (202) 662-1530

- National Rural Housing Coalition, 2001 S St. NW, Washington, DC 20009; (202) 483-1504

- Shelterforce, 439 Main St., Orange, NJ 07050; (201) 678-3110

Further Reading

Three recent collections edited or co-edited by the author of this chapter are an excellent source of background readings.

- *Housing Issues of the 90s* (co-edited with Sara Roseberry), Praeger, 1988. See especially the contributions by William Apgar, on U.S. housing conditions; by Sandra Newman and Ann Schnare, on the relationship of welfare payments to housing; by Emily Achtenberg, on dealing with financially distressed subsidized housing developments; by Rachael Bratt, on Massachusetts' programs to aid nonprofit housing development; and by Michael Stone, on a detailed local (in this case, Boston) program to promote decent, affordable housing, adopting principles embodied in this chapter.

- *Critical Perspectives on Housing* (co-edited with Rachel Bratt and Ann Meyerson), Temple University Press, 1986. See especially the contributions by Kim Hopper and Jill Hamberg, on homelessness; by Michael Stone, on housing and the dynamics of U.S. capitalism; by Ann Meyerson, on deregulation and restructuring of the housing finance system; by Tom Schlesinger and Mark Erlich, on the housing industry; by Peter Marcuse, on the making of housing policy; by Cushing Dolbeare, on housing and the income tax system; by Rachel Bratt, on the public housing program; by Chester Hartman, on the Reagan administration's housing policies; and the chapters on Great Britain, Sweden, "Red Vienna," and Cuba, by, respectively, Steve Schifferes, Richard Appelbaum, Peter Marcuse, and Jill Hamberg.

- *America's Housing Crisis: What Is To Be Done?*, Routledge & Kegan Paul, 1983. See especially the contributions by John Atlas and Peter Dreier, on the tenants' movement in the United States, and by Paul Davidoff, on the entitlement notion in housing.

Chester Hartman is a Fellow at the Institute for Policy Studies. His most recent books are *Housing Issues of the 90s* (with Sara Rosenberry); *Critical Perspectives on Housing* (with Rachel Bratt and Ann Meyerson); *The Transformation of San Francisco*; and *America's Housing Crisis: What is to be Done?*

Reconstructing Education

Platform

- Establish a universal preschool entitlement for low-income children, aged three to five.
- Restore, expand, and redesign federal equity programs to serve all eligible children and aid overall school improvement.
- Establish a school restructuring demonstration program with nation-wide field capacity.
- Create an urban school reconstruction fund.
- Redirect federal aid to the states to rebuild teacher training programs and equalize school funding.
- Create a National Teachers Corps scholarship program to recruit new teachers and promote affirmative action.
- Sponsor youth action campaigns for dropout prevention, drug prevention, and in-school social services, including a National Youth Community Service Corps.
- Create participatory governance incentives to assist teacher decision-making, parent organization, and community-school linkages at the local school level.
- Initiate a national family literacy campaign.
- Expand college assistance to assure that every qualified student in need can enter and finish college.
- Redesign vocational education to promote academic skills, affirmative action, and economic literacy.
- Restore federal enforcement of civil rights and educational equity mandates.

In relatively progressive times, influenced by social activism, the federal government's commitment to public education has been to expand opportunity. The educational mandate has been to broaden the economic mainstream and to promote social equality.

Hence, in the 1960s and 1970s, we witnessed very substantial gains in educational access for long excluded groups, as well as a narrowing of the educational gaps that have been constructed on distinctions of class, ethnicity, race, and gender. The national debate was about the democratic mission of education.

In regressive times, such as the 1980s, the federal government has narrowed access and favored more exclusive and elitist paths to school achievement. Under Reagan, the debate has centered on the marketplace functions of education, on issues of competition and productivity. The administration's goal was to divest the federal government of responsibility for equality, pursued by cutting education funding 16 percent, with particular malice toward equity programs and civil rights enforcement. Fortunately, the administration has been less successful in reaching its ultimate objective, the privatization of public education institutions.

While these last eight years have produced the rhetoric of excellence for all, the reality is a system that is rapidly polarizing. Schools at the top may be pumping up their test scores, but it is not clear that we are producing more thoughtful, informed, or creative minds. Schools in the middle tiers of the system are stagnating or deteriorating, squeezed by shrinking tax bases and by rising numbers of children in need. And in the schools of the inner cities or impoverished rural areas, the bottom is literally dropping out, in catastrophic proportions. If we take the democratic potentials of public education seriously, we are indeed a nation at risk and we have more to fear than mediocrity.

In reaction to the combativeness and negligence of the Reagan administration, serious reform efforts have come from the states and from a host of national commissions, notably the 1983 Bell Commission's report launching the "excellence movement" and the 1986 Carnegie Forum report on the teaching profession.

There is widespread consensus that it's time to overhaul outmoded educational practices and raise standards, but there is no consensus over which direction to take: greater standardization and rigidity in education or more enlightened child- and teacher-centered modes of learning. The reports vacillate between elitism and democracy, unsure if we need to produce a new layer of the technocratic elite or a more empowered citizenry. Quality and equality seem antagonistic goals on the one hand, mutual preconditions on the other.

Resolution of these dichotomies will come in part from ideological battles over the soul of schooling. While the conservative agenda has had a federal mouthpiece in William Bennett, Reagan's Secretary of Education, a progressive agenda has also emerged from the ranks of educators, advocates, and civic leaders awakened to the gathering crisis of inequality. The more decisive resolution, however, will be determined by the resources made available to establish new models of achievement and introduce systemic changes in the bottom and middle tiers of schooling.

Here the federal government's role is pivotal. Its capacity to fund equity interventions, provide financial incentives, arbitrate the terms of debate, instigate new approaches, and activate broader forces for change are all crucial to setting a progressive direction for school reform in the coming decade.

In enacting an education policy agenda, the federal government can also act to empower the constituencies behind the agenda: educators, parents and community, advocates, and youth. One of the ironies of the 1980s is that the preoccupation with corporate management has resurfaced a militant 1960s demand for "maximum feasible participation." What Nixon undid and Tom Peters redid gives us the almost conventional wisdom that genuine school change must come from the bottom up. This reform platform is constructed in the spirit of grassroots change, with emphasis on democratic participation as the means toward specific educational ends.

There is also a growing consensus that to improve education, especially in failing schools, programs should address educational "inputs" and "outputs" as well as the educational process itself. That is, we need to consider the whole child, and the social environments and economic destinies shaping that child, along with the school experience the child encounters. An effective federal education policy would operate on three levels simultaneously: preparing the child for school, serving the child's potential from elementary through secondary school, and providing meaningful opportunities for college or work following graduation. Funding, too, is in need of reform.

Pre-school Preparation

Compounding the direct assault on children's welfare waged by the Reagan administration, several trends make it harder for more children to meet contemporary educational demands: severe economic and social dislocation in industrial and farming communities; continuing change in family structures as more women work and head households; a new wave of immigration, largely from impoverished third world countries; an increase and deepening of poverty, especially among women and children. These conditions underlie some alarming statistics about children now entering school: 30 percent will be latchkey kids, 20 percent will be in poverty, 40 percent will experience broken homes, 15 percent will speak English as a second language, 10-20 percent will have poorly educated or illiterate parents, 15 percent will be physically or mentally handicapped. The correlation between social distress and school failure is high, especially where multiple factors are present. The Committee for Economic Development (CED), in its first-rate study *Children in Need*, estimates that at present 30 percent of children in school are at risk of school failure. By the year 2000, if current trends are not reversed, as many as half of all children will be at risk.

Clearly, educational disadvantage is not an isolated or a vestigial problem. The majority of children in this society need stronger social support systems if they are to enter school ready to learn and stay in school in order to learn. Part of the solution lies in major changes across the spectrum of federal family and social policy, from prenatal care to childcare, from nutrition programs to substance abuse prevention.

In education, the priority must be to address barriers to school success at the earliest moment by dramatically broadening access to preschool education programs. The Head Start experience has clearly shown that early childhood development and enrichment make a big difference in the achievement levels of children and the involvement of parents in schooling; it is also highly cost-effective. CED indicates that for every $1 invested in Head Start, there is a short-run saving of $3 and a long-run saving of $7 in remedial education, welfare, and criminal justice costs. Yet today Head Start serves less than 20 percent of all eligible children.

There should be a preschool education entitlement for all low-income three- to five-year-olds, approximately 2.25 million children. Head Start would be the core building block, extended to three-year-olds and expanded nationwide, keeping intact its integrity as a community-based program with strong parent participation and training.

Equivalent programs for early childhood education and development should also be established through public schools and childcare centers. Federal incentives should also encourage states and districts to provide full-day kindergarten. The Department of Education needs to create an Office of Preschool Education, parallel to its other divisions, to assure the priority, quality, and coordination of these programs, along with Head Start (now located in Health and Human Services). The cost of a full preschool education entitlement, with adequate salaries for teaching staff, would be roughly $10 billion annually.

Restructuring School

For the children of urban America, where dropout rates range from 50-80 percent, the pursuit of educational excellence is a critical imperative. It will take the best we can offer to undo the damage of present elementary and secondary institutions. For the children of middle America, the stakes of school reform may not be as high, but the gains could be just as impressive. The difficulty of reform, across all tiers of schooling, lies more in our political priorities than in educational strategy or program design.

Effective schools and effective classrooms are not a mystery to educators. We know enormous amounts about what kinds of schools work well for all children. While there is no one best or perfect model, effective schools maintain high expectations through environments which are personal, interactive, collaborative, and orderly. School size and class size are human-scale, and teachers have good support staff, in-service training, and adequate preparation time. The learning process emphasizes individual progress and peer cooperation. Mastering academic and social skills, particularly critical thinking skills, replaces testing, tracking, and segregation in motivating students and maintaining classroom discipline. Student diversity is respected and valued as a strength, rather than repressed or tolerated as a liability.

In good schools, teachers have a strong say in working conditions and there is a collegial approach to decisionmaking in the classroom and in the school as a whole. Contact with parents and the community is high, through paraprofessional and volunteer programs, through after-school recreational and cultural programs, and through citizen involvement in local school policy.

Such schools exist. Predictably, they exist most often in the top tiers of the system, in affluent public school districts and in elite private networks. Such schools also exist in some very poor districts, where concerted campaigns for school improvement have opened the doors to innovation and attracted additional resources. These schools prove that children can succeed educationally regardless of socioeconomic status, in defiance of institutional racism. Schools *can* make a difference.

To promote universal quality and genuine equality in education, the federal government must play a role in restructuring school organization from kindergarten through high school. There are five areas from which initiatives can be launched: equity, school improvement, teaching support, youth support, and parent/community involvement.

Federal Equity Programs

We must restore, expand, and fully fund the categorical equity programs which have been the chief targets of cutbacks under Reagan and Bennett. Chapter 1 compensatory education funding currently reaches less than half of all eligible low-income children, chiefly through compensatory reading programs; most math programs have been cut.

Chapter 1 parent advisory mandates must also be strengthened with training and technical assistance. The Follow Through program, intended to develop innovative approaches to compensatory education and sharply cut by Reagan, should be revamped and integrated with Chapter 1 services. To fully fund Chapter 1, focusing on the primary grades, would cost roughly $7 billion annually. CED estimates that every $500 spent in the program produces a saving of $3,000 in the cost of a repeated grade.

Bilingual education and language assistance programs reach only 30 percent of children in need. It must be a priority to reach districts with sharply rising immigrant and refugee populations. Federal efforts to support bilingual education should also focus on overcoming the chronic shortage of qualified bilingual and ESL teachers, through subsidies for certification studies and the active recruitment of bilingual teaching candidates. Parent advisory mandates should be supported with technical assistance in the field.

Special education for the handicapped, while spared the worst cuts, lags far behind the needs of disabled children for appropriate services and equal access. New programs for preschool special education should be rapidly expanded.

Indian education was cut nearly 40 percent from 1981-1987. Funding should be restored with a thorough review—tribal and federal—of program effectiveness. The Women's Educational Equity Program has been cut 66 percent; funding should likewise be restored. Federal assistance for education for the homeless should be greatly expanded, as should the federal oversight role and parent-teacher involvement in such programs. The Department of Education's Office of Civil Rights faced elimination under the Reagan/Bennett administration. Its funding and function need to be fully restored to ensure meaningful compliance and ongoing progress toward equal rights in education, including effective desegregation.

Federal equity programs must not be delivered in ways that do not label, sort, and segregate children. The typical Great Society model for educational equity was an add-on program that brought in new funds but did little to change the educational mainstream. Where the mainstream is already deficient, where schools operate on factory principles, where the school culture is alienating or hostile, additional and separate programs seldom make headway. In many cases, special programs have served as dumping grounds for "hard to teach" children. For instance, discriminatory misclassification in special education has been widespread in urban schools, while noncompliance with special education mandates is common in rural districts.

Tomorrow's equity programs should emphasize broadening the mainstream and giving schools the staff, space, and supportive services they need to make classrooms heterogeneous and individually attentive. They should enrich the school as well as the student, and therefore should go hand in hand with federal school improvement initiatives.

School Improvement

The task of school improvement rests essentially with local schools, districts, and states. It is an organic process of change that must account for the huge variations of history and circumstance in our public schools, as well as the current power alignments. Many urban and rural school systems have yet to enter the 20th century; others have not left the 1950s. While some are grappling with the realities of the 1980s, few are ready to enter the 21st century.

Federal policy cannot substitute for local change, but it can encourage positive models and give aid to struggling systems. One priority should be an activist federal research program that promotes innovative teaching approaches and rising standards in traditionally underserved schools. Field staff for such a program should include educators already involved in school improvement campaigns. Their work should bring new conceptual and organizing skills to local teachers, administrators, and school advocates across the country who are seeking designs for change.

The considerable federal funding now directed to educational research, particularly in the area of standardized norm-reference testing, must be redirected toward alternative forms of assessing achievement. We are in danger of developing a test-driven system, where the pursuit of rising test scores dictates curriculum and teacher time, inhibits the acquisition of critical thinking skills, limits access to broad social knowledge, and devalues heterogeneous classrooms.

Another area for federal action in school improvement can be based on federal aid to the states. Under the Reagan administration, a hodge-podge of categorical grants was lumped into a new block grant—Chapter 2—with the intent of reducing both federal oversight and total dollars. There is no good reason to extend a program that should not have existed to begin with. Chapter 2 monies should be redirected into state aid for teacher training and into state aid to equalize school funding.

At present, discrepancies in funding among districts in a given state can range from $1,500-5,000 per pupil. Schools in poor communities are simply starved of the funds necessary to launch improvement efforts. A federal equity aid program can be contingent on state efforts both to reform funding formulas and provide school improvement assistance to historically underfunded schools and districts.

A complementary program would provide federal incentive grants to states and districts for developing participatory governance mechanisms and support at the local school level. California's School Improvement Program and South Carolina's School Improvement Councils are forerunners of the school-site management approach, which ideally gives teachers, parents, and community members a direct role in evaluating local school performance, setting improvement goals, and allocating discretionary budgets. Demonstration grants could also be given to projects that enhance faculty participation in administrative decisionmaking and parent/voter participation in local school elections.

It is imperative that the federal government aid urban schools in the massive task of rehabilitating school facilities. Billions are needed to rebuild decaying inner-city schools. This job goes well beyond restoring the physical plant in schools where paint peels from the ceilings and there is no running water. Urban school rehabilitation can restructure the school environment, creating human-scale spaces, providing for recreation and culture, and demonstrating respect and hope for students and teachers. It is also an opportunity to train and employ neighborhood residents—especially youth—in reclaiming what should be a community institution.

Teaching Support

In the next five years, half the nation's present teachers are expected to retire or leave teaching. Very little has been done to address this crisis, although some states are recognizing that significantly higher pay, across the board, is necessary to attract and retain qualified teachers. The capacity of government to improve teaching conditions, especially in distressed schools, will also be important to reversing current trends.

Two new federal programs are recommended to address the looming teaching crisis. One is a consolidation and extension of existing teacher training programs—including redirected Chapter 2 funds—to expand the network of local teacher (resource) centers, underwrite career development opportunities for classroom teachers and support personnel, and encourage teacher leadership and autonomy in instruction. Training funds should also promote innovative in-service training programs, with attention to multicultural and cooperative learning techniques.

A second initiative would establish a National Teachers Corps, patterned after the pre-Reagan Public Health Service Corps. With a substantial investment ($1 billion), the federal government can provide teaching candidates with full scholarships in return for service in areas of teacher shortage. This effort should include college and high school preparation programs directed at the recruitment of minority teachers, whose numbers are declining just as the minority student population is rapidly rising.

Youth Support

Drug abuse has been the major focus of youth support programs in this administration, and the problem certainly merits more extensive and realistic programs. Yet, drug or alcohol abuse cannot be addressed in isolation from a host of pressures on today's youth or the appalling lack of counselling and personal support services in most schools.

A federal grant program can assist states and districts to develop or extend holistic, peer-centered programs to deal honestly with drugs, family violence, sexual responsibility, teen suicide, and other issues. Federal incentives can also encourage high-risk schools to develop on-site health and family services in collaboration with other social agencies.

Dropout prevention has emerged as a new reform priority, having received little more than lip service from the administration until this election year. A serious program would support alternative high schools, peer tutoring and adult mentor programs, family counselling programs, and other promising approaches. Re-entry programs should include a federal entitlement to complete high school at public expense, regardless of age.

The federal government can also take the lead in promoting citizenship programs that involve youth in their communities. The establishment of a National Youth Community Service Corps, with grants to participating middle school and high school programs, would help young people combine academic, vocational, and social learning, connect them to the world they are entering, and value their talents and contributions. The Youth Community Service Corps should also include an employment component for high school dropouts and students at risk, adding educational dimensions to the model of the New Deal Civilian Conservation Corps.

Parent/Community Involvement

If it is important to connect youth to communities, it is equally important to connect communities to schools. Three federal demonstration projects can facilitate the participation of families and citizens in the education process, a factor which has proven critical to the transformation of failing schools in underserved neighborhoods.

- A family literacy program, based both in schools and community organizations, would target the 30 percent of adults who are functionally or marginally illiterate *and* their school-age children. The program would link parent and child learning, and would help family members play an active role in children's education at home and in the classroom.

- A federal parent participation program would provide training funds and technical assistance to parent and neighborhood organizations involved in school improvement campaigns. It would also provide funds for continuing education to support low-income parent activists in pursuing educational careers.

- A community-school linkage program would help hard-pressed districts underwrite the use of school facilities for community activities, adult education, childcare programs, nutrition centers, and civic events. Federal incentives would help districts establish all-day school programs.

Post-Secondary

In addition to changing the conditions which determine how children enter school or what they experience in school, we must improve the destinies that currently await students who finish high school. Their probable futures regulate achievement by raising or lowering children's expectations, enlarging or deflating their self-esteem, energizing or sapping their motivation.

These probable futures look discouraging. Job growth is occurring largely in low-wage, unskilled, non-union sectors. In *The Great
American Job Machine*, Barry Bluestone and Bennett Harrison point
out that 58 percent of all new jobs created from 1979-1984 paid less
than $7,000 a year, well below the poverty line. Working-class youth
are moving into dead-end jobs at very high rates. Inner-city and rural
youth experience unemployment rates exceeding 50 percent. Nor is the
picture so bright for college graduates, over half of whom will enter
non-professional jobs outside their field of study.

One fairly obvious priority is to broaden access to higher education as we have done in the past with the GI Bill, the National Defense
Education Act, and the Pell grant program. Thanks to Congress and the
election year, the Reagan administration may exit without a net cut in
college assistance programs, but federal grants and loans have not kept
pace with sharply rising college costs and student need.

To significantly open the doors, to offer a place to every qualified
student, college financial aid must more than double. Grants should be
expanded faster than loans. Grant and loan levels should be raised.
The concept behind the National Teachers Corps should be adopted
in a loan-forgiveness program for students entering human service jobs
in needy communities. Displaced workers should be eligible for higher
education retraining grants. Aid to higher education institutions should
be linked to institutional success in retraining and graduating college
entrants.

It is also time to thoroughly revamp vocational education, both
in adult programs and secondary schools. Federal guidelines for vocational education aid should stress the need for stronger academic components, critical thinking and problem-solving skills, and the
modernization of occupational training. Federal action should attack
the patterns of racial and gender discrimination that still dominate vocational programs. Federal grants should also stimulate programs for
economic literacy beginning in elementary school, programs that
present issues of unionism and workplace democracy as well as issues
of employment.

The federal government must make job development and labor
rights the centerpiece of its economic policy agenda outside the Department of Education. For youth, as for displaced workers, prospects for
a dead-end future or a motivating future will depend on how much we
invest in rebuilding this country's industry, infrastructure, and human
services. Contrary to optimistic predictions, educational achievement
does not create jobs; it only fills jobs that exist. Our work will be in-
complete, and ultimately frustrated, if we do not invest in our children's
future beyond the schoolhouse.

Funding a New Agenda

Funding this platform is quite simple: the next administration must double the present education budget as a first step, and triple it once programs are in full gear. This is actually a modest proposal.

The current annual allocation for the Department of Education is roughly $20 billion, or 2¢ out of every federal income tax dollar. The military receives more than 50¢ out of every income tax dollar. Under Reagan, tax breaks for the richest Americans come to $50 billion annually. Funding education reform is a matter of priorities.

In addition to federal spending, state and local revenues for education should be expanded and restructured. Through programs like the proposed state equity aid, as well as specific incentives and matching grants, the federal government can have some leverage over state spending patterns, and indirectly affect the revenue sources.

The critical reform lies with the states, however. State governments have the power to reduce school dependency on local property taxes and increase the share of state education funding raised through progressive income taxation. At present, most states are falling somewhere in the middle, turning to measures like sales tax hikes and local tax caps. At best, such half-hearted reforms have generated incremental gains for teachers and local schools. At worst, as in California, school funding is falling far behind the levels of need.

The value of these proposals lies chiefly in consolidating the progress achieved through educational innovation and struggle, and in synthesizing a feasible platform from which to launch new offensives for democratic schooling. These proposals are bridges toward a fuller agenda, which will emerge from the practice of reform and from rising educational expectations.

Federal action won't in itself solve the crises in educational quality and equality. But federal action can generate new resources and energy for progressive advances. Particular programs and targets should be chosen where need is greatest and where popular support can be mobilized to reorder priorities and power.

Although we cannot legislate democracy in education, we can open the arenas of education politics to new participants and new issues of contention. We can resist social and economic injustice by holding education to democratic rather than marketplace goals. We can recognize some past achievement and future promise in an education system that, for all its failures, remains community-based and accountable to the common good. The federal government is ground worth reclaiming and holding in the battle for an education system that is truly public, free, and universal.

Resources

Organizations

- The National Coalition of Advocates for Students, 76 Summer St., #350, Boston, MA 02110; (617) 357-8507. NCAS is the umbrella organization of twenty-one youth and education advocacy groups from across the country. The affiliates that are national policy organizations include: the Children's Defense Fund (122 C St. NW, Washington, DC 20001; (202) 628-8787), the Center for Law and Education (236 Massachusetts Ave. NE, Room 510, Washington, DC 20002; (202) 546-5330), and the National Black Child Development Institute (1463 Rhode Island Ave. NW, Washington, DC 20005 (202) 387-1281). State and local affiliates operate in all regions of the country. Among those taking leadership are: Advocates for Children (24-16 Bridge Plaza South, Long Island City, NY 11101; (718) 729-8866), Designs for Change (220 S. State St., Chicago, IL 60604; (312) 922-0317), and the Intercultural Development and Research Center (5835 Callagham Rd., #350, San Antonio, TX 78228; (512) 684-8180).

- The National Education Association, 1201 16th St. NW, Washington, DC 20036; (202) 833-4000. NEA is the largest teachers' union, with 1.8 million members nationwide. In recent years, it has been a major voice defending equity issues and school funding. NEA sponsors a local school reform demonstration project called Mastery in Learning and sponsors model dropout prevention programs through Operation Rescue. Its state and local affiliates vary widely, but a number of local affiliates are actively experimenting with school restructuring, professional reform, and teacher-community coalition building. The Montgomery County Education Association (1776 E. Jefferson St., #220, Rockville, MD 20852; (301) 881-5305) is exemplary of this trend.

- The American Federation of Teachers, 555 New Jersey Ave. NW, Washington, DC 20001; (202) 879-4400. AFT represents 600,000 educators, chiefly in urban school systems. It has been a major voice for increasing teacher authority and autonomy in school decision-making. Like the NEA, its local affiliates vary considerably. The Toledo Federation of Teachers, 321 W. Woodruff, Toledo, OH 43624; (419) 243-8527, has been in the forefront of AFT locals initiating school restructuring programs.

- The National Committee for Citizens in Education, 410 Wilde Lake Village Green, Columbia, MD 21044; (301) 997-9300. NCCE is an informational clearinghouse and technical assistance/training center focusing on federal equity programs and school-site governance programs.

- The Federation of Childcare Centers of Alabama, 3703 Rosa Parks Ave., Montgomery, AL 36101; (205) 262-3456. FOCAL is an organizing and training center serving low-income childcare workers in

Alabama, chiefly black women. An outgrowth of the Head Start program, FOCAL is exemplary as a community-based organization which has gained state policy influence through constituency organizing and its empowerment work around racism and social justice.

Further Reading

- Ann Bastian, Norm Fruchter, Marilyn Gittell, Colin Greer, and Kenneth Haskins, *Choosing Equality: The Case for Democratic Schooling*, Temple University Press, 1986.

- *Children in Need: Investment Strategies for the Educationally Disadvantaged*, the Research and Policy Committee of the Committee for Economic Development, CED, September 1987.

- *Barriers to Excellence: Our Children at Risk*, report of the National Board of Inquiry of the National Coalition of Advocates for Students, NCAS, 1985.

- Jeannie Oakes, *Keeping Track: How Schools Structure Inequality*, Yale University Press, 1985.

- John I. Goodlad, *A Place Called School: Prospects for the Future*, McGraw-Hill, 1983.

- Theodore Sizer, *Horace's Compromise: The Dilemma of the American High School*, Houghton Mifflin, 1984.

- *Becoming a Nation of Readers*, report of the Commission on Reading of the National Institute of Education, National Institute of Education, 1985.

- Stewart C. Purkey and Marshall S. Smith, "School Reform: the District Policy Implications of Effective Schools Literature," *Elementary School Journal*, January 1985.

- Susan J. Rosenholtz, "Political Myths about Education Reform: Lessons from the Research on Teaching," *Phi Delta Kappan*, January 1985.

- Linda Darling-Hammond and Barnett Berry, *The Evolution of Teacher Policy*, The Rand Corporation, 1988.

- *The Forgotten Half: Non-College Youth in America*, report of the William T. Grant Foundation Commission on Work, Family and Citizenship, The Grant Foundation, January 1988.

- *Call to Action: A Briefing Book on the Status of American Children in 1988*, a report of the Children's Defense Fund, Children's Defense Fund, 1988.

- Harold Hodgekinson, *All One System*, Institute for Educational Leadership, 1985.

Ann Bastian is a social policy analyst working with the New World Foundation in New York. She is also a college teacher and consultant, whose recent projects with the NEA and the Jackson for President Committee have focused on national education policy trends. Norm Fruchter is an education consultant and activist, who serves as an elected school board member in Brooklyn's District 15 and as secretary of the National Coalition of Advocates for Students. Colin Greer is President of the New World Foundation and an education historian. The three are co-authors of *Choosing Equality*, an analysis of conservative and progressive alternatives for school reform in the 1980s, which received the American Library Association's 1988 Intellectual Freedom Award.

Vicente Navarro

A New Health Care System for the United States

Platform

- Create a National Health Program to provide comprehensive health coverage, without co-payments or deductibles, and ensure access to quality health care to all citizens and residents of the United States.
- The National Health Program should be federally funded with revenues coming from earmarked corporate taxes and personal income taxes.
- Minimize financial incentive for both undercare and overcare.
- The federal government should have the responsibility of administering the National Health Program (through a National Trust Fund and a National Health Board) and of assuring the provision of comprehensive health coverage to the population. State and local authorities should be responsible for planning health services in their area.
- The National Health Program should assure the accountability of health institutions to the communities they serve. Health institutions receiving federal funds should be governed by a board of trustees accountable to and representative of the community it serves.
- Citizens and residents should be guaranteed a choice of provider.
- Patient advocates must be present in each health care institution, and be responsible for responding to and acting upon the grievances and concerns of patients.

Regarding AIDS, this platform proposes:

- a massive, federally-funded prevention and education campaign
- sufficient funding for all aspects of AIDS research
- a National Health Program to provide needed health care

- the vigorous defense of civil rights, including an end to discrimination against gay people and IV drug users and no mandatory testing
- fulfillment of international obligations, e.g., supporting the World Health Organization's AIDS effort
- establishment of a Federal Commission on AIDS

Health is not a human right in today's United States. Millions of people of all races do not receive the care they need because they cannot pay for it. Among western industrialized nations, only the United States and South Africa lack a national health program that would assure every person the right to develop his or her potential to live a healthy life and obtain access to health care in time of need. This heartbreaking reality is frequently explained and justified by saying that the United States has neither the resources nor the popular will to make health a human right. Both arguments are wrong.

The problem is clearly not a lack of resources. As the wealthiest country ever known, we already spend more on health care than any other nation on earth. Nearly 11 percent of our GNP is spent on health services, making the health sector the third largest economic activity in the nation, after agriculture and construction.

Despite these enormous expenditures, we still have a health care "non-system." No other country faces such skewed priorities, high costs, and poor health care coverage.

- From 1980 to 1985, more U.S. children died because of poverty, hunger, or malnutrition than the total number of U.S. battle deaths in the Vietnam War. These children were the casualties of Reaganomics.

- Today, on average, one child dies of poverty, hunger, or malnutrition every fifty minutes.

- A child from a black or white low-income family has twice the chance of dying during the first year of his or her life as does a child from a higher-income family.

- A migrant farmworker is likely to live slightly over one-half the number of years that a corporate executive lives.

- On average, a worker is killed or dies because of work-related conditions every five minutes.

- Three million families were refused medical care in 1985 because they could not pay for it.

- Twenty percent of Americans could not pay for the medical care they needed in 1985.

- Thirty-eight million people do not have any form of health insurance coverage, public or private; 36 percent of them are children.

- Fifty-nine percent of poor and near-poor blacks and 63 percent of Hispanics were uninsured for all or part of 1984.

- Twenty years after the establishment of Medicare (the insurance program for our elderly) senior citizens still have to pay more than 20 percent of their health expenditures.

- Low-income senior citizens spend 25 percent of their income on medical care. None of the current catastrophic health insurance proposals will correct this situation.

- More than one-third of black women and more than one-fifth of white women receive inadequate prenatal care. This situation has worsened during the Reagan administration.

- Infant mortality is no longer declining at the rate that it has for the last twenty years. The mortality rate of infants aged between 28 days and one year has increased.

- Gaps in infant mortality rates between blacks and whites and between low-income and high-income families are the largest since 1940.

- The number of families refused health care because they could not pay increased by two million from 1982 to 1985.

- Average out-of-pocket health care expenditures have increased.

- The proportion of people who do not have a regular source of health care has increased by 65 percent.

- Federal health expenditures have received unprecedented cuts. For example, Medicare, which represents 7 percent of all federal expenditures, has received 12 percent of all federal cuts. The percentage of federal expenditures going to the care of the elderly and disabled has declined from 7.6 to 7.1 percent, while the percentage for defense has increased from 22 to 26 percent.

- Federal interventions have stimulated hospitals to discharge "unprofitable" cases. The National Opinion Research Center reports that 78 percent of admitting physicians claim to have received pressure from their hospitals to discharge patients.

- There has been further growth in investor-owned hospitals (the hospitals with highest profits), stimulated by new forms of federal payment; 13 percent of all hospitals are now investor-owned. They are concentrated, for the most part, in the South. They provide care that is believed by a majority of physicians (including one-quarter of those working for them) to be inferior to care by nonprofit hospitals.

- Profits in the hospital industry have increased: 81 percent of all hospitals realized profits in 1985, with an average profit margin of 14.1 percent, a margin several times higher than the 3.3 percent after-tax margins reported by *Business Week* for the service sector as a whole.

- More than 40,000 people have been struck by AIDS, of whom half have already died, and another 2 million are infected. Yet we still do not have a mass educational program to halt what is ultimately a preventable disease.

These are the realities of the U.S. health care "non-system." They are frequently put aside as problems of only small sectors of the population. The facts show otherwise. For example, high health care costs and limited health coverage are problems faced by the majority of the U.S. population, not only the poor. For several years, these two problems have been among the top concerns expressed in major public opinion polls. The average person still pays, on average, 27 percent of his or her bill directly out-of-pocket; health costs are the major cause of personal bankruptcy.

Much of this hardship could be avoided. The majority of industrialized countries offer more comprehensive and universal health care coverage, have better health indicators, and provide health services that are more popular than ours; and these services cost much less. Canada is just one example. Canadians pay less in health care than we do, and they get more comprehensive health benefits and are more satisfied with their health care system. Not surprisingly, 72 percent of our population feels that the U.S. health care non-system must change profoundly. Seventy-five percent of Americans feel that the federal government should guarantee health as a human right. No less than 62 percent favor a national health program, even if establishing such a program called for higher taxes.

If the United States does not have a comprehensive and universal health program to promote the health of our people and take care of their health care needs, it is not because the wealthiest country on earth cannot afford it or because the overwhelming majority of Americans do not believe that health should be a human right and that our government should assure that right. It is a result of the power of specific interest groups which hold enormous political power that shapes the nature of our government and its policies.

The root of the problem is the profit orientation of our health care non-system, the economic rationale it sustains, the entrenched interest groups that it reproduces, the enormous waste it generates, and the great power and influence of specific business and professional interest groups in our political, communications, and academic institutions. In 1983, profits in the health sector were: for the drug industry, $5.6 billion; for the medical and equipment suppliers, $1.8 billion; for insurance and other financial institutions, $2.1 billion; and for health institutions (including hospitals) $2.8 billion. Enormous apparatuses are needed to sustain the dynamics of those profits and to reproduce the interest groups they benefit. In 1983, for example, $15.6 billion was spent on insurance overhead, $26.9 billion on hospital administration, $4.1 billion on nursing home administration, $31.1 billion on physicians' overhead, $2 billion on marketing, and $38.2 billion on excessive physicians' income.

These harmful and unnecessary profits and expenditures are central to the problems of wrong priorities, high costs, and limited coverage. They could and should be dramatically reduced or even eliminated. Needless to say, the business and professional interest groups that benefit from high profits and waste will oppose changes, and their political influence is enormous. The Reagan administration has been crowded with individuals who worked for and were part of these business interest groups. Starting from the top: President Reagan used to work for General Electric—a major hospital supplier—appearing in ads opposing Medicare, the program that has been responsible for a decline of 2 percent per year in the mortality rate among senior citizens. A lot of unnecessary deaths would have occurred had the Reagan ads been successful. Vice President Bush used to be a Director of Lilly, one of the largest and most profitable drug and medical equipment companies. The list could go on and on. It is not only the military-industrial complex that rules this administration; the interests of the medical-industrial complex do also, and no political force dares to confront them. Political, communications, and academic establishments prefer to leave things as they are, saying it is what people want.

These power groups, not people's will, shape the nature of our health priorities and our health care. To cite one example of many: the health care non-system in North Carolina, a state that has about the same number of babies born per year as Sweden, but twice as many low birth weight babies and neonatal deaths, due to poverty and malnutrition. North Carolina, however, has twice as many expensive ventilator-equipped neonatal intensive care unit beds as Sweden, with further expansion proposed. It would be much more humane and cost-effective to provide food and other social services than highly expensive curative technology. A neonatal intensive care unit for an infant costs more than $1,000 per day, often amounting to $100,000 per infant, while adequate prenatal care costs only $800. The power of corporate medical technology, in alliance with the state's hospital industry and the federal government (which pays for much of the usage of those beds), leads to the type of service that responds to profit, not need.

The solution to this unhealthy situation is to stop favoring the few—the business and professional interests—over the many—the majority of people who need medical care. We need a National Health Program to guarantee health as a human right.

The main characteristics of the proposed National Health Program are as follows:

The Program should provide comprehensive health care coverage, without co-payments and deductibles, and should ensure access to quality health care to all citizens and residents of the United States. Health benefits should include the provision of and access to preventive, promotional, curative, and rehabilitation services.

The National Health Program should be federally funded. The current system of funding health care, which relies very heavily on premiums, payroll taxes, and fee for services, is highly regressive. These payment systems are unfair to the middle- and low-income families who pay for the majority of health services in the United States. The current system of health benefits coverage, which relates the type and size of health benefits to people's jobs, produces enormous inequities in the distribution of health benefits. Eighty percent of people have their health benefits coverage provided at the workplace. Where unions have been strong (such as in manufacturing), full-time jobs available, and wages good, health benefits coverage has been much more extensive than in those sectors where unions have been weak, jobs part-time, and wages very low, such as in services and retail sales. We face a situation in which the type of health benefits that families or individuals get depends on the place they work. A service sector worker has, on average, 53 percent less coverage than a manufacturing worker.

This diversity and inequality of health benefits is not beneficial to the majority of workers (who are not in manufacturing), nor is it beneficial to workers in manufacturing. Manufacturing workers are very vulnerable to corporate employers' decisions to reduce benefits, increase co-payments and deductibles, or establish two layers of benefits, one for the old-timers and another (with fewer benefits) for newer entrants. Funding health services in this way divides people into different categories of employment as well as into the employed and unemployed. Moreover, it causes people to fear job loss or change—where their health benefits may be lost or reduced—enormously. Seventy-five percent of workers over 45 years of age who lost their jobs in the 1982 recession lost their health insurance as well. The provision of health care in the proposed National Health Program should be based on need rather than on ability to pay or ability to bargain.

The funds to support the Program should be earmarked general revenues coming primarily from:

Corporations: A substantial share of current non-government health care funds is now supplied by private corporations through group insurance packages for their employees. These funds should be shifted to the support of a National Health Program by including a health tax levied on corporations. The size of this corporate tax should be related to the size of the corporate payroll. Since corporations would be saving significant sums currently spent on benefit packages, this tax would shift expenditures but not increase them. Private health insurance coverage overlapping public coverage should be banned, as has been done in Canada, to assure equal access to care.

Personal Income Taxes: General income taxation retains some limited measure of progressivity (despite recent "tax reform" packages that sharply reduced taxes on the wealthy) and provides the broadest and fairest base on which to fund the National Health Program. Collecting funds through taxes is both fairer and cheaper than collecting individual premiums, co-payments, deductibles, and fees.

Health care expenditures under the proposed National Health Program would be considerably less than under the current private system. Thus, a National Health Program, while funded differently from the current private system, should be less costly to both citizens and corporations.

It is estimated that in 1989 under the current system of funding and organizing health services, the United States will spend $591 billion; $145 billion will be corporate-employer contributions, $206 billion will come from individual contributions, and $240 billion from government. Under this system, the majority of Americans will continue to face major problems of high cost and limited health coverage. Most insurance plans will still leave many health benefits uncovered.

Under the proposed National Health Program, the costs of the whole program would be $581 billion, $10 billion less than under the current system. (For a detailed exposition of the costs of the proposed National Health Program, see the Himmelstein and Woolhandler study listed in the resources section at the end of the chapter.) The corporate share, paid in health taxes, and the government contributions from general revenues, would equal current contributions. The greatest savings, however, would be in individual contributions—$196 billion rather than $206 billion. The majority of people would pay much less and they would get much more. They would have all preventive, promotional, curative, and rehabilitative services covered, without co-payments and deductibles. Moreover, people who do not use health services because they cannot pay for them would be able to use them without worrying about how to pay for the services they need. Today there are approximately 106,000 deaths due to underutilization of health services in cases of need. These deaths would be prevented under the National Health Program. It is estimated that with this program there would be a 15 percent increase in utilization of health services, expenses included in the $581 billion total cost. In summary, more people would be using the services they urgently need and none would have co-payments or deductibles.

Providing health care through a National Health Program is much more efficient than a private system, since billing and most insurance overhead costs are eliminated; improved planning would reduce the current wasteful duplication and excess of current facilities, and advance payment to institutional providers would reduce administrative costs. Profit-making by pharmaceutical companies, medical supply companies, and other for-profit health corporations would be reduced, since the government would be the primary purchaser of services.

The system of payment to providers should minimize financial incentives for both overcare and undercare. The current fee-for-service system gives providers incentives for overcare, since the more services they provide, the more money they make. Conversely, the Medicare

DRG system rewards providers for giving too little care, since they are paid according to the diagnosis, the same amount no matter how much or how little they do for their patients.

Hospitals should be shifted from their current fee-for-service reimbursement basis to an annually budgeted basis. The federal government, operating through state and local authorities, should negotiate annual operating budgets with each hospital, based on the size and health care needs of the population served. (In a number of other programs the federal government has shown that it can, in fact, perform such an allocation based upon a variety of statistical indicators.) Hospitals would then know what staff to hire and could plan their service delivery sensibly and cost-efficiently. By eliminating billing and much of the attendant internal cost accounting, annual budgeting could save the 10 percent of total hospital spending now devoted to such activities.

Capital funds for expanding or replacing health care facilities should be allocated by state and local authorities, handled separately from operating budgets. Canada has shown that this is an effective and workable scheme for ensuring equitable access to health care facilities for its entire population.

Physicians should be paid through a combination of salary, capitation, and fee-for-service. The Program should gradually increase the number of salaried physicians, but existing arrangements will undoubtedly have to be retained in many cases. Salary schemes offer the best opportunity for public authorities to ensure the equitable distribution of health care personnel and facilities around the country. Fee-for-service arrangements will be discouraged.

The Program should be federally administered. We have learned from the last twenty years that a National Health Program must be funded and guided by the federal government. This federal involvement is essential to assure adequate funding in poorer areas, to prevent regressive state governments from blocking effective implementation of the Program in their area, and to assure that all people have the same chance to get good care when they need it. Decent health care must be established as a right for all citizens, and this right, like our other constitutional rights, must be guaranteed at the federal level.

While the federal government should be responsible for administering the National Health Program (through a National Trust Fund and a National Health Board) and assuring the provision of comprehensive health coverage to the population, states and local authorities should be responsible for planning health services in their areas. Operating budgets and capital expenditures should be approved at the state and local levels; plans should be developed and approved by state and local health boards. These plans should meet federal guidelines approved by the National Health Board.

Health institutions, such as hospitals and nursing homes, that receive government funds should be required to have boards of trustees that are publicly accountable and representative of the communities they serve. Today, 53 percent of hospital funds and 83 percent of nursing home funds are already tax funds, but their boards of trustees are highly unrepresentative of the populations they serve. These trustees come primarily from the wealthiest 5 percent of our population. This situation must change. Such boards should be representative of their communities. Community participation must be made meaningful and not a token reality. In no other area is community participation more important than in the health sector.

The executive and legislative branches of the federal government should appoint a National Health Board to direct the National Health Program. At the state and local authority levels, the executive and legislative branches of each level of government should appoint their health boards, the top planning authorities at each level of government.

National health policy guidelines should aim to change the orientation of the system, shifting it towards preventive, community, environmental, occupational, and social interventions. These priorities will require a combination of government intervention and citizen participation, in which the populations affected by the health programs play a major role in their governance.

All people should have a choice of provider.

The National Health Program should guarantee quality care by establishing federal norms and standards of good health to be followed by providers receiving funds from the Program. Moreover, the National Health Board, as well as the state and local health boards, will have the task of evaluating the service offered by providers and assuring quality standards.

The National Health Program should mandate the establishment, in each health care institution and each local authority, of patient advocates appointed by the local health board who will have responsibility for responding to and acting upon patients' grievances and concerns. The boards of these institutions should also address grievances and complaints brought to them by patient advocates.

These should be the principles and characteristics of a National Health Program. The proposal put forward here makes sense on moral, human, and economic grounds. The commitment is a principled one, based on an uncompromising position that health is a human right.

AIDS: The Need for a National Health Program*

AIDS is one of the best examples of why we need a National Health Program. By mid-summer of 1987, 40,000 people had been diagnosed with AIDS: half are already dead. It is estimated that nearly two million people in this country are currently infected, and the U.S.

---

* This section is based on the National Rainbow Coalition position paper on AIDS, prepared by Nancy Krieger.

government has predicted that by 1991 270,000 people in the United States will have been diagnosed with AIDS, of whom 179,000 will have died. This number equals half the World War II casualties. AIDS is indeed an overwhelming health tragedy.

Along with the lives it has claimed and will claim, AIDS is also exacting an enormous economic price. In 1986, direct health care costs for AIDS exceeded $1 billion, and by 1991 they may reach $8-$16 billion. The vast majority of AIDS patients are forced to rely on Medicaid, and the bulk of their care is provided by already overwhelmed and underfunded public hospitals. No other disease shows as clearly the problems with our medical care non-system.

In the United States, AIDS has primarily hit the gay and minority communities, killing young people in the prime of their lives. Nearly 70 percent of adults with AIDS are gay or bisexual men, and about 40 percent of individuals with AIDS are people of color, including 75 percent of all women and 90 percent of all children with AIDS. The disproportionate concentration of minorities among these groups reflects the deadly translation of racism to poverty, unemployment, and subsequent high rates of drug abuse (IV drug use is an AIDS risk factor) and ill health. Over one-third of black and Latino men and women with AIDS, as compared with only 5 percent of white men, were infected through IV drug use, while another third of minority women with AIDS were infected because they were the sexual partner of men who used IV drugs.

AIDS is transmitted only between people who have shared intimate, high-risk contact; it cannot be spread by casual contact. People infected with the AIDS virus consequently pose no threat to the public at large. The best way to reduce the spread of AIDS is to encourage people not to engage in high-risk behaviors. Public health experts both here and abroad agree that enacting mandatory testing and quarantine not only would be ineffective, but would represent a massive waste, diverting necessary resources from the broad educational campaigns so urgently needed. In addition, such measures would force those with or at risk for AIDS underground, denying them treatment and perpetuating the epidemic.

Rather than lead the way in a forceful federal campaign to combat AIDS and the hysteria it has engendered, the Reagan administration has exacerbated the political crisis triggered by the epidemic. It has underfunded research, stonewalled frank educational efforts, defaulted on its payments to the World Health Organization (WHO), and gone against the recommendations of its own scientists by implementing mandatory testing without real guarantees of confidentiality for all who fall under federal jurisdiction: immigrants, federal prisoners, patients in Veterans Administration hospitals, plus people in the military, the foreign service, and the Job Corps.

AIDS must be challenged forcefully through the following steps. A massive federally-funded prevention and education campaign should be launched. This campaign must utilize explicit, multilingual, and culturally sensitive materials and must expand the availability of free substance abuse treatment programs. Needle distribution or exchange efforts should also be initiated to discourage AIDS transmission and encourage people to enroll in treatment programs. Sufficient funding for all aspects of AIDS research must be provided. A National Health Program, as outlined above, must be created to provide needed health care. Until these steps are taken, Medicaid and Medicare benefits must immediately be extended to all people with AIDS or ARC (AIDS-related complex), and insurance companies must be prohibited from using the AIDS antibody or any other test to deny applicants coverage. Civil rights must be defended, including an end to discrimination and mandatory testing. International obligations must be fulfilled by supporting the World Health Organization's AIDS effort. A federal Commission on AIDS should be created to develop, advocate, coordinate, and oversee the implementation of federal AIDS policy. This commission should include those most affected by and involved in the AIDS crisis: public health, medical, dental, legal, and educational professionals, men and women with AIDS and ARC, and members of the communities at high risk for AIDS, i.e., the gay community, minority communities, hemophiliacs, IV drug users, and prisoners.

Finally, the motto guiding appropriations for AIDS should be "money for AIDS, not war." Specifically, there should be $5 billion allocated for prevention and $2 billion for research per year, starting immediately. These funds cannot be diverted from necessary ongoing or needed health programs or research; the obscene travesty of pitting different diseases and the people they afflict against one another cannot be permitted. Instead, money for AIDS must come from the bloated U.S. military budget, and health care service must be expanded through creation of a National Health Program.

Resources

Recommended Appointees for a New Administration

- Dr. June Jackson Christmas, psychiatrist and expert on mental health, former President of the American Public Health Association

- Drs. David Himmelstein and Steffie Woolhandler, Harvard University, health services researchers who have done extensive work on the problems faced by the U.S. medical system

- Dr. Daniel Lindheim, counsel to Representative Ronald Dellums (D-CA), an attorney and economist well versed in the economics of health

- Dr. Quentin Young, editor of *Health & Society*, a prominent force in denouncing the problems faced by U.S. medicine

- Dr. David Kotelchuck, expert on occupational and environmental health medicine who has been a proponent of newly revised interventions in occupational health, Professor of Environmental Sciences at Hunter College
- Tony Mazzacchi, a trade union leader and spokesperson for occupational health
- Dr. Ellen Silbergeld, Chief Toxics Scientist of the Environmental Defense Fund and toxicologist who has done major work on environmental health policy
- Dr. Sidney Wolfe, at the Nader group, who has distinguished himself by making specific proposals on how to control the quality of care and regulate the health industry

Organizations

- National Health Commission, The National Rainbow Coalition, 733 Fifteenth St. NW, Suite 327, Washington, DC 20005; (202) 638-0580
- Health and Medicine Policy Research Group, 220 S. State, Suite 300, Chicago, IL 60604; (312) 922-8057
- National AIDS Network, 1012 14th St. NW, Suite 601, Washington, DC 20005; (202) 347-0390
- National Gay Rights Advocates, AIDS Civil Rights Project, 540 Castro St., San Francisco, CA 94114; (415) 863-3624

Further Reading

- Vicente Navarro, *Medicine Under Capitalism*, Neale Watson, 1976.
- Vicente Navarro, "Federal Health Policies in the United States: An Alternative Explanation," *Milbank Quarterly*, Vol. 26, No. 1, 1987.
- "The Need for a National Health Program," The National Health Commission of the National Rainbow Coalition, Washington, DC, 1987.
- David Himmelstein and Steffie Woolhandler, "The Costs of the National Health Program, Appendix 1," in Vicente Navarro (ed.), *A Proposal for a National Health Program*, National Health Commission of the National Rainbow Coalition, October 1987.
- Nancy Krieger and Rose Appleman, *The Politics of AIDS*, Frontline Publications, 1986.
- *Confronting AIDS: Directions for Public Health, Health Care, and Research*, Committee on a National Strategy for AIDS of the Institute of Medicine, National Academy Press, 1986.
- Randy Shilts, *And the Band Played On: Politics, People, and the AIDS Epidemic*, St. Martin's Press, 1987.
- Cindy Patton, *Sex and Germs: The Politics of AIDS*, South End Press, 1985.

Vicente Navarro is Professor of Health Policy of the School of Hygiene and Public Health of the Johns Hopkins University. He has worked as a consultant to many western countries, to the Council of Europe, the United Nations, the World Health Organization, and the Pan-American Health Organization. He has been the founder and president of the International Association of Health Policy and the founder and editor-in-chief of the *International Journal of Health Services*. He has been an elected member of the Executive Board of the American Public Health Association, and a consultant to the National Science Foundation and the National Institutes of Health. He is currently the Chair of the National Health Commission of the National Rainbow Coalition.

William J. Chambliss

Dealing With America's Drug Problem

Platform

- Appoint a high-level commission to review current drug enforcement policies. The commission's charge must be to consider *all* of the consequences of present policies, from international relations to corruption of government officials and law enforcement agencies.

- Establish an education program that will honestly and accurately communicate to the citizens the nature of different types of drugs and their consequences.

- Law enforcement agencies should be directed to communicate objectively about drug abuse problems and cease to propagandize.

- Provide research funds immediately for an evaluation of alternative drug policies in the United States and abroad. Research should compare the effect of the changes in drug laws in those states that have decriminalized marijuana and in those countries that have medicalized heroin and cocaine addiction.

The Assistant Attorney General of the United States, William Bradford Reynolds, inadvertently revealed the root cause of the drug problem in the United States when he said in a 1988 memo to the "Heads of Department Components" in the Department of Justice:

> Overall, we should send the message that there are two ways to approach drugs: the soft, easy way that emphasizes drug treatment and rehabilitation versus the hard, tough approach that emphasizes strong law enforcement measures and drug-testing. Naturally, we favor the latter.

Why the Justice Department should "naturally" favor strong law enforcement measures and drug-testing over treatment and rehabilitation is not clear. But for seventy years, law enforcement agencies in the United States have successfully lobbied for the criminalization of drugs and ever-harsher penalties for users and sellers. The fact that this policy has been a complete and utter failure should give Mr. Reynolds and all of us reason to reconsider our current policies.

The consequences of leaving the problem of drug use to law enforcement agencies are obvious. Since drug use was criminalized in the United States (between 1914 and 1937) there has been a steady increase in the availability of drugs and the number of drug users. In the last twenty years cocaine has become readily available on every college campus and in every office building, not to mention the streets of every city. In the 1980s, the number of people regularly using cocaine tripled in less than three years.

Hand-in-hand with increased use and availability has come wholesale corruption in the governments, military, and law enforcement agencies of Peru, Bolivia, Colombia, Honduras, Turkey, Thailand, Laos, and even the United States. Democratic institutions have been undermined.

Organized crime syndicates have grown wealthy and powerful on the profits from drug smuggling. Political candidates all over the world are bought and sold. Drugs are sold indiscriminately and with no concern for what the additives used to increase profits are doing to consumers. To protect their profits, crime networks employ murder, threats, blackmail, and the purchase of political favors.

Illegal drug use has spread from small enclaves of addicts to every corner of society. The people in the poorest sectors of society spend scarce resources on drugs they cannot afford, but which provide an escape from the boredom and frustrations of their lives. Diseases like AIDS and hepatitis disproportionately affect the poor, as they share needles and seek bargains in inferior products.

Taxpayers support a massive and endlessly greedy law enforcement machinery that keeps promising results but delivers only more misery along with demands for ever-increasing budgets. In the last ten years in the United States, the number of police has doubled, and calls are heard for doubling, tripling, or even quadrupling law enforcement expenditures for drug control. The existence of such a powerful, well armed, and politically persuasive police force in the midst of a democratic society is a development that should be seriously weighed and not accepted as necessary in the aftermath of anti-drug hysteria. If we know nothing else about bureaucracies, we know they will never disappear or curtail their influence voluntarily. Do we want a nation bordering on a police state? Even if this were the only way to stop the drug traffic—which it is not—one wonders if it would be worth it.

The U.S. market in opium, heroin, cocaine, and marijuana now constitutes at least a $130 billion a year business. The growing, manufacture, and distribution of illegal drugs has become one of the largest industries in the world. Whole nation-states—Turkey, Colombia, Peru, and Bolivia—depend upon drug trafficking for their economic survival. (The export of cocaine provides Bolivia with more income than all other export products combined.) Other nations, including the United States, Honduras, Panama, Burma, Thailand, Laos, and Mexico, are so deeply enmeshed economically in the production and distribution of drugs that their economies would be severely threatened and the existing political systems undermined by a major shift in drug trafficking.

Internally, these same nations are either significantly influenced or completely controlled by criminal networks consisting of smugglers, professional murderers, military personnel, cabinet-level ministers, and even heads of state that provide the wherewithal to move the drugs from the hills and farms through the processing laboratories, across borders, and onto the streets. The extent of corruption varies but the impact is similar in every country. In Panama, the head of the government is a known drug trafficker. In Colombia, the government is virtually controlled by a drug cabal. The corruption of the police and military in Thailand and Turkey is directly attributable to the smuggling of opium and heroin and touches almost every facet of life in these countries.

In the United States, the CIA has been either a partner in or organizer of international drug trafficking. It aided and abetted the production and distribution of opium in Southeast Asia during and after the Vietnam War and worked hand-in-glove with drug smugglers from Latin America in order to support the *contras* in Nicaragua. Former members of the CIA oversaw the transportation of opium out of the Laotian hills on airlines controlled by the CIA and helped found a bank in Australia which became one of the world's most important links in the financing of international narcotics and money-laundering. In Honduras, according to testimony presented at congressional hearings, a farm owned by an American which was used as a staging area for the *contras* to attack Nicaragua was also the transfer point for millions of dollars worth of cocaine being shipped to the United States. These shipments sometimes went through military bases and were handled by U.S. military personnel. The Drug Enforcement Administration (DEA), the military, and the FBI cooperate with the CIA to rationalize and facilitate international drug smuggling and in the process any semblance of law enforcement becomes a mockery. Some of the players in this sinister enterprise take advantage of the opportunity to enrich themselves while providing illegal funds for government-sanctioned operations.

All of this derives from general acceptance of the law enforcement definition of reality, which perpetuates ignorance and depends on the creation of myths. One of the most important myths is that heroin, cocaine, crack, and marijuana inevitably lead to addiction and a willingness to sacrifice everything for the short-term pleasure of the drug. Nothing could be further from the truth. That some people become addicted is well established. Equally well established, however, is the fact that most people who use these drugs, even those who use them regularly, do not become addicted nor are they willing to sacrifice their lives or their families to obtain the drugs. A National Institute of Drug Abuse survey of 18-25-year-olds revealed that 8.2 million Americans in this age group had used cocaine. Over five million had used it within the last year, two and one-half million within the preceding month, and 250,000 used it weekly. Only 3 percent of these people reported problems giving it up. With marijuana, the number of people who use the drug is much higher but the proportion of those who report difficulty in giving up the drug, even after a long period of heavy usage, is negligible.

The most highly addictive of these illegal drugs are the opiates and their derivatives, particularly heroin. We do not have good data on the addiction rate among opium users but we do know that where opium is legally available through medical doctors, as it is in Great Britain, addicts are able to function normally so long as they receive regular injections under clinically safe conditions. Most addicts, given that opportunity, sustain their habit with the legal injections. The illegal market in opiates in Great Britain is minuscule.

A comparison of the addictive qualities of these illegal drugs with tobacco and alcohol is revealing. A survey of high school seniors asked those who admitted to using marijuana, cocaine, and cigarettes if they had ever had difficulty stopping. Less than 4 percent reported difficulty stopping cocaine, 7 percent marijuana, and 18 percent of the cigarette smokers answered affirmatively. It is also estimated that 10-20 percent of the people who consume alcohol are problem drinkers. Alcohol contributes to over 200,000 deaths annually, tobacco consumption to over 300,000. The National Council on Alcoholism attributed only 3,562 deaths to illegal drugs in 1985.

Of course, there are many more alcohol and cigarette users than illegal drug users, so these statistics are misleading. Nonetheless, they tell us that the scare tactics of police and politicians are gross exaggerations. While two wrongs do not make a right and one could argue that these statistics suggest that alcohol and tobacco should be illegal as well as other drugs, experience with Prohibition has shown quite clearly that it does not work to criminalize drug consumption. The point is rather the reverse: experience with attempts to criminalize alcohol is a powerful argument in favor of legalizing other drugs as well.

The biggest myth perpetrated by the law enforcement agencies, however, is that legalizing these drugs would increase consumption and generate a host of other problems. The reverse is the case. Many of the problems concomitant with present drug policies would disappear and our ability to help those who are seriously addicted would be enhanced. The high cost of these drugs is entirely due to the fact that they are illegal. Marijuana sells for about $8 a pound in Colombia.

In the United States it sells for about $900 a pound wholesale and two or three times that on the street. Cocaine costs about $4,000 a pound in Colombia and wholesales at $20,000 in Miami. The markup on opium and heroin is even higher. If these drugs were legally available, the cost to people who wished to use them would not drive them to crime, prostitution, poverty, and, in extreme cases, the selling of their personal property and even their children into prostitution to support their habit.

If the drugs were legal, the stigma of criminality would not attach to the user and problem drug-users would seek the help they need. Addicts would not have to share dirty needles, and the spread of AIDS would decline precipitously. Legalization would also facilitate the accurate dissemination of drug information. Most people know the difference between the effects of beer, wine, and whiskey. Possessing this knowledge enables us to rationally choose which to drink under what circumstances. Law enforcement propaganda which lumps all illegal drugs together as equally dangerous makes sensible policies and personal decisions impossible. Furthermore, it reinforces the belief on the part of potential users that everything they hear about drugs is the big lie. Every ghetto twelve-year-old knows that marijuana is very different from cocaine, but they are not told exactly how and why. When they are offered crack or heroin, they do not have the necessary information to consider what the consequences may be.

So long as drugs are illegal, there can be no control over their content. It is impossible to assure a constant supply of equally potent or pure commodities, and people therefore die from taking drugs that are stronger than they are used to or drugs that are impure.

Carefully ignored in all the law enforcement propaganda is the experience of the dozen or so states that have virtually legalized marijuana (among them, Alabama, New York, Maine, California, Nebraska, Mississippi, and Rhode Island). Evidence is spotty, but what there is suggests that the use of marijuana actually declines after legalization. This makes sense. Where it is legal, the incentive to create new markets is reduced and much of the excitement that comes with violating rules disappears.

The evidence is overwhelmingly clear that we cannot permit this insanity to continue. In the past ten years, we have doubled the number of people in prisons, many of them there for possession of drugs. If we double the number of street cleaners, we will find twice as many dirty streets, but the problem of people littering will not be solved. We can double, triple, quadruple the size of our police forces. We can arm them with warfighting weapons. We can arrest ten times as many drug-users and sellers as we did last year and we will still not make a dent in the drug problem nor touch any of the related tragedies that follow from our present policies.

Legalizing drugs will not make them go away any more than legalizing alcohol made it go away. It will, however, offer the opportunity to control the epidemic and cut back on the corruption in government and law enforcement agencies, the devastation of communities, and the wrecking of the lives of an untold number of human beings.

Legalization should not, however, be confused with an open invitation to consume any and all drugs indiscriminately. The highly addictive qualities of heroin make it a dangerous substance for the open marketplace. Allowing medical doctors to administer a sustaining amount to addicts, however, would greatly curtail the profits and go a long way toward solving many of the attendant problems. Cocaine is less addictive than heroin, but it should be available to addicts from medical doctors as well.

One of the deterrents to over-consumption of these drugs, as is the case with alcohol and cigarettes, is their high cost. Even though these drugs can be produced cheaply, a state-controlled system of marketing should retain a fairly high price and use the profits to set up rehabilitation and education programs. Marijuana should simply be legalized. Perhaps the California model permitting people to be in possession of less than an ounce and to grow their own for their own consumption would suffice to limit usage but decriminalize its use. If the profit for criminal networks were taken out of heroin, cocaine, and marijuana, many of the attendant problems described above would disappear.

In considering alternative social policies, it must be remembered that an ideal solution does not exist. We must always weigh the costs and the benefits. The costs of our present drug policies are excessive. Common sense, scientific knowledge, and logic all suggest that legalization is long overdue.

Resources

Recommended Appointees for a New Administration

- Martha Huggins, Chair of Department of Sociology and Anthropology, Union College. Dr. Huggins has an intimate knowledge of Latin America and law enforcement in those countries.

- Alfred R. Lindesmith, Professor Emeritus, Indiana University. Professor Lindesmith has written innumerable articles and two books on opiates, heroin, and the law. He is an internationally recognized authority on drug programs in different countries.

- David Musto, Departments of Psychiatry and History, Yale University. Dr. Musto has written seminal works on drug use and abuse.

- Ethan A. Nadelman, Woodrow Wilson School of Public and International Affairs, Princeton University. Dr. Nadelman has published a seminal article on the impact of criminal law on drug use and abuse.

- Lloyd Ohlin, Harvard Law School. In a career of social policy and research on juvenile crime and prisons, Professor Ohlin has established himself as a leading authority on crime and social control.

- Representative Charles B. Rangel (D-NY). Representative Rangel and his staff have gathered testimony and information on drugs and crime. He has shown more interest in this subject than most members of Congress.

- Joseph Scott, Director of Black Studies, University of Washington, Seattle. An internationally recognized authority on black teenage lifestyles and the culture of the black community.

- Robert B. Seidman, Boston University Law School. Professor Seidman is one of the world's leading authorities on drafting legislation to effect social change.

- Kurt Schmoke, Mayor of Baltimore. Mayor Schmoke has given top priority to the drug problem in American cities and is very knowledgeable about drugs in minority communities.

- Lisa R. Stearns, Associate Director, Legislative Drafting Unit, Columbia University. Ms. Stearns is an experienced legislative drafter who has written model legislation for dozens of organizations, states, and congressional committees.

- Daniel Vietz, attorney, Columbia, MO. Mr. Vietz is on the Board of Directors of NORML (National Organization for the Reform of Marijuana Laws).

Organizations

- National Council on Crime and Delinquency, 77 Maiden Lane, San Francisco, CA 94108; (415) 956-5651

- American Society of Criminology, 1314 Kinnear Rd., Columbus, OH; (614) 292-9207

- Academy of Criminal Justice Sciences, Northern Kentucky University, 402 Nunn Hall, Highland Heights, KY 41076; (606) 572-5634

- National Organization for the Reform of Marijuana Laws, 2001 S St. NW, Washington, DC 20009; (202) 483-5500

Further Reading

- David Musto, *The American Dream*, Yale University Press, 1984.

- Ethan Nadelman, "U.S. Drug Policy: A Bad Export," *Foreign Policy* Spring 1988, pp. 83-109.

- Alfred R. Lindesmith, *Opiates and the Law*, Indiana University Press, 1969.

- Alan A. Block and William J. Chambliss, *Organizing Crime*, Elsevier, 1982.

- Patrick O'Malley, Lloyd Johnson, and Jerald Bachman, "Cocaine Use Among American Adolescents and Young Adults" in *Cocaine Use in America: Epidemiological and Clinical Perspectives*, Nicholas Kozel and Edgar Adams eds., National Institute of Drug Abuse Research, monograph 61, Government Printing Office, 1985.

- Lester Grinspoon and James Bakalar, *Psychedelic Drugs Reconsidered*, Basic Books, 1979.

- John Kaplan, *The Hardest Drug: Heroin and Public Policy*, University of Chicago Press, 1983.

William J. Chambliss is Chair of the Department of Sociology at George Washington University and President of the American Society of Criminology for 1988-1989. He is the author of *On the Take: From Petty Crooks to Presidents* and *Exploring Criminology*.

Ross Capon

New Directions
in Transportation Policy

Platform

- Urban transportation must be improved with respect to safety, energy efficiency, mobility for those without cars, and environmental impact via: financial incentives promoting smaller cars; restoration of previous funds cut from the federal transit program—preferably through a gasoline tax increase with exemptions for car-owning poor; federal encouragement of land-use policies consistent with pedestrian and transit use rather than dependency cyon private auto use.

- The nation should strive for a more balanced intercity passenger transportation system which fully utilizes trains that can relieve air congestion and which includes a nationwide train network that is coordinated with intercity bus services.

- Increase funding for intercity rail passenger services and feeder bus services, preferably through a unified transportation trust fund.

- Freight carriers should pay the full costs they impose on publicly owned infrastructure or, at a minimum, all modes should be treated equally.

- Important rail lines which otherwise would be abandoned should be acquired by public agencies.

- Unified transportation trust fund money should be available to states for rail freight projects.

America's highway and aviation systems suffer from increasingly serious problems relating to congestion, environmental pollution, energy supplies and efficiency, mobility for the poor, safety, and the proliferation of auto-dependent real estate developments. These problems could be alleviated by improving mass transit and rail services and by public policies encouraging "human-scale" developments consistent with pedestrian and transit rider needs.

Unfortunately—and notwithstanding some stunning success stories—rail remains largely unexploited. This is partly because, while rail systems' full financial costs are easily measured and are usually paid by one or a few entities, the financial costs of road and air are widely dispersed among users and various levels of government. Rail's benefits—including environmental and energy efficiency and positive impacts on development patterns—are harder to measure and have been of little interest to the Reagan administration. Meanwhile, far from encouraging land-use patterns consistent with "balanced transportation" and pedestrian needs, President Reagan—by increasing federal spending on highways and cutting spending on mass transit—has encouraged auto-dependent "suburban moonscape" development.

Similar local-level pressures stem from intense competition among jurisdictions to attract developers. Furthermore, most requirements imposed on developers to date—minimum parking space provisions and funding for road construction—merely intensify America's drift toward auto dependence. Finally, auto-oriented developments requiring no coordination with transit systems seem easier to build, though office developers might change their views if they fully understood the savings (from reduced parking space needs) inherent in transit/pedestrian-oriented developments.

In short, public policy has focused largely on trying to relieve congestion through expansion of road and air capacity, while ignoring or misusing land-use controls. America needs "balanced" transport and development policies which make best use of existing resources: the highways and airports already built, the weedgrown rail lines that could be restored, and the light rail lines that could be built on urban arterial roads. As the following "snapshots" suggest, such policies are both sensible and unusual.

• Since the San Diego trolley began operating in 1981, it has proved an economic and political success: ridership far exceeds what buses previously carried, fares have consistently paid about 90 percent of operating costs, and, as Mayor Maureen O'Conner said, "Everybody loves the trolleys. The only problem is we can't [build new lines] fast enough… People *are* giving up their second cars and they are commuting to work on the trolleys. It's not just the senior citizen and the low-income household but it's the professionals as well that are using the trolley. In the South Bay area, if we didn't have a trolley, there'd be gridlock."

• Having defeated lengthy environmental lawsuits, Maryland is widening I-270 from six to twelve lanes at a cost of $125 million, even though the road is paralleled by underutilized transit lines. On

California's urban freeways, average rush-hour speed is 23 mph and, by the year 2000, is expected to drop to 15 (half that on some freeways).

- Amtrak carries over one-third of New York-Washington air-plus-rail traffic, with no trains exceeding 125 mph (vs. 186, 180, and 155 planned for French, Italian, and German trains, respectively; France already has 168 mph trains). Trains limited to 110, 100, 90 and 79 mph have impressive market shares on the New York-Albany, New York-Boston, Los Angeles-San Diego, and San Francisco-Bakersfield lines.

Problems

Stimulated by cheap gasoline and cheap parking, increasingly large single-occupant autos dominate commuting patterns even in urban areas with good transit, whereas much urban travel could be accommodated by mass transit and light, energy-efficient, two-passenger cars.

Federal transit funding dropped 30 percent from FY1981-1988 under President Reagan, whose proposals for more severe cuts were resisted by Congress. Many urban freeways were built with 90 percent federal funds, but Reagan officials insist transit is a "local problem." They seem indifferent to the tangible benefits of improved public transit: cleaner air and water; energy efficiency; mobility for people without cars; land conservation; safety; economic efficiency.

The Reagan administration resisted construction of well designed, new rail transit lines although they are far more effective in attracting auto users and positively influencing development patterns than are buses and carpools. In southern New Jersey, a single rail line handles about 30 percent more passengers than the network of twenty-eight bus routes serving the rest of the state's Camden/Philadelphia suburbs. From 1985 to 1987, the number of commuters entering downtown Washington rose 1.8 percent but those in carpools dropped 9.3 percent.

For years, federal tax law allowed full deductibility for employer-provided parking but no deductibility for employer-provided transit passes. A 1984 law made a small improvement: up to $15 per month of employer-provided transit fares can be tax-free, but, if an employer gives more than $15 of benefits, tax deductibility is lost for the entire amount!

Reagan budgets for FY1986-1989 had no money for Amtrak. Perennial Amtrak foes such as Senator William L. Armstrong (R-CO) and U.S. Chamber of Commerce President Richard Lesher will force Amtrak management to waste time debating yet again whether Amtrak should exist, even though, in FY1987, Amtrak passenger-mileage rose and its revenue-to-cost ratio improved for the sixth consecutive year. With a 1988 appropriation 35 percent below the 1981 level, however,

Amtrak lacks rolling stock for existing demand, and prospects are dim for replacing its small, intensively used fleet.

Truck safety is a major problem, which may worsen if the government grants an industry request to lower the allowable driving age from twenty-one to eighteen. Meanwhile, the much safer freight railroads have steadily lost market share to trucks, a trend likely to continue as the road network expands, allowable truck sizes increase, rail lines are abandoned, and rail managements withdraw assets from the industry.

A 1982 law increased the size of trucks allowed on interstates and established guidelines for permitting the largest trucks to use other roads as well. This was a *quid pro quo* for user tax increases the law also included, but trucks were not paying their full costs before 1982. As of 1985, the Department of Transportation estimated trucks over 75,000 pounds gross weight paid just 65 percent of their cost responsibility; rail-competitive trucks generally pay even less. On many key routes, railroads compete with domestic water carriers which paid no infrastructure use charges before 1980 and since then have paid no more than 10 percent of their infrastructure costs.

Highways may command too large a portion of current transport spending, but road maintenance gets too little. The 1982 gas tax increase was promoted mainly as a means of improving maintenance, but about half of the dollars were made available for new construction. Earmarking all aviation and most highway use taxes for construction and maintenance of air and road facilities assures a constant stream of funds for such projects, pushing policymakers toward road and aviation rather than transit and railroad choices. The "most specific" funding approach means, for example, that ticket tax paid to fly from Washington, DC to New York can be used to build airports nationwide, but not to improve rail service that could reduce congestion at the airport the traveler used.

"Balanced transportation" might exist anyway if, decades ago, trust funds had been established for railroads and transit. Unfortunately, the opposite happened, largely because road and air facilities then were publicly owned while most railroads and rail transit lines were private. Railroads were taxed while tax dollars went to road and air projects. Also, General Motors, Firestone Tire & Rubber, Phillips Petroleum, Mack Manufacturing (the truck builder), and Standard Oil of California were convicted in 1949 of conspiring to destroy electric mass transit systems nationwide.

Some Solutions

In urban areas, use of transit and carpools must be encouraged by increasing the cost of single-occupant auto commuting and increasing federal transit funding. One obvious method: a gasoline tax increase with some or all of the proceeds going to transit.

Efficient transit projects must be encouraged. The Reagan crackdown on rail transit was partly a reaction to "gold-plated" metros providing fast service—encouraging long-distance commuting—when the need was for light rail on existing highway and rail rights-of-way, stopping more often than metros and thus providing good service for shorter trips. (Reagan ignored similar faults in the highway program, as when he reversed courageous Carter decisions against completion of beltways around Richmond, Virginia, and Dayton, Ohio.)

The new administration should promote some or all of the following techniques and should reduce transport funding for all modes in regions which ignore these strategies and fail to achieve a reasonable level of urban transport efficiency:

- as in Singapore, charge a fee to low-occupancy vehicles entering business districts during morning rush hours;

- electronic road-use fees, varying by time of day;

- raise parking fees; increase the proportion of parking spaces available only to smaller cars and charge less for those spaces; use tax deductibility and gas-guzzler taxes to reduce the average size of the auto fleet;

- assess developers for a big part of the land value created by publicly-funded transit facilities or, for highway-dependent projects, the full costs of the associated infrastructure; and

- correct the tax deductibility inequities discussed earlier regarding employer-subsidized parking and transit fares. (Rep. Barbara Kenne ily [D-CT] and Sen. Alfonse D'Amato [R-NY] have appropriate bills.)

Airport landing fees should vary by time of day. Airlines—already allowed to sell some landing "slots" to each other—should be required to pay the government for them in the first place. The appropriateness of continuing to use general funds to support air traffic control operating costs attributable to airlines and general aviation should be reviewed. Amtrak needs a larger rolling stock fleet and track repair program. The aviation trust fund would be a logical source for funds to invest in air-competitive rail services, but a unified transportation trust fund might be more viable politically.

Rural transport includes 11,000 rural transit systems (long-distance trains and intercity buses)—serving 86 percent of the nation's counties. These are heavily used by the elderly and others without cars. Legislators representing rural states strongly support the first two systems, which helped federal transit aid and Amtrak survive the Reagan era's darkest days. The Department of Transportation's rural transit funding dropped from over $70 million in 1981 to $58.6 million in 1986; it rose to $75 million in 1987, but this may not continue because two favorable factors—a backlog of unused funds and states' willingness to transfer funds from small urban to rural programs—may not last.

Although long-distance trains are also heavily used by those travelling between the major air-competitive city-pairs, air and bus deregulation have increased the number of communities where Amtrak offers the only public transport. At a minimum, the Amtrak network should expand to include routes serving Columbus, Ohio; Nashville, Tennessee; Louisville, Kentucky; and Oklahoma City, Oklahoma. States should be free to use federal highway funds to subsidize such service as well as intercity bus service that would otherwise be lost.

The most obvious need is to treat all modes equally with respect to infrastructure user fees, whether by increasing truck and water carrier payments or by public acquisition of rail infrastructure. A national weight-distance tax (payments increasing with vehicle weight and miles travelled) would do the best job of matching truck-user payments with relevant road costs. While truck deregulation has led to unreasonably low driver wages, comparatively high rail wages and the limited ability of rail management and labor to modernize work rules have contributed to the decline of rail's market share. Public right-of-way ownership could increase rail freight productivity by eliminating the monopoly which unions and management both hold over most rail infrastructure, a monopoly unique to railroads (and pipelines).

Vermont is one example of preserving rail freight. It acquired rail rights-of-way, provided capital funds to improve them, and contracted with private firms that operate the service. Thanks to plentiful federal highway dollars, Vermont is the exception. Unfortunately, Vermont's investment is threatened by the deterioration of a key connecting line (that already forced cancellation of the state's only Amtrak train). The deterioration may benefit the line's owner because—while north-south traffic now uses a different route—a competing north-south railroad relies on "trackage rights" over the deteriorating line in Vermont. This illustrates a weakness of private infrastructure ownership.

The federal interest in preserving rail freight service—based on safety, energy efficiency, and reduced road wear—argues strongly for making rail freight projects eligible for unified transportation trust fund money.

Resources

Recommended Appointees for a New Administration

- Alan S. Boyd, Chief Executive Officer, Airbus Industrie of North America, first Secretary of Transportation under President Johnson. Boyd negotiated international aviation treaties for President Carter and served as President of Amtrak.

- Barry Commoner, Director, Center for the Biology of Natural Systems, Queens College, New York, and former presidential candidate. A tireless advocate for greater reliance on rail systems and small automobiles.

- Matthew A. Coogan, a Dukakis appointee, transportation under-secretary in Massachusetts with knowledge regarding all modes of transportation.

- Thomas Downs, former City Administrator, Washington, DC, new head of the Triborough Bridge and Tunnel Authority (agency of New York's Metropolitan Transportation Authority). Previously served as head of the District of Columbia's Department of Transportation and with the Urban Mass Transportation Administration.

- Louis Gambaccini, Assistant Executive Director for Trans-Hudson Transportation, Port Authority of New York and New Jersey. Former New Jersey Secretary of Transportation who was offered the position of Urban Mass Transportation Administrator by President Carter.

- David Gunn, President, New York City Transit Authority. Formerly Director of Operations, Massachusetts Bay Transportation Authority (MBTA). Prior to that, he was MBTA's first Director of Commuter Rail Operations and helped save Boston's commuter rail system.

- Judith E. Harris of Harris and Kahn, Philadelphia. She is a longtime member of the Southeastern Pennsylvania Transportation Authority's Board of Directors.

- Thomas Larwin, General Manager, Metropolitan Transit Development Board, San Diego.

- James R. Mills, Chairman, Metropolitan Transit Development Board, San Diego. Former California State Senate President *Pro Tem*, considered "father" of the successful San Diego trolley and California's ambitious program of support for Amtrak services, including the nation's largest network of dedicated feeder buses linking Amtrak trains to key off-line points; former member of Amtrak Board.

- Frederick P. Salvucci, Massachusetts Governor Dukakis's only transportation secretary. Formerly transportation aide to Boston Mayor Kevin White.

- Ronald C. Sheck, Director, Transportation Programs Division, New Mexico Highway and Transportation Department. Former Professor of Geography and Planning at New Mexico State University (Las Cruces) whose first position in Santa Fe was Director of the Transportation Department's Planning and Development Division under Governor Toney Anaya. Oversees efforts to convert three Amtrak stations in New Mexico into intermodal public transport terminals incorporating local and intercity buses, taxis, and elderly/handicapped services. Staff Director for State Transportation Authority efforts to develop new rail lines to coal-producing regions.

- Eugene K. Skoropowski, Chief Operations Planning Officer, Southeastern Pennsylvania Transportation Authority (SEPTA). Previously Chief Railroad Services Officer, Massachusetts Bay Transportation Authority (MBTA). Transportation involvement began as a civic activist fighting to save Boston's commuter rail system; he represented the City of Melrose on MBTA's Advisory Board.

- Vukan R. Vuchic, Professor of Transportation Engineering, Department of Systems, University of Pennsylvania, Philadelphia.

Organizations

- American Public Transit Association, 1225 Connecticut Ave. NW, Washington, DC 20036; (202) 828-2800

- Campaign for New Transportation Priorities, 236 Massachusetts Ave. NE, Suite 603, Washington, DC 20002; (202) 546-1550

- Center for Auto Safety, 2001 S St. NW, #410, Washington, DC 20009; (202) 328-7700

- Insurance Institute for Highway Safety, Watergate 600, Washington, DC 20037; (202) 333-0770

- National Association for Transportation Alternatives, 725 15th St. NW, Suite 900, Washington, DC 20005; (202) 628-2537

Further Reading

- Barry Commoner, *The Poverty of Power*, Knopf, 1976.

- Jonathan Kwitny, "The Great Transportation Conspiracy: A juggernaut named desire," *Harper's*, February 1981.

- Steven Morrison, "The Equity and Efficiency of Runway Pricing", *Journal of Public Economics*, Vol. 34, October 1987, pp. 45-60, North Holland Publishing, Amsterdam, Netherlands.

- Boris S. Pushkarev with Jeffrey M. Zupan and Robert S. Cumella, *Urban Rail in America, An Exploration of Criteria for Fixed Guideway Transit*, Indiana University Press, 1982.

- George Rucker, "Public Transportation: Another Gap in Rural America," *Transportation Quarterly*, July 1984.

- Bradford C. Snell, *American Ground Transport: A Proposal for Restructuring the Automobile, Truck, Bus, and Rail Industries*, Presented to the Subcommittee on Antitrust and Monopoly, Committee on the Judiciary, U.S. Senate, U.S. Government Printing Office, 1974.

- Richard M. Stanger and Vukan R. Vuchic, *Lindenwold Rail Line and Shirley Busway: A Comparison*, Highway Research Record 459, pp. 13-28, Highway Research (now Transportation Research) Board, 1973.

- Laurence E. Tobey, "Costs, Benefits, and the Future of Amtrak," *Transportation Law Journal*, Vol. XV, No. 2, 1987.

- Vukan R. Vuchic, "Urban Transit: A Public Asset of National Significance," *Urban Resources*, Vol. IV, No. 1, pp. 3-6, 63, Metropolitan Services, University of Cincinnati, 1987.

- Vukan R. Vuchic, "The Auto v. Transit Controversy: Toward a Rational Synthesis for Urban Transportation Policy," *Transportation Research-A*, 18A, No. 2, pp. 125-133, Pergamon Press, 1984.

- Vukan R. Vuchic, *Urban Public Transportation Systems and Technology*, Prentice-Hall, 1981.

- Joseph Yance, "Airline Demand for Use of an Airport and Airport Rents," *Transportation Research*, December 1971.

Ross Capon has been Executive Director of the consumer-oriented and consumer-funded National Association of Railroad Passengers since 1976. He oversees the Campaign for New Transportation Priorities, established by the Association in 1986 to promote mass transit in general as well as fairer public policy treatment of freight railroads. From 1971 to 1975, he served as a special assistant to the Massachusetts Secretary of Transportation and Construction.

Mark Ritchie and Kevin Ristau

Agricultural Policy: Back to the Future

Platform

- Higher prices for farmers in the marketplace through higher support loan rates and the elimination of costly deficiency payment subsidies.
- Effective supply management of major farm commodities to balance production with demand and reduce wasteful surpluses.
- Conservation of soil and water resources through an expanded Conservation Reserve Program and the implementation of proper supply management designed to reduce the pressure on farmers to adopt intensive methods of production.
- International trade agreements to achieve higher world prices, eliminate world hunger, and stop agricultural trade wars.
- Stable reserves of farm commodities, insulated from the market, to protect consumers from shortages and excessive food costs.
- Targeted Entry Programs designed to increase the number of full-time commercial family-size farmers.
- Legislative and regulatory initiatives to ensure that all farmworkers can achieve just conditions of employment, occupational safety, and good working conditions.
- Servicing of high value, specialty, and growth markets through diversification of the agricultural base by developing alternative crops and new uses for existing crops.

"The farm crisis is over. The 1985 Farm Bill is working." Pronouncements like these are often featured in news articles and reflect current conventional wisdom. Conventional wisdom, however, often has little basis in reality.

Farmers are going broke even faster now than before the 1985 Farm Bill was enacted. The American Bankers Association reports that over 235,000 farms have been lost in the last two years. This is an average of 2,500 farms per week—up from the 2,100 farms per week lost in 1985.

The main promise of the 1985 Farm Bill—that lowering U.S. farm prices would increase export earnings—has not been fulfilled. Although there has been a 2.5 percent increase in export volume, the value of our exports has declined from $31.2 billion in 1985 to $28.0 billion in 1987, a 10.3 percent loss.

The current rural crisis can be traced through a variety of turning points: the collapse of farm prices in the early 1980s, the dramatic increase in farm debt in the 1970s, and the dismantling of Depression-era commodity price programs during the 1950s. These events should all be seen as part of a recurring cycle of crisis. In the first phase of such a cycle, prices for commodities fall below the costs of producing them. In the second phase, farmers are forced to borrow in order to cover the losses caused by those low prices, hoping all the while to hold on until "times get better." In the third and final phase, farmers find themselves unable to repay those debts, and are thus forced to sell out and leave their land.

During the late 1800s and early 1900s, this cycle caused a number of rural depressions or "panics" in the United States. Seeing these economic crises as a threat to their survival, family farmers organized political movements to protect themselves and to lobby for changes in the government policies that were exacerbating the crisis. In North Dakota, for example, farmers formed the Nonpartisan League, which gained control of the state legislature in 1916. To break the bank monopoly, they established the nation's first and only state-owned bank. To protect themselves from exploitation by grain monopolies, they established a state-owned wheat mill. Farmers, working with labor, played a key role in winning progressive control over state legislatures in almost a dozen states.

The political efforts at the state level, however successful, did not affect the national crisis of falling prices and the huge surpluses created by these low prices. Without help from Washington, state governments could not control the price-fixing of multinational grain monopolies; nor could they help farmers balance supply with demand. By the 1920s farmers recognized the need to set prices and control production at the national level. The most important early U.S. federal farm legislation, the McNary-Haugen Bill, was passed by Congress three times in the 1920s, but vetoed twice by President Coolidge and once by President Hoover.

It took almost a decade to win the necessary federal legislation. Often referred to as the parity farm program, this legislation successfully placed a floor under prices, and also balanced supply with demand through effective surplus management.

The parity program had three central features: (1) It established the Commodity Credit Corporation (CCC), which made loans to farmers whenever prices offered by the food processors or grain corporations fell below the cost of production. This allowed farmers to hold their crops off the market, eventually forcing prices back up. Once prices returned to fair levels, farmers sold their crops and repaid the CCC with interest. By allowing farmers to control their marketing, the CCC loan program made it possible for them to receive a fair price from the marketplace without relying upon subsidies. (2) It regulated farm production in order to balance supply with demand, thereby preventing surpluses. Since government storage of surpluses was expensive, this feature was crucial to reducing government costs. (3) It created a national grain reserve to prevent consumer prices from skyrocketing in times of drought or other natural disasters. When prices rose above a predetermined level, grain was released from government reserves onto the market, driving prices back down to normal levels.

From 1933 to 1953 this parity legislation remained in effect and was extremely successful. Farmers received fair prices for their crops, production was controlled to prevent costly surpluses, and consumer prices remained low and stable. At the same time, the number of new farmers increased, soil and water conservation practices expanded dramatically, and overall farm debt declined. Even more important, this parity program was not a burden to the taxpayers. The CCC, by charging interest on its storable commodity loans, made nearly $13 million between 1933 and 1952.

Parity legislation conflicted with the economic interests of a number of powerful corporations and banks. For example, government intervention to stabilize grain prices hurt grain corporations and speculators who benefited from large fluctuations in the market. Effective supply management meant that fewer acres were planted, reducing the potential for increased sales of pesticides and fertilizers by chemical and oil companies. Finally, farmers with stable, secure incomes were less likely to borrow large amounts from insurance companies or banks.

As early as 1943, corporate, government, and academic policymakers began planning for postwar expansion of energy- and capital-intensive methods of production. Their political objective was to achieve greater control over agriculture by the industrial and financial sectors of the economy. To accomplish this, millions of farmers, especially poor southern blacks, would have to be forced out of agriculture. Not only would this mass relocation encourage the expansion of industrial-type agriculture, it would also free a huge labor force to fuel the industrial boom planned for the North.

The primary strategy developed by the corporate planners to force farmers off their land was to lower their commodity prices to levels below the cost of production. To enforce lower prices, however, they first had to repeal the parity legislation won by farmers in the 1930s.

In the early 1950s, the corporate planners launched an all-out political war against the parity legislation. They labeled supply management programs "socialism," an effective tactic popularized by Senator Joe McCarthy. University professors were drafted into a national propaganda effort to convince both farmers and the general public that fewer farmers were needed, and that the parity legislation was standing in the way of "modernizing" agriculture.

By 1954, the corporations had won. CCC loan levels were reduced and the Secretary of Agriculture was given discretionary power by Congress to lower farm prices to "market-clearing" levels in order to "get government out of agriculture." This marked the beginning of the most recent cycle of the farm crisis, culminating in the depression we are now facing.

Almost immediately, farm prices began to fall, and they have continued to decline in real terms (with the exception of two years in the early 1970s) since repeal of the parity legislation. As prices fell, many farmers were forced out. Farm population dropped by nearly 30 percent between 1950 and 1960, and another 26 percent between 1960 and 1970.

In response to political unrest, Congress passed a new farm program in the early 1970s. It was decided that the farmers who had managed to survive would be maintained on a direct federal income subsidy program. Under this program, Congress set a target price for farm products that was somewhat higher than the dramatically reduced CCC loan levels. If prices fell below this target level, participating farmers received a check from the government—a "deficiency payment"—to make up the difference.

Let's look at corn as an example. The current CCC loan rate is around $2 per bushel; the target price is about $3. This means that taxpayers are forced to make deficiency payments for the difference— roughly $1 per bushel on corn. But since it costs more than $3 for the average farmer to grow a bushel of corn, most farmers are still losing money on every bushel harvested.

The result of this deficiency payment system is that grain traders, corporate feedlots, and foreign buyers are allowed to buy grain at prices more than $1 below cost of production. We spend huge sums of taxpayers' money to compensate farmers for part of their losses caused by this subsidy to the grain trade; then we force farmers to borrow enormous sums of money to cover the rest of their losses.

This new farm program set the stage for the second phase of the farm crisis cycle—the infusion of massive amounts of credit to cover annual losses caused by the low prices set by federal policy. As long as inflation was pushing up the paper value of farmland, farmers could keep operating on borrowed money from lenders who believed land values would continue to rise indefinitely.

In the winter of 1978-79, over 40,000 protesting farmers came to Washington with a prophetic message. They warned Congress that agriculture based upon paper land values could not be sustained, and that farm prices needed to be raised to avert a rural collapse.

This message was ignored by most policymakers. As predicted, farm debt continued to rise, finally peaking at over $225 billion in the early 1980s—an increase of almost 1,000 percent over the $20 billion total farm debt before the introduction of the target price program in the early 1970s. Interest payments on this debt now exceed net farm income, amounting to almost 30 percent of production costs for many farmers. As more and more capital was drained from agriculture through interest payments, the conditions were created to set in motion the third and most devastating phase of the farm crisis cycle—the forced liquidation of family farms, with transfer of ownership into the hands of corporations, banks, speculators, and the federal government.

In 1981, land prices began to fall, forcing the most vulnerable farmers into bankruptcy or foreclosure. As their land and machinery went to auction, values were forced down for everyone else, causing a downward spiral of falling land values throughout the nation. Farmland prices have fallen over 50 percent, and almost 20 percent of the farming population has been displaced since 1981. Farm prices are lower in constant dollars than during the worst years of the Depression.

The main alternative to the 1985 Farm Bill was a proposal introduced by Senator Tom Harkin (D-IA) that was similar to the parity program of the 1930s and 1940s. Its central features included raising the price floor set by the CCC loan rate so that farm prices would at least equal the costs of production, and having farmers vote on the specifics of a supply management program that would control production in order to reduce surpluses. Subsidies would be totally eliminated, saving taxpayers between $12 and $14 billion per year.

One argument often made for keeping farm prices low and then supplementing farmers with tax dollars is that it keeps food prices down for low-income consumers. Some argue that the current farm program, which is paid for with federal taxes, is generally progressive, whereas the supply management proposal, by shifting costs to consumers, would be regressive, falling hardest on the poor. This argument ignores the fact that most heavily subsidized U.S. crops are not grown for American consumers but are shipped overseas to the Soviet Union, Europe, Japan, and the Middle East, which means that U.S. taxpayers are subsidizing foreign buyers.

Paying farmers a fair price would result in a one-time increase in food prices of only 3 to 5 percent. Since the supply management proposal also contains provisions for doubling the funds available for food assistance, the poor would not be hurt by this small increase in food prices. (It is worth noting that in 1985, the entire Congressional Black Caucus voted for supply management and higher prices.) Another argument for keeping farm prices below the cost of production is to keep U.S. crops competitive on the world market. This argument needs to be examined closely in order to understand the role that imports and exports play in the world economy.

A number of major farm commodity organizations contracted with the Food and Agriculture Policy Research Institute in 1985 to project grain export sales under different price levels. Based on their calculations, there would be only a slight drop in the volume of exports if prices were raised to a break-even level; because of increased prices, however, actual export earnings would be much greater.

For example, the Institute projected that corn set at current levels of around $2 per bushel would give the United States an export volume of 2.2 billion bushels, with earnings of roughly $4.4 billion. However, if the price of corn were set at $3.60 (slightly over the present cost of production), it would generate total sales of 1.6 billion bushels and the new value of those bushels would be over $5.76 billion—nearly 25 percent higher export income under higher prices.

Why does it work this way? For one thing, the demand for food is inelastic—price changes cause little change in demand one way or the other. In addition, the United States has a large portion of the world's grain storage facilities. Since most importers cannot store more than one month's supply of grain, they have to buy on a month-to-month basis; since most exporters, outside the United States and Canada, also lack major storage facilities, they are forced at harvest to sell all of their crops.

What this means is that the United States is, for up to six months of every year, practically the only country that can meet the month to month needs of the world's grain importers. The Soviet Union buys huge quantities of wheat, corn, and soybeans from the United States because it has nowhere else to turn.

Furthermore, because the United States dominates world food trade, domestic prices become world prices. The United States ships about 70 percent of the world's soybeans, 65 percent of the corn, and 30 percent of the wheat. (By comparison, the Middle East ships only 40 percent of the world's oil exports.) Because of this U.S. dominance, any U.S. price increase is met with a similar increase by all other supplying nations. Likewise, any attempt by the United States to lower its prices below those of other exporters results in equal drops in prices around the world. This causes great harm to the export earnings of all exporting countries. Since many grain exporters have enormous debts to U.S. banks, they must try to generate the same export earnings from their crops, no matter how low prices fall. The result is a downward price spiral in which all nations suffer.

The task of establishing a sound and democratic agricultural policy is not a hopeless effort. Other nations are supporting family farms and have developed policies to accomplish that objective. For example, we could follow the lead of the Netherlands, nearly fourteen times more densely populated than the United States, highly industrialized, with a comparable standard of living. Yet the percentage of its population still farming is nearly eight times that of the United States. Along with other countries in Europe, the Netherlands has consistently set farm prices at levels adequate to cover the cost of production in order to protect its farmers, its land, and its economy.

Whether the United States is to pursue a similar course will be determined by the new administration and congressional debates of the next few years. Unless we reestablish a fair world price for all commodities, as well as a system for managing production levels, we will be unable to prevent the increasing concentration of land ownership and control in the hands of a few.

Resources

Recommended Appointees for a New Administration

- Leland Beatty, Director, Farmer Assistance Programs, Department of Agriculture, Texas
- John Berry, Jr., President, Burley Tobacco Growers' Cooperative Association
- Carolyn Brickey, staff, Senate Agricultural Committee
- Dr. Frederick Buttel, Professor of Rural Sociology, Cornell University
- Cesar Chavez, President, United Farmworkers of America
- Dr. Kate Clancey, Professor of Human Nutrition, Syracuse University
- Cheryl Cook, staff, National Farmers' Union
- Isao Fujimoto, Professor of Rural Sociology, University of California, Davis
- John Kenneth Galbraith, economist, Harvard University
- Merle Hansen, President, North American Farm Alliance
- Lynn Hayes, attorney, Farmers Legal Action Group
- Elbert Harp, President, National Sorghum Growers Association
- Jim Hightower, Commissioner of Agriculture, Texas
- Anne Kanten, Assistant Commissioner of Agriculture, Minnesota
- Dan McGuire, President, Nebraska Wheat Board
- Jim Nichols, Commissioner of Agriculture, Minnesota
- David Ostendorf, Director, Prairiefire Rural Action
- Ralph Paige, Director, Federation of Southern Cooperatives
- Lorette Picciano-Hanson, staff, Interfaith Action for Economic Justice
- Harvey Joe Sanner, President, American Agriculture Movement
- Andrew Schmitz, Professor of Agriculture and Resource Economics, University of California, Berkeley

- John Stencel, President, Rocky Mountain Farmers Union
- Dixon Terry, National Co-chair, League of Rural Voters
- Doug Zabel, Director of Policy and Research, League of Rural Voters

Organizations

- League of Rural Voters, P. O. Box 8468, Minneapolis, MN 55408; (612) 827-6055. Washington Office: 100 Maryland Ave. NE, Suite 500, Washington, DC 20002; (202) 544-5757
- National Save the Family Farm Coalition, 80 F St. NW, Suite 714, Washington, DC 20001; (202) 737-2215
- Texas Department of Agriculture, P.O. Box 12847, Austin, TX 78711; (512) 463-7476
- Minnesota Department of Agriculture, 90 W. Plato Blvd., St. Paul, MN 55107; (612) 297-2200
- Prairefire Rural Action, 550 11th St., Des Moines, IA 50309; (515) 244-5671
- National Farmers' Union, 600 Maryland Ave. SW, Suite 200 West Wing, Washington, DC 20024; (202) 554-1600
- American Agriculture Movement, 100 Maryland Ave. NE, Suite 500, Washington, DC 20002; (202) 544-5750
- Federation of Southern Cooperatives, 100 Edgewood Ave. NE, Atlanta, GA 30303; (404) 524-6882
- Western Organization of Resource Councils, 412 Stapleton Bldg., Billings, MT 59101; (406) 252-9676

Further Reading

- U.S. Department of Agriculture, "History of Agricultural and Price-support Programs, 1933-1984," 1984.
- Food and Agricultural Policy Research Institute, University of Missouri, "An Evaluation of Proposed Program Designs for the 1985 Farm Bill," 1985.
- James Wessel, *Trading the Future,* Institute for Food and Development Policy, 1983.
- Prairiefire Rural Action, "The Continuing Crisis in Rural America: Fact vs. Fiction," 1987.
- Prairiefire Rural Action, "The Fate of the Land: Rural America's Continuing Crisis," 1988.
- Mark Ritchie and Kevin Ristau, "U.S. Farm Policy," *World Policy Journal,* Winter 1986-87, pp. 115-134.
- Mark Ritchie and Kevin Ristau, "Crisis By Design: A Brief Review Of U.S. Farm Policy," League of Rural Voters Education Project, 1987.

- Mark Ritchie, "The Loss of Our Family Farms: Inevitable Results or Conscious Policies?" Center for Rural Studies, 1979.

Mark Ritchie, a farm and trade policy analyst for the Minnesota Department of Agriculture, is also founder and co-chair of the League of Rural Voters. Half of his time in 1987 was spent in Europe working toward international trade agreements that would achieve higher world prices and an end to agricultural trade wars.

Kevin Ristau farmed in Southern Minnesota for ten years before being forced out of farming in 1984. In addition to writing articles on farm policy for various publications, he has written and produced a number of multi-media educational tools for the League of Rural Voters. Ristau is currently Field Director for the League and lives in Washington, DC.

Communications Policy: Putting Regulation in Its Place

Platform

Broadcasting

- Reinstate the Fairness Doctrine, which requires stations to air a wide range of views and reduces the power of advertisers, networks, or stations to manipulate public opinion.
- Institute a well-funded public broadcasting system.
- Reinstate station ownership and trafficking restraints.
- Protect the interests of children through requirements of child-oriented programming and limitations on advertising.

Cable

- Vigorously enforce existing anti-trust laws in the cable industry.
- Repeal the Cable Communications Policy Act of 1984 and allow fair municipal regulation of local cable systems.

Newspapers

- Rather than attempting to stop chain ownership and joint operating agreements among local newspapers, support government subsidies for innovative news services and magazines, practices widely adopted in Europe.

Telephone

- Establish a means-tested federal subsidy program to ensure universal access to a minimum level of telephone service.

- Develop policies allowing all citizens equitable access to new communications and information services.

———

The Reagan administration has based its communications policies on an ideological commitment to the superiority of free-market competition over government regulation. The problem is that Reagan-era officials at the Federal Communications Commission and in Congress have too often pursued deregulation as an end in itself, without considering all its effects.

The centerpiece of a new agenda is recognizing that competition is a means, not an end. Where competition alone does not achieve public interest goals, government regulation is legitimate and desirable. The new agenda should put forward a more balanced appraisal of competition, supporting government action where appropriate. Part of the new communications policy agenda involves undoing deregulatory initiatives of the FCC; part involves using regulation and subsidies to shape a communications system that actively fosters knowledgeable participation by the citizenry in a revitalized democracy.

The central goal of communications policy should be to make useful information as widely and inexpensively available as possible. What makes communications policy vitally important to all other policy goals is that good information is necessary for the public to act in its own best interests—for democracy to be genuine. The typical condition of the American public is political ignorance and apathy. This renders Americans susceptible to manipulation; it makes them more likely to treat politics as a spectator sport, to accept bad policy decisions with passive resignation or active enthusiasm. Information empowers the citizenry, and an informed public enhances the autonomy of government from narrow organized interests. When the average person can readily obtain useful information, it is much easier to mobilize the public pressure and involvement that usually enables positive change in politics.

In the past, communications policy functioned largely to defend the economic interests of broadcasters and telephone companies. In return for monopoly or oligopoly and the extraordinary and stable profits this allowed, the industry provided subsidies and accepted certain limitations on its economic and political power. For broadcast companies, this meant carrying low-profit or no-profit public affairs programming, agreeing to limits on the number of communications properties they could acquire, and refraining from using stations as exclusive pulpits for their own political views. For telephone companies, it meant using a part of the monopoly profits to keep the cost of local telephone service low and confining their investment activities to a narrow sphere (for example, staying out of the computer industry).

At least in theory, producers lose economic protection and consumers gain wider choices and lower prices under deregulation. For example, to keep cable television from siphoning off the audiences and ad revenues of broadcasters, the FCC long restricted cable to the least lucrative rural markets. Now the commission allows cable everywhere and consumers can receive dozens of television channels. In telephone, where government policy restricted competition with AT&T for long distance service, in recent years it has often encouraged MCI and its fellow giant-slayers; long distance calls are cheaper than ever. A lot of regulations remain on the books, especially in the telephone industry, but the clear trend has been toward lifting virtually all of them and relying only upon sluggishly enforced anti-trust law to keep markets competitive.

This is as far as many federal policymakers have analyzed the issue. They reason that once regulatory protection is gone, assuming markets remain competitive, competition will provide the best possible outcome. They believe that the outcomes of market competition comprise the public interest by definition. This notion fails to recognize that ideas are not just another consumer good. Even in conventional economic terms, their analysis neglects the external or unintended benefits and costs the "idea market" creates. A new agenda recognizes that the public interest in a healthy supply of diverse ideas is more compelling than the public interest in a diversity of laundry detergents and cheeseburgers. More important, diverse ideas are unlikely to emerge from economic competition alone—or from traditional forms of regulation.

Under deregulation, the public has lost policy benefits that were once part of the regulatory treaty with the communications industry. For example, the subsidies for public affairs programming and restrictions on the economic and political activities of broadcast corporations have eroded; the cost of local telephone service has escalated.

My recommendation is to reverse the anti-democratic effects of some deregulatory initiatives and enhance the democratizing promise of communications through government intervention. This requires challenging the reigning premise of the 1980s: that the superiority of market competition—and the need to protect rights identified by a dubious but widely held reading of the First Amendment—requires minimizing active government involvement in communications. Those who seek an improved communications system must defend the contrary proposition: that government can advance rather than threaten the core values of democracy. That doesn't mean reversing all deregulation, but rather melding regulation and competition in a way that is pragmatic and humane, making regulation work for the public interest where it can, but not clinging to outmoded and politically infeasible regulatory strategies.

Perhaps the most important and misguided act of the Reagan-era FCC was abolishing the Fairness Doctrine. Congress tried but failed in

1987 to reverse the decision via legislation. The doctrine requires that broadcasters devote time to controversial issues of public importance and offer reasonable opportunities for different views on these issues to be aired. In the past, the commission ignored the first part. The real effect was limiting the power of broadcasters to control the flow of ideas in their communities by airing only views they or their advertisers approved. The FCC believes the plentitude of television and radio stations now provides enormous diversity of views and prevents any one station from exerting significant power over the opinions of a well informed citizenry. The commission provided no relevant evidence in support of these propositions; no wonder, for empirical research finds little.

Freed of fairness restrictions, broadcasters can, for example, cover a referendum on nuclear power by relying exclusively on nuclear industry spokespersons. Since the doctrine covered commercials, stations can now accept pro-nuclear ads exclusively; they can refuse even to sell time to anti-nuclear forces, let alone provide free reply opportunities. As another example, broadcasters can now air one-sided editorials on the importance of capital punishment, placing an emotional issue on the agenda and putting a candidate who opposes the death penalty on the defensive while enhancing the chances of a pro-penalty candidate. (Under regulations still in force, they cannot attack one candidate by name without giving the opponent some opportunity to reply.) There may be some commercial restraints against such practices; viewers might tune out obviously crusading stations. But stations in many markets can probably do pretty much as they please; and in most, broadcasters can push one or two key issues or candidates around election time even if they can't get away with a year-round political slant. The Fairness Doctrine must be reinstated, with both its parts vigorously enforced. Failure to perform by its standards should be grounds for stations to lose their licenses.

The most important new initiative, potentially even more useful to democracy than restoring the Fairness Doctrine, is a large, well funded public broadcasting service. The examples of the Canadian Broadcasting Company and British Broadcasting Company show that a country can enjoy a public service that is relatively autonomous. Funding should come from general revenues—not, as often proposed, from a fee paid by commercial stations. The latter proposal dooms itself by guaranteeing a concentrated, highly motivated source of political opposition: the commercial broadcast industry. Obtaining revenues from taxpayers as a whole diffuses the resistance.

Although public broadcasting may be somewhat susceptible to government influence, so are the commercial networks, and a generously funded public service would be less vulnerable to the corporate influence now so pervasive at PBS than the three commercial networks. Given the cutbacks on unprofitable programming at the big three, a vital public broadcasting service is more important than ever, especially for news and children's programming.

The other major area of FCC deregulation was in ownership and sale requirements. The commission believed that raising the number of television stations any one corporation could own from seven to twelve would allow the formation of networks to compete with ABC, CBS, and NBC. In fact, all that has apparently happened is an increase of ownership concentration in the industry and a takeover of each of the big three networks by new owners more interested than previous proprietors in profit-maximization and less in public service. Freer trading in broadcast properties has also meant an escalation in station prices. Those who happened to acquire licenses at the right time have been enriched, with no compensation to the public, whose airwaves licensees have been using. Although it seems unlikely that existing station groups could be forced to divest of any holdings, the old rules should be reinstated and applied to all future station acquisitions.

Children's programming is the one area where the FCC's actions (and acquiescence to them by Congress) is least explicable. Local stations and the networks ought to face clear restrictions and disclosure rules on advertising during children's shows. Numbers of ads should be limited, commercials should be clearly labeled and differentiated from programs, and direct tie-ins between shows and products (which have led to programs that are essentially 30-minute toy advertisements) should be prohibited. Advertising probably can't be eliminated completely, despite the inherent distastefulness of manipulating young children for business gain, because commercials are the chief source of funds for good programs. Stations should also face requirements of a minimum number of hours of programming per week aimed at children.

Most Americans believe that market competition is as good a thing for newspapers as it is for other products. But research shows that as often as not newspaper competition has bad effects or no effects on the quality or independence of journalism. Many of our best papers are monopolies in their towns (the *St. Petersburg Times*, *Atlanta Journal and Constitution*, and *Providence Journal-Bulletin*, for example). Other fine papers are monopolies in practice; it's unlikely that the *Washington Post* would deteriorate if the theoretically competitive *Washington Times* died. Nor would the *Boston Globe*, *Los Angeles Times*, or *Miami Herald* score fewer journalistic coups if their weak competitors vanished. In any case, there's no politically feasible way to stop the trend toward newspaper chains and newspaper monopoly. Even if there were, restricting chains or joint operating agreements (where two separately owned papers share printing and other facilities) would have no clear payoff.

It would be far better to push a policy of subsidizing nonprofit print and video news services and magazines. Some of these outlets might be affiliated with political parties, which could revive the party as an instrument of mass political identification and involvement; others would be independent. Such subsidies are commonplace in European democracies, most of which enjoy vigorous parties and suffer no shortage of diverse political debate. While government subsidies for media may seem superficially to clash with First Amendment values, they actually serve the goals of diversity and enlightenment.

As in other areas of the economy, an enormous amount of vertical and horizontal integration has occurred in cable television without any intervention by anti-trust authorities. Unlike in the newspaper industry, this consolidation may pose a clear and practically irreversible threat to the public interest. The largest cable companies routinely own program services like Cable News Network or Nickolodeon, often in partnership with one another or with broadcast companies. As a result, for example, Time, Inc. owns American Television and Communications (ATC), one of the largest operators of cable systems, and Home Box Office (HBO) and Cinemax. Subscribers to systems owned by ATC sometimes have trouble obtaining movie services that compete with HBO and Cinemax. The largest companies also own an increasing share of all cable systems. In some cases bigness may not be bad; in others it probably is. Under the recent regime, bigness has simply been irrelevant to policymakers, and it shouldn't be. The policy should be to enforce the anti-trust laws already on the books in ways that prevent abuse of economic power.

The story of what has happened to local regulation of cable television systems illustrates how the courts and Congress, not just the FCC, have contributed to unfortunate communications policies during the 1980s. Congress passed the Cable Communications Policy Act of 1984, stripping most of the power local governments had to regulate cable systems. Courts have reinforced this law by striking down some local government regulations as infringements on the First Amendment. These policies have made cable virtually an unregulated monopoly in most communities. While cable does face competition from "free" broadcast television and from videocassette rental, the unusually high rate increases and strong performance of cable corporations' stocks since deregulation suggest that cable systems are now a secure source of high profits. It is true that some municipalities abused their regulatory powers and demanded unreasonable concessions from cable companies (e.g., that they provide free communication networks for government agencies). These wound up saddling companies—and consumers—with unnecessary costs.

The ideal policy would be for Congress to restore local municipal powers, with some limitations to prevent flagrant overregulation. However, it is impossible to predict or control how the courts will apply the First Amendment, and consumers may have to live with paying rates that are too high. In the absence of a policy that all Americans should have access to newer communications technologies, poor persons may continue without cable service altogether. While most cable fare is hardly worth fighting for, cable does offer news, health, arts, and children's services with real merit.

The most direct effect on consumers of the AT&T breakup and other changes in telephone policy has been an increase in local service costs and a decrease in long distance rates. Most policymakers believe long distance rates had been artificially high and subsidized local rates. The pertinent point is that there is little political hope of reversing the trend toward higher local rates. A new agenda must establish telephone service as a necessity and the right to a reasonable level of service as worthy of public support. The policy should be a means-tested federal guarantee of telephone service to all Americans who want it.

Such a federal "lifeline" policy could have an important political side-effect. Once everyone can obtain service, the industry will almost certainly redouble its efforts to deregulate long distance and even local rates. In both of these cases, public interest groups ought not to say no automatically, which they sometimes have in the past. They should demand that all relevant information and policy goals be weighed before deregulation is promulgated. They ought to remember that the spread of innovative computer and communication technologies encouraged by deregulation can enhance productivity, and new communication services can potentially democratize information by making specialized or detailed data more widely available to nonexperts, to ordinary people at home.

It is not clear how poor people will afford access to the new technologies. Eventually, the goal should be not merely ensuring universal access to plain old telephone calling, but making advanced communication and information services readily available. There are, of course, competing priorities. Important as information is, food, jobs, housing, and education might come ahead of communications. But mobilizing support for new government initiatives in employment, schooling, and the rest will require an informed public, and that requires an improved communications system. A progressive communications policy deserves a high place in the priorities of a new administration.

Resources

Recommended Appointees for a New Administration

- Douglas Bennet, President of National Public Radio. Bennet's ability to keep NPR afloat and even vital after its near bankruptcy testifies to a skill and commitment that would serve the public well in a policy position.

- Kathy Bonk, long associated with the communications efforts of the National Organization for Women. Bonk is a sophisticated Washington insider as well as an expert on policy.

- Barry Cole, a former consultant to the FCC and co-author of a standard book on broadcast regulation. Cole now teaches law and policy at Columbia and the University of Pennsylvania and is also the author of a major study of telephone regulation.

- Benjamin Compaine, previously Executive Director of the Harvard Program on Information Resources Policy and now an entrepreneur in the communications and information industries. Compaine is an expert on all communications media who sees their interrelationships clearly. His most recent writing has been on the implications of new technologies for literacy.

- Charles Firestone, former professor at UCLA and a communications law specialist with a public interest orientation.

- Oscar Gandy, Professor of Communications at Howard University, an expert on the policy issues and the larger concerns of democratic communications.

- Henry Geller, former chief counsel to the FCC and head of the National Telecommunications and Information Administration under Carter. Widely considered the most knowledgeable communications law and policy expert, Geller is legendary for his sensitive grasp of the issues and ability to suggest innovative solutions. The manifest choice for FCC chairman in a Democratic administration.

- Louise McCarren, former Chair of the Vermont Public Service Commission, respected throughout the field for her intelligent advocacy of deregulation that serves consumer interests.

- Eli Noam, a professor of business and law at Columbia, now on leave at the New York State Public Service Commission. Noam is a leading academic expert on cable television and telephone economics.

- Robert Pepper, widely respected by all sides in the policy arena, is currently at the FCC's Office of Plans and Policy. He has written on broadcast news, cable, and telephone regulation.

- Michael Rice, Director of the Aspen Institute's communications program. Rice has been the motivating force behind important, forward-looking studies of television policy and telephone regulation. As a sometime producer of public broadcasting programs, he would bring a unique perspective to a policymaking position.

- Lee Selwyn, president of the consulting firm Economics and Technology, Inc. Selwyn applies sophisticated economic reasoning to issues of telephone regulation and often challenges conventional wisdom.

Organizations

The public interest movement in communications policy has lost some of its energy and clout (i.e., funding). Ralph Nader remains the most visible and effective advocate. Three active groups are:

- Media Access Project, 1609 Connecticut Ave. NW, Washington, DC 20009; (202) 232-4300
- Consumer Federation of America, 1424 16th St. NW, Suite 604, Washington, DC 20036; (202) 387-6121
- Office of Communication, United Church of Christ, Media Reform Unit, 3136 17th St. NW, Washington, DC 20010; (202) 331-4265

Further Reading

- Stanley Besen *et al.*, *Misregulating Television*, University of Chicago Press, 1985.
- Gerald Brock, *The Telecommunications Industry: The Dynamics of Market Structure*, Harvard University Press, 1981.
- Barry Cole and Mal Oettinger, *Reluctant Regulators: The FCC and the Broadcast Audience*, Addison-Wesley, 1978.
- Benjamin Compaine *et al.*, *Who Owns the Media?*, Knowledge Industries Publications, 1982.
- Robert M. Entman, *Democracy Without Citizens: The Dilemma of American Journalism*, Oxford University Press, forthcoming.
- Robert Horwitz, *The Irony of Regulatory Reform: The Deregulation of American Telecommunications*, Oxford University Press, 1988.

Robert M. Entman is Assistant Professor of Public Policy Studies and Political Science at Duke University and Associate Director of its Center for Communications and Journalism. His book, *Democracy Without Citizens: The Dilemma of American Journalism*, will be published in 1989 by Oxford University Press.

Provide for the Common Defense...

Richard Barnet

Cobwebs and Catchwords:
Rethinking National Security

Platform

• The National Security Council should be replaced by a council in the White House which is charged with weighing military and non-military threats to the security of Americans. The highest officials concerned with education, the environment, and industrial policy should be members as well as the secretaries of Treasury, State, and Defense. The purpose of the new body is to develop a long-range national planning process which integrates economic, social, environmental, and military considerations and assists the president in making budget choices for a real security strategy.

Because he is rethinking Soviet global strategy and radically shifting tactics, Mikhail Gorbachev is challenging the United States to re-examine its own objectives and strategy. The new openings in international politics being created by his bold approach to Soviet security problems—a simultaneous effort to repair relations with the United States, Europe, China, Japan, and the Muslim nations of the third world—offer new opportunities and pose new risks. If the United States continues to fight the Cold War, it is likely to find itself outflanked and isolated. More important, it will miss a historic chance to end the insanity of the arms race and to start demilitarizing international relations.

There is a second reason why developing a new grand design for foreign policy is more critical than at any time in the last forty years. After fifteen years of slow and erratic economic growth, the domestic costs of the Cold War have become intolerable. For many years the productive system, the educational system, and the physical environment on which all else depends have been denied needed investment of capital, imagination, and presidential attention on the grounds that the endless acquisition of weapons and the maintenance of a global military establishment had a prior claim. The irony is that unexamined national security policies, designed to protect the people of the United States from foreign coercion and interference, have had the unintended effect of reducing the quality of life at home, constricting choices about how to organize and develop the country, and giving foreign citizens increasing control over the United States.

The deficits incurred in large measure in the pursuit of national security pose great risks to U.S. security, but the overwhelming response so far has been to limit expenditures for schools, assistance to poor women and children, environmental protection, preventive health measures, libraries, even police and fire protection, on the theory that in a time of hard choices, social spending has less to do with keeping the United States "strong" than military expenditures.

Over the past forty years, the guardians of the republic have developed a special language to talk about the national interest—words like "threat," "commitment," and "deterrence." Such words gained currency in the early postwar era when the root assumptions of Cold War strategy were first embraced. Each word artfully conceals a whole world view which people unconsciously adopt whenever they use them. Other words, such as "friend," "enemy," or even "nation," though part of the foreign affairs vocabulary since the beginning of the republic, no longer have the meanings they had in the prenuclear world. Thus the grammar of national security often serves to obscure what we are protecting and what we are protecting it against. By talking about national security as primarily a matter of foreign policy and the economy as primarily a matter of domestic policy, the side-effects of defense strategies are hidden and debate about how to balance foreign obligations and domestic needs is avoided.

Connections between national security strategy and mounting insecurity are becoming too clear to ignore. The U.S economy is increasingly tied to a world economy over which the United States exercises less and less control. We are dependent on foreign investors to finance our budget deficit (which we incur in large measure because of military expenditures), and to lure their money we raise interest rates. To sell otherwise non-competitive goods, we devalue the dollar, but this causes the standard of living of millions of Americans to decline. With the end of America's competitive edge in the world economy, there has been a decline in real wages for thousands of workers who have exchanged high-paying industrial jobs for low-paid jobs in the service sector. Many families are dropping out of the middle class altogether as dreams of homeownership, or even affordable housing, recede. Having incurred huge obligations payable in dollars, much of it for defense, and having failed to offer attractive enough goods and services for the holders of dollars, the United States finds that its IOU's are being redeemed for pieces of the nation itself. Some of our richest farmland, choice city blocks in metropolitan areas, and major U.S. corporations are passing into foreign hands.

The conventional response is to convene another "blue ribbon" gathering of Cold War veterans to modernize the official vocabulary. Not long ago a distinguished Pentagon panel called the Commission on Integrated Long-Term Strategy (which included Henry Kissinger, Zbigniew Brzezinski, and William Clark, all former National Security Advisers) offered the mystifying term "discriminate deterrence" as the conceptual breakthrough to extricate the United States from its security dilemmas. (The term is a tasteful way of describing a strategy based upon threatening to drop nuclear weapons on Asians, Africans, and Latin Americans unlucky enough to live in embattled, strategic places.) This new addition to national security lingo will not solve the problem which politicians and strategists keep struggling to avoid: How can the United States develop a deeper, broader, and more imaginative understanding of what our core interests actually are?

The real choices facing the United States in 1988 have almost nothing to do with the arcane matters which provide employment for Cold War strategists. Far more basic questions of national identity and purpose are at issue: What is the mission of the United States at the dawn of the 21st century? To fight communism? To be the architect and guarantor of a new global order? To build an island of prosperity and freedom in a world of accelerating misery? To force changes in the Soviet Union? The answers to such questions do not depend upon knowledge of classified facts but upon wisdom and judgment. How the questions are answered will set the course for the United States in the 21st century, now just twelve years away. Thinking about fundamental choices and goals is never easy, but we make it much harder than it needs to be because the words we habitually use to talk about national security keep getting in the way.

Since the National Security Act of 1947, the term "national security" has become a talisman. In the name of national security, telephones are tapped, mail is opened, countries are invaded, U.S. citizens are put under surveillance, Congress is deceived, the Secretary of State, perhaps even the president, is deceived, and in the Nixon era, high crimes and misdemeanors were committed. But in no statute is there a definition of national security. In forty years, no politician has told us what is meant by those magic words. It has been considered enough to say that the United States has enemies, and that the way to deal with enemies is to acquire and from time to time use armed force against them. The only even quasi-official definition of national security I have found is in a dictionary prepared for the Joint Chiefs of Staff:

> a. a military or defense advantage over any foreign nation or group of nations, or b. a favorable foreign relations position, or c. a defense posture capable of successfully resisting hostile or destructive action from within or without, overt or covert.

This obscure government document merely reflects the conventional understanding in the corridors of power. Security is treated as a scarce commodity. If I have more of it, you must by definition have less of it. The inevitable result is that each player seeks more security by making his potential adversaries more insecure. This is obviously a recipe for permanent war in one form or another. At times this truism is recognized. Sometimes governments talk about "interdependence" and "common security." But the institutions of government and official rhetoric normally operate as if the pursuit of security were a contest.

In the late 1980s, we have lost our sense of what "national security" is because we are confused by the meaning of "nation." Nationalism is still the strongest political ideology in the world, but what a "nation" actually is today differs dramatically from what it was in 1789 when George Washington first took the oath of office, or even what it was in 1948. Any sensible national strategy must begin with some conception of the national interest, whether explicit or not, which is based on a series of assumptions about what a "nation" is, what it can do, and what costs it may safely incur. Normally these assumptions are unstated and undebated.

Usually, "national security" suggests that a nation is a distinct entity which can act on the outside world without inevitably feeling the boomerang effects. One of the consequences of seeing foreign policy as a succession of confrontations with winners and losers is that the defeats are ignored and the victories—such as the overthrow of the Shah in 1953, the invasion of Grenada, the bombing of Libya—go unexamined. The price tag is neither calculated nor disclosed. Nor is the transient nature of the triumph noted. The price tag of the war prevention system we call "deterrence" has caused some of our inner cities to look as if the war had already happened. That prime objective of modern warfare, the demoralization of the civilian population, has been accomplished in a substantial number of farming communities and city neighborhoods throughout the nation by our own efforts without outside assistance. They are the consequences of choices U.S. leaders have made about scarce resources. This usually involves a choice about what to ignore and whom to abandon.

The word "nation" is misleading in another respect. It implies that each constituent part of the whole owes its primary loyalty either to the government in Washington or to the American people, who, under the Constitution, are sovereign. But in a commonwealth as divided as the United States has been from the start, the system never worked quite this way; national loyalty is much more complex. We have assumed, for example, that what is good for the largest U.S. corporations and banks is good for the people, on the theory that their wealth redounds to the strength of the nation. But, increasingly, decisions on the part of banks to make quick profits by foolish loans to third world nations have helped to create a world debt problem which poses a threat to the U.S. economy. U.S. corporations producing goods in

Taiwan or Korea are now an important part of the "foreign competition" which has forced a disastrous trade deficit upon the United States. The internationalization of the U.S. economy is not a scandal but a fact of life, a more or less inevitable result of the growth of capitalism and the world economy. The scandal is that neither laws nor official rhetoric recognize the transformation that has occurred, and the nation grows weaker under the illusion that national boundaries protect us. A rethinking of national security policy requires looking at the domestic consequences of alternative military and economic policies and understanding the connections better, but the federal government has no effective way to do this because the arbitrary separation of foreign and domestic policy is scrupulously maintained.

All this suggests that "defense" is a much more complex process than the word implies. The seductive image the word throws up before our mind's eye is a piece of real estate with a fence around it and perhaps a snarling dog or two; nations can be guarded either by putting up a shield (SDI) or more usually by arranging to fight potential intruders on their turf and not ours. But borders are hopelessly permeable. They cannot stop nuclear missiles, drugs, or illegal aliens. As the Iran-*contra* affair showed, secrets cannot be kept in or embarrassing information from abroad kept out.

The more apt analogy is the human body defending itself against disease. The primary strength of a nation comes from within. Its essence is spirit, not hardware. Like people, nations are inescapably vulnerable. How well they ward off outside attack depends upon their inner health as much as on their ability to control the surrounding environment. Sensible preventive health measures call for keeping the immune system strong as well as reducing the risks of contamination. Like the human organism, every defensive response has side-effects. Yet we have no institutions within the government to evaluate or even note the political, economic, and social side effects of the measures we take for national defense.

"Power" is another word we use too easily in thinking about security. A major function of the military is to back up diplomatic efforts to achieve U.S. interests; armed might is considered a useful instrument for convincing other nations that our solutions to international problems ought to be taken seriously.

The unthinking equation of military hardware with national power ignores the reality of the last forty years. There appears to be a steadily diminishing relationship between the ability to destroy and the ability to achieve political objectives, at least for great powers with much to lose. There have been many occasions and many provocations for the use of military force; there have been many enemies proclaimed and many acts of aggression committed: the Berlin blockade, Soviet military intervention in Hungary, Czechoslovakia, and Afghanistan, terrorist attacks against U.S. citizens, etc. But the actual commitment of U.S. military forces to battle has rarely been successful.

The last clear-cut victory was General Douglas MacArthur's triumphant landing at Inchon, a victory which was undone a few months later by the Chinese entry into the war. (That the bungled operation in Grenada, an island of 100,000 people with a barely functioning government and a token army, should have been an occasion for Americans to "stand tall" suggests how victory-starved we have become.) Vietnam, the disastrous rescue mission to Iran, and the failure of "low-intensity" wars to achieve their stated objective in El Salvador and Nicaragua suggest that the U.S. security problem may be rooted in some basic misconceptions about the proper missions of the armed forces in today's world. As the ability to destroy has increased, so have the political constraints.

The reason for military failures is not lack of bravery or skill, low pay, or wrong weapons but stubborn realities which greatly inhibit the successful use of force by great powers. Most of the threats which the armed forces have been asked to address with weapons—either by shooting them or supplying them to others—have been essentially political in nature, and they have not responded well to either approach. The tens of thousands of lives sacrificed trying to subdue North Vietnam and the twenty billion dollars' worth of sophisticated military hardware supplied to the Shah of Iran to keep a U.S. peace in the Persian Gulf are prime examples of assigning the military impossible tasks. (This reality does not work against the United States alone. Asking the Soviet military to pacify Afghanistan was an equally quixotic assignment which has also ended in failure.) It has become clear since the Vietnam war that the U.S. people will not support large scale military adventures abroad unless an overwhelming case can be made that national security requires it. The Reagan administration called this allergic reaction to foreign military intervention "the Vietnam syndrome." It reflects not pathology but intuitive realism about the limits of military power in the nuclear age. It is a real constraint on the use of military power as long as the United States remains a democracy.

The only deployments of military force in recent years which could be said to generate political power were situations where force was introduced as a bargaining chip in a political negotiation. The Reagan administration argues that deployment of the intermediate range missiles in Europe led to the INF agreement, and that the $630,000,000 in covert military aid to the Afghan resistance last year and the $150,000,000 in aid to the *contras* in Nicaragua were the decisive factors in bringing about the prospect of a Soviet pullout from Afghanistan and a liberalization of the Sandinista regime in Nicaragua. Given all the factors involved, it cannot be demonstrated one way or the other whether the U.S. contribution to the harassment of the governments of Nicaragua and Afghanistan made a crucial difference. But let us assume it is true. An important conclusion follows: for a great power, the only effective military option in a world of nuclear weapons is a relatively limited show or use of force on someone else's territory, preferably with young men from some other country doing the fighting and dying. The Soviet experience in Afghanistan, like the U.S. experience in Vietnam, shows how constrained superpowers are in fighting their own wars, not only by domestic opinion but by the risks of escalation and the pressures of other nations. In each of these cases, the superpower abandoned its original war aims despite having an abundance of hardware and troops to throw into the war.

The recent report of the Commission on Integrated Long-term Strategy, convened by the Department of Defense, recognizes this point and recommends more emphasis on "low-intensity" warfare in the third world. "Low-intensity" war is a euphemism for subsidizing the *contras*, the *Mujahideen* of Afghanistan, or the army of El Salvador to fight what are perceived to be U.S. battles in strategic places. But surely a strategy that bases the safety of the richest nation in the world on the sacrifices of desperately poor people in distant lands is a cynical and corrupting form of dependence unworthy of that nation.

Measured by the ability to produce beneficial changes in the international environment, the power of the United States has declined rather precipitously in the last decade, in part because of changed circumstances, in part because of a failure of nerve. The Reagan administration, despite its big military buildup, has been unable to bring weight to bear on the two prolonged wars of the Middle East, that between Iran and Iraq and the continuing struggle among Israel, the Palestinians, and the Arab states. One index of this loss of power is that national security managers have become so conflicted in their policy goals—at once wishing to bring peace but also to punish other nations deemed to be "enemies"—that they are unable to use U.S. power to help settle dangerous conflicts. Indeed, the United States has at times aided both sides in the Iran-Iraq war, apparently in the short-sighted belief that the war somehow serves U.S. interests to keep two "enemies" busy.

What sort of power is the United States seeking? Power to do what? What is the connection between the exercise of power abroad and the creation of space for development at home? Until we begin to have a national discussion about these questions, the word "power" will remain an empty vessel. Meanwhile, at a time when international agreements and institutions for managing the world economy are urgently needed, the United States is playing a passive role. Yet, as the world's largest debtor nation, the United States has the most to gain from reforms to stabilize monetary arrangements and establish a new set of agreements and institutions regulating world trade.

Or take the word "friends." The cooptation of this word into the vocabulary of national security is particularly offensive. Free citizens choose their friends. If a government insists upon choosing friends for us, it has some obligation to exercise better taste. Over the years "friends" like Anastasio Somoza, Ferdinand Marcos, Ngo Dinh Diem, and the Shah of Iran have trooped to Washington to be toasted on behalf of the American people by a succession of presidents. If the government wishes to make the case for giving these and other dictators U.S. money and guns, it should make that case on grounds of self-interest. But because this case often cannot be made, ideology and sentimentality take over. A murderous, vulnerable leader of some third world country is proclaimed a "friend" either because he rents us bases, pursues communists in his country where they exist, calls his enemies communist when they are not, or votes "correctly" in the United Nations. Once "friend" status has been extended, it cannot be easily withdrawn. It is a matter of "honor" to stand by political leaders who have been declared friends, except when "national security" dictates that they be eliminated, as in the case of the former friend Ngo Dinh Diem, the president of South Vietnam, whose overthrow was engineered after a wink from the U.S. ambassador.

The friendship argument has been used to goad members of Congress into supporting the *contras* after all arguments based on *realpolitik* collapsed. The heavy artillery version of the argument is expressed in terms of "commitments." As the Iran-*contra* episode shows, it matters a good deal who makes "commitments" on behalf of the United States. Some "commitments" are made by bureaucrats without legitimate authority, like the Poindexter-North crowd. Other "commitments" were made properly but in radically different times and should be re-examined. The leaders of the military establishment are right to say that it is difficult, even impossible, to cut the military budget without cutting our "commitments."

The first step is to bring the "commitments" into the light of day. Most U.S. taxpayers have not even heard of many of them. Few know why they were made in the first place, and even fewer know what difference thirty to forty years may have made with respect to these obligations. If changes in the basic commitments which the nation has made to its own citizens—Social Security, veteran's benefits, etc.—have to be reconsidered because of budgetary constraints, surely decades-old commitments to foreign leaders can also be re-examined. No duly authorized commitment should be abandoned lightly. Many are based not on treaty obligations, but on executive decisions, on statutory provisions slipped into laws enacted years ago with little or no debate, and sometimes just on bureaucratic momentum. For example, the Senate has not considered the foreign-policy implications of the military installations constructed in recent years in Oman, Kenya, and Somalia. The case for each must be made anew in the light of current realities. A comprehensive review would also consider alternative commitments the United States should now be making.

"Enemies" is another troubling word. It is a term of war but now is used to describe nations with whom the United States maintains diplomatic relations while simultaneously seeking the overthrow of their governments—Nicaragua, for example. The more diplomatic and frequently used word is "adversary," the standard State Department word to describe the Soviet Union. "Adversary" suggests conflicting interests and a willingness to pursue those interests to the damage of the United States. That is a fair description of the Soviet government. The problem is that the description fits even better other governments which are our allies. The policies Japan pursues for its own prosperity now hurt the United States more directly and more deeply than the revolutionary ambitions of the Soviet Union. Is Japan an adversary? Is West Germany? Should the United States once again treat these allies as "enemies?" Obviously not. The concept of adversary needs to be rethought.

It sometimes appears that the purpose of United States policy toward the Soviet Union is to force the leaders in the Kremlin to give up a dream which we say they have but which they deny having, i.e., world domination. But dreams are evanescent and quite beyond the reach of even the most advanced reconnaissance satellites. Nothing is easier for an "evil empire" than to publicly disown aggressive dreams. There is no reason for us to feel one whit safer when it does so. Arming against a bad dream we impute to the Soviet Union is a hopeless exercise and a recipe for bankruptcy. The Soviet Union is an adversary not because of its dreams but because of its military "capabilities" and because of specific behavior which has caused alarm, such as the interventions in Czechoslovkia and Hungary and the invasion of Afghanistan. It is within the power of the United States to modify both Soviet military potential and political behavior, but only by modifying its own and by building a new relationship with the Soviet Union based on considerable mutual self-interest.

The United States has forgotten the aims it embraced when the Cold War began. As the Soviet Union moves toward strengthening its own society by making it less arbitrary and brutal, some U.S. leaders cannot decide whether this is good news or bad. George Washington warned against "passionate attachments" which let habit and emotion rather than reason decide who is friend and who is foe. If ever there was a time for a consensus on what the Cold War is about—whether it is a struggle to contain military aggression, defeat a "threatening" ideology, or humble what used to be the only contender for global power—it is now. Examining old habits of mind and passionate attachments to "friends" and "enemies" would enable the United States to bring commitments and resources into balance. Rethinking the purposes for which power is sought can help reverse our decline in influence and credibility.

This is a nation where winning is important. Since most other nations also look upon international politics as a game, it is perhaps utopian to think that the United States could come to consider our fragile planet in another way. Yet the U.S. community could not have been built had there not also been a real capacity for cooperation. Teamwork made survival on the frontier possible in the 19th century and the development of mass production in the 20th. Surely, it is not too much to hope that U.S. citizens will come to see that the national security game has changed.

A new and better definition of national security would be something along these lines: "a desired state of physical safety, economic development, and social stability within which there is space for individuals to participate in building a community free of both foreign coercion and manipulation by government." (Citizens are not secure if the strategy to keep foreign enemies at bay causes the government to impugn the patriotism of politically active citizens and to treat them as enemies to be watched.) A sensible definition of national security which could survive the mumbo jumbo of electoral politics will emerge, if at all, only through the processes of democratic debate. The United States is still immensely strong and its possibilities enormous. The society and economy are maturing. The path to decline is not inevitable. But choices must be made, and they should be made on the basis of judgments about what has worked and what has not to advance U.S. interests.

What is needed are leaders who will help write new rules and then live by them in cooperation with other nations. We can begin the process of rethinking national security by taking advice from Confucius. The beginning of wisdom, he said, is to call things by their right name.

Resources

Recommended Appointees for a New Administration

- James Chace, former managing editor of *Foreign Affairs*, co-author of *America Invulnerable*
- George McGovern, Fellow at the Institute for Policy Studies, former member of the Senate Foreign Relations Committee, presidential candidate, 1972
- Peter Weiss, Vice President of Center for Constitutional Rights
- Richard Ullman, professor of government, Princeton University
- Patt Derian, former Assistant Secretary of State in the Carter administration

Organizations

- Committee on National Security, 1601 Connecticut Ave. NW, Washington, DC 20009; (202) 745-2450
- National Security Archive, 1755 Massachusetts Ave. NW, Washington, DC; (202) 797-0882
- SANE/FREEZE, 711 G St. SE, Washington, DC 20003; (202) 546-7100

Further Reading

- Andrew Cockburn, *The Threat: Inside the Soviet Military Machine*, Random House, 1983.
- David Holloway, *The Soviet Union and the Arms Race*, Yale University Press, 1983.
- Jonathan Kozol, *Rachel and Her Children*, Crown Publishers, Inc., 1988.

Richard Barnet is a founder and Senior Fellow at the Institute for Policy Studies. He has taught at Yale and the University of Mexico, and during the Kennedy administration was an advisor in the State Department. He is the author of, among other books, *The Alliance, The Lean Years: Politics in the Age of Scarcity, Global Reach: The Power of Multinational Corporations*, (co-authored with Ronald E. Muller), and *The Giants: Russia and America.*

Saul Landau

A Non-Interventionist Policy
for the 1990s

Platform

Central America and the Caribbean

- Follow the letter and the spirit of the Central American Peace Plan, signed in August 1987. It is supported by almost every nation in the world, the UN, and the OAS.

- The United States must end its support of the *contras*, withdraw U.S. troops from the region, and dismantle the recently built bases in Honduras.

- The United States must cease its covert operations and rely instead on diplomacy and multilateral, not bilateral, solutions to Central American as well as Caribbean problems.

- Restore relations with Cuba, drop the economic embargoes against that island and Nicaragua. Trade should not be used as a political faucet, to be turned on and off depending on the actions of a particular government.

Asia

- End the Cold War with Vietnam, Laos, and Cambodia, and resolve through diplomacy the issues that stand in the way of normal relations.

- Demilitarize the border between North and South Korea and stop exacerbating the tensions that constantly threaten war between the two Koreas.

- Remove U.S. military bases from the Philippines, the outposts and logistical props of U.S. intervention from the Middle East to the Pacific Basin.

275

Africa

- Recognize that Namibia will be independent, that majority rule will prevail in South Africa, and end the CIA war against Angola. Support the UN-proposed solution of Namibian independence and the withdrawal of Cuban troops from Angola and South African troops from Namibia.

Middle East

- Work for an end to the senseless and dangerous Iran-Iraq war via a multilateral policy in the Persian Gulf, not a unilateral one that implies that the United States alone is responsible for the safety of oil transport.

- Support UN-sponsored peace talks on Afghanistan and stop the CIA support (hundreds of millions of dollars a year) of Afghan rebels whose principles are anathema to most Americans. The United States should support multilateral efforts to help prevent the "Lebanonization" of Afghanistan.

- Slash U.S. weapons sales to the Middle East and support an international peace conference to work toward a resolution of the Israeli-Palestinian conflict.

Aid

- Replace the bulk of U.S. aid which is military in nature with developmental aid. U.S. aid should assist countries with coherent development plans—ones that are both ecologically sound and contain provisions for social justice—not be treated as an exchange for concessions to U.S. entrepreneurs, pro-U.S. votes in international organizations, or costly and abrasive U.S. military bases. "Security-related" assistance, which grew to two-thirds of total U.S. aid from 1982-1987, should be eliminated.

- Aid policies should conform to UN guidelines. Bilateral aid should be replaced by multilateral assistance, with high priority given to agencies like the International Fund for Agricultural Development that try to reach the poor majorities with their programs.

The UN and Other Multilateral Agencies

- The United States must reaffirm its support for the institutions of international democracy. The United Nations and its various affiliates can emerge in a post-Cold War climate to achieve their mandate: ensuring peace and the rule of law, the basic requirements for security and development.

We have wasted our substance for thirty years and more fighting some phantom Russian. We've neglected America in favor of Russia. It's time we thought about America. I say get our own house in order. To thine own self be true.

> *I. I. Rabi, writing in the* New York Times, November 18, 1985
> Rabi won the Nobel Prize in Physics in 1944 and
> was a key figure in making the first atomic bomb.

If we examine our foreign policy over the past decades, we see a series of debilitating wars, in Korea, "in the wrong place, at the wrong time, against the wrong enemy," and in Vietnam, "a tragedy" that left its "syndrome" infecting the body politic. There was the "Bay of Pigs fiasco," a "missile crisis," a terrifying arms race, and regional crises abounding. In the mid-1970s, Senate hearings revealed that the CIA had been illegally meddling in other nations' affairs, sponsoring coups, assassinations, surreptitious drug-testing, and conducting illicit surveillance against U.S. citizens. Under President Carter there was "humiliation": despite our immense arsenal of nuclear weapons, we were powerless when the Iranians took and held the U.S. Embassy staff hostage in 1980. Most recently, the Iran-*contra* affair has once again enshrined illegality as national policy, embarrassed our government internationally, and called into question the basis for policymaking.

The foundations for the policies of the 1980s were established in the late 1940s on the premise that the Soviet Union and international communism threatened freedom everywhere and that Soviet expansionism had to be contained indefinitely. The Soviet Union, licking its wounds after losing an estimated 20 to 30 million people in World War II, with as many more wounded, facing the rubble of 200 cities destroyed, massive hunger, and social chaos, could hardly have been in a position to launch an invasion of Western Europe, much less threaten the United States, which possessed a monopoly on nuclear weapons until 1949. Yet, beginning with the National Security Act of 1947, U.S. leaders created an apparatus that became a kind of state above a state in order to combat the Soviet threat to Western Europe and the rest of the "free world." In addition to the immediate military threat the Soviets supposedly posed to "free" Europe, western propagandists also attributed to them the fantastic powers of being able to fashion revolutions throughout the third world. The ideologists of Cold War posited that the Soviet Union exercised control over the various anti-colonialist and nationalist movements that had been brewing in the countries of Asia, Africa, and Latin America for many decades. In national security circles these independence movements became transformed into potential tentacles of Soviet expansionism.

In the course of two decades, the Soviets did become strong enough to aid some third world revolutions, albeit not at the level these movements had anticipated. Yugoslavia broke from the Soviet hold in 1948; North Korea, angry at lack of Soviet support during the Korean War, moved away from the Kremlin; China, supposedly married to the Soviets eternally, rudely separated from Moscow in the early 1960s; and various Eastern European states have been able to maneuver enough to convince the United States to award them "most favored nation" status. (Roumania, probably the most repressive of the Eastern European states, continues to maintain such a position with the United States.) Other nationalist governments, like those in Egypt, Ghana, Somalia, and Indonesia, either replaced Soviet aid and advisors with U.S. support or diversified their economic and military dependency.

The ideologists of the national security state adjusted to these "aberrations" and continued simply to insist that combating the Soviet threat was the equivalent of the defense of freedom. From the end of World War II through 1987, our government spent some ten trillion dollars on national security (ten times the size of third world debt). The United States has sustained a standing army of three million for much of that period. Over 3,000 military bases have been built at home and in forty countries abroad. More than 25,000 nuclear weapons are ready to be launched from bombers, submarines, and land launching pads to stop the communists. Yet the people of the United States do not feel more secure as a result of this massive expenditure, and the variety of military interventions that have been carried out in the third world in the name of fighting communism have not hurt the Soviet Union, but rather noticeably damaged the social fabric of our own country.

Indeed, Cold War anti-communism has led the United States into global entanglements, with troops and bases dotting the map. Anti-communism provided the impulse for atmospheric, and later underground nuclear testing, for the fashioning of CIA clandestine, illegal, and immoral operations, including assassination, coup-plotting, drug-testing, and mind-altering experiments on the American public. Intervention in the affairs of other nations became a normal, indeed habitual way of life—all in the name of fighting communism.

At home, the FBI became a national political police, to hunt down "communists," "subversives," and a variety of "fellow travelers" and "pinkos." New anti-communist institutions emerged inside and out of government. In the late 1940s, the Attorney General's list of "subversive organizations" printed for the public the names of the alleged communist enemies, while the Subversive Activities Control Board monitored them.

Anti-communism turned U.S. priorities around. The most dramatic statement about its impact on American society has been the economy. For forty years, an arms race and national security crises have absorbed a lion's share of the budget. Yearly U.S. deficits that fuel the soaring national debt, the current disparity between military and domestic spending, the massive investment in the so-called defense industry—all are a result of anti-communism as the official state ideology, the pillar of Cold War policy.

From the end of World War II, intervention became a continuous, almost reflexive policy. Unlike the gunboat and dollar diplomacy of an earlier era, Cold War thinking assumed that revolutionary, liberation, or independence movements were not only *ipso facto* contrary to U.S. interests, but, should they win power, would constitute a serious crisis for Washington, because the Soviet communist enemy supposedly was sponsoring them. Instead of portraying the rise of third world nationalism accurately as a diverse and complex set of movements fashioned to restore peoples' lost places in history, U.S. intelligence analysts tended to characterize third world reform and revolution as Soviet-inspired at worst and suspicious at best, therefore demanding of U.S. counter-action.

Such interpretation of events in Guatemala, the Congo, Cuba, Vietnam, the Dominican Republic, Chile, Angola, and elsewhere corresponded to the premise of the defense budget itself: the threatening tentacles of the communist conspiracy stretched to all continents. No amount of weaponry and military preparedness was ever "enough."

Instead of thinking about foreign policy as a way to increase domestic well-being, a series of presidents and their national security bureaucracies built policies designed to hurt the enemy, rather than help the U.S. public. The recent flood of Central American refugees, fleeing from the results of U.S. policy in that region, should not be a surprise. Back in 1961 when the CIA-backed invasion of Cuba failed to overthrow the Cuban government, the U.S. public had to suffer the brunt of what CIA Chief Allen Dulles called "the disposal problem," the incorporation into our society of thousands of Cubans who had been trained in dirty war and nasty intelligence techniques. Small wonder that the boomerang effect was felt: some of the right-wing Cubans later engaged in large-scale drug and other criminal enterprises; others turned up as terrorists who were involved in the assassination in Washington, DC of former Chilean Ambassador to the United States Orlando Letelier and an American colleague. Miami, where most of the Cubans settled, became a kind of U.S. Casablanca, drenched in intrigue and violence. Its CIA-created population was a direct consequence of the failure of the Bay of Pigs invasion to unseat Castro.

The undoing of President Nixon, sparked by the Watergate break-in, exemplifies the boomerang effect. The burglars were CIA-trained Cubans. According to the FBI, CIA-trained Cubans also murdered dissidents in their own community, assassinated a member of the Cuban UN delegation, and were responsible for bombings, arson, and murders throughout the United States and other parts of the world.

Similarly, U.S. troops who fought in Vietnam not only wreaked havoc on the people and land of Southeast Asia, but brought home to the United States a new set of problems that has caused a long-term disruption of society, infusing it with a kind of pain, sorrow, and confusion.

After forty years of Cold War intervention in Latin America, Asia, Africa, and Europe, the notion of the United States continuing to control events in the third world to preserve a way of life congenial to U.S. policy has become unrealistic. There are scars on the body politic. Public opinion polls have consistently shown that a considerable sector believes "covert actions" are unproductive, partly as a result of the ongoing series of scandals that follow from them. The tactics, the policies, indeed the very strategy of the Cold War have become unsuitable.

While national security planners have thought little of the disastrous results of low-intensity warfare on the civilian populations of Central America and other covert battlefields, the local residents are left to suffer immense and long-range consequences of U.S. crisis-management policies. The U.S. public has read about the effects of Agent Orange, sprayed on Vietnamese forests to deprive the Viet Cong of refuge, on the health of those GIs who had skin contact with the chemical. The effects on the Vietnamese people and their land, while less publicized, have been devastating.

These facts have had little impact on the anti-communist fanatics in the national security apparatus. Since 1981, President Reagan has maintained an ongoing series of dirty wars in Latin America, Asia, and Africa which have brought grief and hardship to the peoples of Nicaragua, Angola, Afghanistan, and Cambodia, and have produced a sense of embarrassment and failure for the United States. The anti-communist fixation has proved impractical, unaffordable, and inhumane. It is time for a redefinition, according to both budgetary realities and the shared sense of the U.S. public for the values of true democracy and human rights. It is time for a change—a fundamental one.

The policies of the past forty years have been costly; there is a generation of bills to pay for giving budgetary priority to military expenditures. Political aspirants continue to respond reflexively in favor of a "strong defense" without addressing the questions of who is or might be threatening U.S. security. A non-Cold War language with which to discuss foreign and defense policy is still inchoate. But there are signs that the Cold War curtain is being lifted from the policy stage. New Soviet leadership, major nuclear weapons agreements, and multilateral peace initiatives in the third world have further isolated the diehard Cold Warriors from majority thinking. Our challenge is to define U.S. interests without allowing the Cold War crisis ideology to freeze our progress.

Dismantling the Cold War Foundations

To build a new policy foundation, the bases for the past four decades of Cold War must be discarded because they are unfounded in the facts of modern politics, and thereby destructive to us as a nation. The new policy order must be derived from the real political world and from the organic history of this country. The implications are both vast and encouraging.

An end to the Cold War would mean at least a major reduction of nuclear weapons, since U.S. defense would no longer be nuclear-centered, and the concomitant terror under which the people of the world have lived would be removed. In addition, by stopping the manufacture of nuclear weapons, radioactive contamination of the environment would be reduced.

Cold War and nuclear "defense" have gone hand-in-glove with anti-communism, an ideology that cannot be sustained, given the facts of change in the Soviet Union and the declining budgetary possibilities for military expenditures in the United States. By extension, the Cold War policy toward third world revolutions would also be revised to regard them as inevitable results of long-term processes in former colonial states, not as plots hatched in Moscow.

U.S. policy must accept the need of peoples removed from the course of modern history to reenter it. Often, revolution provides the only means to do so, and revolutionary ideology, the inspiration and unifying force for initiation into modern nationhood, will and indeed must sound radical. The words "Marxism-Leninism," however, do not need to set off alarm bells in Washington. An understanding of revolutions, based on our own experience and that of other countries, should prepare us to accept these processes and deal with them patiently and maturely. Revolutions do not necessarily threaten U.S. interests, and the anti- or counter-revolutionary axiom that has operated for many decades can be discarded along with other Cold War baggage. In China, Yugoslavia, and the Soviet Union, "Marxism-Leninism" remains official ideology. It is not threatening to U.S. security.

The Foundations for a New Policy

The removal of these ingredients from the U.S. foreign and defense establishment leaves the elite policy circles with no coherent basis for formulating their overseas programs. The task of defining national interests should not be on their shoulders, but upon the citizenry, the appropriate defining body.

To design a new policy requires a national discussion and debate, one that ought to have been held after the Vietnam War but that got lost in recriminations and accusations. One of the obstacles to such a discussion in the past has been the existence of the national security state apparatus that has insisted upon the notion that there exists a permanent and eternal communist threat to U.S. security—and therefore a degree of secrecy that vitiates serious discussion. The dropping of the idea of permanent enemies, and consequently permanent allies to fight those enemies, allows for a flexibility in foreign policymaking that was absent during the Cold War. But where to find methods and guidelines for new policy?

To begin such a challenging endeavor, the participants in the discussion can both look ahead to the real threats that face the nation and backwards for guidance on how to meet them, for methods organic to their historical experience.

George Washington and the conservative Founding Fathers affirmed, logically, that foreign policy should follow from domestic needs. The Cold War period reversed that assumption and made domestic policy subject to the U.S. global mission. Because of the humiliating demise of the Reagan administration and its exaggerated ideological posturing, new possibilities have opened for popular participation in political life. The Jesse Jackson campaign has dramatized the fact that many millions of Americans are open to hearing new ideas and language about national priorities and meaningful values about a new politics.

Jackson has essentially affirmed the belief that each individual is worthy, and does not need either to identify with false notions of Cold War patriotism, or to indulge in drugs in order to achieve meaningful identity. Jackson has underlined a national credo of democracy, justice, equality, and human rights, a set of values that make a solid underpinning for policy. If such an ethos begins to pervade the body politic, then it will demand of lawmakers that both domestic and foreign programs follow those guidelines.

U.S. policymakers have shown little respect for the sovereignty and self-determination of weaker nations, albeit in the name of defending freedom and democracy U.S. troops and the CIA have crushed movements that aspire to those very goals. The U.S. public has reacted with confusion and pain to many of the counter-revolutionary moves over the past four decades. A solid consensus has not been and indeed cannot be reached by continuing in the imperial mode, no matter what high-sounding rhetoric is employed.

Ironically, the United States does face serious threats to its security, ones that are also faced by other nations. The global environment is now an accepted reality. Acid rain produced by U.S. companies destroys trees and bodies of water in areas beyond U.S. borders; clouds of pollution that formed over Central America have poisoned Minnesota lakes, and the ravaging of Brazilian jungles has affected rainfall patterns thousands of miles away. The thinning of the ozone layer, the warming pattern, the advancing desert in Africa all have become accepted global concerns.

While environmental consciousness has grown in the United States, there has not been a corresponding growth in understanding methods to apply that awareness globally.

The attacks on the United Nations over the past decade have seriously weakened not only the UN itself but the confidence of the populace in multilateral solutions. Once again a return to the trust in multilateralism that was present at the end of World War II might lead to a resuscitation of the UN and with it a policy that could accomplish foreign and defense policy goals that coincide with U.S. values and real economic interests.

Without the idea that the United States is or should be number one, a concept that brings forth the feeling of game-playing rather than a people moving forward in a historical process, how do we project our interests? With the guiding proposition that foreign policy should serve domestic purposes, grandiose visions of keeping or making the world free from this or that abstraction become inane. Nevertheless, a substantial institutional structure has been created to ensure reproduction of the national security theme in policy.

Some four million people work directly for national security agencies, most of them in the armed forces. Many millions more depend upon military installations for their livelihood; indeed, entire cities and even regions have military-based economies. The number of people employed directly by the defense industry whose earning capacity depends on the ongoing production of conventional, chemical, or nuclear weapons runs into the multimillions.

The mighty U.S. economy and the government policy of global interventionism have been marriage partners, but the conditions that allowed that union to take place and endure for some four decades have changed. Intervention is no longer practical; the $300+ billion military budget has become preposterous.

A common-sense guideline is that foreign policy should promote domestic peace, prosperity, and stability—and not aim primarily at hurting a foreign government. Let us retreat to historically-rooted notions of policy, ones that not only increase trade and protect our people and territory, but above all conform to the laws and treaties that our government has sworn to uphold. Government, by being law-abiding, sets an example.

Pursuit of human rights and democracy, however, must be accompanied by realistic economic policies, ones guided by a notion of national interest that stretches beyond short-term ideologies like anti-communism. While maintaining the preservation of the environment as a constant factor that underlies all policies, the economics of the future must take into account peace and stability factors as well.

Parts of the third world need assistance, and it is in the long-term U.S. interest to provide it—but in forms different from Cold War bilateralism, and with assumptions that diverge from the axioms of the last four decades.

Let us assume that the United States, Japan, and Western Europe are entering a post-industrial world, which means a drastic transformation of the global labor force and technological changes of a depth and rapidity never before experienced. This has already caused major alterations in trading and commercial patterns, which may well accelerate in the future. Let us assume that the global environmental destruction of the past half century will require serious attention and that freedom to develop will go hand-in-glove with ecological consciousness.

Adjusting to New Realities

How then to break away from intervention as a way of life toward the third world and into another policy?

In several areas of the world, ongoing or new revolutions and liberation movements present challenges for policymakers. The national security response calls for automatic hostility at the ringing of the revolutionary bell anywhere. Indeed, progressive or nationalist changes in the third world have constituted the bulk of national security "emergencies." Instead, those whose training in diplomacy includes the reading of history should replace the crisis managers. Those who look at history as a process have a context for understanding events as they unfold.

The change in policy thus also requires a change in the structure of the foreign policy apparatus, and that, in turn, calls for clear guidelines around which a public consensus can form.

Two obvious principles emerge as guidelines for future policy: human rights and international law. These notions have received vast amounts of lip service from heads of state, but, like other concepts that are patently just and useful, they too must correspond with the political reality of their time.

The age of U.S. hegemony over much of the third world, the American Century vision, the century-old control over our spheres in Central America and the Caribbean have passed into history. No amount of bluster, jingoism, or right-wing nationalism is going to bring Latin America back under Uncle Sam's thumb; nor would there be popular support, should a president attempt such folly.

Led by President Reagan and British Prime Minister Thatcher, UN agencies with mandates to help third world development, such as UN ESCO, UNICEF, and IFAD, have been badly assaulted, their achievements belittled and their budgets slashed. The wisdom that lies in the UN's aid and development staff has been discarded by the United States and many of its European allies. Multilateral aid requires UN coordination so that there is continuity while governments—including the U.S. government—change.

There are proper forms of engagement for the United States, which will remain a great and powerful nation. Future U.S. influence, however, should correspond not only to its might but to its maturity. In multilateral forums, the United States might well exercise more influence for democratic and ecologically sound development than it has by intervening unilaterally, or acting bilaterally in the interests of control.

The national security managers have defined U.S. interests as informal hegemony. Such "heedless self-interest was bad morals," as President Franklin Roosevelt said in his second inaugural, and "bad economics." Intervention and the Cold War have proven both morally and economically bankrupt. If "our goal is to again influence history rather than observing it," as John F. Kennedy said, we must begin to think of projecting power through law, not covert action; order and stability through international agreement, not unilateral fiat. "The empires of the future," said Winston Churchill, "are the empires of the mind." We have devoted the brains and finances of this nation to military control; it is time to cultivate our intelligence at home by pursuing sensible policies abroad.

Resources

Recommended Appointees for a New Administration

- Professor Richard Fagen, Political Science, Stanford University, author of *Forging Peace: The Challenge of Central America*
- Professor William LeoGrande, Government, American University, author of *Cuba's Policy in Africa, 1959-1980*, and co-author of *Confronting Revolution: Security Through Diplomacy in Central America*
- Gayle Smith, Co-ordinator of the Relief of Tigray-Ethiopia, and author of numerous articles on Africa for the *Boston Globe, Toronto Globe and Mail*, and the *Miami Herald*
- Patricia Weiss, professor at University of California, San Jose, expert on immigration and refugee policy Professor
- Carmen Diana Deere, Economics, University of Massachusetts, co-author of *Transition and Development: Patterns of Third World Socialism*

Organizations

- Policy Alternatives for the Caribbean and Central America (PACCA), 1506 19th St. NW, Suite #2, Washington, DC 20036; (202) 332-6333
- TransAfrica, 545 8th St. SE, Washington, DC 20003; (202) 547-2550
- Middle East Resource and Information Project, 1470 Irving St. NW, Washington, DC 20010; (202) 667-1188
- Southeast Asia Resource Center, 712 G St. SE, Washington, DC 20003; (202) 547-1114

Further Reading

- Richard Barnet, *Intervention and Revolution*, Meridian, 1980.
- Morris J. Blachman, William M. LeoGrande, and Kenneth Sharpe, *Confronting Revolution: Security Through Diplomacy in Central America*, Pantheon, 1986.
- Philip Brenner, *From Confrontation to Negotiation: U.S. Relations with Cuba*, A PACCA Book, Westview Press, 1988.

- Richard Fagen, *Forging Peace: The Challenge of Central America*, A PACCA Book, Basil Blackwell, 1987.
- Peter Kornbluh, *Nicaragua: The Price of Intervention*, Institute for Policy Studies, 1987.
- Walter LaFeber, *Inevitable Revolutions*, W.W.Norton, 1984.
- Saul Landau, *The Dangerous Doctrine: National Security and U.S. Foreign Policy*, A PACCA Book, Westview Press, 1988.
- Lars Schoultz, *Human Rights and United States Policy Toward Latin America*, Princeton University Press, 1981.

Saul Landau is a Senior Fellow at the Institute for Policy Studies. His published books include *The New Radicals* and *To Serve The Devil* (with Paul Jacobs), *Assassination on Embassy Row* (with John Dinges), and *The Dangerous Doctrine: National Security and U.S. Foreign Policy*. He has taught history, sociology, film, and politics at several universities, including the University of California, at the Santa Cruz and Davis campuses. He has made more than forty films for television and theatrical release, including *Paul Jacobs and the Nuclear Gang* (1980), with Jack Willis, and the feature-length 1988 documentary, *The Uncompromising Revolution: Cuba and Castro in Middle Age.*

U.S.-Soviet Relations: The New Realism

Platform

Disarmament Principles

In the first months of a new administration, the U.S. and the U.S.S.R. should negotiate the following principles and the framework for arms reduction and disarmament. Jointly, they would suggest that other states cooperate in reaching early agreement on common security and general disarmament in a peaceful world in accordance with these principles.

The goal of arms negotiations on partial reduction is to achieve agreement on a program which will ensure that:

- a general framework single treaty is constructed so that disarmament is general, including conventional and nuclear forces, so that war and armed conflict are no longer instruments for settling international problems

- such disarmament is accompanied by the establishment of reliable procedures for the peaceful settlement of disputes and effective arrangements for the maintenance of peace in accordance with the principles of the United Nations Charter

- partial agreements shall be part of an overall step-by-step 15-year treaty program of general disarmament.

The program for common security and general disarmament shall ensure that states will have at their disposal only those nonnuclear armaments, forces, facilities, and establishments as are agreed to be necessary to maintain internal order and protect the personal security of citizens; and that states shall support and provide agreed staffing for a United Nations peacekeeping contingent.

The common security and general disarmament treaty shall contain the necessary provisions for citizen support, participation, and human rights to assure proper adherence to the objectives and terms of the treaty program.

The terms of the treaty program shall apply to the military establishment of every nation for:

- disbanding armed forces and dismantling military establishments (including bases), ceasing the production of armaments as well as liquidating them or converting them to peaceful uses;

- eliminating all stockpiles of nuclear, chemical, bacteriological, and other weapons of mass destruction and ending the production of such weapons;

- eliminating all means of delivery of weapons of mass destruction;

- abolishing the organization and institutions designed to further the military effort of states, ending military training except for purposes of internal order and use according to the purposes and objectives of a proposed common security and general disarmament program;

- discontinuing military expenditures not in keeping with the terms of the treaty program.

The disarmament program shall be implemented in an agreed sequence, by stages until it is completed, with each measure and stage carried out within specified time limits. Transitions to a subsequent stage in the process of disarmament shall take place without interruption and according to the specifications of the treaty. To promote the objectives and implementation of the treaty program, a Coordinating and Verifying Commission shall be appointed to resolve questions of compliance and effectiveness of measures taken pursuant to the treaty program.

An ongoing verification study will be undertaken jointly by the parties to assure that measures in the next stage, when appropriate, are ready for use. The signatories will initiate a series of verification studies in preparation for a verification and disarmament organization which will establish the nature of such an organization and the types of studies to be undertaken. They will include anthropological, political, economic, statistical, military, psychological, historical, scientific, and other disciplines which will give proper meaning to inspection and verification principles.

Although certain asymmetries and incommensurable characteristics will arise within each stage of implementation of the treaty program (because of the different design of weapons, the configuration, and size of forces), no state or group of states shall gain military advantage of the other. Security is to be ensured equally for all and is to be a common property of all nations.

All disarmament measures shall be implemented from beginning to end under such strict and effective international control as would provide firm assurance that all parties are honoring their obligations. To this end, citizen participation in each nation will be encouraged to assure that the terms of the treaty program are carried out. Furthermore, national leaders will be asked to communicate on a regular basis to their nations to report on the progress and implementation of the treaty program. They will encourage each institution and agency of government to assure strict compliance with the terms of the treaty program. Each nation will be encouraged to pass legislation which will assure such personal accountability on the part of government officials.

During and after the implementation of general disarmament, the most thorough control shall be exercised, the nature and extent of such control depending on the requirements for verification of the disarmament measures being carried out in each stage. To implement control over and inspection of disarmament, an International Disarmament Organization (including all parties to the agreement) should be created within the framework of the United Nations. This organization and its inspectors shall be assured unrestricted access without veto to all plans as necessary for the purpose of effective verification. The parties shall formulate legal standards and legal instruments to assure that the disarmament process will continue and that penalties will be applicable where violations are found.

Progress in disarmament shall be accompanied by measures to strengthen institutions for maintaining peace and the settlement of international disputes by peaceful means, including the use of nongovernmental organizations, scientific institutes, labor unions, universities, and churches to assure successful compliance with the terms of the treaty program and the construction of a peaceful world system. In accordance with the principles of the UN Charter, during and after the implementation of the program of general and complete disarmament, steps shall be taken to maintain international peace and security, including the obligation of states to place at the disposal of the United Nations an agreed number of peacekeeping contingents necessary for an international peace force to be equipped with agreed types of armaments. The character of the international peace force shall be formulated on the basis of recommendations of the Military Staff Committee of the UN Security Council, which is charged with the responsibility of preparing an international security program.

Arrangements for use of the international peace force should ensure that the world community is able to protect the integrity of the disarmament process as outlined in the treaty program, and punish nations that violate the purposes and principles of the United Nations.

States participating in the negotiations should seek to achieve and implement the widest possible agreement at the earliest possible date. The stages of the program shall continue without interruption until fulfillment of the total program has been achieved. Efforts to ensure early agreement on partial measures for disarmament should neither prejudice progress on the treaty program nor inhibit the efforts of this program. Any partial steps should be incorporated in the overall framework for common security and general disarmament.

The United States and the Soviet Union shall invite other nations to join them in an international conference to formulate ideas and actions to bring about the purposes and objectives of common security and general disarmament. The United States and Soviet Union shall urge other nations to join them in seeking completion of the general disarmament treaty program negotiations and partial implementation before the year 2000 so that the treaty program and its specific aspects can be implemented quickly and expeditiously.

———————

As a general rule in international affairs, statesmen and diplomats follow a time-honored principle, "If it's not broken, don't fix it." This is sound advice for those who believe it is possible to freeze the future. It is poor advice for the end of the 20th century, where changes on the international and domestic scene are continuous, necessary, and often tumultuous. As conservative a man as Secretary of State George Shultz has grasped this fact, but his attempts at shifting U.S. policy toward the Soviet Union merely scratch the surface of what needs to be and can be done.

The extraordinary, energetic leadership of Mikhail Gorbachev may help Americans see the Soviet Union more clearly. Nevertheless, even with Gorbachev's presence, Cold War habits will be hard to unlearn. The period ahead requires that the United States and the Soviet Union understand each other and their past relations better. Given the bureaucratic and institutional predilection for backward "geostrategic" thinking, a future administration could easily fall into the rhetoric and blindness of the Cold War, where myths and misunderstandings have been the coin of public discussion. Even though sporadic attempts have been made since 1945 to improve U.S.-Soviet relations, we have understood the Soviet Union in cartoon terms. Rather than approach that country as a sprawling, highly pluralistic, economically underdeveloped, and proud nation caught in 20th century tragedy and frozen dogma, we have acted as if it were a cross between Satan and Atlas, all-powerful and enormously clever and evil, where everyone marches lockstep at the command of the party.

It does not take a leap of historical imagination to see that both nations have lost the Cold War. Ironically, the vanquished of World War II, Germany and Japan, became the beneficiaries, indeed the victors, in the Cold War. Unfortunately, U.S. foreign policymakers have not adjusted to this stubborn fact of international politics. Conservatives and their academic supporters continue their Cold War attitudes, hoping to use Gorbachev's *perestroika* as a means to "liberate" the Russian people for very obscure objectives. This group favors a Pressure Strategy.

The Pressure Strategists, like Harvard's Richard Pipes and the Heritage Foundation, believe that the Soviet Union is basically weak, much like the Ottoman empire, that it has little internal regenerative strength, and that a "victory" for the West is possible through a policy of military buildup and economic isolation. According to this view, each attempt at liberalization within the Soviet Union should be taken as a sign of Soviet weakness. The U.S. response should be military with political probes that would further roll back the Soviet hold on Russia and Eastern Europe. The idea of "rollback," so popular rhetorically with John Foster Dulles during the Eisenhower administration, has continued as a secondary theme of American foreign policy since the United States sponsored probes into the Soviet Union and East Europe early in the Cold War. The probes were often undertaken by different exile factions, some of whom were fascist in ideology.

A variation of the Pressure Strategy is espoused in the national security documents of the late Carter and early Reagan eras. Proponents of this view, such as Zbigniew Brzezinski, hold that the Soviet Union can be dismantled through a decapitation and balkanizing strategy which will encourage non-Russians within the Soviet sphere of influence to seek independence, autonomy, or legal rights. As Alexander Yanov, a former Soviet historian and now U.S. professor, has put it,

> For example, the religion of 55 million Muslims, the nationalism of 50 million Ukrainians and 10 million Balts, not to mention 40 million Poles, are all potential targets for U.S. exploitation of political unrest within the Russian empire. The "dismantling" view will gain currency among conservative groups as non-Russians struggle for greater autonomy in their affairs. Thus, the Latvian, Armenian, and Estonian experiences will become rallying cries within the United States for militant action against the Soviet Union.

According to Yanov, the strategy of balkanization and decapitation is a "godsend" to the Russian new right, which is increasing in size and thrives on the idea of Russian nationalism and purity, Western "corruption," anti-semitism, and fears that their homeland is going to be invaded by the West. There is no question that Gorbachev and the liberalizers will face difficult political moments as they attempt restructuring of the economy simultaneous with a new definition of citizenship within the Soviet Union.

The third, more official view of the Soviet Union is expressed by those within the universities and the Council on Foreign Relations who have adjusted to the Cold War and who believe in a management strategy. They point to history, saying that there have been some forty years without hot war because nuclear weapons force both sides toward a relationship of competitive management. The assumption is that there is very little the United States can do to influence the direction of events within the Soviet Union and that to try would be an error because it would require changing our own commitments and purposes.

What is missing from these established positions are the dynamic possibilities now present in world politics and within the Soviet Union. These possibilities could cause a shift in relationships at least equal to the U.S. shift toward China in 1971. As the Soviet Union turns to greater democratization both in its economy and political process, European perceptions will change substantially. One result is that changes in style and thrust of Soviet policy will require the U.S. to rearrange its alliance relations, reconsider in less ideological and more pragmatic terms its real needs and interests, and adopt an attitude which eschews needless confrontations with the Soviet Union. For example, the U.S. will need to recognize the obvious: that the Soviets want trade and we need markets. Either we trade with the Soviets or we will be sacrificing another market to the Japanese, Germans, and Swedes due to outmoded political assumptions. Trade can become an instrument to end the Cold War.

There need not and should not be any passionate attachment in international affairs to any particular nation or cause except those specifically agreed to, such as the UN Charter. In other words, primary emphasis for a new administration would be to reestablish the role of international institutions which seek to end the war and Cold War system. Such a goal requires a significant change in attitude and the realization that a number of the steps taken during the Cold War in U.S.-Soviet relations need reconsideration and retracing. It should be noted that by improving relations with the Soviets we do not have to hinder our relations with other nations. International relations is not a zero sum game, although U.S. policymakers have often been attracted to that metaphor. The position which I hold is called the New Realism. It sees the U.S. role in the world in flux and in need of redefinition. The cornerstone of this change will be rebuilding the international system and changing our relationship to the Soviet Union to one in keeping with our national interest rather than ideological pretension.

For such an *entente* to occur it is necessary to be aware of those elements in the past which caused enmity between the two sides. The reasons began early, when the Bolsheviks pulled the Russians out of World War I. This happened a few months after the U.S. entered the war on the side of the allies. The Soviet government concluded it had little choice but to sign a separate peace treaty, for the Russians had lost 3.7 million men in the war and millions more Russians died of starvation. Lenin's slogan of "bread, land, and peace" had caught the imagination of the Russian people and there was no turning back from it. Almost immediately, the U.S. joined with other nations in an ill-fated intervention in Siberia, which amounted to little more than a failed defense of the remnants of the Tsar's forces.

But these early incidents were only one side of the story. While the U.S. did not officially recognize the Soviet government until November 1933 and there was considerable fear of "bolshevism" in western media and governments, the fact is that many Americans, including U.S.

corporations, helped the Soviet Union in its development during the 1920s. Indeed, some analysts have made the argument that the communists learned more from the way that Henry Ford set up an assembly line than they did from Karl Marx's theories of capital.

Both nations turned inward during the 1930s; the United States committed to economic and social reconstruction, while Stalin and his henchmen involved themselves in terrifying purges against dissidents and old bolsheviks. They claimed that the purges were the key to industrialization and economic development.

The pressures caused by Hitler's invasion of the Soviet Union and the worldwide struggle against Nazism gave life to the idea that an American-Soviet entente was possible. As Henry Trofimenko, a Soviet professor of diplomatic history, pointed out,

> As to the problems the Allies had to tackle, they were often far more complex than those currently depicted as "insoluble." They concerned the lives of whole nations, the joint elaboration and co-ordination of military operations on an unprecedented scale, the adoption of a single policy toward the enemies, their attitude to the conquered, the postwar organization of the world, and the principles and forms of post-war cooperation among states. These problems were resolved quickly and in a businesslike manner. Despite the complexities, difficulties, and even substantial differences in interests, compromises were found that suited all parties concerned.

The abrupt end of lend-lease disagreement over Poland, the emergence of the U.S. as the single superpower, with attendant hubris, the decision of the Soviet government to mask its weakness in bluster and distrust, the omnipresence of U.S. nuclear weapons and bases which ringed the Soviet Union, and the arteriosclerotic nature of Soviet life when compared to the West helped to reinforce American elite and popular attitudes toward the Soviet Union during the end of the Stalin period. These early conditions blinded us, so that little significance was attached in the United States to positive changes which took place in Soviet life after Stalin's death. Gorbachev's rise to power was not an accident. It came at the end of a long party and bureaucratic struggle to transform the Soviet Union from a benighted and deformed state to one which sought a measure of stability and economic growth in its governance. The ascent has not been an altogether smooth one.

What have been the overriding and deadening political assumptions which guided American policy since 1947? The first was the belief that the United States should relate to the Soviet Union as a permanent enemy. This was not a simple decision, for it meant two changes in American foreign policy.

One was that the United States would alter the legacy left by George Washington that our country should have neither permanent friends nor permanent enemies in its foreign affairs. The second was that the Second World War period of cooperation with the Soviets would be erased from the popular mind. From thence forward our leadership was to assume that what is "bad" for the Soviet Union is "good" for the United States. Thus, throughout the Cold War period we have arranged our foreign policy actions along the lines of knee-jerk antagonisms. The result is that our ideological predilection has been in direct conflict with the Soviets in every important sphere of relations. The reason American leaders adopted this view related less to our vital interests than to the bureaucratic illusion that the world was a huge checkerboard, with nations nominated as pawns rather than autonomous entities with their own history and needs. Our adversary, the Soviet Union, was to be continuously tested in the game of geopolitics, but curiously never really defeated. (If, for example, the Soviets are having trouble in Estonia, the United States asserts its "right" of free passage in the Baltic Sea to show the Estonian dissidents that the U.S. supports them and will not forget them: a cynical game, since the U.S. will do even less for the Estonians than it did for the Hungarians in 1956.)

The second assumption is not geopolitical but eschatological. It is that the struggle between the United States and the Soviet Union is religious in character, reminiscent of the 100 Years War of Catholicism versus Protestantism. The amassing of military force and psychological will must go on because the struggle is over which ideology is closer to "God" or the ultimate spirit of history. But this view is betrayed in practice by both nations, and even the most militant of Cold Warriors can no longer deny reality. There is a wide variety of communisms and capitalisms and the internal economic character of the nation is not necessarily a guide to whether it threatens the United States. Polycentrism is more than ever the character of international affairs, and all the nuclear missiles in the world, marxist tracts, and capitalist material goods will not change that reality back to a two-power-bloc system. Since Cold Warriors are notoriously slow at recognizing political, social, and cultural changes in the world, they are enamored of instruments which ostensibly are meant to keep things as they are. Thus, they put their faith in weaponry and technology, not realizing that both these ingredients force even greater change among nations. Except for spasm periods (1949-51, 1961-62, 1979-82), most Cold Warriors have held that military force must not overwhelm the requirement of self-control with the Soviets. But the costs of the U.S.-Soviet Cold War have not been adequately tallied. The United States has spent $6 trillion on the Cold War and its frozen version of the Soviet Union. It has sacrificed 110,000 armed forces personnel and suffered 400,000 wounded for wars which were, in part, an outgrowth of artificial boundaries that stemmed from not resolving differences at the end of World War II.

Change is imperative because the Cold War has had costs that could be terminal to constitutional democracy. For example, we have been relatively thoughtless in changing the character of our government, increasing secrecy in order to assure the appearance of consensus and endorsing military adventurism in the name of anti-communism. A new president will have to decide whether to embrace a defense and foreign policy system which keeps the institutions and assumptions of the Cold War reproducing themselves like paramecia. A new administration will have to decide whether Gorbachev offers the United States a chance to escape a world view which straps us to the stone of constant threat and fear. That administration will also have to find a moral voice to successfully challenge those within U.S. life who, fearful of modern times, are prepared to risk war for their view of a fundamentalist, ethical purity. As I have suggested, this form of reaction is also present in the Soviet Union, where forces of Russian nationalism and fundamentalism hope to destroy the current liberalizing direction. But there are far stronger social forces in the Soviet Union which seek closer, normal relations with the West. The policy of *detente* was favored by the Soviets through much of the Cold War. For the Soviets this was nothing new. Even at the beginning of the Cold War the Soviets sought to make clear the limits of their grasp. The historian D. F. Fleming pointed out that, "Near the end of the Second World War Stalin scoffed at communism in Germany, urged the Italian Reds to make peace with the monarchy, did his best to induce Mao Tse Tung to come to terms with the Kuomintang, and angrily demanded of Tito that he take back the monarchy, thus fulfilling his bargain with Churchill."

The Soviet leadership sought respect from the United States, and in exchange it was prepared to limit its interests and commitments, staying out of the way of the United States. The Soviets played second fiddle to the international symphony led by the United States. They knew that the changes wanted by third world or Eastern European nations often stemmed from ideas which the United States stimulated either directly or through example. In contrast, U.S. foreign policy has been conservative and restorationist, fearful of international social change. This tendency caused us to generate governmental institutions whose mission was to attack change, especially when it seemed to threaten the status quo or ruling elites that were linked to U.S. business and military interests.

The *detente* of the rascals, that of Nixon, Kissinger, and Brezhnev, men whose reputation in public life was made on the basis of generating fear or corruption, fell apart soon after they left power. The reason for the failure of *detente* from the Soviet side was the collapse of the Shah's government and the emergence of Khomeini in Iran, an unstable situation in Poland, and the inability of President Carter to gain agreement from the Senate for the SALT II treaty. The result for the Soviets was a monumental foreign policy blunder on a scale proportionate to the American intervention in Vietnam. The Soviet-"invited" intervention in Afghanistan destroyed the possibilities of the rascals' detente. The United States, which used trade as a carrot in its relations with the Soviets, turned off the trade enticement. The Soviet managers and planners who had sought liberalization within the Soviet economy through heavy trading and technical assistance were again checkmated by international politics. They had made the mistake of gearing their economic planning to substantially increased trade with the U.S. as a means of fulfilling their own technological development. The atmosphere between the two sides, from 1979-1984, again became poisonous and the respective national security institutions of both nations reinforced each other in their competing weapons claims and needs. Yet sober analysts knew that the Soviet increase in long-range missiles or the Reagan dream of SDI was no answer to the security of both nations. It was obvious that the arms race itself was the single most dangerous dynamic between both nations, which made a mockery of each side's security and any ideas they had for a nation free of the burden of military institutions and armaments. Sir Solly Zuckerman, the former science advisor to a number of British prime ministers, put it well when he said, "The arms race can bankrupt the superpowers without adding anything to their respective military strengths. Deterrent systems today cost tens of times more than they did twenty years ago, when the political state of deterrence was just as operative as it is today. From the point of view of political/strategic value nothing has been gained." It is painful to note that much has been lost in resources through feeding military and defense economic institutions which protect national security in ways that are not dissimilar from protection rackets. Mutual deterrence has become a shared protection racket of both sides' military establishments. This is hardly a stable way of conducting international affairs or freeing up internal energies for domestic needs.

A new administration should seek to develop a new system of defense and disarmament, one which transforms the military, bureaucratic systems of both sides. This objective is well within the grasp of creative statecraft. It requires renouncing the technological forces of violence in the world because their value for specific political objectives, from the point of view of the West and the Soviet Union, is minimal. Even non-nuclear, "conventional" warfare and military assistance has its limits. The Soviets have learned this in Afghanistan, just as the United States was treated to the same lesson in Indochina.

The Soviets are no longer convinced that the amount of material and military assistance they provided to the third world has resulted in very much gain, either for their brand of socialism or their idea of "correct" state-to-state relations. The lesson is that it is possible to obtain good relations in the third world without much direct investment; less is more in order to assure that superpower confrontations do not occur in the third world. Conservatives and Democrats nevertheless urge a buildup of conventional force and small nuclear weapons efforts to avoid conflicts in the third world. This is a recipe for disaster and flies in the face of our own experience and need for domestic reconstruction.

The evidence is clear. The Soviets want to end the Cold War and, like ourselves, their internal needs require that they do so. The question is whether a debilitating *folie à deux* can be transformed into a more healthy set of bilateral and world relations. This question can be answered operationally, for there are specific steps which can be taken that will enhance world security, and even the U.S. position in the world. These steps, however, must take account of Soviet fears and interests. What are they?

Throughout the Cold War, concern about Germany's long-term intentions has never been far from the Russian mind, whatever the person's age and however far the Russian is from the Kremlin's walls. It is hardly surprising, therefore, that besides the issue of nuclear weapons the direction Germany will take in the next generation is of great importance to the Soviet Union. The *detente* of the rascals sought to freeze Europe and the German role through NATO and the Warsaw Pact. For at least twenty-five years before Gorbachev, the Soviets were uninterested in any plans of military disengagement along the lines either of the Polish Rapacki plan or the disengagement plans of George Kennan. But mutual military disengagement has now become a real possibility. Indeed, both the Soviet and the Polish governments have offered disengagement plans, with the Soviets calling for a cutback of a 1.25 million troops now stationed in Eastern and Western Europe. If a new administration sought such negotiations in the context of a larger arms and security settlement which precluded a regional arms race in Europe, real gains to world—and U.S.—security achieved.

Until now neither the Democratic nor Republican leadership has been prepared to consider an alternative security structure to NATO, or to substantially change the alliance into a joint security system with the Warsaw Pact. The harsh economics of increasing trade deficits, a citizenry angry at the decay of the quality of life, and astronomical costs for new weaponry will change this reality. Economic considerations will press the United States toward rapprochement, just as the Soviet government is being pressed in that direction for the same reasons. The costs of U.S. presence in Western Europe run in the neighborhood of $160 billion a year. These burdens seem anachronistic given the prosperous condition of Western European nations. Yet there are dangers to U.S. security if France and Germany unite to mount their own nuclear weapons "defense"—just as the U.S. has nothing to gain from Japanese rearmament.

There is no value to further nuclear buildup anywhere in the world. All nations have their antagonists and interests, and each conflict could become a tinderbox for world war if war preparation continues to be the rule of international relations. A new administration could champion the continuation of a nonproliferation treaty, a treaty originally signed by nonnuclear nations on the promise that nuclear weapons nations would rid themselves of nuclear weapons. The nonproliferation agreement is merely a stopgap measure. It does not speak to the continuing crisis of insecurity caused by the war system.

A new administration must formulate a framework for common security and general disarmament. Without concrete, cumulative steps—first by the superpowers and then other nations—humanity will continue to be trapped in an unaffordable militarism at best and terrifying wars at worst. The nations, and especially the superpowers, will be trapped in a political version of the second law of thermodynamics. Each step taken forward without changing the framework will not result in significant positive change, because the nations will not have had a "roadmap" as to how to proceed. The decline for all nations will continue precipitously. In financial terms, the result will be expenditures of astonishing amounts of money on armaments as the bottom half of humanity sinks further into a swamp of misery.

There are signposts for both the United States and the Soviet Union which, if followed, will prevent the two from falling backwards. They are found in international law, ethics, the UN Charter and Covenants, and specific cases of mutual agreements which have worked for both nations in the past, such as the Austrian State Treaty. Thus, for example, multilateral organizations such as the World Bank and GATT should be opened to Soviet participation.

Certain arguments will have to be rejected as casuitical. The tiresome academic debate of whether political tensions cause arms races or arms races cause tension is irrelevant because both political differences and arms races are utterly intertwined with each other, especially as they relate to U.S.-Soviet relations. The reality of this intertwining relationship can be seen in third world conflicts and local interventions, where military assistance from opposing sides increases tensions to the point of war. This fact requires that the United States and the Soviet Union work through the United Nations in ending the anarchic tendency for "intervention at will" which has gripped many nations. Because the United States and the Soviet Union have played down international law and non-intervention in their own activities, other nations have felt quite unrestrained in their interventions. A new administration would do much for U.S. national interest by pressing for international legal standards which renounce unilateral interventions and make use of international agencies such as the UN.

At the end of the Second World War, the United Nations Relief and Rehabilitation Agency, an allied effort for European rehabilitation, had enormous positive effect. Its successor, the Marshall Plan, also had a powerful effect, for it helped to restore the West European economy. Its serious flaw was that it became linked with the Truman Doctrine, in which the United States tied itself to the role of world policeman. Nevertheless, the idea of multilateral economic and social responsibility for development is a good one and is especially relevant to 21st century problems around technology, damage to the world's atmosphere, starvation, and world debt.

There is almost no world leader who has not decried the foolish waste of funds for armaments as billions of people live at starvation's edge. Problems of starvation and development cannot be dealt with unless there is focused attention to general disarmament and common security. Hence, the most important activity in diplomacy with the Soviet Union and other nations is developing a common approach to security and disarmament. In 1961, in part as a propaganda exercise, but also because there had already been a felt need for it, the American and Soviet emissaries, John McCloy and Valerian Zorin, signed an agreement for negotiating general and complete disarmament. This phrase has been referred to in at least a half dozen treaties between the United States and the Soviet Union. Yet not since 1962 have there been any serious negotiations on general disarmament. A new administration will have the choice of continuing the battle of arms control, pursuing the elixir of SDI, or pursuing the path of general disarmament through the Arms Control and Disarmament Agency (ACDA), as well as other agencies of government. It is sad but true that in recent years the ACDA became the justifier of weapons systems and military force rather than the governmental instrument to come forward with ways and means of bringing about disarmament. A new administration will need a far different set of advisors in ACDA, including greater openness to the peace movement and that part of the scholarly community which seeks comprehensive answers to the war system. After a generation of arms control it is obvious that requirements for limited agreements are as complex and onerous as they would be for a comprehensive disarmament arrangement which encompassed conventional and nuclear forces.

Judging from past negotiated agreements with the Soviets, a 15-year common security and general disarmament program with the Soviets could be achieved. However, the treaty program, even with a strong president, will require massive citizen support to negotiate and sustain. Is there a greater gift which political leadership and citizen action could offer the 21st century than taming the dogs of war and ending the terrible weight of the arms race?

Resources

Recommended Appointees for a New Administration

- Stephen Cohen, Professor of Russian History, Princeton University, author and specialist on the Soviet Communist Party

- Alexander Yanov, Professor of Political Science, City University of New York, specialist on Soviet government and Russian culture

- John Mercer, Harriman Institute, Columbia University, scholar of Soviet Affairs

- William Arkin, Fellow, Institute for Policy Studies, expert on nuclear and conventional forces
- Norman Birnbaum, University Professor, Georgetown University, expert on European affairs
- Seymour Melman, Professor Emeritus of Engineering, Columbia University, authority on inspection and the economics of conversion
- Betty Lall, Council on Economic Priorities and Cornell University, expert on disarmament and Soviet affairs
- Burns Weston, Professor of International Law, University of Iowa Law School, expert on disarmament
- Louis Sohn, former State Department advisor, Professor of International Law, University of Georgia, leading authority on international law and security, drafted Law of the Sea Treaty
- Henry Richardson, Professor of International Law, Temple University, former member of the National Security Council staff, and expert on common security
- Joane Landy, Director of Peace and Democracy East and West, New York, NY
- George McGovern, former member of the Senate Foreign Relations Committee, 1972 Democratic Party presidential candidate, and Fellow of Institute for Policy Studies
- Raymond L. Garthoff, Senior Fellow of Brookings Institution, former U.S. ambassador
- David Cortright, Co-director of SANE-Freeze, author, and expert on developing national consensus
- Representative Patricia Schroeder, (D-CO), Member of House Armed Services Committee

Organizations

- SANE-FREEZE, 722 G St. SE, Washington, DC 20003; (202) 546-7100
- Committee on National Security, 1601 Connecticut Ave. NW, Washington, DC 20009; (202) 745-2450
- Coalition for a New Foreign Policy, 712 G St. SE, Washington, DC 20003; (202) 546-8400
- George Kennan Institute of Russian Studies, Woodrow Wilson Center, Smithsonian Institution, 1000 Jefferson Dr. SW, Washington, DC 20001; (202) 357-2415

Further Reading

- Richard Barnet, *The Giants: Russia and America*, Simon and Schuster, 1977.

- Alexander Yanov, *The Russian Challenge*, Touchstone Books, Basil Blackwell, 1987.

- Marcus Raskin, *The Common Good* (Chapter Five: Securing the Nation), Routledge & Kegan Paul, 1986.

- William Arkin, Thomas Cochran, and Milton Hornis, *Nuclear Weapons Data Book*, Volume 1-4, Ballinger, forthcoming, 1988.

- *Collected Speeches of Michail Gorbachev*, Moscow Publishing House, 1988.

- Raymond L. Garthoff, *Detente and Confrontation: American-Soviet Relations from Nixon to Reagan*, Brookings Institution, 1985.

Marcus Raskin is co-founder and Distinguished Fellow of the Institute for Policy Studies. He was a special staff member of the National Security Council in the Kennedy administration and presently heads a joint U.S.-Soviet study on disarmament. He is the author of, among other books bearing on the subject, *Politics of National Security* and *Notes on the Old System*.

Ronald V. Dellums and Daniel N. Lindheim

Toward Increased Defense Sense

Platform

In order to create a rational military budget:

- Reduce the risk of nuclear war through arms control negotiations and restrictions on new nuclear weapons funding.

- Reorient the present force structure emphasis away from third world intervention and preparation for World War II-style land wars in Europe.

- Eliminate overlapping and unnecessary weapons and procurement inefficiencies and abuse.

- Fully fund military personnel and family benefits.

- Establish programs for economic conversion and military toxic waste clean-up.

Such revisions can produce a $200 billion savings over the next four-year presidential term.

The most important task facing the next administration is determining the size and direction of the military budget. The military budget is the principal instrument of U.S. foreign and military policy. The programs it funds determine whether U.S. policy is based on the simplistic Cold War ideas of the last four decades or on principles of self-determination, independence, and respect for human rights. These programs also determine whether we will continue to stand on the brink of war and nuclear destruction or move toward a world of peace and stability. In large measure, the military budget also shapes the nation's domestic agenda. It claims such a dominant share of total budget resources that military funding decisions determine whether resources will be available for addressing crucial domestic concerns.

The military budget defines the country's national security priorities. The United States has legitimate security interests and the government should allocate the resources needed to defend those interests. National security is not promoted, however, by present policies where hundreds of billions of dollars a year are spent in preparation for wars that cannot be won and may well result in the destruction of the planet. Equally important, national security requires ensuring that the economy is strong, that people are healthy and well educated, and are able to contribute meaningfully to the development of the society.

A military budget for an incoming administration committed to these notions of national security is outlined below. It first addresses the context in which debate on the next military budget will take place. This is followed by a brief discussion of the principal elements of such a budget alternative. The point is that by challenging a few critical assumptions about national defense policy, a substantial restructuring of the present military budget is possible, with potential savings of many hundreds of billions of dollars.

The Military Budget: The Big Context

The Reagan Buildup: Dollars Over Policy

Increasing the military budget was one of the highest priorities and achievements of the Reagan administration. By its third budget year, the military budget had increased more than 75 percent, or $100 billion. The $295 billion recently approved for FY1988, the current budget year, and the $300 billion proposed for FY1989 are more than double the $144 billion approved for FY1980.

In theory, funding levels and directions are determined by policy objectives or "missions," which themselves are based on formal commitments as well as changing perceptions of national security requirements. Unfortunately, during this period of massive spending increase, most debate focused on dollar amounts and growth rates, not considerations of strategy and substance.

To justify the increases, the administration complained of a "decade of neglect" in U.S. military spending, particularly as compared with supposedly high rates of growth in Soviet spending. The assertion that a major buildup was necessary was accepted with relatively little inquiry or debate. In fact, U.S. military spending has risen every year since FY1976; and Soviet spending growth, according to CIA estimates, was far below the administration's claims, barely exceeding the rate of inflation.

The debate was essentially an auction. The administration sought to maximize spending growth; the opposition limited itself to bidding for slightly lower rates. The bidding war created enormous military budget increases and effectively altered budget priorities. The result was a military share which now accounts for over half (51.4 percent) of the available federal budget as compared with a less than one-third share (31.9 percent) in FY1980. These calculations exclude interest on the national debt and programs separately financed through the earmarked Social Security Trust Fund (Social Security and Medicare).

If high levels of spending are necessary to ensure national security, then sufficient money should be provided. If they are not necessary, then reductions should be made, even substantial ones. But these should be determined by debating policy priorities, not by arbitrary rates of spending or growth. The threat to national security does not change by 3 or 5 or 10 percent per year, and there is no reason to feel compelled to allocate scarce budget resources in such terms.

Constraints on Future Military Budgets

The incoming administration will be seriously constrained in its ability to set new military policies as well as to either increase or decrease spending patterns and levels. Unprecedented budget deficits, caused by the military budget increases as well as by substantial tax benefits provided for the wealthy, have made deficit reduction a pressing new priority. This has placed a political limit on future military spending. The administration and the Congress are finally realizing that large increases in the military budget are inconsistent with even minimum levels of funding for non-military programs. This realization prompted the late 1987 "budget summit" on deficit reduction and is reflected in the administration's FY1989 budget request, which capped new military programs at $299.5 billion, a level substantially below what the administration had previously planned to request from the Congress.

At the same time, the new administration will be constrained in its ability to substantially reduce the level of military spending. First, military spending increases, which are unprecedented in peacetime history, have substantially altered what is considered politically acceptable. For example, the administration's FY1982 proposal, at the time considered the cornerstone of the Reagan revolution, would be dismissed as involving radical reductions if offered today.

Second, despite the Intermediate Nuclear Forces (INF) Treaty and prospects for strategic arms reductions, the Pentagon, with congressional blessing, is already committed to financing new generations of expensive nuclear weaponry, including the MX, Trident II, and cruise missiles, the B-1 and Stealth bombers, and the irrational Strategic Defense Initiative (SDI) program. In addition, military spending advocates are calling for further conventional arms buildups to of fset supposed Soviet advantages they claim result from the INF Treaty.

Third, regardless of actions taken by the next administration, more than $270 billion in additional military spending has *already* been approved, primarily for major weapons systems and the massive Navy shipbuilding program. These "obligated" and "unobligated" balances are monies which have already been appropriated, but which will not be spent until the next administration's term in office, and as such will place pressure on that administration's budget deficits.

Budget "Cuts"

In every year of the large spending increases, the administration and the media have spoken of military spending "cuts." In fact, there has not been a spending cut during the Reagan administration's term in office. The only "cuts" have been from proposed increases, not from prior year spending. For example, the $33 billion "cut" touted in the administration's FY1989 budget request simply masks one more such increase. Some argue that since the military budgets approved by Congress in the FY1986-1988 period increased by less than the rate of inflation, these increases constitute cuts. This might be a legitimate argument, except that over the entire Reagan term, inflation-adjusted "real growth" in the military budget has been almost 40 percent, almost 4 percent real growth each year.

The Alternative Program

Most criticism of the military budget, particularly by congressional liberals and public interest groups, tends to focus on either individual weapons programs such as MX and SDI, or on well publicized procurement scandals, like the $600 toilet seats. While the procurement problems are outrageous, and many individual weapon systems must be opposed, these account for a minor part of the military budget.

The military budget basically funds two activities—developing and purchasing military equipment, and paying people to operate and maintain this equipment—all allocated in support of various "missions" and policy objectives. To substantially affect the level and direction of military spending, either the purpose of these forces must be challenged or the requirements to meet these objectives must be redefined. Changed policies would lead to alterations or reductions not only in troop levels, but in the monies allocated toward their support, including weaponry, equipment, and installations.

In what follows, many aspects of present policy, and monies allocated in support of these policies, are questioned. In particular: nuclear policies and the need for new generations of weaponry; naval strategy and the supposed need for a 600-ship navy; NATO policy and the consequent enormous resource commitment. We believe that different policies, with correspondingly different sets of spending decisions, would provide for a secure national defense, at lower spending levels, without sacrificing personnel benefits or readiness.

The alternative would result in appropriations, over the next four-year term, of some $200 billion less than Congressional Budget Office projections of the cost of continuing current policy. The calculations made in reaching the $200 billion figure are based on very conservative assumptions as to the rate at which a new administration could affect policy. In fact, much larger reductions could be made without jeopardizing national security. Thus, it is a proposal well within the realm of political viability for the incoming administration and not a description of what ultimately should be. This does not lessen our resolve to bring about a substantial restructuring in the military budget, but it takes as its guide the basic principle that people must be reached where they are, and not where one wants them to be. It is an effort to take a realistic first step in the right direction.

Reduce the Risk of Nuclear War

The only value of nuclear weapons is to prevent their use. This is the view of every responsible military thinker and policymaker. While some nuclear weaponry may be necessary as a deterrent to nuclear war, existing inventories of well over 25,000 warheads are far more than sufficient for that purpose. Present efforts to "modernize" the U.S. nuclear arsenal do not add to deterrent needs. Instead, they are costly, in some cases highly destabilizing, and should be opposed.

The administration has muted its early rhetoric about fighting and winning a nuclear war. Nevertheless, it has actively sought both nuclear warfighting and first-strike capabilities. These would be of value only on the mistaken belief that nuclear weapons, on the scale of those dropped on Hiroshima and Nagasaki, can actually be used in battle.

Systems such as the land-based MX and submarine-based Trident II (D-5) missiles do not enhance deterrence. What differentiates them from prior systems is their ability to destroy Soviet missiles in their silos. Were there a Soviet first strike, Soviet silos would be empty and the added capability would be useless. Thus, they add little to existing deterrents based on retaliatory capability. Instead, their power, range, and accuracy provide the United States with a first-strike capability. This creates strategic instability and might push the Soviets toward preemptive attack in the event of extreme crisis.

This argument goes beyond the "vulnerability" arguments which were the basis of mainstream opposition to a fixed silo MX. For example, many MX opponents, who based their opposition on MX vulnerability, still support the mobile, and thus less vulnerable, "rail-mobile" MX or "Midgetman" systems, or the submarine-based Trident II, which is essentially an "invulnerable" MX. Similarly, opposition is independent of recent reports on the technical problems facing the MX system. Instead, the argument is that purchasing additional nuclear weapons, including the less vulnerable systems, offers no improvement in security.

The INF Treaty presents an important opportunity to begin the process of reductions in both nuclear and conventional weaponry. While the Treaty itself only affects "intermediate" missiles (and does not even address warheads) and would reduce the nuclear missile inventory by less than 4 percent, it is a first step. The present START talks may extend this process to strategic weaponry. The next administration must aggressively pursue negotiations to substantially reduce the nuclear arsenals of the superpowers.

The START negotiations, laudable as they are, are also part of the danger of much force modernization in the context of arms control reduction. There is tentative START agreement to limit each side to 4,900 warheads on land and at sea. With development and deployment of the Trident II missile, each Trident submarine will carry (for arms control counting purposes) 192 warheads. We now have 500 MX warheads (50 missiles with 10 warheads apiece) and some 900 Minuteman launches, each with either 1 or 3 warheads.

The United States has purposely placed the majority of its strategic nuclear force in submarines because of their virtual invulnerability. However, START reductions, in the context of MX and Trident II deployment, mean that we would be limited to between 14 and 20 submarines, depending on what was done with the Minuteman force. Thus, the combination of Trident II deployment and START limitations necessarily increases reliance on land-based missiles, and leads us to greater vulnerability and greater instability. In the short, the world would be far safer with elimination of both the MX and Trident II.

The SDI ("Star Wars") proposals are also misguided. The idea of a defensive shield against nuclear weapons sounds attractive; however, the defensive capability of SDI is illusory and much of the supporting rhetoric is dishonest and contradictory. First, the administration continues to propagandize the idea of a laser-based population shield. Most SDI funding, however, is actually directed at developing systems to protect missiles, not people, and uses existing technologies. This means that rather than moving away from reliance on the threat of mutual assured destruction (MAD) to prevent nuclear war, the president's asserted justification for SDI, it would simply reinforce the present MAD reality and the idea of prevention through deterrence. Second, while the president has made much of the program being nonnuclear, substantial funds have been provided for SDI nuclear programs, including the X-ray laser and orbiting nuclear reactors.

Most scientists argue that the scientific, engineering, and computer problems associated with the exotic versions of SDI make it impossible in the next decades and highly improbable thereafter. Even assuming, however, the technical feasibility of the most exotic of the laser technologies, no SDI can "render nuclear weapons impotent," as the president has asserted. This is because SDI is directed at intercepting ballistic missiles. It does not offer, even in theory, protection against cruise and other low-trajectory missiles, bomber attacks, or small "backpack" or other "tactical" weaponry.

It should be noted that a defensive SDI could be used offensively as well. In addition to shooting at missiles or other targets, it could be used to blind or destroy satellites, thereby threatening opposing command and control systems. This is the apparent basis of the Soviet concern about SDI; in particular, that it might be part of a nuclear war-fighting plan.

Finally, SDI would violate both the terms and the logic of the 1972 Anti-Ballistic Missile (ABM) Treaty. While debate exists concerning at what point SDI "tests" would technically violate the Treaty, it would necessarily be violated in the next few years. More important, SDI would lead to the same offensive and defensive arms races that the ABM Treaty sought to avoid. The ABM Treaty was signed because the parties understood that without it there would be a missile defense arms race, and a corresponding offensive arms race to overwhelm the developing defensive systems. SDI is, at a minimum, an ABM system and the logic of ABM applies directly to any SDI.

The following specific reductions and eliminations are proposed (four-year savings over next administration in parentheses):

No additional MX funding ($8 billion); cancel Trident II ($13 billion); limit sea- and ground-launched cruise missiles ($6 billion); cancel Midgetman ($10-15 billion); no additional Trident submarines ($5 billion); eliminate SDI, replace with basic R&D ($20-25 billion); limit Stealth to R&D ($15-20 billion); terminate chemical and biological weaponry ($4 billion); limit atomic warhead production ($8+ billion); end anti-satellite (ASAT) program ($4 billion); establish programs for enhancing verification for nuclear weapons testing ($3 billion increase).

Reorient Present Conventional Force Priorities

For four decades, the United States has maintained security allian-ces with Western Europe and Japan. These continue to be vital, but the argument for such vast U.S. resource commitments may no longer apply and the terms and requirements of these and other foreign policy com-mitments should be reassessed. First, increasing budget pressures place limits on what the government can spend; second, there is increasing discomfort about the perception of inequality in the contributions and responsibilities of the various parties; most important, there appears to be a possibility of improved relations with the Soviet Union (e.g., the INF START negotiations, Gorbachev's statements and actions). This provides an extraordinary opportunity for initiating reduction in this part of our military spending, as well as that of the Soviet Union. The next administration must seize this opportunity to not only reduce the threat of nuclear war, but to bring about substantial conventional reduc-tions as well.

European Land War Preparation

According to Department of Defense reports, well over half of the U.S. military budget is devoted to preparations for fighting a World War II-like extended land war against the Soviet Union in Europe. With the INF Treaty, there will be increased pressure for such preparations. The probability of such a war, however, is close to zero.

First, present NATO forces are credible deterrents to any significant Warsaw Pact aggression. While the relative NATO/Warsaw Pact balance is complex, recent reports from both the Senate Armed Services Committee and the International Institute for Strategic Studies indicate that a rough conventional balance exists. There is no massive NATO force inferiority and no justification for a further conventional arms buildup in Europe. Moreover, the buildup argument presumes the absurd notion that the only deterrent to a Soviet invasion of Western Europe is NATO conventional parity and forward-deployed U.S. troops.

Second, while the INF Treaty will eliminate the SS-20, Pershing, and GLCM missiles from Europe, both Warsaw Pact and NATO conventional forces in Europe are still equipped with nuclear weapons. It is inconceivable that a U.S./USSR war in Europe would remain conventional for long, yet preparation for extended conventional war is presently one of the highest military spending priorities.

The real priority is to reduce the number of troops on both sides. The presence of 325,000 U.S. troops in Europe is unnecessary as a deterrent. It also increases the risk of U.S. troops becoming "trip-wires," thereby escalating otherwise less threatening confrontations. In addition, for budgetary as well as security reasons, we must put on the table the issues of whether our European allies should increase their financial and physical participation in NATO defense. Even absent negotiations, the United States could safely remove substantial portions of its troops currently based in Europe. We propose removing some 20 percent of these troops over the next four-year term, but far greater reductions are possible if the next administration aggressively pushes negotiated reductions.

The following specific reductions and eliminations are proposed (four-year savings over the next administration in parentheses):

Reduce the U.S. European presence by two divisions, decommissioning one and returning the other to the United States ($10-15 billion); limit hardware predicated on preparation for extended land war in Europe (e.g., M-1 tank, Bradley) ($8-10 billion).

Limit Third World Intervention

The proper U.S. defense policy is to defend U.S. security interests, not to intervene militarily in and against third world countries. Much of the spending buildup has gone to support administration efforts to create the 600-ship navy, particularly the increase from 13 to 15 aircraft supercarrier battle groups. These battle groups, the primary instrument of the Navy's "forward offensive strategy," are of little use, however, against the alleged target, the Soviet Union. A recent Congressional study indicated that a carrier battle group is probably the world's most tempting target for tactical nuclear weapons (i.e., the battle group could easily be destroyed and there would be little chance of unintended damage).

In reality, the buildup's primary purpose is third world intervention. Most recently, three carrier groups were deployed against Libya, while last year two were deployed against Nicaragua. Devoting such an extensive part of the naval budget to these forces is inappropriate and expensive. The number of battle groups should be immediately reduced back to thirteen, with a further decrease to a maximum of ten battle groups to take place over the next term. This would reduce the number of battle groups forward-deployed at any one time from between four and five to three.

The administration has also given priority to the creation of Rapid Deployment and Special Operations forces. These forces are oriented toward "low-intensity conflict," the euphemism for actions like the Grenada invasion. This is part of a changing military strategy which envisions U.S. armed intervention throughout the third world (e.g., Central America). The problems of the third world are not military ones, and the next administration should disband, or at least limit, the further growth of these units.

The following reductions and eliminations are proposed (four-year savings over the next administration in parentheses):

Provide funding to equip thirteen battle groups in the short term, with force and equipment modernization limited to a maximum of ten carrier groups, involving the following: retire two deployed CVN carriers ($4 billion); defund the two FY1988-approved CVN carriers ($6 billion); limit purchases of battle group ships ($9 billion); reduce battle group airplane purchases ($8 billion); limit other related battle group purchases ($11 billion); reduce Navy, Air Force and Marine Corps personnel to FY1980 levels ($15-20 billion); disband Rapid Deployment and Special Operations forces

Efficiently Fund Necessary Systems

The massive increase in military funding has led to plans based on the availability of funds, rather than on necessity or mission. Too many programs are over-bought. Moreover, inter-service rivalry has led to unnecessary levels of duplication, with the consequent purchase and production of inefficient, and more costly, numbers of both necessary and unnecessary systems.

The Pentagon and Congress must determine which systems are necessary, and then purchase them in the most efficient way possible. This will of necessity result in the cancellation of certain systems, while increasing production of others deemed of higher priority. For FY1988, the House and Senate Armed Services Committees took initial steps in this direction; however, the final appropriation, based on the "budget summit" agreement, restored funds for most of the previously cancelled systems.

Similarly, budgetary excess has led to the development of ever more sophisticated systems at enormous capital and maintenance costs and requirements. Approval of such high-cost and high-tech systems should be closely scrutinized, particularly when the improvements over existing models are marginal. In addition, simple tactical considerations of quantity (i.e., more lower cost items) may be superior to a lesser number of expensive, high-tech systems.

Congress has finally become alarmed at the Pentagon procurement system. The publicity surrounding Pentagon purchases of dime-store hardware items for thousands of dollars has forced Congress to insist on initial reforms in this area. These must go much further. In particular, sole-source contracts must be limited, and competitive contracts increased. The "revolving door," whereby high Pentagon officials and defense contractors simply rotate seats, must be severely constrained. Greater control over quality, efficiency, and cost must be exercised by the Pentagon in all of its contract dealings. Moreover, whistle-blower protection must be assured.

Real reform, however, requires a radical change in the relationship between the Pentagon and the major U.S. military contractors who benefit from this relationship. Military contracts are a major source of profits for many of the largest U.S. corporations, and making the process more efficient, and presumably less profitable, will require substantial political commitment.

Fully Fund Personnel and Family Programs

Force levels should be reduced for policy reasons. All remaining forces, however, must be properly supported. This requires substantially improving living and other "quality-of-life" conditions for all members of the services and their families. In particular, more and better family housing and dependent programs are needed.

Economic Conversion and Military Toxic Waste Clean-up

The burden of a decision to eliminate or reduce certain weapon systems should be a national one. The cities and towns where those particular systems are produced should not be forced to shoulder the effects of necessary changes in national policy. Military systems should be supported strictly on their military merits and not on the basis of the number of jobs involved. Thus, the proposal includes monies for funding approximately 150,000 new jobs annually in areas where workers on military programs are displaced as a result of weapon systems cuts. This is an initial step in the longer-term process of reducing present economic dependence on military spending and on forcing decisions on military systems to be based on their military rationales.

Military sites are major sources of toxic waste dumps and environmental pollution. Substantial efforts are needed to begin the process of removing the dangerous conditions present in many of these sites. The proposal includes $2-3 billion per year to initiate such a program.

The budget alternative was calculated by taking the FY1988 House-passed Appropriation bill as its base. Adjustments were then made to reflect various policy differences as discussed in the text. The principal reductions from the House bill were in nuclear weapons and military personnel. The improvement in military family programs, and the creation of new programs for economic conversion and toxic waste clean-up, resulted in increases from that bill. These programs were adjusted for inflation for FY1989, and then projected forward for the FY1990-1993 period using Congressional Budget Office (CBO) assumptions.

As indicated in Table 1, implementation of this alternative would reduce new appropriations by slightly more than $200 billion as compared with CBO projections of continuing current policy for the four-year (FY1990-1993) period of the next administration. Despite the substantial savings, the alternative would still spend more in each year of the next administration, even after adjusting for inflation, than every military budget in the postwar period, excepting the periods of the Korean and Vietnam Wars and the most recent Reagan years. This is an indication of the impact of the Reagan administration on what is now considered politically viable.

Table 1

	Proposed Alternative As Compared With Continuing Current Policy (in billions of dollars)						
	FY88 actual	FY89 estimate	FY90	FY91	FY92	FY93	FY90-93 total for next administration
				next administration			
Alternative Proposal	—	268	276	284	293	303	1156*
Congressional Budget Office Projection of Current Policy	291	308	320	333	347	361	1361
Difference	—	40	44	49	54	58	205

* Includes $26 billion over FY1990--1993 period for major new economic conversion and toxic waste cleanup programs discussed in text.

Resources

Recommended Appointees for a New Administration

A new administration could tap a large universe of excellent people. Many of the persons involved in the organizations mentioned below would be excellent choices, as would a limited number of members of Congress, congressional staff, and Pentagon officials. Much of the work of many of these organizations is accomplished through collective effort and to list just a few names would necessarily omit too many first-rate people. For that reason we offer no list of suggested high officials.

Organizations

- Arms Control Association, 11 Dupont Circle NW, Suite 900, Washington, DC 20036; (202) 797-6450
- Arms Control and Foreign Policy Caucus, 501 House Annex 2, Washington, DC 20515; (202) 226-3440
- Brookings Institution, 1775 Massachusetts Ave. NW, Washington, DC 20036; (202) 797-6000
- Business Executives for National Security, Inc., 21 Dupont Circle NW, Suite 300, Washington, DC 20036; (202) 429-0600
- Cato Institute, 224 2nd St. SE, Washington, DC 20003; (202) 546-0200
- Center for Defense Information, 10 Massachusetts Ave. NW, Washington, DC 20005; (202) 862-0700
- Center for Economic Conversion, 222C View St., Mountain View, CA 94041; (202) 968-8798
- Coalition for a New Foreign Policy, 712 G St. SE, Washington, DC 20003; (202) 546-8400
- Committee for National Security, 1601 Connecticut Ave. NW, Suite 301, Washington, DC 20009; (202) 745-2450
- Congressional Budget Office, Second and D Streets SW, Washington, DC 20515; (202) 226-2621
- Council on Economic Priorities, 30 Irving Pl., New York, NY 10003; (212) 420-1133
- Council for a Livable World, 100 Maryland Ave. NE, Washington, DC 20002; (202) 543-4100
- Defense Budget Project, 236 Massachusetts Ave. NE, Washington, DC 20002; (202) 546-9737
- Federation of American Scientists, 307 Massachusetts Ave. NE, Washington, DC 20002; (202) 546-3300
- Friends Committee on National Legislation, 245 Second St. NE, Washington, DC 20002; (202) 547-6000
- Institute for Defense and Disarmament Studies, 2001 Beacon St., Brookline, MA 02146; (617) 734-4216
- Institute for Peace and International Security, P.O. Box 2651, Cambridge, MA 02238; (617) 547-3338
- Institute for Policy Studies, 1601 Connecticut Ave. NW, Washington, DC 20009; (202) 234-9382
- International Institute for Strategic Studies, 23 Tavistock St., London WC2E 7NQ, England

- Jobs With Peace, 77 Summer St., Boston, MA 02110; (617) 338-5783
- Natural Resources Defense Council, 1350 New York Ave. NW, #300, Washington, DC 20005; (202) 783-7800
- Physicians for Social Responsibility, 1601 Connecticut Ave. NW, Suite 8, Washington, DC 20009; (202) 939-5760
- Project on Military Procurement, 422 C St. NE, Washington, DC 20002; (202) 543-0883
- SANE/FREEZE, 711 G St. SE, Washington, DC 20003; (202) 546-7100
- Stockholm International Peace Research Institute (SIPRI), Bergshamra S-17140, Solna, Sweden
- Union of Concerned Scientists, 26 Church St., Cambridge, MA 02138; (617) 547-5552
- United Campuses to Prevent Nuclear War, 309 Pennsylvania Ave. SE, Washington, DC 20003; (202) 543-1505
- Women's International League for Peace and Freedom, U.S. Section, 1213 Race St., Philadelphia, PA 19107; (215) 563-7110
- Women Strike for Peace, 105 Second St. NE, Washington DC 20002; (202) 543-2660
- World Policy Institute, 777 United Nations Plaza, New York, NY 10017; (212) 490-0100

Further Reading

- Ronald V. Dellums, *Defense Sense: A Search for a Rational Military Policy*, Ballinger, 1982.

Persons interested in alternative budgets should consult the following:
- Josh Epstein, *The 1988 Defense Budget*, Brookings Institution; Earl Ravenal, *Defining Defense*, Cato Institute Press, 1984; *Reducing the Deficit: Spending and Revenue Options*, Congressional Budget Office.

Various organizations publish newsletters, journals, and papers concerning military issues. The Defense Budget Project provides timely analyses of military budget issues. The Council on Economic Priorities publishes newsletters and books on various issues, including economic conversion and SDI. SANE/FREEZE produces numerous short documents, particularly concerning nuclear weapons. *The Defense Monitor*, published by the Center for Defense Information, analyzes major weapon systems and military policies. The Union of Concerned Scientists produces various material, including excellent *Backgrounders* on topical issues. The Federation of American Scientists publishes *Public Interest Report*, which focuses on test ban issues and SDI. The Institute for Defense and Disarmament Studies publishes a wealth of important material, including a newsletter, *Defense and Disarmament News. Arms*

Control Today, the journal of the Arms Control Association, and the *Bulletin of Atomic Scientists* both regularly publish excellent articles on a range of defense issues. In addition, the weekly publications *Aviation Week and Space Technology, Defense Week,* and *Defense News* (all accessible to the general reader) provide timely and detailed information.

Ronald V. Dellums has represented the 8th Congressional District of California since 1971. A veteran of the U.S. Marine Corps, he holds a B.A. from San Francisco State and an M.S.W. from the University of California at Berkeley. He is a senior member of the House Armed Services Committee and is Chair of its Subcommittee on Military Installations and Facilities. He was the first member of Congress to introduce legislation to terminate the MX missile (1979) and SDI (1985). In each year since 1982, he has introduced comprehensive military budget legislation as alternatives to those incorporated in the Budget and the Defense Authorization bills.

Daniel N. Lindheim holds a Ph.D. from the University of California at Berkeley and a J.D. from Georgetown University Law Center. He has extensive professional experience in a range of fields including economics, planning, and public health and was for many years a senior project economist at the World Bank. He is a member of the State Bar of California and has been on the staff of Congressman Dellums since 1979.

Promote the
General Welfare...

Richard Falk

Strengthening the Rule of Law in Foreign Policy

Platform

The United States has an excellent opportunity to strengthen national and international security at this time by reviving its commitment to the Rule of Law. Under Reagan this commitment was weakened at great cost to the well-being of the country. The Gorbachev initiatives give American political leadership an unexplored opportunity to rebuild and extend the resources of international law and the United Nations. Specifically:

- The United States should increase its participation in the UN and shape its foreign policy by reference to the Rule of Law, including respect for the Constitution at home and international law abroad.

- The United States should immediately reconsider its rejection of the Law of the Sea Treaty, the World Court judgment in the Nicaragua case, and the two Geneva Protocols of 1977 on the humanitarian Law of War.

The Reagan years have done more to damage the standing of international law and the United Nations than has any presidency since 1945. This shameful record coincides with an equally impressive Soviet turnaround on the very same issues. Odd as it may sound, Gorbachev's leadership and advocacy of a stronger United Nations as well as his concrete proposals across a wide spectrum of international law and arms control concerns have seized the initiative from the United States on the stage of global reform. It is Moscow, not Washington, that is providing the peoples of the world with some basis to hope for the avoidance of warfare and nuclear destruction, for a safer and more equitable world, and for more institutionally centered management of conflict based on strengthening the peacekeeping capacities of the United Nations.

These Soviet developments are welcome, and we can only fervently wish that this unexpected internationalism issuing forth from the Kremlin will be sustained and extended in the years to come, and that other governments will follow suit. At the same time, it is an occasion for lament here at home. Since its independence, America's identity has been associated with the promotion of peace and justice around the world. Its prominent role in such activities as founding the UN, promoting human rights, and providing humanitarian aid has given it an international prominence which has sustained, in some degree, an idealistic self-image. There have been tensions and contradictions from the beginning, associated with the genocide of Indian nations and the institution of slavery. Yet an abiding kind of idealism had until recently kept our sense of national purpose, including a claim to moral leadership in international affairs, credible. The erosion of this leadership antedates Reagan, and can be traced back to the critiques of Wilsonian idealism in the pre-World War II years and to the notion that peace can be achieved by appeasement. The rise of realism in the years after 1945, conceiving international relations as governed primarily by power relations among sovereign states, on the basis of learning the lessons of Munich under the stern tutelage of such teachers as Dean Acheson, George Kennan, and Hans Morgenthau, pushed the pendulum on security policy far in the opposite direction, producing a permanent disposition toward war and intervention and an implicit conviction that only preparing for war preserves the peace. Reagan's militarist view of national security is merely an extension of these developments, abetted by the ideological enthusiasms of the Cold War and challenged by revolutionary movements in several third world settings.

Hiroshima and Vietnam suggest the problematic U.S. willingness to unleash virtually limitless violence against civilian sectors of an enemy society during war. Military policies, however, were separated in American political experience from policies needed to develop a safer and more equitable system of world order than those associated with the interplay of ambitious rival sovereign states. Until Reagan, the uneven performance of U.S. military policy abroad was overshadowed by the seemingly abiding and sincere support for the application of international law and for a strong United Nations. With Reagan, a new surge of unilateralism has come to the fore, partly, to be sure, as antidote to Carter's supposedly ineffectual presidency. Carter was cleverly held responsible for the perceived U.S. decline during and after the Reagan presidential campaign. Such a partisan indictment led quite naturally to the view that the United States should start acting like a superpower—that is, militarily and at its own discretion.

In this spirit, the United States has used covert and overt force against other countries: Grenada (1983), Libya (1986), and Nicaragua (throughout the 1980s). Belligerent defiance of international law has been coupled with a series of harsh, dismissive attacks upon the United Nations: American withdrawal from UNESCO; U.S. refusal to submit either the Law of the Sea Treaty or the Geneva Protocols on the Law of War to the Senate for ratification; U.S. repudiation of the World Court as a result of its adverse rulings on U.S. policies in Nicaragua. The image of U.S. foreign policy on normative issues has become almost entirely negative, even if some small steps in the opposite direction have been taken, such as ratification of the Genocide Treaty and some support for democratizing movements in such selected third world countries as Haiti, the Philippines, and Argentina. In addition, the Reagan administration has shifted ground somewhat on arms control, regarding the INF Treaty as one of its major accomplishments, and on international financial institutions (the International Monetary Fund and the World Bank), which for better or worse were finally considered, even by this supply-side administration, as necessary instruments of world capitalist stability.

But the picture that has taken shape is not a mixed one. The image of U.S. government internationally rests on the gut issues of international life (use of force in foreign policy, reliance on nuclear weapons) and overall attitudes toward the United Nations. On both counts, Reagan's record is dark and foreboding, especially when contrasted with Gorbachev's attitudes and actions over the last several years.

These developments offer the next administration both challenges and extraordinary opportunities. Pragmatic steps in a different direction by the U.S. government could quickly erase the present damaging image. The larger opportunity is to test the sincerity and depth of the Gorbachev proposals by superseding an arms race with a peace race. Such an exciting option is available to the next president; although it contains risks of domestic backlash and international disappointment, these risks could be met by careful planning and bold, visionary leadership. The country seems ready for some bold, positive steps, especially if this shift in diplomatic direction were coupled at home with a vigorous program of economic reconstruction. Such a combination of moves would not only give leadership back to the United States, but could begin to put into place a global problem-solving framework far more responsive to the needs of the citizenry of this country and to the actual realities of international relations at the end of the 20th century. This combination of developments, if accompanied by a new, more solid detente with the Soviet Union, could create a genuine optimism about the future, an attitude that has not been present since the victory over fascism in World War II.

The reversal could begin with symbols and practical functions. It would be of immediate benefit for the United States to return to UNESCO and renew the U.S. commitment to the United Nations in the areas of peace and security. Additionally, it would appear desirable, and relatively non-controversial, to reverse Reagan's destructive stand on the great law-making treaty governing the use of the oceans, carefully negotiated for a decade to achieve a balance of benefits for all states. Ratifying this treaty as a formal policy would build confidence in the peaceful negotiating abilities of the leaders of the world. A similar, but more controversial, effort to extend the humanitarian law of war to situations of civil strife and revolutionary warfare would be helpful. Reactionaries will, no doubt, portray the well-balanced Geneva Protocols of 1977 as somehow "soft" on terrorism and liberation movements, especially as the treaties honor the rather minimal and altogether humane impulse to let such fighters receive the benefit of POW status in the event of their capture.

There are other areas where innovation is needed. The Reagan administration deserves some credit for negotiating an international agreement designed to safeguard the ozone layer against further depletion. It would be a self-interested contribution to world health for the U.S. government to implement such standards in an utterly serious manner that went beyond treaty requirements. Similarly, new steps could be taken to promote improved safety standards and procedures relating to nuclear energy facilities. Finally, the next president could address terrorism by renouncing all forms of support for political groups that do not respect the innocence of civilian life and by committing U.S. foreign policy to work for the restoration of the rights of dispossessed and abused peoples, making recourse to terrorist opposition both unnecessary and counter-productive.

But symbolic and functional innovation are not enough. The biggest challenge is to carry out U.S. foreign policy within the limits set by law, both domestic and international. The immediate proving ground for such commitment is the redesign of policy toward Central America. To begin with, by arming and financing the Nicaraguan *contras*, the U.S. government is flagrantly violating domestic neutrality laws as well as the international prohibition against forcible intervention into the internal affairs of sovereign states. The American political mainstream, including the Democratic Party, has not been willing to subordinate foreign policy to the regulation of international law. Hence, at this stage it may be difficult even for a Democratic president to show respect for the well-reasoned and moderate judgment of the World Court in *Nicaragua v. United States* that decided in June of 1986 that any further support for the *contras* was illegal. But the United States could show some good faith by establishing peace with Nicaragua, dissolving support for the *contras*, and negotiating an overall settlement that acknowledged the relevance of the World Court findings. Beyond this, Reagan's repudiation of the jurisdiction of this judicial arm of the United Nations should be quickly replaced by agreement to submit international legal disputes to the World Court in the event they cannot be resolved by diplomacy.

Beyond current policy lies the overall challenge of a fragile structure of world order. A new leader in the United States, especially with receptive Soviet counterparts, could breathe new life into the whole idea of collective security and peacekeeping under UN auspices. The sorry spectacle of conflict and bloodshed in the Middle East and Africa suggests the potential for conflict-resolving missions, especially if reinforced by superpower cooperation and anti-interventionism. A more energetic attempt could be made to end the Iran/Iraq war and to promote practical schemes for Namibia's political independence. One could even envisage an arrangement among the superpowers and participants in the annual economic summit to reallocate 1 percent per year from respective defense budgets to UN operations, giving the organization a greater measure of financial independence in relation to its target members.

Among the most successful and visible UN efforts in the 1970s were its conferences about global-scale problems such as environment, population, food, and human rights. Preparation for and participation in these conferences was itself educational for policymakers around the world, and events themselves provided the media with an occasion to disseminate information on world problems. Social movements also used these gatherings to disseminate more drastic versions of the problems being addressed and to publicize their demand for more radical strategies of response, thus broadening the general debate and what was discussed at official levels. Regardless of their substantive result, these UN-facilitated conferences began a multifaceted global dialogue on critical policy issues that were not conceived earlier to be the stuff of international relations.

In the 1980s this function has been virtually suspended. The United Nations is in eclipse, but it could be revived through energetic U.S.-led initiatives. The UN membership would be responsive to the United States resuming constructive participation after almost a decade of negative participation and withdrawal. There is an obvious and growing need for a forum on global-scale problems where policymakers can exert pressure on elites as well as shape a coherent, if not common, problem-solving approach.

Of course, the policy climate on every issue of global concern might not always be congenial to the wishes of even a reform-minded leadership in Washington. Demands from the third world associated with debt relief, shifts in terms of trade, price supports for commodity exports, and restrictions on multinational corporations might cause tension and controversy. Demands to support the anti-apartheid campaign or to secure a homeland for the Palestinian people would create difficulties. The United Nations was never expected to be immune from the conflicts taking place in international political life. On the contrary, the United Nations was intended to serve as a forum for discussion among adversaries and, to the extent possible, to facilitate conflict resolution by peaceful means.

The change in the U.S. stance toward the United Nations does not reflect its flawed character or its irresponsible manipulation by the

Soviet bloc or the third world. It is mainly a frustrated reaction to operating in a post-colonial world that no longer automatically defers to American leadership. Perhaps, in retrospect, the early dominance by the United States in the United Nations was costly, creating a misleading set of expectations. If the organization is to serve the world, and not some sector of it, then it needs to reflect the tensions that exist, and not ignore them or allow a single state to possess so much influence as to be able to convert the organization into an arena for its own foreign policy even when its actions are difficult to reconcile with the UN Charter. Early U.S. influence in the United Nations made it appear that later alternative policy outcomes were "anti-American" or "politicized." The United States was foolishly opportunistic during this early period, using its political muscle to deny mainland China UN representation long after its tenure was secure and after most governments were ready to work things out.

The United Nations is not now, nor has it ever been, an adversary structure of the sort portrayed by the far right, typified by the Heritage Foundation. U.S influence in the organization remains even now extraordinarily great across a wide range of issues. Remarkably, despite its record of interventionist diplomacy, the United States still retains considerable diplomatic capability to induce and reinforce mediation and compromise in regional conflict zones. A creative leadership in the White House, especially one that renounced the unilateralism of the Reagan years, could quickly rebuild the tarnished image of the United States and become once more a constructive force.

It would require leadership, not merely a flip-flop on policy. Anti-internationalism has grown beyond Reaganism, and is made credible for the public by periodic outbursts of anti-U.S. terrorism, by a perception of European allies (except Thatcher's Britain) as wimpy on issues of international order, and by a mainstream elite sense that the passivity induced by the so-called "Vietnam syndrome" is detrimental to international stature of the United States.

Time (2/29/88), in its coverage of the 1988 presidential election campaign, criticized Michael Dukakis'

> instinctive tendency to latch onto the most dovish stances...his policies are not only mushy, they seem downright unsophisticated. He bases his opposition to even humanitarian aid for the Nicaraguan *contras* on his reading of "international law" rather than on calculations about U.S. interests.

Note that international law is put in quotes to express editorial scorn, while the words humanitarian aid are allowed to stand uncritically despite the record of deviations. Why mushy and unsophisticated? Might not adherence to international law be the best way for the U.S. government to uphold order in a fragmented world, especially in light of the evident Soviet retreat from interventionism? The unexamined premise remains that the U.S. government is more effective when it retains the option to act lawlessly in world affairs.

My own reading of world events illustrates that lawlessness has a high price both internationally and in terms of domestic support for foreign policy. The Bay of Pigs, the Vietnam War, and the Reagan Doctrine, especially as applied to Central America, are all instances of flagrant violation which have resulted in defeat abroad and backlash at home. Comparably serious dislocation of national political life can be associated with such other legally dubious undertakings that appeared to reach their goals: CIA interventions in Iran (1953) and Guatemala (1954), armed intervention in the Dominican Republic (1965), and the aerial bombardment of Libya (1986). The United States would be both more secure and influential if it had built its post-1945 foreign policy around a serious commitment to accept the Rule of Law as a constraint on foreign policy.

We are currently being held captive to a consensus that regards "law" and the "United Nations" as mere distractions from real calculations about power and international interests. Yet tough-minded adherents to this consensus become neurotically jumpy about the slightest suspicion of Soviet arms control violations. Of course, we need to rely on Soviet assurances if we are to enter long-term relations with them that obligate both governments to act in specified ways. But to do this, we need to regard international law as a source of authority that is entitled to respect even when it *inhibits* our foreign policy. Respecting such inhibitions, especially in uses of force, could easily have saved us from past costly misadventures. From the Bay of Pigs to the Gulf of Corinto, U.S. violations of international law cast a shadow over our country's image, weaken the diplomatic reputation of the United States in world arenas, and cause countless American citizens to oppose, even resist the implementation of policy. If these consequences are coolly considered, they are incentives to encourage a legal foreign policy.

The main reason why we should renew our commitment to the Rule of Law internationally has to do with the character of the world, not recalculations of interests. International legal order and an increasingly empowered United Nations are truly required to reduce the menace of global chaos and disaster today. Given the realities of fragile and complex interdependence among nations, of global-scale environmental issues, and of controversial internal abuses of human rights, ample space exists to fashion common standards and global procedures. The wholeness of the planet requires disciplined participation by member states drawn from all sectors. International integration is a matter of objective circumstance, not vague aspiration. To portray U.S. national interests in this spirit, especially to the extent a new positive relationship is being forged with the Soviet Union, would find a supportive public, provided the new look is expressed in positive, hopeful, prudent terms and provided such a shift was not connected with the perceptions of geopolitical defeats.

In the background is the growing realization that both the United States and the Soviet Union are currently challenged to manage their own separate, yet connected, processes of relative decline in a difficult, vulnerable world order, with both the global economy and a sustaining ecological balance in jeopardy. This phase of waning empire, in a nuclear setting, is itself a daunting prospect, but it will be even more so if we fail to make use of the very substantial opportunities for planetary oversight that now exist. Leaders are most admirable when they convert daunting prospects into occasions for reformist breakthroughs. World conditions in the late 1980s offer the next set of leaders just such a crisis of opportunity.

Resources

Recommended Appointees for a New Administration

State Department
- Burns Weston, Professor of Law at the University of Iowa, co-author of *International Law and World Order*
- Tom F. Farer, Professor of Law at the University of New Mexico, former Chairman of the Inter-American Human Rights Commission

United Nations
- Edith Brown Weiss, Professor of Law at Georgetown University, author of books on science, technology, and public policy
- Saul Mendlovitz, Director of the World Order Models Project, New York
- Peter Weiss, Vice President of the Center for Constitutional Rights

International Court of Justice
- Leonard Boudin, practicing lawyer in New York, associated with some of the most important international constitutional cases in the last two decades

Arms Control and Disarmament Agency
- Randall Forsberg, Director of the Institute for Defense and Disarmament, Cambridge, Massachusetts, founder of FREEZE
- Robert Johansen, Director of the Institute for Peace Studies, University of Notre Dame, author of *The National Interest and the Human Interest*

Organizations

- World Policy Institute, 777 UN Plaza, New York, NY 10017; (212) 490-0010

- Institute for Policy Studies, 1601 Connecticut Ave. NW, Washington, DC 20009; (202) 234-9382
- World Order Models Project, 777 UN Plaza, New York, NY 10017; (212) 490-0010

Further Reading

- Francis Wormuth and Edwin Firmage, *To Chain the Dog of War*, SMU Press, 1986.
- Louis Henkin, *Foreign Affairs and the Constitution*, Norton, 1975.
- Louis Henkin, *How Nations Behave*, 2nd edition, Columbia University Press, 1979.
- Richard Falk, *The Promise of World Order*, Temple University Press, 1987.
- Stanley Hoffman, *Duties Beyond Borders*, Syracuse University Press, 1981.
- Francis Boyle, *Defending Civil Resistance Under International Law*, Transnational Publishers, 1987.

Richard Falk is Albert G. Milbank Professor of International Law and Practice at Princeton University. Over the years he has worked with several presidential candidates as a foreign policy advisor. His most recent books are *Revolutionaries and Functionaries: The Dual Face of International Terrorism* and *The Promise of World Order*.

Seymour Melman

Why Economic Conversion?

Platform

- Develop an economic conversion program with sufficient planning time to select new products and equipment, identify raw materials sources, and retrain the labor force.
- Decentralize the economic conversion planning process.
- Eliminate cushioning management subsidies.
- Establish by law an alternative use committee (half selected by management, half by workers) at every military-serving facility and base.
- Retrain managers and engineers for product design that seeks cost-minimizing simplicity within the limits of reliable performance.
- Provide funds for worker relocation, where necessary.
- Provide income support for workers to cover lag time between the end of military production and the start of civilian work.
- Enact H.R. 813, a bill to "facilitate economic adjustment of communities, industries, and workers through reduction or realignment of defense or aerospace contracts, military facilities, and arms export and for other purposes" introduced by Representative Ted Weiss (D-NY), 1987.

Economic conversion is the planning and implementation of a changeover of factories, research laboratories, bases, and allied facilities from military to civilian application. After enduring a warlike economy for more than forty years, the American people need economic conversion planning for the following vital purposes:

- to make possible the physical reconstruction of U.S. industry, infrastructure, and environment that have been depleted by the war economy

- to give confidence in the ability to carry out the production cutbacks that are a core part of an agreed disarmament process

- to make disarmament an opportunity rather that a penalty for the largest number of people whose working lives will have to be converted to civilian skills and tasks

Economic conversion is dramatically different from what was called *reconversion* at the close of World War II. At that time, factories that had turned from civilian to military production for the duration of the war reverted to their former activities. They were able to reapply the old machines and more often than not the former workforce to the production system that had been there before, turning out familiar products, getting raw materials from familiar suppliers, selling to familiar markets. The situation now is altogether different. Factories and laboratories producing military goods and services were for the most part brought into being for those purposes; they have no civilian history. A large part of today's personnel have spent their entire careers in military-serving operations.

Economic conversion has three functions. One is to move production facilities from military to civilian use, thus directly diminishing the power base of warmaking institutions. Another is to reverse the erosion of competence in civilian industrial production that has been caused by the spread of cost-maximizing practices from the military to the civilian sphere. Lastly, conversion offers economic opportunity to the people of the war economy institutions while the reversal of the arms race proceeds.

The Managerial Power Base of the Warmaking Institutions

What is the meaning of "the power base" of warmaking institutions? In the United States, about 120,000 persons comprise the central administrative office of the U.S. military-serving industrial system, located in the Department of Defense. It is an office equivalent to the top decisionmaking entity of a multidivision, multiplant firm; it formulates general policy, designates the principal managers of main subdivisions, and polices policy compliance among the divisions. The central administrative office of the Department of Defense stands in relation to 37,000 prime contractors as does the central administrative office of General Motors to the divisions of General Motors. It is the largest such central administrative office in the U.S. economy and very possibly the largest such body in the world.

Warmaking institutions have mobilized the largest labor force under one management. They have the largest research and development staffs subject to one management. The R & D sections of the

Department of Defense and its allied agencies consume from 70-75 percent of the total R & D budget.

We are indebted to President Eisenhower for calling attention, in his farewell address of January 7, 1961, to the fact that during every year of the previous decade, the fresh capital resources made available to the Department of Defense exceeded the cumulative net profits of all U.S. corporations. That state of affairs has continued from 1961 to the present day; a modern military budget is a capital fund, and warmaking institutions wield the largest finance capital fund in the U.S economy. From 1946 to 1980 the budgets of the Department of Defense totalled $2,001 billion. The budgets executed and projected for the period 1980-1988 were to be $2,089 billion. If control of finance capital is a means of exerting economic and political power, then it is only too clear that the U.S. warmaking institutions have enjoyed an unprecedented measure of it.

Costs to Society

Capital in an ordinary industrial enterprise is of two sorts: fixed and working. Fixed capital is the money value of the land, buildings, and machinery. Working capital is the money value of all other resources that must be brought to bear to set the enterprise in motion. Funds applied to a modern military budget provide precisely the set of resources that are conventionally identified as fixed and working capital. Such funds do that on behalf of a set of military products that have the unique characteristic of contributing nothing to ordinary consumption (i.e., to the quality of life). Neither can they be used for further production.

Due to that peculiarity of the military product, the aggregate cost to the whole community of the capital resources so used has a set of characteristics almost entirely overlooked in our economic textbooks. The first cost to the whole society is the direct resources allocated to the military function. A second cost is measured by the civilian use-value—goods and services for consumption or for production—which are foregone when the resources are used for military products. For the whole community, that value is approximately equal to the cost of the direct inputs from the military budget. There is a third cost: when capital resources are used for new civilian production on a continuing basis, there is usually improvement in the design of the means of production. Economists call this an increase in the marginal productivity of capital. But when capital resources are used for purposes that cannot be applied to any further production, that increment of productivity of capital is lost, forever. There is yet a fourth kind of social cost. A large part of knowledge that is generated on behalf of the military has unique application to military technology and is not relevant elsewhere; hence it is lost. A fifth kind of cost, while unmeasurable, is quite important. As a large labor force is trained for the military, it becomes accustomed not to minimizing cost but to maximizing cost, and to offsetting that maximized cost with maximized subsidies. Such practices are possible only when carried out by a privileged ward of the state, with almost unlimited resources made available by tapping the income of the whole society. A labor force so trained develops what Thorstein Veblen genially called a trained incapacity—in this case for civilian work. To my knowledge, no one has yet attempted an aggregate measure of the above mentioned social costs of the military.

How the Military Further Depletes the Civilian Sector

Returning to the basic idea of the military budget as a capital fund, it is important to compare that budget with another capital fund, Gross Domestic Fixed Capital Formation, which is the money value of new civilian capital items put in place in a given year: school buildings, factories, machinery, roads, waterworks, libraries, and the like. From data on national income assembled by the staff of the United Nations one can calculate the capital fund made available for the military in a number of countries for a given year as a ratio per $100 (or francs or yen, etc.) of capital represented by new civilian capital formation, whether privately or publicly funded. For the last year of such available data, 1983, the ratios of military expenditures for every $100 of civilian gross fixed capital formation were: United States, 40; United Kingdom, 31; France, 16; Sweden, 12; West Germany, 13; Japan, 3.3. (For the USSR there are no official data. My estimate, which I will be pleased to discard when proper data are offered, is 66.)

These relationships are informative. The very low ratio of military to civilian use of capital in Japan and West Germany is a fundamental clue to the modernity of their industrial plant and equipment, their rapidly developing civilian technologies, and their ability to sustain a rapid rise in wage rates together with competitive competence.

A further estimate in this area is truly startling. It is based on the planned U.S. military budget for 1988. I compared that budget with an estimate, derived by simple statistical extrapolation, of the Gross Domestic Fixed Capital Formation in the same year. The U.S. ratio I arrived at for 1988 is 87:100. If the present trend of military buildup continues, if the intense use of capital by the Pentagon prevails, it is entirely likely that the competence of U.S. industry will be irreparably destroyed, that the quality of the civilian production system will be so degraded as to be an important factor in reaching what I described in *Profits Without Production* as a point of no return.

The military budget as a capital fund influences productivity growth. The United States, from 1865-1965, paid the highest industrial wages in the world, and its industries were able at the same time to turn out products of a quality and at a price that made them saleable both domestically and abroad. That was possible because high wages were offset by progressive mechanization of work and improvement in the organization of work. As a result, there was growing productivity. After 1965, following a period of growing military budgets, U.S. productivity growth dropped sharply. According to a December 1984 report of the U.S. Bureau of Labor Statistics on trends of manufacturing productivity and labor costs from 1960-1983, eleven countries—Canada, Japan, Belgium, Denmark, France, Germany, Italy, the Netherlands, Norway, Sweden, and the United Kingdom—all had higher average rates of productivity growth than the United States, whose average annual increase was only about 2.6 percent.

The ratio of military to civilian use of capital obviously has profound consequences for work mechanization, plant modernity, and increasing or slowing productivity growth. As cost-minimizing was replaced in military industries by cost-maximizing, the classic process whereby endless detailed improvements were made in manufacturing productivity was stalled.

The mechanism of cost minimizing in U.S. industry used to work as follows: the wages of labor, a major cost item, would rise for various reasons—market forces and union bargaining among others. The users of labor in cost-minimizing firms would move to offset the wage increase by mechanization of work, by better organization of work, by product redesign. This meant that wages could rise more rapidly than the prices of product-machinery. In turn, this meant that the users of machinery were being offered new, more efficient equipment at prices that were progressively more attractive. So a continuing process encouraged the broader, more intensive use of machinery in place of manual labor. The effect: an improvement in the average productivity of labor. This pattern was characteristic of the United States, and of Great Britain until 1950. Now that pattern has been essentially transformed. By 1978, the United States had the oldest stock of metalworking machinery of any industrialized country. To be sure, this was not caused only by the fact that the Department of Defense had become a major purchaser of machine tools and a major sponsor for machine tool R & D, thus causing cost-maximizing to infect the interior operations of the machine tool industry. There was also a general transformation in the emphasis of U.S. industrial management, away from competent production and toward straight moneymaking by all manner of financial devices.

How a Permanent War Economy Counters Productivity Growth

A definable set of conditions favors productivity growth: cost-minimizing within the machinery-producing industries; cost-minimizing among machinery users; wages rising faster than machinery prices; availability of finance capital at modest interest rates; R & D to innovate new means of production; stable rates of production; management oriented to production; availability of a competent surrounding infrastructure as a support base for production. The effect of the military economy in its normal operation has run counter to every one of these requirements for productivity growth. As a result, U.S. firms have become less able to offset cost increases and unable to supply even the domestic market at acceptable levels of price and quality. By 1980, 27 percent of our automobiles were imports; so too were 25 percent of machine tools (by 1986 it was 49 percent), 15 percent of steel mill products, 87 percent of black-and-white television sets, 47 percent of calculating machines, 22 percent of microwave ranges and ovens, 34 percent of integrated microcircuits, 24 percent of x-ray and other irradiation equipment, 74 percent of motion picture cameras, 51 percent of sewing machines (by 1984, 100 percent of the household type), 100 percent of radios, 22 percent of bicycles, and 50 percent of shoes (by 1987, 86 percent).

Every one of these percentages also means that about the same percentage of domestic employment in those industries has disappeared. That is what accounts for the several million jobs lost in the U.S. industrial economy.

Misleading Statistics

There is a discrepancy between the national employment figures issued by the government and the details of life in particular industries, cities, and regions. The military economy prospers; there are boom conditions in the industries and regions that seek to employ engineers and skilled workers for the Pentagon's needs. The evidence is in job announcements in newspapers in Los Angeles, Boston, and New York City. But there is no boom condition in Homestead, Pennsylvania, where the works of the U.S. Steel Corporation are blacked out and where the neighboring works of the Mesta Machine Company, once supplier of steel mill equipment to U.S. industry, have been dismantled.

Again and again it is essential to differentiate among the published aggregate figures for economic activities. For example, on December 22, 1984, an AP dispatch reported that, according to the Commerce Department, orders for durable goods posted their biggest gain in more than four years—an 8.3 percent November increase. Next paragraph: more than half the gain was attributed to a 99.4 percent increase in the volatile military orders category. In other words, the headline reads "Durable Orders Surge 8.3 Percent," but the small type tells us more than half was in readily manipulated Pentagon orders.

The High-Tech Industries

Depletion has occurred not only in the so-called smokestack industries, but also in the highest of all the high-tech—the computer industry. An instructive example is one of the most popular, fastest selling, and important computers, the IBM Personal Computer. On the back of the cathode ray tube box is printed "made in Taiwan" or "made in Korea." The label on the lower box says "made in the U.S.A.," but the disk drive is made in Singapore or Hong Kong, and the chips, made in Japan, are also assembled abroad. The keyboard and power unit are made in Japan. What is left in the United States is production of the outer case and assembly of the main working components. Indeed, for the R & D-intensive industries as a group, the 1980s saw a sharp reversal of position. In 1980, the high-tech industries showed a balance of payments that was favorable for the United States. By 1986, that had become a net deficit.

This situation is troublesome, not for some nationalist reason, or because of the desirability of economic self-sufficiency, but because in order to live, a community must produce. There is no theory or experience from which to infer that it is possible on any sustained basis for a community to have its production done for it by someone else.

Product Unreliability

There is a further problem for which the military economy is responsible. The military trains engineers and production workers to accept product unreliability. Military products have been made increasingly complex, to the point that complexity necessarily reduces reliability. That happens because the reliability of a set of linked components is the product of the reliability of each of the separate components. Since no person-made device is ever 100 percent reliable, the combination of more and more components degrades the reliability of the whole mechanism or system.

In military experience it is normal for 45 out of 100 F-15s, the first-line fighter plane of the U.S. Air Force, on the average, to be in repair at any given moment. If M-1 tanks are on maneuvers, they can be kept running only by heroic maintenance efforts and by the immediate availability of spare parts. On the anti-aircraft Aegis cruiser, software is crucial to the operation of the control systems for the weaponry involved, but the software has a high failure rate. Other parts of the system can be expected to function only 45 percent of the time.

Such unreliability, which has become acceptable in the military, is completely unacceptable in civilian operation. If a trolley car or subway goes out of service 45 percent of the time, if it fails frequently on the tracks, it will block the right of way; it will inconvenience a whole community; it will immediately come to the attention of many witnesses. There will surely be a great public outcry for relief from an intolerable situation. When aerospace technology and modes of organization were applied to the production of trolley cars (as was done by the Boeing-Vertol Co. outside Philadelphia), it becomes clear why the military-industry approach won't work in the civilian economy. Boeing-Vertol had to drop out of the trolley car business because it was confronted by massive lawsuits from the Massachusetts Bay Transit Authority. The trolley was handsome; it was a pleasure to ride in when it functioned, but a remarkable array of things went wrong. Those things were built-in weaknesses, the direct result of a mode of organization and operation that is systematically pursued in military industry, and notably in the aerospace industry. That is why economic conversion, which includes retraining personnel from military to civilian competence, is essential.

One of the standard practices of the military industry is called concurrency. In the civilian economy, when a new product is projected, it customarily goes through a set of functional stages: the concept; research; design; prototype use; prototype tests; discovery of faults. It is redesigned, retested—perhaps several times. Only after the prototype meets the desired performance standards is the order given to produce. Not in the land of the Department of Defense. There, concurrency is practiced, indeed ordered by the regulations of the Secretary of Defense. Concurrency means carrying out all these steps in parallel. You discover defects after you have produced and used the product, whereupon you change the design for items yet to be produced and retrofit those already made.

This is probably the most expensive way ever formulated of building anything, and is a major component of the cost-maximizing managerial hierarchies governed by the Pentagon. In the Pentagon, such procedures "work," as they escalate costs and thereby justify ever-larger military budgets (for details of these mechanisms, see *The Permanent War Economy*). As this becomes the habitual behavior of military engineers and managers, and to some degree production workers, they become unable to function in a civilian economy. This is why occupational retraining for economic conversion is not an arbitrary idea. It is indispensable if the workers engaged in military economy are to function competently in a civilian environment.

Planning For Economic Conversion

What are the strategic components of economic conversion from military to civilian economy? First, it must be planned well in advance. To establish an alternative civilian use for a military industrial enterprise of any size, one needs a lead time of at least two years. This period is required for selecting new products and production equipment; identifying sources of raw materials; retraining the labor force. For firms (or division of firms) with an all-military background, the selection of new products is crucial. What marketable civilian products can be produced most competently by people or equipment hitherto employed entirely by the military?

Second, economic conversion planning must be decentralized. If attempted from a national center it will fail, because it is not possible to oversee from a remote headquarters the myriad of specific data that must be taken into account in a plan devised for a given enterprise.

Third, the whole activity must be carried out without subsidy to the managements involved. A continuance of subsidy means a continuance of cushioning for what in the civilian realm would be gross incompetence.

Fourth, it is essential that every military-serving factory and base be obliged by law to set up an alternative use committee, half of its members selected by management, half by workers (all grades), with responsibility and authority for planning alternative products, production, and marketing systems for the plant, laboratory, or the base facility. This procedure must be mandatory because otherwise the managements involved, and even some of the engineers or production workers, would resist engaging in such planning.

Fifth, managers and engineers must be retrained. Military-serving managers are expert in the politics and diplomacy of dealing with the Department of Defense; they couldn't sell a folding bed to Sears, Roebuck to save their lives. Engineers who have been trained to create products of escalating intricacy, without regard to cost, must be taught a new approach to product design that seeks cost-minimizing simplicity within the limits of reliable performance. Research and development must be disciplined so that people who have been accustomed to making lavish use of resources paid for out of the federal pocket will discover economical ways of doing their work. Some of the production workers will need to be retrained, but probably a smaller proportion than among engineers and managers.

Sixth, economic conversion planning must include funds for worker relocation, because parts of typically oversized administrative and engineering staffs at the Pentagon—serving factories and bases—will have to be moved to other locations.

Seventh, even with the most thorough advance planning, there is bound to be a lag between the end of the military production and the start of civilian work. Some income support for workers will therefore be required.

What can ex-military-serving firms produce? For a start, they could examine the list of manufactured products now being imported to the United States, asking: which of these products are producible in our facilities and could that work be done at acceptable price and quality? There is also the challenge of competing against producers already in the field. In addition, U.S. industries will require vast capital investment, as will U.S. infrastructure. In 1982, the editors of *U.S. News and World Report* reckoned that the crumbling infrastructure could be repaired at a price of $2,500 billion. U.S. military budgets (spent and planned) 1980-1990 exceed $2,900 billion. By 1988, the further deterioration in infrastructure and the lessening purchasing power of the dollar (since 1982) indicate that $3,000 billion is a more appropriate estimate for the cost of repairing U.S. infrastructure. At an average of $30,000 per person-year, this indicates a requirement for 100 million people-years of work to meet the requirement. Such an immense activity will have far-reaching effects in many U.S. industries as the demand for machinery of every sort rises in order to meet vast construction requirements. It is more than likely that the U.S. labor force will prove to be too small, especially in the skilled occupations, for carrying out this task before the turn of the century.

H.R. 813

At the time of this writing, the set of requirements for conversion planning as enumerated here are incorporated in the text of a bill introduced by Representative Ted Weiss (D-NY), and supported by more than fifty colleagues. In 1987, it was designated H.R. 813, a bill to "facilitate economic adjustment of communities, industries, and workers through reduction or realignment of defense or aerospace contracts, military facilities, and arms export and for other purposes." The importance of H.R. 813 is twofold. First, it outlines a coherent, urgently needed, and constructive approach that is an economic alternative to the arms race. Second, with planning for economic conversion underway, both the government and the people will have fresh political will to negotiate and implement the reversal of the arms race.

The components of H.R. 813 meet each of the requirements outlined above for competent economic conversion planning. It is worth underlining that the planning process defined in this proposed law provides not only for highly decentralized authority and responsibility for planning the future use of factories, laboratories, and bases, but it also includes the core of the planning process that is needed for defining the great array of new expenditures for infrastructure repair in every city, county, and state. One of the main obligations of the national commission defined under this proposed law is the task of encouraging the governments of cities, counties, and states, as well as federal departments, to undertake capital investment planning in all the areas of public infrastructure that are their responsibility. The consequences of fulfilling this mandate will be a great array of workable capital investment plans that translate into immense new future markets and work opportunities in the U.S. economy.

Addressing disarmament and economic conversion will allow us to strike at the heart of the single most dangerous political process of our time: the antagonistic cooperation whereby the warmaking institutions of the United States and the USSR have reinforced each other and generated larger budgets, larger military economies, larger stocks of more dangerous weapons, and in doing so have justified more centralism and more authoritarianism in each society. There is no single public issue that is as crucial for the survival of society as disarmament and economic conversion.

Resources

Recommended Appointees for a New Administration

- John E. Ullman, Professor of Management and Engineering at Hofstra University, author of basic monographs on industrial conversion planning problems

- Bernard Roth, Professor of Mechanical Engineering at Stanford University, expert in robotics and redesign of industrial facilities
- Warren Davis, astrophysicist at MIT, key person in groupings of scientists and engineers concerned with problems of retraining engineering/science personnel for civilian specialties following long military research and/or industrial experience
- William Winpisinger, President of the International Association of Machinists, expert in all aspects of blue-collar worker transitions from military to civilian work
- Ernest Fitzgerald, industrial engineer and cost analyst, leading expert on operation of military firms and industrial practices, with extensive industrial experience in both civilian and military economy
- Dr. Greg Bischak, economist with specialized knowledge about the nuclear industry, in particular problems of civilian utilization of facilities and firms
- Professor Lloyd J. Dumas, industrial engineer and economist, has done extensive research and writing on conversion from military to civilian economy, including articles and books that deal with U.S. and international aspects of these topics
- David McFadden, historian with specialized knowledge about the role of governments in decentralized organization and functioning of economic conversion operations
- Robert DeGrasse, Jr., economist with substantial research and publications on characteristics of military economy, especially the relation between military economy and industrial efficiency

Organizations

- National Commission for Economic Conversion and Disarmament, 715 G St. SE, Washington, DC 20003; (202) 544-5059
- Center for Economic Conversion, 222C View St., Mountain View, CA 94041; (415) 968-8798
- Jobs With Peace, 76 Summer St., Boston MA 02110; (617) 338-5783

Further Reading

- H.R. 813, a bill introduced to the 100th Congress, 1st Session, January 28, 1987, by Congressman Ted Weiss (D-NY).
- *Jobs From the Sun: Employment Development in the California Solar Energy Industry*, California Public Policy Center (304 S. Broadway, Room 224, Los Angeles, CA 90013), February, 1978.
- Lloyd J. Dumas, *The Overburdened Economy*, University of California Press 1986.

- Curtis B. Eaton, "Do Defense Engineers Have Social Reemployment Problems?" *Monthly Labor Review*, 94, July 1971, pp. 52-54.

- Suzanne Gordon and David McFadden, eds., *Economic Conversion: Revitalizing America's Economy*, Ballinger Publishing Co., 1984.

- W.F. Gutteridge, *Problems of Conversion of Scientists and Technologists in the Event of Disarmament*, Department of Languages and Social Science, Lancaster College of Technology, Coventry, England, 1967.

- Seymour Melman, *Barriers to Conversion from Military to Civilian Industry—in Market, Planned, and Developing Economies*, prepared for the United Nations Center for Disarmament, Ad Hoc Group of Governmental Experts on the Relationship Between Disarmament and Development, April 1980 (available from Professor S. Melman, 304 Mudd, Columbia University, New York, NY 10027).

- Seymour Melman, *An Economic Alternative to the Arms Race: Conversion from Military to Civilian Economy*, The National SANE Education Fund, 711 G St. SE, Washington, DC 20003, 1987.

- Seymour Melman, ed., *Conversion of Industry from a Military to a Civilian Economy*, a series in six volumes, Frederick Praeger Special Studies, 1970: M. Berkowitz, *The Conversion of Military-Oriented R&D to Civilian Uses*; A. Christodoulou, *Conversion of Nuclear Facilities from Military to Civilian Uses*; J.E. Lynch, *Local Economic Development After Military Base Closures*; D.M. Mack-Forlist and A. Newman, *The Conversion of Shipbuilding from Military to Civilian Markets*; Seymour Melman, ed., *The Defense Economy*; J.E. Ullman, ed., *Potential Civilian Markets for the Military-Electronics Industry*.

- Seymour Melman, *The Permanent War Economy*, Simon and Schuster, 1985.

- Seymour Melman, *Profits Without Production*, A.A. Knopf, 1983.

- U.S. Comptroller General, *Problems Associated with Converting Defense Research Facilities to Meet Different Needs: The Case of Fort Detrick*, Report to Congress, B-160140, February 16, 1972.

- P. Wallensteen, ed., *Experience in Disarmament: On Conversion of Military Industry and Closing of Military Bases*, Report No. 19, June 1978, Department of Peace and Conflict Research, Uppsala University, Uppsala, Sweden (note: contains major review article on conversion literature, papers on U.S., U.K., and Sweden, and bibliographic appendices).

- C. Wong, *Economic Consequences of Armament and Disarmament—A Bibliography*, Center for the Study of Armament and Disarmament, California State University, Los Angeles, 1981.

Seymour Melman is Professor Emeritus of Industrial Engineering at Columbia University and Chairman of the National Commission for Economic Conversion and Disarmament. He conducted early studies on the way economic factors determine the design and use of technology, and resulting productivity. His *Profits Without Production* is a combined analysis of the role of private and government managers and the effect of their policies and institutions on productivity and industrial competence. A new book, *The Demilitarized Society*, is currently in press.

The United States in the World Economy: Aid, Debt, and Trade

Platform

Aid for Development

- The United States sends approximately $14 billion in aid to the underdeveloped world, most of it through bilateral channels (the Agency for International Development-AID), the rest through multilateral channels (the World Bank, regional development banks, and the United Nations). The United States should slash security-related assistance to the third world, which now accounts for over two-thirds of U.S. bilateral aid.

- AID must be reorganized so that popular organizations in the recipient countries are involved in the design and implementation of aid projects. Far greater emphasis must be placed on integrating the needs of women, the poor, and the environment into projects. More multilateral aid should be channeled through UN agencies like the International Fund for Agricultural Development (IFAD) which place priority on smaller projects that benefit the poor.

- Reagan administration priorities of emphasizing export-oriented growth and privatization, which have exacerbated oversupply, falling raw material prices, and inequality, should be eliminated. The United States should work in the World Bank and the regional development banks towards more project lending and away from loans conditioned on the export-oriented, privatization agenda. These "structural adjustment" loans increase inequality in a stagnant world economy and often reinforce anti-democratic institutions (e.g., a December 1987 World Bank loan to Chile which will help finance Pinochet's "re-election" campaign).

- The United States should support reorganization in the World Bank and the regional development banks to reduce headquarters staff and increase field representatives who work with indigenous organizations in project design and implementation.

Finance and Debt

- The extreme exchange rate instability of the 1980s must end. Limiting exchange rate movements to a specified band is a possible short-term correction.

- The United States should cooperate with other nations to replace the dollar as a universal standard of exchange with a standard based on a basket of major currencies, a step which would introduce a more equitable stability in international monetary markets.

- The United States should work with other governments to establish a multilateral facility that will purchase third world debt from banks at a discount and pass on the discount to developing countries in the form of debt relief.

Trade

- The tax, trade, and investment incentives which lead U.S. corporations to produce overseas should be eliminated in order to encourage corporate investment in U.S. communities and infrastructure.

- The United States should enforce the laws which condition trade and investment on foreign countries' adherence to internationally recognized standards of worker rights.

- Repression of worker rights should be codified in the General Agreement on Tariffs and Trade (GATT) as an unfair trade practice.

- In the longer-term, the enormous imbalances that characterize trade will be corrected by the shift from export-oriented development toward wage/income-led growth as deficit countries produce more and more of what they now import.

The postwar *Pax Americana* succeeded in creating an integrated global economy and increasing world production. But its record has been less noteworthy in achieving balanced growth and an equitable distribution of benefits. The promise of global prosperity and security, put forward with such bold confidence forty years ago, seems ever more elusive today. The vulnerabilities of the free trade system have emerged with particular force in the 1980s: sluggish world growth, persistent trade and capital imbalances, worsening inequities between and within nations, and an alarming increase in debt and speculation.

These maladies interact to produce a vicious cycle in which social needs and living standards are sacrificed in both debtor and creditor nations, developing and developed alike. While third world peoples must endure wrenching poverty to prove their creditworthiness to international financial institutions, U.S. workers are expected to lower their wages closer to third world standards in order to become "competitive" with today's successful exporters.

The tragedy is that this harsh pattern is rooted neither in economic necessity nor natural scarcity, but in policies that benefit a few powerful interests. These problems have less to do with economic theory and its application than with the lack of commitment to principles of economic and political democracy and the will to carry them out.

The world economy has changed markedly over the past two decades. Communities, regions, and nations have become more interconnected as trade and lending between countries has increased. These connections have exacted a heavy toll on workers, farmers, and the poor the world over.

Private corporations and banks have been the driving force of this interdependence. Large transnational corporations have grown rapidly in agriculture, industry, media, and other areas of the economy. Along with large banks, they have become increasingly unaccountable to the general public and to the communities in which they originated.

Transnational corporations have exported part of the manufacturing base of industrial countries to underdeveloped countries in what has become known as "the global assembly line." Corporations went global to take advantage of governments which denied basic worker rights, where wages were comparatively cheap, especially as regards women workers. In the process, millions of manufacturing jobs have been destroyed in the United States. Job retraining and education programs have proved woefully inadequate.

New technologies permit the production of more goods with less labor, leading to a growth of unemployment and underemployment. In the United States, the fall in industrial jobs has been matched by a rise in service jobs (fast food, retail, computer, janitorial) which are large-ly low-paying in nonunion shops where job security and benefits are minimal. Many of the new jobs involve women working out of their homes in conditions of low pay and the absence of rights. In short, the quality of work in the United States has been declining.

As transnational corporations moved into the underdeveloped world, they and multilateral institutions like the World Bank pushed countries into export-oriented development strategies dependent on borrowing. After over a decade of heavy borrowing, many underdeveloped countries found that by the early 1980s (when interest rates rose and raw material prices collapsed) they could no longer meet even service payments on their debts. The creditor banks and governments used the International Monetary Fund to make new loans and refinancing agreements contingent on strict austerity programs. These programs place the burden of debt repayment squarely on the shoulders of poor and working people, by freezing wages, cutting government price subsidies (on rice, cooking oil, beans, and other essential items), and trimming subsidized credits in rural areas.

Simultaneously, the United States underwent a debt crisis of its own. During the 1970s, the same fall of raw material prices that sent the third world into a tailspin left U.S. farmers hundreds of millions of dollars in debt to the banks. When both experienced problems repaying their debts in the 1980s, banks turned their lending toward businesses and consumers, who are building up alarming amounts of shaky debt.

Indeed, the practice of Reaganomics has been rooted in greed: redistributing resources from poor to rich and from future generations to current consumers. The consumer bonanza which boosted real personal consumption by $300 per worker each year was not based on increased investment and output in the U.S. economy. The 23 percent rise in personal consumption over the first six Reagan years was accompanied by only a 17 percent rise in GNP. The difference was covered by imports and by a consumer debt boom that has no rival in any country. Consumer debt has now reached $3.2 trillion, over three-quarters the level of GNP. On top of spiralling consumer and corporate debt, the U.S. government has built up an enormous debt as its military and other spending consistently outpaces government receipts. The Reagan years present a grim decline of fortunes: whereas in 1981 foreigners owed the United States $141 billion more than Americans owed them, by 1987 a reversal became evident. U.S. foreign debt hit $400 billion in 1987 and is moving on a trajectory that will push it past $1 trillion in the early 1990s. The United States has become a nation of debtors.

The United States has also encouraged governments in other countries to divert resources from socially useful activities toward the military, to the point where many of them are quite dependent on the military for jobs and exports. Many underdeveloped countries have either stepped up domestic production of weapons or raised military imports in order to keep their own populations under control.

At the same time, there is a dangerous trend of governments reducing their role as providers of a social safety net for the most vulnerable segments of society. A fanatical adherence to an ideology of free markets and privatization has been engendered by U.S. policy in many countries precisely at the moment when workers and the poor, displaced or marginalized by the rapidly changing economy, need assistance the most. There is an urgent need to shift government priorities away from military spending and toward the provision of services which the free market deems unprofitable yet society deems essential.

The effects of these shifts toward exports, military spending, and growing concentration of private economic power have been devastating for the poorer majorities in most countries, especially since the early 1980s.

Four aspects of the economic crisis of the 1980s stand out:

Stagnation

Output and trade slowed markedly as heavy lending, largely to third world elites, fed stagnation and a cycle of increasing, unserviceable debts. Further, the corporate practice of exploiting the underdeveloped world as low-wage producers stunted the growth of demand for goods and services. This decline in consuming power was fed in the industrialized countries by unemployment induced by runaway shops and labor-saving technological innovations. Stagnation, in turn, bred protectionism.

Growth of trade slowed from average annual rates of 8 percent in the 1950s and 1960s, to 5 percent in the 1970s, to just over 2 percent in the 1980s.

Debt and Speculation

Governments responded to stagnation with even greater deregulation and, in the United States, tax cuts for corporations. Corporations and banks used the tax breaks to feed a flurry of highly speculative investments. The U.S. economy increasingly resembles what *Business Week* has called "the casino society": the large-scale diversion of the nation's productive resources into short-term, highly speculative investments.

According to the proponents of supply-side economics, the massive tax cuts that Reagan bestowed on corporate America in 1981 were designed to spur productive investment that would generate jobs, incomes, and new tax revenues. In practice, however, the nation's corporations channelled these tax handouts into a vast array of highly speculative financial instruments such as futures markets, stock options, leveraged buyouts (whereby funds borrowed for the takeover of a company are secured on that company's assets), and mergers and acquisitions. To finance these wholly unproductive operations, U.S. corporations have accumulated a debt of $1.9 trillion, a figure that has been growing at over 10 percent a year.

The result of this enormous amount of money rushing into speculative activity was that, from 1979 to 1986, productivity growth slipped from an already low 0.6 percent a year in the 1970s to 0.4 percent. This has catastrophic consequences for industrial America as it lumbers into the last decade of the century.

Imbalances Among Countries

Banks continue to squeeze debt service out of the underdeveloped world, leading to a perverse resource flow from poor to rich countries that grows yearly. Trade and financial imbalances between the United States and other industrialized countries have likewise grown to dangerous proportions.

By 1985, the United States suffered a trade deficit of $150 billion, one-third of which was with Japan, a third of which was with Canada and Western Europe, and one-third of which was with the third world. Most of the U.S. deficit with the third world is with Asian countries, a deficit which has steadily grown over the last decade under the impetus of U.S. trade, investment, and tax incentive programs, and exploited work forces overseas. The dynamics are clearly visible in U.S. trade with Taiwan. The United States registered a $16 billion deficit with the island in 1986. The biggest Taiwanese exporter is none other than the U.S. transnational, General Electric. Not far behind are Texas Instruments, Digital Equipment, General Instrument, Atari, Wang, Sears, K-mart, and dozens of other U.S. firms.

General Electric and other firms move to Taiwan because, in addition to incentives from the U.S. and Taiwanese governments, worker rights there are systematically violated. Assembly workers receive barely subsistence wages for eight-hour to twelve-hour days. They live in crowded company-owned dorms with no air-conditioning, despite 100 degree heat. Health and safety regulations are lax or nonexistent. Strikes are all but illegal and the few unions that do exist are government-controlled. The resulting trade imbalance cannot be righted without dismantling the underlying incentive structures and establishing worker rights.

Inequities

Third world debt provided record dollars to pad the bank accounts and lifestyles of third and first world elites, while IMF austerity has hurt mainly poor and working people. Service economies in the industrialized world likewise breed greater inequalities.

Poverty and hunger have grown across the world during the 1980s, especially among women and children. Underdeveloped countries are marked by the growing shantytowns that surround major cities as people leave rural areas. In the United States, homelessness is on the rise in cities, rural communities are in rapid decline as farms go bankrupt in record numbers, and poverty grows around huge plantation-like farms in the southwestern United States. Unemployment is on the rise across the world. In short, there are increasingly few opportunities for meaningful lives and work for young people everywhere. Educational and training opportunities are likewise on the decline.

The increasing capital mobility and nonaccountability of large corporations have eroded worker rights in both the South and the North. The transnational corporations have won major concessions from U.S. workers by threatening to pick up shop and move to whichever third world country wins the competition for the most repressed work force. It is increasingly the case in the North, as has long been true in the South, that one can hold a job yet live in poverty.

The fragile environment and natural resource base of many countries are being destroyed. Some western corporations have moved into the underdeveloped world primarily to take advantage of weaker environmental regulations.

More just resolutions of the calamities of the 1980s—stagnation, debt and speculation, imbalances, inequities—must begin with the understanding that they are not the result of mismanagement or some temporary downturn. They have grown from the logic of the institutions, public and private, which have emerged to dominate the postwar global economy. In their present form, these institutions do not serve the interests of sustainable development and real security. The institutions themselves must be examined and changed.

Principles of democratic participation, responsiveness to human needs, public accountability, and social equity are essential to a just and workable policy in the post-Reagan era. The application of such principles to international economic relations and national policies is undeniably a tall order—one that demands a determined political will and mobilized public commitment. But the alternative to such an effort is the increasing misery and starvation of a stagnant world economy deeply divided by region, sex, class, and race—the very situation in which Reaganite free-trade orthodoxy and market mystification have stranded us.

The six principles outlined below comprise the foundation upon which a platform of sustainable growth and social justice can be built. They are the critical touchstones of a policy to overcome the stagnation, imbalances, inequities, and speculation that have characterized the U.S. and world economies in the 1980s.

- Economic democracy means developing institutions and practices that are responsive to the needs and participation of a majority of citizens.

- Attention to basic human needs and worker rights should replace the present emphasis on export-led growth in both industrialized and underdeveloped countries.

- Public accountability of multilateral financial and development institutions as well as private banks and corporations must be instituted in both industrialized and underdeveloped nations.

- Universality of participation in multilateral financial and development institutions should be encouraged along with an end to discrimination against nations whose social and economic systems differ from those of the dominant industrial nations.

- Multilateralism must become more than a linguistic fact by giving the underdeveloped nations, with over three-quarters of the world's population, a representative vote in the international economic institutions.

- Equity at an international level must guarantee fair returns to nations producing raw materials; at the individual level, concern for workers' rights must bring greater equality to income and power distribution.

Resources

Recommended Appointees for A New Administration

Aid/Development Issues

- Robert Browne, Staff Director of House Subcommittee on International Development Institutions and Finance, former U.S. Executive Director at African Development Fund

- Susan George, Fellow of the Transnational Institute and author of *How the Other Half Dies*

- Sheldon Annis, Fellow of the Overseas Development Council and visiting lecturer at the Woodrow Wilson School of Princeton University

- Frances Moore Lappé, co-author of *Food First* and co-founder of the Institute for Food and Development Policy

Finance/Debt Issues

- Howard Wachtel, Professor of Economics at American University and author of *The Money Mandarins*

- Al Watkins, Consultant to the United Nations Economic Commission for Latin America, former international economist at the Joint Economic Committee of Congress

- Robin Broad, Resident Associate at the Carnegie Endowment for International Peace, former international economist at the Treasury Department

- Jane D'Arista, former staff director at the House Energy and Finance Subcommittee on Telecommunications, Consumer Protection and Finance

Trade

- Ray Marshall, Professor of Economics at the University of Texas, former Secretary of Labor in the Carter administration

- Lee Price, international economist for the Joint Economic Committee of Congress, former economist at the UAW

- Bill Goold, co-author of *Trade's Hidden Costs* and administrative assistant for Representative Don J. Pease (D-IL)

Organizations

- Joint Economic Committee of Congress, U.S. Senate, Washington, DC 20510; (202) 224-5171

- Institute for Food and Development Policy, 145 Ninth St., San Francisco, CA 94103; (415) 864-8555

- Overseas Development Council, 1717 Massachusetts Ave. NW, Washington, DC 20036; (202) 234-8701

- Bread for the World, 802 Rhode Island Ave. NE, Washington, DC 20018; (202) 269-0200
- Interfaith Action for Economic Justice, 110 Maryland Ave. NE, Washington, DC 20002; (202) 543-2800

Further Reading

- John Cavanagh, Fantu Cheru, Carole Collins, Cameron Duncan and Dominic Ntube, *From Debt to Development: Alternatives to the International Debt Crisis*, IPS Books, 1986.
- Howard Wachtel, *The Politics of International Money*, TNI Issue Paper No. 2, Amsterdam, Transnational Institute, 1987.
- Giovanni Andrea Cornia, Richard Jolly, and Francis Stewart, eds., *Adjustment with a Human Face*, A Study by UNICEF, Oxford University Press, 1987.
- Lester Brown, ed., *The State of the World*, annual publication of the Worldwatch Institute.
- United Nations, Department of International Economic and Social Affairs, *World Economic Survey 1987*, 1987.
- Archibald Gillies, Jeff Faux, Jerry Sanders, Sherle Schwenninger, and Paul Walker, *Post-Reagan America*, World Policy Institute, 1987.

John Cavanagh is Director of the World Economy Project at the Institute for Policy Studies. He is a former international economist at the United Nations Conference on Trade and Development and the World Health Organization. His recent books include (as co-author) *From Debt to Development* and *Trade's Hidden Costs.*

Jerry Sanders is academic coordinator and professor of Peace Studies at the University of California, Berkeley. He is a co-author of *Post-Reagan America*, a contributing editor of *World Policy*, and author of *Peddlers of Crisis.*

Robert S. Browne

Shaping an African Policy

Platform

- Assist beleaguered African economies to return to a sustainable growth path: by effective measures to reduce the African debt overhang; by reallocating the U.S. foreign assistance budget, channelling assistance to areas of greatest need; by allowing greater input from aid recipients in the design and structuring of development strategy.

- Seek independence for Namibia by mobilizing the United Nations to enforce this unanimous objective.

- Terminate U.S. support for efforts to overthrow the government of Angola: by extending diplomatic recognition to the Angolan government; by terminating U.S. support for the Angolan rebels; by initiating UN efforts to end South Africa's occupation and subversion of Angola.

- Take strong steps toward ending apartheid by expanding, strengthening, and internationalizing the sanctions program and by exploring the feasibility of extending direct assistance to the African National Congress.

Sheltering a half billion people, occupying the globe's largest land mass, and harboring what may well be the world's richest agglomeration of mineral resources, Africa is a continent which the United States cannot ignore. In 1987, however, U.S. bilateral assistance for sub-Saharan Africa came to less than $900 million, hardly double the $492 million which the U.S. allocated for tiny El Salvador (population five million) and less than one-third the sum allocated to Israel (population four million).

Clearly, the cause for this disparity was not that Africa did not need foreign assistance. United Nations figures indicate that twenty-eight of the world's thirty-five poorest countries are in sub-Saharan Africa, where poverty, hunger, and disease are endemic. Africa's illiteracy rates are the highest in the world; its agricultural practices are generally low-yielding; physical and social infrastructures are grossly inadequate; the industrial sector is virtually non-existent; the workforce is mainly unskilled; management tends to be inexperienced; the economies are undiversified (based on a single crop) primary commodity exporters, and heavily dependent on imports of food as well as of consumer goods and capital inputs. During the past decade most African economies have experienced chronic balance-of-payments deficits and about two dozen of them are carrying so severe a debt burden that it is unrealistic to expect they can ever fully repay their debts.

In addition to this litany of debilitating economic problems, much of Africa is plagued with political quarrels and instabilities and with repressive governments, exemplified by the ongoing conflicts within Ethiopia and the Sudan, by the border disputes in various parts of the continent, and above all, by the nightmare of apartheid in South Africa and by South Africa's attendant subjugation of Namibia.

The relative neglect of Africa by the United States arises from our failure to perceive a sufficiently close linkage between Africa and U.S. interests. Five million El Salvadorans live only 900 miles from Texas, whereas the half-billion Africans are 4,000 miles from our shores. Other considerations might be the fact that the International Development Administration (IDA, the World Bank's soft loan window) is allocating about half of its resources to Africa and the fact that the European countries tend to view Africa as within their "sphere" and therefore are tacitly assigned the primary responsibility for providing assistance to that continent.

This cavalier attitude toward so crucial a segment of the world is extremely short-sighted. Although one cannot easily imagine a situation in which Africa could, on its own, pose a direct military, economic, or even political threat to the security of the United States, Africa's sheer size bears mention, and fifty African votes in the United Nations constitute that body's largest single voting bloc. More important, however, is the fact that Africa's numerous unresolved problems provide endless opportunities for creating international tensions. The risk of conflagration is great within Africa, and history is replete with examples of innocuous events becoming global conflicts. It is demonstrably in U.S. security and economic interests that instability be kept to a minimum within Africa, that African nations retain friendly relations toward the United States, and that African economies realize their great potential both as markets for U.S. products and as suppliers of highly desired raw materials and commodities. Accomplishing these objectives depends on African economic growth and development.

Realistically, there are only a limited number of avenues through which the United States can have a positive impact upon Africa's problems. The continent's internal political quarrels, violations of human rights, and the political instability which characterizes many of its regimes can be booby traps for foreigners. The most useful policy for the United States is to afford maximum support to the Organization for African Unity, which has performed reasonably well in providing an all-African forum within which to settle intra-African disputes. On the other hand, Africa's debilitating debt and stagnant development, and the South Africa-created problems of apartheid, Namibian independence, and the destabilization of the southern Africa region are all problem areas in which the United States could play a major constructive role.

Although Africa's debt of some $180 billion is modest by comparison with total third world debt of more than $1 trillion, it is a more burdensome debt because of the fragility of African economies. Unlike Latin America's debt, Africa's debt is not owed to commercial banks but primarily to governments and to other official institutions such as the World Bank and the International Monetary Fund (IMF). Since 1980, this debt has been endlessly rescheduled, a process which simulates relief but in reality merely postpones the problem for a few months at a time, while adding to its magnitude. Meanwhile, many African countries are experiencing debt service-to-export ratios averaging in excess of 50 percent, which means a serious net outflow of capital. For a capital-starved region such as Africa to be forced into becoming a net supplier of capital to the rest of the world is morally unconscionable as well as economically unsound and politically dangerous.

A number of western creditor countries have recognized the impropriety of forcing Africa to become a net capital exporter and have taken steps to forgive African loans and call for a more reasoned approach to resolving Africa's debt problems. The United States, however, has simply urged others to be generous and encouraged the World Bank to allocate a higher portion of its soft loans to Africa. For 1988, the already modest 1987 level of U.S. aid to Africa has actually been reduced, and our relative share in the replenishment of funds for the African Development Fund, a major funding agency for African development, has shrunk. Meanwhile, a congressional effort to legislate a five-year moratorium on African debt repayments to the United States remains stymied at the time of this writing, and in any case has received little encouragement from the administration.

The new administration should aggressively seek to write off a sizeable portion of Africa's debt. Such a policy would enable the excessively debt-burdened countries of Africa to regain their creditworthiness, to once again become capital recipients, and thus to return their economies to positive growth paths.

Proposals to postpone repayment for twenty or more years should be afforded serious consideration, although any solution short of complete forgiveness of at least a portion of this debt is of only marginal benefit. The most effective method for easing the African debt problem is via an issuance of special purpose SDRs (Special Drawing Rights) by the IMF earmarked for this purpose, as recommended in the omnibus trade bill, a step that would not add to the U.S. budget deficit. There is considerable support within the international community for such a solution, but the negative stance of the United States toward any further issuance of SDRs has led most nations to feel that this solution is unachievable. A new president could turn this completely around.

Although writing off a substantial portion of its debt would end a major drain on Africa's scarce resource base, the flow of external resources to Africa must also increase. The need for budget stringency here in the United States will restrain the new president from calling for large increases in foreign aid appropriations. It is imperative, however, that the new administration undertake a thorough review of how foreign aid monies are allocated, noting especially the disproportionately large amounts going to a handful of countries based on political criteria, and the minuscule amounts going to a host of countries, mainly in Africa, which desperately need these funds. Holding sacrosanct aid for Israel and Egypt, which together garner about 40 percent of our non-military foreign aid budget, can be justified neither on grounds of need nor security, and indeed little effort is made to do so. The appropriation is voted unquestioningly, as if mandated by an unseen force.

There is, of course, a great deal more to economic development than transferring funds from first world donors to third world recipients via the World Bank. The development strategy which the donor community has been prescribing for Africa has not proved effective, and the time is overdue to allow the recipients to play a major role in shaping aid programs intended for their benefit.

For eight years, Africans have been expressing dissatisfaction with the overemphasis on the export-led development strategy which donors urge them to pursue despite disappointing results and discouraging prospects. Yet Africans' call for a more self-reliant approach to development has elicited little support within the donor community. To be sure, Africans have not demonstrated great dedication to this alternative strategy themselves, but they have pointed out that, as recipients, they are in a weak position to insist upon a strategy which the donors do not favor. There would seem to be an excellent opportunity for a new U.S. president to move bilateral aid programs in the direction of encouraging and strengthening the sub-regional institutions and intra-African cooperation which are regularly cited as the *sine qua non* for effective, self-reliant development.

The president who takes office in 1989 can be assured that conflicts in southern Africa will constitute ongoing, critical items on the foreign policy agenda. The question of Namibia's independence is the least complex of these issues because it has been unambiguously ruled upon by both the United Nations and the World Court. With legal opinion, international political opinion, and popular, moral opinion all lined up against South Africa's occupation of this territory, there can be no justification for continued occupation. It is one of the few issues on which East and West, North and South all agree. That no effective action has been taken is a testimony only to cowardice. Meanwhile, the delay has not only enabled South Africa to continue to drain Namibia of its resource base, in open violation of the edict laid down by the World Court, but it has also permitted South Africa to pursue a policy of destabilization, indeed overt invasion and occupation, of Angola with impunity.

There is an unparalleled opportunity here for a bold and imaginative president, perhaps in concert with both eastern and western bloc nations, to transform the United Nations into a "do something" organization, by informing South Africa in no uncertain terms that it must either relinquish that territory in accordance with the unanimous wishes of the world community or face serious consequences. The president should take the lead in persuading the United Nations to mobilize the necessary support, whether military or economic, to make this threat credible. It is a unique opportunity not only to remove a long-standing injustice on the world political scene but also to restore some respectability to the flagging image of the United Nations, an image which we have done little to help in recent years.

An independent Namibia would place a territorial wedge between South Africa and Angola and thus impede South Africa's incursions into and occupation of Angolan territory as well as its support of the Angolan rebels. An independent Namibia would, however, be in no position to repel such incursions across its territory, so it probably would be necessary to pursue a complementary strategy for the removal of South African troops from Angola.

A first step would be for the United States to extend diplomatic recognition to Angola. As a duly constituted (although not elected) government, Angola is recognized by some 145 countries, including all of Africa. Major U.S. corporations operate there quite profitably and the Angolan government has demonstrated unstinting cooperation with the U.S. government. The United States nevertheless has chosen to send clandestine and overt military support to the Angolan rebel forces who are fighting alongside South Africa in an attempt to overthrow the government and thwart its development efforts. The bloodshed, especially the suffering imposed on civilians, has reached massive proportions and its repercussions extend into several neighboring countries. U.S. association with this mayhem and subversion has gravely damaged the U.S. image throughout Africa, especially in southern Africa where our national interests may be at their maximum.

Recognition of the Angolan government and a complete reversal of our policy there are the necessary first steps. In concert with the United Nations, the president should then demand that South Africa withdraw from Angolan territory. At this point, a negotiated cessation of South African support for the rebels should be possible, but if not, an international police force detailed to the Caprivi strip of Namibia could effectively cut off South African support for the rebel movement and lay the foundation for reducing the Angolan struggle to a national framework.

Unquestionably the most difficult aspect of the southern Africa problem is the elimination of apartheid within South Africa itself. The general case for non-intervention in the internal affairs of other nations is a policy to which the U.S. is well advised to subscribe. In general, our past history of such interventions does not do us credit. Apartheid, however, transcends national boundaries. Although it may have been a self-contained, basically internal policy at its inception, apartheid has over the years expanded into an international struggle. South Africa has fastened the culture of apartheid on neighboring Namibia and, in the name of apartheid, is currently waging overt and covert war on Angola and Mozambique, as well as carrying out destabilization measures and committing violent acts against its other neighbors. It justifies this aggression as necessary to protect its apartheid system against South African expatriates who are attempting to assault apartheid from abroad. Thus, South Africa has internationalized the apartheid issue and has invited the intervention of the world community into the struggle.

The 1986 congressional sanctions against South Africa were a useful first step toward a peaceful resolution to this excruciating conflict, but they were much too modest and suffered from a lack of genuine administration support. A new president should expand the sanctions initiative, enlist our allies' support, and pursue it aggressively until it either does the job or proves ineffective. The possibility that it is now already too late to end apartheid by peaceful means must also be considered. The Afrikaners have proved remarkably intransigent to all reasonable efforts to reach a peaceful accommodation, and the world cannot avert its eyes forever from the daily violence being inflicted upon South Africa's black majority. The new president must give serious thought to extending official support to the beleaguered black South Africans who are directing the daily struggle against apartheid, principally the African National Congress.

Resources

Recommended Appointees for a New Administration

- Millard Arnold is an attorney who has a sustained history of involvement with African issues. He has been particularly involved with human rights in South Africa and with entrepreneurship and private investment in Africa. He is currently with the firm of Land, Lemble, and Arnold.

- Robert Berg was Director of Evaluation for AID from 1977-81. Subsequently, he was Senior Fellow at the Overseas Development Council, 1982-85, and is currently President of the International Development Conference. He was Co-Director of the Committee on African Development Strategies and is Senior Consultant to the Review of U.S. Economic Cooperation Policies for the 1990s, a major project being carried out under the direction of Michigan State University.

- Goler Butcher served as Assistant Adminstrator of AID for Africa during the Carter adminstration. She continues to be active in African affairs from her post as Professor in the Howard University School of Law.

- Thomas Callaghy is Associate Professor of Political Science at Columbia University and Research Associate at Columbia's Research Institute of African Studies. He has a long history of observing and commenting on African affairs.

- Willard Johnson is Professor of Political Science at Massachusetts Institute of Technology, where he has specialized in African affairs for nearly two decades. He has travelled and lived in Africa and produced extensive research and publications, mainly in the field of development.

- Carol Lancaster was Deputy Assistant Secretary of State in the Bureau of African Affairs during the Carter adminstration. She subsequently returned to academia as Director of the African Studies Program at Georgetown University. She is currently on leave to the Institute for International Economics.

- Donald McHenry is Professor at the School for Foreign Service, Georgetown University. He was the U.S. Ambassador to the United Nations and a senior member of that delegation throughout the Carter administration.

- Ronald Walters is Professor of Political Science at Howard University. He has been an activist in African affairs for many years, as well as a researcher, scholar, and author.

- Ernest Wilson, III, is Professor of Political Science at the University of Michigan and Director of the Center for Research on Economic Development. He has lived in Africa and conducted research related to economic development strategies.

Organizations

- Washington Office on Africa, 110 Maryland Ave. NE, Washington, DC 20002; (202) 546-7961

- American Committee on Africa, 198 Broadway, New York, NY 10038; (212) 962-1210

- TransAfrica, 545 8th St. SE, Washington, DC 20003; (202) 547-2550

• Africare, 440 R St. NW, Washington, DC 20001; (202) 462-3614

Further Reading

• Robert Browne and Robert J. Cummings, *The Lagos Plan of Action vs. the Berg Report*, Brunswick Publishing Company, 1984.

• Adebayo Adediji and Timothy Shaw, eds., *Economic Crisis in Africa*, Lynne Reiner Publisher, 1985.

• Gerald K. Helleiner, ed., *Africa and the IMF*, IMF Publisher, 1986.

• Robert J. Berg and Jennifer Seymour Whitaker, eds., *Strategies for Africa Development*, University of California Press, 1986.

Robert S. Browne is Staff Director of the House Subcommittee on International Development Institutions and Finance. He has served as Executive Director at the African Development Fund in Abidjan, Côte d'Ivoire and as a Program Officer in the U.S. foreign assistance program in Southeast Asia. He has traveled extensively within Africa and written on a variety of issues related to African economic development. For ten years, he headed the Black Economic Research Center in New York City.

Geoffrey Aronson

Resolving the Arab-Israeli Conflict: A Plan of Action

Platform

Military Affairs

- Establishment of a multinational pact to ration arms transfers to the Middle East
- Establishment of a multilateral agreement through the Paris-based Coordinating Committee (COCOM), which formulates export controls for the western democracies and Japan, to increase control and verification procedures regarding transfer to the Middle East of nuclear-related technology and materiel, including ballistic missile technology
- Adherence to the Nuclear Nonproliferation Treaty (NPT) by all parties to the Arab-Israeli conflict, together with their simultaneous pledge, enforced by appropriate verification procedures, to refrain from the manufacture or use of chemical or biological weapons

Economic Affairs

- Creation of a multi-billion dollar economic development plan, including renegotiation of debt held by Israel, Egypt, Jordan, and Syria
- Termination of all economic and trade boycotts

Diplomatic Affairs

- The convening of an international peace conference, including the five permanent members of the United Nations Security Council and Israel, Egypt, Lebanon, Syria, Jordan, and the PLO
- Implementation of the "territory for peace and recognition" formula articulated in UN Security Council Resolution 242

- Execution of a UN-sponsored plebiscite on the West Bank and Gaza Strip to determine the form of Palestinian sovereignty

---

For a generation, the Middle East has been a prime arena for Cold War competition. A spiralling regional arms race, wars of increasing destruction, the militarization and complementary impoverishment of domestic economies, and the growing power of repressive internal security institutions are the fruits of this contest.

With the necessary commitment and imagination by a new administration, however, the Middle East can be transformed from a potential new Balkans to the showpiece for a new spirit of international and regional cooperation.

In order to give substance to such a vision, U.S. unilateralism must end. This requires, first and foremost, recognition of the positive role which the Soviet Union must play in any regional settlement. If there is to be any chance of peace, prosperity, and freedom, the next U.S. president must accept the Soviet desire to collaborate in leading the region's antagonists away from war and toward peace.

Such a decision will reverse a policy which for almost forty years has been based upon a refusal to accept the legitimacy of Soviet interests in the Middle East and the exclusion of the Soviet Union from U.S. diplomatic initiatives. This policy has degenerated into a base strategy of arms sales diplomacy, pursued by both superpowers, and in times of crisis, into heightened levels of superpower confrontation.

The pattern of zero sum rivalry must end. U.S. and Soviet recognition of this requirement was symbolized by their joint declaration of October 1977. After more than a decade of quiescence, the banner of a cooperative approach to the resolution of the Arab-Israeli dispute should be raised again.

Despite what must necessarily be a cautious estimate of the ability of any outside power to shape the region according to its preferences, the United States needs to promote a bold, comprehensive program aimed at defusing military confrontation, resolving Arab and Israeli demands, and promoting economic development. The resolution of these issues requires a level of integrated, multilateral cooperation which the principals to the conflict alone cannot provide. This program demands leadership from the United States and the U.S.S.R. and the support of their allies for a break with a time-worn strategy of belligerence and noncooperation.

Arms sales have been the calling card of diplomats for generations. In the Middle East, however, as in nowhere else, arms sales diplomacy has borne its most bitter fruits. According to the Arms Control and Disarmament Agency, the Middle East is the most lucrative market for weapons transfers in the world, accounting for almost 50 percent of worldwide weapons sales.

This extraordinary accumulation of weapons has made Israel and its antagonists less secure. Fragile economies have become hostage to the requirements of funding tremendous military budgets, distorting and militarizing national economic priorities. Investment and spending are skewed by the desire to achieve ultimate but ever-elusive military security.

Domestic politics also become captive to military dictates. Military regimes in the Arab world are the most obvious examples of this trend, but the political institutions of Israel and Egypt also are weakened by inordinate military power.

An enterprising U.S. policy must seek to end this spiral of weapons-driven insecurity by capping the conventional arms race in the region through multilateral agreement; controlling the sale of sensitive nuclear technologies; and minimizing the threat posed by chemical, nuclear, or biological weapons.

There is a precedent for such an agreement in the Middle East: the Tripartite Declaration of May 1950. The Declaration was an integral part of a more comprehensive Big Power guarantee of Middle East frontiers. In fact, the Middle East is the only arena in the postwar era where self-restraint·on arms transfers was initiated by the western powers.

A multilateral arms rationing agreement, including the United States, the European Economic Community (EEC), China, and the Soviet Union, would be a central element of an American diplomacy of peace, prosperity, and independence. The value of arms transfers, as the measure of friendship and commitment, and as the litmus test of superpower patronage, would be reduced. An enforced and verifiable end to the arms race, linked to economic and diplomatic initiatives, would echo positively throughout the economic and domestic political arenas of the region's nations.

Unfortunately, concentration on conventional arms alone will not adequately address the military capabilities which currently exist in the Middle East. The United States must confront the proliferation of unconventional arms, from nuclear weapons to chemical and biological stocks, as part of its comprehensive strategy toward the region.

Israel's nuclear capabilities are well known. There are authoritative reports that sophisticated surface-to-surface missiles are already deployed in the Negev Desert and Golan Heights.

Iraq's nuclear pretensions prompted Israel's destruction of the Osiraq reactor in mid-1981. Today, hardly a week passes without some reference to the Arab world's need to develop a nuclear counter to Israel's existing and ever-improving arsenal.

An Office of Technology Assessment report warned that both Egypt and Iraq could have a nuclear weapons capability by year 2000.

Unlike the static Cold War confrontation in Europe, the nations of the Middle East have demonstrated their readiness to resort to war in pursuit of their national interests. The addition of nuclear stockpiles in such an environment would add a new, chilling dimension to future conflict, and make a diplomatic resolution of the Arab-Israeli conflict that much more complex.

A Nuclear Free Zone in the Middle East, an idea supported at various times by both Israel and Egypt, is a real possibility within the context of an overall settlement of the Arab-Israeli conflict. Adherence to the Nuclear Nonproliferation Treaty (NPT) by nations that have yet to do so, as well as rigorous inspections by the International Atomic Energy Agency, will calm Arab fears of Israel's existing nuclear option, which animates their desire to imitate its achievement, and to strive for cheaper chemical or biological substitutes, both of which are legitimate subjects of Israel's concern. A coordinated effort to monitor the purchase of nuclear weapons-related equipment and materiel is an important factor in stopping the flow of nuclear-related materiel and technology to the region.

A generous program of economic development is an integral feature of the diplomacy of peace and the promotion of independence, freedom, and prosperity. The United States, EEC, Japan, and the Soviet Union are all heavily invested in the region, as aid donors or as creditors. The International Monetary Fund and the World Bank have historically played a role in the region's economic development. Subsidies granted by the nations of the Arab Organization of Petroleum Exporting Countries to the "confrontation states" annually run into the billions.

These funds are, however, hostage to the military institutions which dominate the priorities and productive resources of Middle East nations. The U.S., for example, has given more aid to Israel, with its population of 3.5 million, than it allocated to all of Western Europe, with a population over 100 million, during the Marshall Plan. What is there to show for such an investment? Israel's GNP has stagnated for a decade, and it is currently more than ever an economic ward of the United States. And as the current uprisings in the West Bank and Gaza demonstrate, U.S. aid has not assured Israel of the security it deems so important. The economic health and dependence of Syria and Egypt on their respective superpower patrons are, if anything, worse.

A joint U.S.-Soviet commitment to terminating the addiction of their Middle East allies to military aid and to containing militarism will enable all the countries in the region to begin reasserting control over their economic well-being. An internationally subscribed program, coordinated by a newly chartered Middle East Development Organization, should be an integral part of this effort.

Freedom, prosperity, and independence are impossible objectives in the Middle East as long as the Arab-Israeli conflict remains unresolved. Today the dispute is focused upon the territories captured by Israel in the June 1967 war and the related issue of Palestinian self-determination.

The parameters of a diplomatic settlement have been clear for some time: peace between Israel and its Arab neighbors; recognition by Arab states of Israel and recognition by Israel of the Palestinian right to self-determination; and withdrawal from the territories captured in 1967.

The Arab world, which for so long refused to recognize the reality of Israel, is today prepared to accept such a settlement. The United States, whose support for the status quo has been a constant policy since 1967, must now realize, as many Arabs and Israelis already do, that perpetuating the current state of affairs prevents peace, obstructs democracy and freedom, and precludes economic and political independence.

The model of U.S.-Soviet collaboration in promoting a peaceful settlement of the conflict according to these principles can be found in their joint chairmanship of the Geneva Peace Conference following the October 1973 war and the Joint Declaration of October 1977.

In the context of an international conference, the new U.S. administration should support bilateral negotiations along the following lines:

For the Golan Heights:
- complete Israeli withdrawal to the Armistice Line and the restoration of Syrian sovereignty

- the creation of demilitarized zones on the model of the separation of forces agreement implemented on the Golan Heights after 1973

- agreement to end the state of belligerency

- recognition of the Armistice borders as "secure and recognized borders"

- establishment of a timetable and framework for the signing of a Syrian-Israeli treaty of peace.

For the West Bank and Gaza Strip:
- complete Israeli withdrawal to the Armistice Lines except for mutually agreed upon border adjustments

- demilitarization of the two areas as well as the creation of limitation of forces zones on the Jordanian border

- creation of a temporary UN trusteeship to assume responsibility for internal security, and to supervise the transition of these areas to Palestinian rule

- agreement to an end of the state of belligerency between Israel and Jordan

- recognition of the Armistice borders as "secure and recognized borders" dividing Israel from the newly created Palestinian or Palestinian-Jordanian state

- establishment of a timetable and framework for the signing of Jordanian-Israeli and Palestinian-Israeli treaties of peace.

For Jerusalem:

- shared sovereignty and/or mutual administration of an open city of Jerusalem are best suited to reconcile Israeli, Arab, and international demands. As part of an agreement, the five permanent members of the Security Council will agree to establish diplomatic relations with Israel and to move their embassies in Israel to Jerusalem.

The aforementioned elements of a forward-looking and imaginative U.S. policy offer the prospect of resolving an issue which has become a danger not only to Arabs and Israelis but also to international peace. A U.S. policy formulated along these lines provides for a reduction of the fears of both Arabs and Israelis of conventional and unconventional attack; a mechanism for the peaceful resolution of disputes; and a resolution of Arab grievances and Israeli demands for recognition and security.

Peace rather than war, independence in place of dependence, and prosperity instead of pauperism will signal the renaissance of this once glorious region and will serve as a testament to a new era of U.S. leadership and diplomacy.

Resources

Recommended Appointees for a New Administration

- William Quandt, Senior Fellow at the Brookings Institution, formerly with the NSC during Carter's administration

- Ian Lustick, Associate Professor of Government at Dartmouth College

- Ann Lesch, Assistant Professor at Villa Nuovo University, Pennsylvania

- Dr. Yaya Sadovski, Research Associate at the Brookings Institution

---

Organizations

- The Middle East Institute, 1761 N St. NW, Washington, DC 20036; (202) 785-1141

- Center for Contemporary Arab Studies, Georgetown University, Intercultural Center, 3795 O St. NW, Washington, DC 20057; (202) 687-5793

Further Reading

- *World Military Expenditures and Arms Transfers*, annual report of the Arms Control and Disarmament Agency.

- Leonard Spector, *Nuclear Proliferation in the Third World*, annual report of the Carnegie Endowment for International Peace.

- *MERIP*, bimonthly Middle East report, Middle East Research and Information Project.
- *The Middle East Military Balance*, Jaffee Center for Strategic Studies, Tel Aviv University.

Geoffrey Aronson is a specialist on Middle East affairs and a Visiting Scholar at the Institute for Policy Studies. He has worked and travelled widely throughout the region, writing for numerous magazines and newspapers, including *Le Monde Diplomatique*, *The New York Times*, and *The Washington Post*. He is the author of *From Sideshow to Centerstage: U.S. Policy Toward Egypt* and *Creating Facts: Israel, Palestinians, and the West Bank*.

Robert L. Borosage

NATO: From Containment to Common Security

Platform

- Our European allies must bear a greater share of the burden of their own conventional defense. After consultation with our allies, a new administration should announce a gradual reduction of U.S. conventional forces in Europe and dedicated to Europe.

- Simultaneously, NATO must challenge the Soviet Union and the Warsaw Pact to draw down conventional forces in both alliances, focused on reducing offensive forces and deployments and on reciprocal, asymmetrical cuts in areas of technological advantage (e.g., Soviet tanks).

- The president must use the resources gradually freed by a lower commitment in Europe as part of a program to rebuild America and strengthen its economy.

After forty years, the NATO Alliance faces dramatic reconstruction. In the next decade, any administration—no matter how conservative or progressive—will seek to alter the U.S. role in NATO. For a progressive administration, however, reconstruction of NATO offers the possibility of moving beyond the Cold War to a new era of common security.

NATO's strategic dilemma has existed since the Soviet Union gained nuclear parity with the United States. Once the USSR could clearly retaliate against a U.S. nuclear attack, the immorality of defending Europe by threatening to destroy it—and the United States—became apparent. As Henry Kissinger expressed it (once out of office), mutual suicide cannot be made to appear as a rational option...Our European allies should not keep asking us to multiply strategic assurances that we cannot possibly mean, or if we do mean, we should not want to execute because if we executed them we risk the destruction of civilization.

As the U.S. nuclear guarantee seemed less and less rational, NATO adopted a policy of "flexible response," wedding tactical and intermediate nuclear weapons to increased conventional forces. But the lunacy of the implausible response to the presumed threat remained. European governments were much happier with a U.S. nuclear guarantee that might prevent war from ever occurring than with spending the money for the conventional forces necessary to win in the remote possibility that war actually occurred. European publics mobilized against the deployment of Cruise and Pershing missiles and opposed continued U.S. nuclear presence. The result has been stalemate. With the INF agreement to remove the missiles, the trend toward denuclearization in Europe led NATO strategists to demand spending levels on conventional forces that governments are unlikely to approve and deployments of new short-range nuclear weapons that publics are unlikely to accept.

For the United States, even current levels of spending are increasingly difficult to bear. By the end of the Reagan administration, the growing divorce between U.S. commitments and our ability to meet them meant that the U.S. could no longer sustain what analysts began to call the European "free-riders." With pressure growing to cut the military budget, NATO began to attract attention for the same reason that Willie Sutton said that he robbed banks—because that is where the money is. Although experts differ, in 1985 the Pentagon estimated that the NATO commitment consumed 58 percent of its defense budget—some $160 billion. With one-third of the Army's standing divisions in Europe and another third with European defense as their primary mission, NATO reconstruction offers the possibility of significant annual spending savings. The debt which will be the primary legacy of the Reagan administration will make such savings necessary and attractive.

At the same time, the European allies—now our leading trading partners and economic competitors—spend significantly lower proportions of their gross national product on the military than does the United States. As economic rivalries intensified during the 1980s, the fact that Europeans spent less on the military while maintaining better health care, unemployment benefits, education, and old age security became a natural target for populist resentment at home.

Moreover, there is little doubt about the Europeans' capacity to provide an adequate conventional defense, if they so choose. The West Germans field the best land army on the continent; the French and British maintain significant nuclear forces and naval and air forces. Although conventional wisdom holds that the Soviet Union possesses an overwhelming superiority in conventional forces, most careful analyses—such as those issued by the International Institute for Strategic Studies in London, or a recent study by Senator Carl Levin (D-MI)—suggest that there is a rough balance in conventional forces in Europe.

Given these realities, it is not surprising that there is overwhelming support for significant cuts in U.S. spending on NATO. Neo-conservative Irving Kristol and libertarian Earl Ravenal have also called for the United States to quit the alliance. National security mandarins such as Henry Kissinger and Zbigniew Brzezinski have called for pullbacks of 100,000 U.S. troops from Europe (to be used as part of a global Rapid Deployment Force). Progressives, led by Rev. Jesse Jackson and Representative Patricia Schroeder (D-CO), have gained increasing liberal support for "burden-sharing" that would allow dramatic reductions in U.S. forces dedicated to NATO.

Reconstruction of NATO could be part of a more profound challenge to the Cold War as well. Although Europe hosts the greatest array of conventional and nuclear forces in the world, it has been a zone of relative stability and peace since the building of the Berlin Wall in 1960. Instability has arisen either from internal upheaval—1968 in France, Italy, and Czechlosovakia, Solidarity in Poland in the 1980s—or from the military face-off itself, exemplified by the turmoil caused by deployment of SS-20s, Cruise, and Pershing missiles.

Peace has broken out in Europe. German *Ostpolitik* led to a formal recognition of the postwar boundaries, including East Germany. Agreements in Helsinki and Stockholm have created a range of routine "confidence-building measures": prior notification of major military maneuvers, exchange of observers, crisis control coordination. Detente took greater hold in Europe than between the great powers, with trade, travel, and communication growing steadily, limited only by the economic incompetence and political insecurity of the Warsaw Pact governments.

Europe, the centerpiece of the Cold War, the heart of militarized containment, has the potential to be the centerpiece of a new policy of common security and disarmament. The INF Treaty represents a first step in a disarmament process that could lead to denuclearization of Europe, a standdown of conventional forces on both sides, and the construction of common security arrangements and common sense relationships.

A progressive administration would surely seek to pursue this future. Soviet General Secretary Mikhail Gorbachev has written that war in Europe is impossible because it raises the specter of hundreds of Chernobyls that would destroy the continent. He has called for dramatic reductions in military forces on both sides, including "asymmetrical cuts" in those weapons where one side has a disproportionate advantage. He claims to seek a process in which both sides build down in parity rather than up for advantage. Given the Soviet need for economic revitalization, dramatic reductions in Warsaw Pact commitments might well be an economic imperative. Surely a progressive administration would put Gorbachev to the test.

A progressive president could announce—after consultation with the allies—that the United States will reduce its responsibility for the conventional defense of Europe. A five-year program to withdraw a significant portion of U.S. forces—say, three divisions—from Europe and reduce the number of heavy divisions dedicated to immediate European deployment could then be outlined. At the same time, the allies could take responsibility for their own conventional defense, with a European appointed to command NATO forces, and the Europeans taking a greater role in arms reduction talks with the Soviet Union and the Warsaw Pact.

Initiating this policy would spark a dramatic political debate on both sides of the Atlantic. In the United States, establishment strategists—the keepers of the Soviet threat—would decry isolationism and appeasement. In Europe, conservative voices would denounce U.S. weakness and call for large increases in military spending. The Soviets would surely launch a peace campaign, seeking to woo the Europeans toward neutrality and forestall a conventional buildup. Yet, the following fears seem unlikely to materialize.

The central defense of the status quo is that if the United States does not sustain (indeed increase) its commitment to NATO, the allies will be cowed by Soviet military power and will drift into accommodation and neutralism. Ironically, this argument implies that we spend over half of our military budget preparing for an attack that no one believes is plausible primarily to bolster the morale of our allies.

Soviet domination of West Europe is equally implausible. Gorbachev has implicitly admitted that the USSR is already overextended in Europe. Maintaining control over restive East European populations has been taxing enough. The backward Soviet economy and repressive and stunted political culture hold no attraction in Western Europe. Soviet military bluster would be counterproductive in the West, as amply demonstrated in the Cruise and Pershing debates, and Soviet attempts to woo the Europeans are clumsy at best.

Making Europe responsible for its own conventional defense would present the USSR with difficult choices. A hostile Cold War posture would surely produce a Western military response, leaving the USSR facing a stronger European force as well as the United States, China, and an evolving Japan. A disarming response would increase the restiveness among Eastern European populations. Ironically, the USSR has a far greater stake in the status quo in Europe than either the United States or its European allies.

Fears of "the Finlandization of Europe" reflect concern that a reduction of the U.S. role in NATO would lead to more independent European political and economic policies. But economic recovery and competition have already expressed themselves in greater European independence. Europeans have openly opposed U.S. policy in the Middle East, criticized U.S. war on Nicaragua, and refused to cooperate with U.S. efforts to isolate the Soviet Union economically. A Europe less dependent upon the United States for its military defense would surely be even more independent, but the difference will be a matter of degree at best. Political, cultural, and economic affinities will keep the allies cooperating.

Although NATO's stated purpose has been to contain the Soviet Union, its unstated aim has been to contain Germany and tie the German military to outside authority. One great fear about a reduced U.S. role in NATO is that it will feed militarist sentiments in West Germany. Since the West Germans already have the most modern conventional forces on the continent and face a declining population base, U.S. reductions could spark a movement to develop German nuclear weapons. This would alarm not only the Soviets, but the French, British, and other allies as well.

The very threat of German nuclear weapons would induce the Soviet Union to embrace a disarming process in Europe. Faced with the choice of a powerful West Germany seeking its own nuclear weapons or a denuclearized Europe with a conventional stand-down on both sides, Soviet leadership would surely choose the latter.

The French would also act resolutely to forestall German nuclear armaments. Indeed, the growing Franco-German military cooperation is an example of Europeans already acting on the assumption that the United States will reduce its commitment significantly.

Finally, substantial portions of the German public would protest development of nuclear weapons, making their deployment enormously costly. Green Party activists would launch direct action. The Social Democratic Party has already embraced efforts to develop a nuclear-free corridor in Central Europe. The Free Democrats have led efforts to respond affirmatively to Gorbachev's peace initiatives. The willingness of the conservative Kohl government to dismantle Pershing I missiles for the INF accord suggests that German opinion is on the side of denuclearization and disarmament.

The most difficult concern for a progressive president will be the domestic reaction to U.S. troop reductions in Europe. National security mandarins will wage a vicious red-scare campaign against the program. Their target would probably be to use NATO troop reductions to gain resources for the Rapid Deployment Force and global intervention.

Irving Kristol makes that argument the most brutally, suggesting that the United States adopt a policy of global unilateralism, acting on its own to police the world, and leaving pusillanimous allies to wallow in their social democratic domesticity. Both Kissinger and Brzezinski view U.S. troop withdrawals from Europe as desirable at a time of limited budgets in order to increase interventionist forces for U.S. "global responsibilities." The recent high level strategic review report,

Discriminate Deterrence, suggests that the U.S. policymakers place far greater emphasis on preparation for low-intensity wars throughout the globe than on the unlikely threat of a Soviet attack in Europe. Liberal security advisors suggest that it is safer to leave U.S. troops in Europe as a way of constraining ill-advised adventures elsewhere.

This concern makes it imperative that a progressive president define foreign military policy clearly, speak for it boldly, and tie it to domestic priorities. A policy of drift, of compromise, or of step-by-step measures will only embolden the opposition and make support for demobilization more difficult. Here too, the Soviet Union will have a significant stake in cooperation. A threatening Soviet posture in Europe or an adventurous one elsewhere will surely lead to limiting the reductions in U.S. forces and increasing their redeployment to interventionist missions.

A progressive president will argue about real security, which requires that we get our fiscal house in order, rebuild our economy, retrain our workers, and reinvest in America. Economic strength is the core of true security.

Once the troops are removed, and the sky does not fall in, part of the mythic dimension of the Cold War may be dispelled. Soviet troops will not stream across the Iron Curtain; Western Europeans will not fly the flag of neutralism. If conventional force reductions and denuclearization follow, a warmer relationship also will follow. Nothing could do more to change the terms of debate about the U.S. role in the world and the possibility of building a structure of peace and reducing the weapons of war.

Europe has enjoyed the blessings of peace for over forty years. Our allies have recovered from the devastation of World War II and have become our leading trading partners and economic competitors. Relations between East and West have stabilized. The postwar borders have been ratified; trade, travel, and financial flows have increased.

Today we spend over $150 billion a year—more than half our military budget—defending our European allies against a threat that all agree is remote. This staggering sum entails great sacrifices from the American people, and exacts a great tax upon our economy. Our European allies spend significantly less than we do on military defense. With twice the gross national product and one and one-half times the population of the Warsaw Pact nations, they can provide for their own conventional defense.

The United States should adopt a five-year program of conventional force reductions from Europe. NATO should be encouraged to appoint a European as commander-in-chief of NATO forces; Europeans should take the lead in the conventional force negotiations in Vienna.

The United States challenges the Soviet Union to enter into negotiations that will create a zone of peace in Europe, bringing military realities in line with already existing economic and political realities. We call for dramatic reductions of conventional forces on both sides, to be accompanied by conventional force redeployments and denuclearization of Central Europe. Together, we can turn Europe from the Cold War and a costly arms race to common security and disarmament.

Resources

Recommended Appointees for a New Administration

Secretary of State
- Paul Warnke, Director of the Arms Control and Disarmament Agency under Carter, chief negotiator of SALT II, now a partner in Clifford and Warnke

Secretary of Defense
- Stanley Weiss, President of Business Executives for National Security

Ambassador to NATO
- Mortimer Zuckerman, publisher of *U.S. News and World Report*

Head of the Arms Control and Disarmament Agency
- Randall Forsberg, Director of the Institute for Defense and Disarmament Studies

Special Advisor to the National Security Council on NATO
- David Calleo, Professor at Johns Hopkins University

Organizations

- Transnational Institute, Paulus Potterstraat 20, 1071 DA, Amsterdam, The Netherlands; (020) 62-66-08
- Institute for Peace and International Security, P.O. Box 2651, Cambridge MA 02238; (617) 547-3338
- World Policy Institute, 777 UN Plaza, New York, NY 10017; (212) 490-0010
- Institute for Defense and Disarmament Studies, 2001 Beacon St., Brookline, MA 02146; (617) 734-4216

Further Reading

- Mary Kaldor and Richard Falk, *Dealignment*, Basil Blackwell, 1987.
- David Calleo, *Beyond American Hegemony: The Future of the Western Alliance*, Basic Books, 1987.
- Zbigniew Brzezinski, *Game Plan*, Atlantic Monthly Press, 1986.
- Henry Kissinger, "A Plan to Reshape NATO," *Time*, March 5, 1984, pp. 20-24.

- Melvin Krauss, *How NATO Weakens the West*, Simon and Schuster, 1986.

- *END Journal*, (England) A Continuous Revision of European Politics and Ideas for the Peace Movement.

Robert L. Borosage was from 1978-1988 Director of the Institute for Policy Studies, where he is a Senior Fellow. He is currently on leave as senior policy advisor to the Jackson for President Campaign. He co-edited (with John Marks) *The CIA Files.*

And Secure the Blessings of Liberty to Ourselves and Our Posterity...

Robert Gottlieb and Helen Ingram

Which Way Environmentalism?
Toward a New Democratic Movement

Platform

- Provide national support for state and local land use planning as a means to control ground, air, water, and other forms of pollution.
- Re-focus efforts on source reduction rather than treatment of pollutants.
- Expand social governance of the production process to structure environmental protection and other social goals into the industrial decionmaking process.
- Restructure fiscal incentives that now support hazardous and environmentally destructive technologies and resource projects.
- Increase public input into decisions about production and the direction of the industrial order.
- Halt the export of pollution and pollution-prone social choices.
- Reverse the trend toward privatization of public resources and replace narrow notions of economic efficiency with accountability as a measure of bureaucratic performance.
- Create a National Health Service Corps to provide community education about the source of toxics, their risks, and how they can be avoided.

Environmental policy today is at a crossroads. Attempts by the Reagan administration to undo the legislation and regulatory policies established during the 1970s have backfired. Environmental groups have grown in numbers and reach, and Congressional initiatives have increased. In some cases, this has led to more legislation, greater funding for environmental programs, and increased regulations.

Yet environmental problems have, for the most part, remained intractable. Legislative and regulatory approaches have often been inadequate in addressing a growing set of concerns that touch the very fabric of our urban and industrial society. Target dates, such as those established by the Clean Air Act, have come and gone, without anticipated goals having been reached. While the current regulatory approaches look to tradeoffs, cost-benefit analysis, and risk assessment procedures, among others, to try to reduce or at least contain the degradation at hand, it is not even clear whether such goals will ever be met for particular contaminants, such as ozone, in those cities, such as Los Angeles or Denver, where dirty air appears to have become a permanent fixture of the urban design.

The basis for environmental policy continues to evolve around how best to accommodate the dual objectives of environmental protection and economic growth. Government policymakers are continually beset by the apparently conflicting pressures regarding environmental degradation, reindustrialization (whether high tech or old tech), job creation, and community fears regarding environmental and/or economic decline. Policy questions frequently are posed as a choice between contrasting objectives: jobs versus community versus environment. Those environmental groups who accept such a framework are faced with either selecting the route of tradeoffs and compromise, and accepting some level of degradation as an inevitable byproduct of industrialization, or choosing the environment over jobs and economic growth; that is, either enter the corridors of power and likely alienate part of the environmental constituency or be considered marginal in terms of the present political discourse. It is an unhappy predicament somehow incommensurate with the overwhelming public sentiment in favor of large-scale and more definitive action to address hazardous wastes, air and water contamination, pesticide use, solid waste disposal, and countless other environmental problems of our contemporary urban/industrial society.

The established environmental movement of the 1970s and 1980s prided itself on developing a legislative and regulatory agenda over the years. This consisted of specific initiatives in a range of policy areas, much of which translated into laws and administrative programs designed to protect the natural environment. The most recent efforts, such as the 1985 *Environmental Agenda for the Future* put together by the ten largest established environmental groups, represented an elaboration of this already developed program. Their approach, furthermore, has been dictated by the politics of the lobbyist, where agreements are crafted by various interest groups in a give-and-take process in which the giving often exceeds the taking when the power of money is involved.

There is, however, a more grassroots-oriented environmentalism on both a more local and unyielding basis. These movements will frequently insist that a particular project such as an incinerator or a power plant be stopped. They exhibit less willingness to compromise, although their focus is usually limited to the specific matter at hand. Thus, they develop little by way of national program or agenda. Still, many of these movements have begun to make tentative efforts toward developing networks and coalitions. In the process, they have established the outlines of a statewide or national approach, albeit one confined to particular issues.

A national environmental strategy and set of policy goals and objectives remain imperative in face of a declining environment and untempered forms of industrialization. Between the political constraints of the national lobbyist and the limits of a localized campaign, there needs to emerge a form of action—and theory—that links grassroots mobilization with attacking the structure of the problem on the state, national, and even international levels. Such an approach—a new environmental politics—would indeed entail the obvious ("think globally, act locally"), as well as the less obvious ("think globally, act globally") and the most immediate ("think locally, act locally").

Programs and improvements come about largely through the influence of social movements and community action. Legislative initiatives, regulatory actions, and court interventions have been framed in part by the public's concern and activity; such is likely to be the case in the future as well. Environmental "improvements" in this light reflect the state of environmental politics.

Most environmental groups, however, have gone a more exclusive route of institutional engagement and compromise in the arenas of legislation, administrative regulations, electoral politics, and litigation, rather than organizing and establishing a presence with and through the public. The largest of these groups, either in membership size, access to funding sources, or both, have become most recognized by policymakers on the national and statewide levels as representative of the "environmental point of view," and are solicited by media outlets, elected officials and their aides, and members of the bureaucracy for their opinions and positions. This interaction is often framed by the importance of expertise and the role of scientists in evaluating issues affecting the natural environment and the impact of technology. Though environmentalism as a social theory seeks to address the system of living organisms, including human society, in an integrative manner, these environmental organizations took an issue-by-issue approach, within a setting highly dependent both upon expert knowledge and narrowly defined political action. One strand of the intellectual heritage of the environmental movement, that associated with conservation as it was defined by such figures as Gifford Pinchot, who espoused scientific forestry, is highly elitist. While classic conservationists believed in "the greatest good for the largest number," specific applications of the concept were to be made by specialists with appropriate training. Thus, harvesting of forests was to follow the forester's calendar, for sustained yield and water resource development was to be determined from a hydrologic perspective taking into account whole river basins rather than simply responding to narrow, parochial constituencies. Consequently, conservation became synonymous with the growth of bureaucratic power and agency dominance over land and water resources.

By the 1960s, conservation as a popular movement had significantly narrowed. Leadership, such as it was, came mostly from federal agencies. Rod and gun clubs concerned themselves with outdoor recreation. A small band of preservationists dedicated to wilderness and scenic resources depended upon the financial support of the wealthy few. The explosion of public concern for the environment in the late 1960s and early 1970s took classic conservationists somewhat by surprise. Happenings such as Earth Day which mobilized thousands of people across the nation hardly fit their more genteel style.

Under the effective and sometimes brilliant entrepreneurship of leaders such as David Brower of the Sierra Club, some established conservation groups were able to incorporate hundreds of thousands of new members concerned more with the ecosystems and pollution of the human environment than with preservation. The cost of such growth was often internal struggles. New groups sprang up, including those devoted particularly to litigation, which thus appeared at first more "adversarial." Competition for money and membership intensified. For the most part, however, the fractionalized environmental movement of the 1970s remained in the mold set in the Progressive Era—taking up issues serially and with the overarching conception that a correct, scientific approach existed.

During the 1970s, these environmental organizations were successful in establishing what came to be called the "environmental agenda," aided largely by the enormous swelling of public environmental sentiment. This included the major legislative initiatives of the decade, such as the Clean Air Act, Safe Drinking Water Act, the Endangered Species Protection Act, the Resource Recovery and Conservation Act, and the Comprehensive Environmental Response, Conservation, and Liabilities Act (better known as Superfund). These bills and several others signed into law during the 1970s sought to address the problems of pollution and contamination as well as the protection of scenic and natural resources.

Environmental organizations also developed a series of complex and interactive relationships with a host of new administrative bureaucracies such as the Environmental Protection Agency and the Council on Environmental Quality, complementing the relations established by the previous generation of conservationists and preservationists with such agencies as the National Park Service, the Soil Conservation Service, and the U.S. Forest Service. Environmental

groups were also successful in transforming a range of legal rulings and
legislative initiatives, such as the California Friends of Mammoth ruling
in 1972 and the 1969 National Environmental Policy Act, into a whole
new field of environmental law where, for example, the production
and review of environmental impact statements became an industry
unto itself.

The election of Ronald Reagan seemed to threaten that agenda.
The new administration, under the banner of deregulation, attempted
to either reduce or restructure bureaucracies, limit spending levels for
"clean up" legislation, and separate certain key constituencies such as
hunters and fisherman and the tourism trade as a whole from the scenic
protectionists among the environmental groups. While Jimmy Carter
had overestimated the clout and reach of the environmental groups,
particularly in the West, Ronald Reagan underestimated the elevation
of environmental values among the public at large. The hard-edged
rhetoric used by the President and certain of his key officials, such as
James Watt and Anne Gorsuch, during much of Reagan's first term, had
the immediate effect of reinvigorating environmental organizations,
many of which had been ready to proclaim the end of the Environmental Decade. Most of the administration's attempts to halt expenditures, roll back legislation, or delay implementation of regulations had
only limited success. In certain instances, such as passage of the Safe
Drinking Water Act Amendments in 1986, Congress, responding to the
strong public concerns that had evolved around the issue of
groundwater contamination, restructured this legislative initiative to
forestall Reagan administration regulatory backbiting, specifically refer-
ring to the efforts of the Office of Management and Budget to undermine EPA standard-setting.

For the most part, however, environmentally sensitive legislators
were too busy fighting the Reagan administration's attempts to march
backward to push forward with new laws or approaches. Reauthoriza-
tions of existing laws became pitched battles, with changes mostly a
matter of detail. Much of the significant policymaking of the Reagan
years took place within the bureaucracy, far from public, and often
from Congressional, scrutiny. It is not surprising that the development
interests tended to fare best in restricted forums where legal and technical expertise, which can be purchased, are at a premium.

Rather than insisting upon opening agency forums and broadening conflict, some environmental groups actually cooperated in restricting public access. A great deal was made of new opportunities for
negotiation and environmental mediation. Emphasis was put upon finding common ground for agreement, not upon distinguishing environmental and development viewpoints. Leaders of environmental groups
were congratulated for their growing maturity, reasonableness, and
sound management of what had become large-scale organizations. Instead of publicly regretting the lack of substantial accomplishment in
cleaning up the environment, environmental leaders satisfied themsel-

ves that the network of regulatory laws put in place in the 1970s was not dismantled.

The apparent failure at full-blown deregulation and dismantling of legislation, however, did not prevent the emergence of a number of new or revised approaches, some of which were embraced by both Reaganites and environmental groups. These placed the environmental issue on the level of competing technologies and reallocation of resources and minimized the role of both the government and public action. Reaganites emphasized the move toward privatization and private markets in place of government intervention, a position which attracted those environmentalists who had come to focus on government subsidies as a major source of environmental abuse. In the area of solid waste management, for example, growing environmental concerns over landfills, which in turn contributed to the price escalation of the fees per pound of waste, helped stimulate the reappearance of the incineration industry. Privatization-oriented measures, such as tax breaks and the reduction of federal grants, aided that shift, which the environmental movement was slow to address. During the late 1970s, in fact, several environmental groups even welcomed the development of this "waste-to-energy" technology, only to modify their positions later as community and neighborhood groups, worried about air contaminants, hazardous ash residue, and local neighborhood impacts, took the lead in opposing this newly touted technical solution.

The focus began to shift to the private sector as the problems of regulation, expensive and inefficient subsidies, and the costs of clean-up multiplied. Water markets, for one, were identified by some in the water industry—that unique collection of public agencies and private interests—as the best way to salvage long-standing water policies designed to stimulate irrigated agricultural production and urban development. A number of environmental groups identified with this approach, calling it a "win-win" alternative to the construction of new and potentially environmentally destructive facilities. Yet markets also allowed pricing inequities to continue, even providing an additional benefit for those landowners wishing to either bail out of the system or maneuver to obtain an additional profit from arrangements that had amounted to billions of dollars in federal transfer payments to western agriculture. The buyers, meanwhile—the rapidly expanding urban complexes in places like San Diego, Denver, and Phoenix—saw markets as the way to sustain development plans in the face of newly emerging "slow growth" movements. These movements were different from the environmental constituencies, more distinctly neighborhood- and community-oriented, focused on the urban and industrial environment, though not unsympathetic to fears about abuse of the natural environment.

These new social movements have compounded the complexity the environmental agenda. They have raised concerns about toxics and hazardous wastes. They worry about residential groundwater contamination and carcinogenic water disinfection byproducts more than protecting in-stream flows. They have placed questions of housing, transportation, air quality, and even economic development on the agenda, which the traditional environmental agenda either had failed to address or addressed inadequately. These questions, however, are fundamental environmental issues. They reflect patterns of industrialization and urbanization, the primary sources of environmental degradation.

Environmental issues are social issues; the natural environment and the human environment are intricately linked in this industrial age. Some groups have begun to connect apparently disparate concerns such as environmentalism and feminism into a new discourse that places the abuses of industrialization in the context of daily life. Furthermore, unlike the traditional agendas of the nationally-oriented environmental organizations, the focus of many of these community, neighborhood, and various "single issue" groups is local. Their issues are as much about community and democratic control as about "natural" environmental degradation, where the focus tends to be on national and bureaucratic solutions.

These divergent forms of environmental politics help to develop larger perspectives on the environment and future political approaches. Traditional environmentalism, aside from its long-standing interest in scenic protection, has developed as a crisis-oriented, reactive form of politics, seeking to address questions of "clean-up" and more effective regulation of the extraordinary brew of new products and production processes that have heightened the potential of large-scale environmental deterioration. Though this environmentalism also seeks to promote concepts of conservation and "source reduction," these are often articulated in the form of programs to make urban and industrial interests more efficient in their operations, rationalizing rather than restructuring the production process.

In contrast, the more populist, grassroots environmentalism promotes the concept that the needs of the community, and, in its more radical form, the workplace, take precedence. Traditional environmentalism has focused primarily on protecting nature and rationalizing the system while reducing its more obvious environmental abuses. Grassroots environmentalism, dealing with everyday problems from toxics to growth, has questioned how the system functions, at least on a local and single-issue level. Up to now, what both movements have lacked is an examination of how particular environmental crises and community problems are rooted in the structure and control of production and development decisions.

A new environmental approach, one that is beginning to emerge particularly in the "toxics" movements, needs to and has indeed begun to focus on the democratic control of such decisions. This approach involves questions regarding the choices of new technologies and the introduction of new products. It presumes that "risk" choices are political in nature and not exclusively technical and therefore outside the public domain. It centers not just on the consequences of development, such as transportation or housing impacts, but the structure of development and the shaping of the urban environment. It explores not just issues of "conservation" and "source reduction" to minimize resource depletion or the use of hazardous substances, but raises questions of funding and pricing priorities that help determine the choice of resources and "toxics use reduction" strategies that address the choice of technology and technical process.

The difficulties in building such an approach and developing a more systematic grassroots environmentalism are numerous. The existing nationally-oriented environmental organizations, though influenced by the grassroots groups, still adhere to an organizational framework that is dependent on lobbying, litigation, and expertise. Furthermore, the impact of the Reagan years, which has caused increases in their membership rolls and expectations about their influence and programs, has made these environmental groups even more dependent on outside funding sources such as foundations and various sectors of industry, as well as a style of organization that emphasizes managerial rather than organizing skills. In fact, some environmental leaders tend to regard grassroots movements as potentially dangerous to their current respectability as reasonable negotiators. At times they accept the characterization of local residents concerned with their quality of life as expressions of NIMBY (not in my back yard) rather than as an authentic set of criticisms. The lack of scientific sophistication of grassroots movements becomes an embarrassment to environmental leaders who have inherited their conservation forerunners' respect for expertise.

While environmental organizations have become more bureaucratized (or "professionalized," as some of its leaders like to say), there has also developed a more militant, direct action wing of environmentalism. These groups, such as Earth First! and the various advocates of "deep ecology" and "bioregionalism," essentially criticize the national environmental organizations for their more conservative tactics but not their agendas. This infusion of militancy and a kind of "moral witness" approach similar to earlier forms of 1960s counterculture politics has in fact served to reinforce the notion of environmentalism as a movement about nature and not about industrialization and urbanization.

Some of the more militant "eco-activists," influenced by the acerbic and brilliant writer Edward Abbey, have adopted a kind of environmental "naturism." They decry Mexican immigrants as a population scourge and divorce their concern about nature from concerns about social inequities and the exploitation of human beings.

The new grassroots movements are thus outside the definitions of environmentalism. They share an instinct for social change and reform, but lack a single, coherent history and set of objectives. Their popularity and ability to survive and accomplish limited goals despite severe odds, however, testifies to the ways in which they resonate politically with the public at large, much in the way that the public has demonstrated allegiance to environmentalism, especially when it is defined in terms of a response to the hazards of industrialization and urbanization. Many of these groups, in fact, see themselves distinct from and occasionally hostile to environmental organizations that have largely failed to take up the issues involved. Unlike several Western European countries, where such movements have been able to embrace the symbol of environmentalism in "green" movements and parties, grassroots environmentalism in this country still functions as a particular kind of constituency group or single-issue movement, with little opportunity to make common cause with related movements, and beyond that to create the analysis and program that centers on the structure of production and development.

What is most striking about these grassroots movements is their democratic thrust, similar in some ways to the emergence of the student, civil rights, and women's movements a generation earlier. Instead of embracing expertise, they have become examples of how to develop "self-taught experts." Instead of seeking to lobby or litigate more effectively, they have become advocates of popular action and citizen law suits, influencing legislative debate by their mobilizing efforts rather than lobbying skills. They have become organizations of members, in neighborhoods and communities, rather than groupings with organized mailing lists and membership dues which are situated in offices that take the place of communities. Most important, they have begun to demand an accounting of how actions by industries and developers, the government as well as the private sector, affect people in their day-to-day lives and impact both the environments around us and the larger natural—and social—environment.

There is a rich historical tradition related to what can be called a democratic and populist environmentalism. These were the movements that emerged in the late 19th century to address the extraordinary abuses of early industrialization and urbanization, when issues of foul air, dirty water (which killed thousands of people in countless epidemics of infectious diseases), the horrendous noises and din of the new industrial and urban order, the suffocating and overcrowded cities, and the problems of rotting and infected foods dominated the urban and industrial landscape. Rivers, streams, mountains, and wilderness were, to be sure, casualties of this new order, part of the same package of development. The movements that emerged—public sanitarians, municipal housekeepers, social feminists, both "sewer socialists" and radical syndicalists, and a range of other reformist and revolutionary movements of the moment—represented an environmental tradition much as John Muir and Gifford Pinchot did with their romantic and utilitarian impulses.

Today, the issues of the industrial and urban order are more complex and yet more extensive in their impact on peoples' lives and environments. The new grassroots movements of the 1980s are part of a range of efforts that seek to address the consequences of this order, whether in terms of nuclear politics, economic dislocation, or the problems of the environment writ large or small. In this sense, environmentalism can be seen not as an "interest group" seeking better regulation or protection of scenic resources, but as an essential component of a new democratic politics. It is a politics where "risk" is no longer just a question of what contaminant we are prepared or not prepared to live with, but a question of dealing with the hazards of an undemocratic society where the decisions that affect our lives are made elsewhere.

To achieve the goal laid out in this chapter, the following specific proposals are put forth:

- National support for state and local land-use planning. The key to controlling pollution, particularly of resources that are exposed to degradation through different media, such as groundwater and air, is regulating land-use. Groundwater can be protected only by preventing damaging activities in recharge areas. Urban air pollution cannot be controlled without attention to urban sprawl, locations of shopping centers and housing developments, and transportation corridors. Land-use decisions are essentially location-specific, and are best made at the grassroots level with full knowledge of local circumstances. There has been enormous political resistance to national land-use planning. Much can be done at the national level, however, to encourage, reinforce, and prevent the subversion of state and local efforts. The federal level can supply economic incentives and technical assistance. The federal government should not preempt stronger state and local pollution controls by asserting less stringent federal standards. There should be an upward cascade of standards that allow the strictest standards to prevail.

- Establish a focus on "source reduction" rather than the current and exclusive focus on "treatment." Many environmental laws and programs have emphasized "cleaning up" the environment rather than reducing a specific hazard to the environment, which is a more complex and politically charged approach. "Source reduction" directly targets the production process itself.

- Develop the means toward greater social governance of the production process. We need a new national definition of productivity and we need a new emphasis on the social as opposed to the private nature of production. In such a setting, the protection of the environment and the public's health as well as other social goals ("the right to work," equity considerations, providing jobs with purpose and satisfaction, etc.) are structured into the industrial decisionmaking process.

- Establish a more environmentally supportive fiscal policy. Many of the more hazardous and environmentally destructive technologies and resource projects, such as nuclear power, waste incineration, and large-scale hydroelectric and water storage facilities, have depended heavily on various forms of economic subsidies. These have ranged from insurance programs (the Price-Anderson nuclear ceiling) and taxation advantages (use of Industrial Development Bonds) to more direct government intervention in promoting certain approaches (the Bureau of Reclamation's water development policies). These fiscal programs need to be reevaluated. They can be ultimately restructured not only to eliminate subsidies but to create disincentives for the environmentally hazardous technology.

- Create a more democratic structure of input and decisionmaking. Decisions about production and the direction of the industrial order, as currently made, are fundamentally anti-democratic and exclude the public from any essential input, despite the social consequences of such decisions. Citizen movements have emerged which have insisted on greater public input, such as citizen utility boards which monitor the activities of the investor-owned utilities.

- Halt the export of pollution and pollution-prone social choices. The United States allows the export of pesticides and toxics banned in the United States, even while evidence suggests that such damaging substances come back to haunt our population through imported products. More fundamentally, the United States needs to reconsider the kinds of cultural choices it is exporting in foreign aid and through our influence on such international agencies as the World Bank. The prevailing notion of development is making the rich nations richer and the rich within poor nations richer, while worsening the lot of common people. Further, this socially atavistic industrialization is spreading pollution to previously healthful areas of the globe.

- Reverse the trend toward privatization of public resources, and replace narrow notions of economic efficiency with accountability as a measure of bureaucratic performance. One of the responses of the Reagan administration to budgetary problems has been to sell public facilities at fire sale prices and to lease out to private enterprise the provision of services in national parks and forests. Privatization is resulting in organizations which are less concerned with long-term maintenance of resources, less open to public scrutiny, and less sensitive to public needs and participation.

- Renew the fervor of environmental agencies and create a National Health Service Corps. The Environmental Protection Agency is not spinning out of control as it was during the Gorsuch days, but it has lost much of even the limited élan which characterized it in the early 1970s. Numbers of committed individuals have left agencies at all levels because of budget and personnel cuts and a negative working environment. Respect for public service to protect the environment needs to be restored and good people recruited to natural resource and environmental agencies. Among the new activities that should be established is a National Health Service Corps which would provide community education about the sources of toxics, their risks, and how they can be avoided.

Resources

Recommended Appointees for a New Administration

- Martin Strange, Department of Agriculture. Strange is currently active with the Center for Rural Affairs, based in Walthill, Nebraska. He and his organization have been extremely effective and articulate critics of the midwestern version of the industrialization of agriculture and its associated environmental hazards.

- Molly Coye, OSHA. Coye is currently the Director of the State of New Jersey's Health Department and is a well known advocate of worker health and safety.

- Barry Commoner, EPA. Commoner, well known author and political figure, is currently focussing his research on the hazards of solid waste and hazardous waste incineration.

- Ellen Widess, Office of Pesticides—to be created. Widess has been heavily involved in the pesticide issue in both California and Texas, where she is State Director of Pesticide Regulation.

- Eula Bingham, Department of Public Health—to be created from the current Department of Health and Human Services. Bingham, head of OSHA in the Carter administration, remains a champion of the public health rights of citizens, including disadvantaged and at-risk groups.

- Dick Kamp, Office of Transboundary Resources and Environment—to be created. Kamp is a key activist in the Border Ecology Project, which shut down the Phelps Dodge copper smelter that had been endangering health of residents of Southern Arizona and Sonora Mexico for decades. He also helped to convince the Mexican government to install pollution controls on new and expanded smelter facilities. Efforts are now directed at controlling illegal dumping of toxics along the United States/Mexico border. Kamp's skills and perspective would be enormously useful in dealing with the stalled acid rain control efforts with Canada.

- Lee Botts, Assistant Administrator for Water Programs, EPA. Botts, formerly Executive Director of the Lake Michigan Federation, is an important grassroots organizer protecting the Great Lakes.

- Robert Ginsburg, Office of Groundwater Policy, EPA. Active in bringing attention to hazardous waste dumps and the need to clean them up in Lake Calumet, a smoldering underground dump which burned and spread toxic fumes for months.

Organizations

- Citizens' Clearing House for Hazardous Wastes, P.O. Box 926, Arlington, VA 22216; (202) 276-7070
- Border Ecology Project, Box 5, Naco, AZ 85620
- National Campaign Against Toxic Wastes, 20 East St., Suite 601, Boston, MA 02111; (617) 423-4413
- Center for Rural Affairs, Box 405, Walthill, NE 68067; (402) 846-5428
- Hazardous Waste News, Environmental Research Foundation, P.O. Box 3541, Princeton, NJ 08543-3541; (609) 683-0707
- California Action Network/California Institute for Rural Studies, Davis, CA; (916) 756-6555

Further Reading

- Nick Freudenberg, *Not in our Backyard*, Monthly Review Press, 1985.
- David Dickson, *The Politics of Alternative Technology*, Universe Books, 1974.
- Barry Commoner, "The Environment," *The New Yorker*, June 15, 1987.
- Walter A. Rosenbaum, *Environmental Politics and Policy*, Congressional Quarterly Press, 1985.
- Norman J. Vig and Michael E. Kraft, *Environmental Policy in the 1980s: Reagan's New Agenda*, Congressional Quarterly Press, 1984.
- Lois Gibbs, *Love Canal, My Story*, published for the Citizens' Clearing House for Hazardous Waste, State University of New York Press, 1982.

Robert Gottlieb is the author of four books: *A Life of its Own: The Politics and Power of Water* (forthcoming, 1988); *America's Saints: The Rise of Mormon Power* (co-author); *Empires in the Sun: The Rise of the New American West* (co-author); and *Thinking Big: The Story of the* Los Angeles Times*, Its Publishers, and Their Influence on Southern California,* (co-author). He is currently teaching in the UCLA Urban Planning Program and writes for a number of publications, including *The Wall Street Journal.*

Helen Ingram is a professor of political science at the University of Arizona at Tucson. She is the author of a number of books and articles on environmental and natural resources, including: *Water and Poverty* (co-author) and *Saving Water in A Desert City* (co-author). She has recently written on the environmental movement (with Dean Mann) for a book entitled *Environmental Politics and Policy: Synthesis of the Literature,* edited by James C. Lester.

Michael H. Goldhaber

A Call for a Humane Technology

Platform

- Use our technological prowess for the equal benefit of all our citizens, for deepening our democracy, for opening new opportunities to all, for increasing the economic self-sufficiency of communities, and for international cooperation and development.

- Begin work on a free, federally-financed telecommunications and information system, with ample capacity for use by all citizens, to be fully operating no later than 1999. This system shall include: capacities for high-resolution, two-way television conversations; open, immediate access to all publications, recordings, and films now stored in libraries, to most government information sources, and to large-scale computing facilities; and direct access to executive and legislative offices at all levels of government.

- Revamp our intellectual property laws to better serve the goal of encouraging and supporting artistic expression and beneficial innovation, while removing the restrictions on free speech and access to information such laws presently entail. Add requirements for concise Social Impact Statements for inventions.

- Create an Agency for Social Goals-Directed Technologies, which would directly and indirectly stimulate the development of technologies to meet important needs now neglected in our technology system.

We Americans are justly proud of our technological prowess, which often shapes our hopes and dreams, yet we also often rightly fear where technology will take us. We lose sight of the fact that people cause technological change. As a society, we can and should control

385

what these changes will be. Wisely developed, new technology can strengthen our economy, improve our options for democratic dialogue, extend possibilities for social equality, help promote international cooperation and peace, and enrich individual lives. When they are badly managed, however, similar technological changes can help impoverish the majority, stifle debate, enlarge inequality, increase global tensions, and add confusion and uncertainty to our lives. Each new technology, from a humble toothpaste tube to a space station, changes both what people can do and what they cannot, in much the same way that a law changes how people may act. We cannot have democracy if people have no say in constructing laws. Likewise, we cannot have democracy without a considerable degree of public control over the direction of technology.

As the pace and scope of technological change keep increasing, the importance of good technology policies keeps growing. The U.S. government is by far the world's largest single sponsor of technological innovation. Beyond that, it also establishes the environment for most private sector innovation both here and abroad. The current furious pace of technological innovation can easily undercut any government program, no matter how good or important, that has no technological component. And, of necessity, the government responds to the social consequences of new technologies, whatever their source.

There is ample precedent, then, for government involvement in shaping the direction of technology and dealing with its consequences. However, government policies are now substantially misdirected. Current government research and development programs are heavily weighted in favor of military over civilian technology. Existing civilian-oriented programs are heavily weighted towards research, the results of which are almost exclusively of use to those corporations with extensive technical capacities of their own. Government departments more attuned to constituencies such as labor, cities, or the poor have virtually no capacity to influence technological development.

Ironically, what both major parties have viewed as the chief goal of technology policy—improving American competitiveness—can only backfire, as it has before. In both arms races and business races, the more we try to use technology to stay ahead, the faster our competitors can catch up. Technology, especially as it has developed in this country, is a means for standardizing and routinizing tools and tasks, relying on science rather than craft wisdom as its ultimate knowledge base. This means technological methods are inherently transportable and reproducible elsewhere. Technology therefore works to undercut advantages based on local tradition or other geographical particulars. When we designed long-range missiles so as to be able to strike at the Soviet Union, they felt the need and had the capacity to match us, rendering our own cities vulnerable to foreign attack for the first time. Similarly, when we built a system of highly productive factories and made advances in transportation and communications to increase our exports, our economic competitors imitated our best factories and have used the international channels we created to swamp us with goods they produce. It was geography that conferred upon the United States both its relative military security and its economic independence and strength. Our attempts to benefit from long-range arms and long-range commerce have only helped lead us to nuclear insecurity and balance-of-payments deficits.

Regardless of what we may intend, global technological development must be cooperative. Other nations, whether friends or enemies, have little choice but to build on and augment our own innovations. We cannot escape from their growing similarity to us in technological terms. As the largest innovator, then, we are in the best position to choose whether the global system will be cooperating in annihilation or in human growth, whether we shall beggar each other through growing world unemployment or move together towards a world in which each person can have a role. Do we cooperate to build instruments for extending authority and social control, or do we cooperate in providing the means for heightened participatory democracy?

Among the currently favored means of increasing economic competitiveness are automation and other steps to increase industrial productivity. For an individual company or nation, increasing output may seem to be beneficial, but there are serious drawbacks for the world as a whole. Quite obviously, increases in productivity will create unemployment unless they are matched by increases in consumption or decreases in the average work day. But consumption cannot rise without limit, even when real prices drop, for consuming anything requires time and attention, as well as the infrastructure necessary to make use of the item to be consumed (for cars, this infrastructure includes roads, gas stations, parking lots, etc.). A shift to new kinds of goods can take up some of the slack, but if consumption patterns change too fast cultural chaos results.

These limits on consumption hold true not only for the well-off, but even more for the majority of the world's people who are very poor. Most third world countries lack the infrastructure needed to make use of the types of mass-produced consumer goods the industrialized world most easily can export, and even at current levels of export the third world is in danger of being swamped culturally. New forms of consumption are incompatible with traditional social roles, the loss of which is a tragedy inadequately described in economics terms as "massive unemployment." Third world countries that are able to import production facilities as well as consumer goods may slightly ease their own unemployment situation, but only by adding to the pace at which worldwide production levels can outstrip world consumption capacities.

Nor is lowering the work week feasible once it already is short enough to allow a significant number of people to hold two jobs. These people can outbid others for scarce goods, raising the work time required to maintain a decent living standard. Our standard work week reached forty hours some forty years ago, and has stuck there despite enormous productivity increases and rising unemployment. Only in illusion can any amount of automation now reduce the work week further—barring very major changes in the way society functions.

Then, too, increases in productivity usually affect only some tasks, so more and more workers—when not unemployed outright—end up with the leftover lower productivity tasks — often with low pay and low social status. Whether an individual's productivity rises or falls, the new technologies often damage working conditions, lessening personal control over the pace and character of the task, making it boring, and removing pride in work. The conclusion has to be that increasing productivity is not a worthwhile goal unless carefully balanced with other changes and protections.

For much of the post-World War II period the problems with increasing productivity were masked in the United States by three factors: 1) there were wide areas of this country not yet saturated with goods such as automobiles; 2) we were able to transfer the negative effects such as unemployment to other parts of the world, especially the third world; 3) we added to demand without competing with the outputs of ordinary industries by engaging in Keynesian "wasteful" spending, especially for "defense" and space exploration.

However, in most of this country, by the mid-1960s, problems with further saturation by automobiles and related goods began to outweigh benefits. Around that time also, the effects of attempting to establish global markets were coming home to roost. In a global economy, our Keynesian spending serves to benefit other industrial countries; likewise, industrial competitors can cut into our markets at home and abroad. Similar structural crises have happened before, such as the period of the late 19th century when railroad growth began to slow down. Part of the apparent solution in the past was a massive cultural and social transformation centered on new technology. In oversimplified terms, the automobile plus electric power and telephones allowed a vast reshaping of our way of life—even physical changes in the relation of homes to workplaces; activity such as construction associated with reshaping was essential to an economic boom.

In looking to new technology for a parallel revitalizing of our now sagging economy, many have looked to information technologies—ranging from fiber-optical telecommunications cable to personal computer software to supercomputers. Developments in these fields hold great promise. Information and its exchange are the lifeblood not only of any economy but of democracy. Deployed in the most democratic way, the new technologies could offer everyone access to an almost unlimited abundance of information resources and openings for social interconnections. But there is a serious problem. If information technology is to be the basis for growth of a private-enterprise economy such as ours, then information itself must be privatized—turned into property sold only to those who can afford it. If that happens, democracy itself will be available only to the relatively rich. Furthermore, access to the newest, most versatile forms of information technology—such as cellular radio, video-conferencing, and desktop publishing—allows the fortunate few to create new wealth by producing and "broadcasting" information in new ways. Without access to the leading technological edge, others become relatively poorer. Social and economic inequalities deepen.

Jobs become more polarized as well. Work related to information creation tends to be well rewarded and fulfilling while other kinds of work are reduced to rote tasks that require little creativity or inventiveness. Early roots of this inequality stem from unequal access to the new technologies that begin in childhood; for instance, middle-class children now are likely to have their own computers; poor children are lucky to have even very restricted access to computers in school. Access to telephone services is even more unequal.

The more important information becomes to our economy, the more serious the problems in treating it as an essentially new kind of property—"intellectual property" protected by patents, copyrights, and other legal devices. Unlike earlier kinds of property, this one can be anywhere. To protect it requires intrusions upon rights of privacy, large-scale violations of the freedoms of speech and expression, and denial of free access to the communications system and to data banks of legitimate public interest.

Our intellectual property laws need major revision, which may involve finding new ways to serve their original purpose—encouraging beneficial innovation. While the fast pace of innovation is not always desirable, much is certainly essential if we are to overcome our deepening problems.

The proposals below are an integrated approach to best utilizing the emerging possibilities of technology in order to help build a more humane society. Priorities for government-backed research and development will be turned around, so that pro-human technologies can be developed according to the needs and desires of the constituencies involved. Small-scale organizations would derive more benefit, facilitating community-based production, which also would be aided by a universal-access information and communication system. Changes in intellectual property laws would be necessary for this to work, but the new system would make beneficial innovation and free expression easier. An economy so improved would be far more robust, more equal in its rewards, and more forgiving of mistakes and bad luck. It would not require a high level of international trade to work. Without the inherent tensions dependence on trade brings, a more cooperative world order could flourish. The same changes would obviate the economic need for wasteful weapons spending.

Current policies that emphasize weapons development assume that development of humanly beneficial technologies should either be left to private industry or will emerge as "fallout," by accident, from the military programs. These assumptions are silly at best. Beneficial technologies are much too important to be left to chance. No matter how well-meaning corporate executives may be, in the end they are governed by the bottom line. They will develop only that for which they can see a ready market, and that usually means initial innovation must be aimed toward private use by the most well-off consumers or other large corporations.

If the government is to represent all the people, it must see to it that other constituencies—and the needs of the nation as a whole—are addressed more directly in the innovation process. To achieve this, other government departments will have to be accorded substantial funding not only for research but for development. Programs will have to be targeted toward specific kinds of needs, such as more satisfying working conditions, greater opportunities for democratic discussion and debate, more resources for poor communities, greater independence for the handicapped, etc. If these goals are to be accorded more than lip service, some institution within government must be held accountable. One clear way to do this would be to designate a new office in an overall Agency for Social Goals-Directed Technologies for each distinct goal. These offices must be able to influence the direction of scientific research, as well as engineering, in ways likely to aid their particular projects.

The constituencies to be affected should play active roles in every stage of developing specific technologies. Since these are mostly very large groups, this sort of involvement is unprecedented, so several different ways of achieving it will have to be tried. For example, randomly selected grand jury-like panels of members of low-income communities could be asked to decide on goals for technologies that would aid their communities. These should be allowed their share of failures without over-hasty condemnation.

Some additional needs that should be addressed in this program include gender-neutral job design, full employment, worker self-management, improved living standards for low-income households, improving the social environment for children, developing alternative market forms, intelligible technologies, and third world village development. Explanations of what might be involved in these programs may be found in my book, *Reinventing Technology: Policies for Democratic Values.*

The development of modern technology in a context of international cooperation (rather than competitiveness) would allow increased equality, independence, and mutual respect among nations. A free exchange of information and ideas would heighten international understanding, allow all wealth in the form of information to be shared, and dramatically improve the quality of life all over the world. Poorer countries would benefit most from truly free exchange, as they would be allowed to pick and choose technologies that best meet their particular needs and that are best suited to locally available skills and resources. With freely available expertise, plans, and technical information, each country or region would be in a position to fill its own needs without having to be dependent on trade. Trade would not have to cease, but with effective means for substituting for imports, no nation or region would be threatened with undue dependence, and would have little reason to build up a huge trade surplus. With economic independence, political independence could survive as well.

The United States should take the lead in developing this technical basis for international cooperation, helping design and build a free international communications system, making our sources of information accessible to other countries, advancing technologies for small-scale, local production, and substituting for scarce local resources. With a clear commitment of this sort, we could influence other countries to join in furthering the process.

To maintain democracy, we need the best possible means for sharing information, for allowing each person to communicate with others and to express his or her own ideas. Since information can be shared without being used up, the more it is shared, the greater our per capita wealth as well. Equal access to communications and information resources would have been desirable at any time in our history, but now, with information technology so well developed, unequal access is more of a block to democracy and equality than ever. Even long-distance telephone charges seriously impair the social, political, and economic options of all but the very well-off.

Ironically, the same technology that now intensifies inequality could, in fact, permit a viable, intensive, completely free communications and information system. We possess both the resources and technical competence to guarantee to every citizen by 1999: unlimited access to two-way, high-resolution television; immediate access to considerable computer power, to data banks, to libraries holding virtually every book, film, or recording; direct interaction with distant experts; participation in political and other "meetings" and forums; direct access to most government offices, and so forth.

Access to an information network such as this would allow people from widely varying backgrounds a chance to participate in the political process, maintain social ties, come to understand one another and share scarce resources. For our geographically mobile and culturally diverse country, this would greatly strengthen the social fabric, rescuing many from loneliness, isolation, or alienation, and so help reduce homelessness, mental illness, and crime.

We owe it to ourselves to establish this system and make it as rich and flexible as possible. Its cost would be minuscule in comparison with the enormous benefits, including immediate economic benefits. To operate for free, the system would have to be tax-supported, but it would not have to be run by some unfeeling, inefficient bureaucracy. Private companies and democratically run cooperatives could vie for subsidies—on the basis of quality of service, as decided by individual users.

The new communications and information system itself would necessarily make a wide variety of creative resources available to everyone. It will also facilitate many kinds of group efforts at innovation as well as widen opportunities to disseminate and debate new ideas of all sorts. It would make possible a system, similar to what now is used to pay recording artists for airplay of their works, to reward creators in general. Since expense for much creative work would be reduced, and since government policies should not intentionally foster enormous concentrations of wealth, moderate stipends can be offered on a graduated scale, depending roughly on the number of times a given work is requested—with some per person total ceiling.

For inventions with high development costs, a system of intellectual claims should assure adequate reimbursement for all aspects of development. Current patent laws have this as a goal, but they also permit innovating corporations to establish effective monopolies which allow such high prices for many new products that only the well-off can benefit from them. In the case of most utility industries, it has long been recognized that the government must regulate prices to counteract monopoly power. A similar method of control would make the patent system much fairer; it would also allow the public to benefit from products combining the inventiveness of competing firms. Companies holding intellectual claims similar to patents would be required to grant licenses to other firms at prices regulated so as to assure wide availability of the innovation while allowing adequate but not excessive returns on development costs.

Alternative ways to finance development of inventions are also needed; these should include grants or use of government-provided facilities and other direct aid. All products, processes, techniques, or computer programs would have to be fully disclosed to be accorded intellectual claim protection. Additionally, brief Social Impact Statements would be required. Clearly negative impacts could be denied protection. To protect free speech, and encourage dissemination of innovative ideas, this category of innovation should no longer be protected by the courts as trade secrets.

Resources

Recommended Appointees for a New Administration

Two jobs stand out, for very different reasons. One is the President's Science Advisor. Like other members of the Executive Office of the President, the function of the Advisor depends on who is president. The right person could exert effective leadership in the massive changeover needed. Possible candidates are:

- Congressman George Brown (D-CA), longtime Chair of the House Committee on Science and Technology, is totally familiar with, but not totally accepting of, the present ways of Washington technologues.

- Professor Barry Commoner, head of the Center for Biology of Natural Systems, Queens College, New York, and former presidential candidate.

- Professor Vera Kistiakowsky, Massachusetts Institute of Technology, one of the few women who has achieved significant status in the male-dominated area of science and technology, while still being outspoken enough to have established a public position in relation to the social consequences.

- Dr. Paul Raskin, physicist and director of the Energy Systems Research Group, a Boston consulting firm specializing in energy policy for the third world.

The other office of special note is Undersecretary of Defense for Research and Engineering:

- Dr. Richard Garwin of IBM, a longtime Pentagon advisor who has, to his credit, offered spirited opposition to many military research excesses, especially Star Wars. While probably not in tune with many of the proposals here, he might be the best choice for this difficult post, since his credentials would command considerable respect from the powerful and ingrained military-industrial establishment he would be assigned to rein in.

Organizations

- Center for Technology and Democracy, P.O. Box 146516, San Francisco, CA 94114; (415) 648-5742

- Computer Professionals for Social Responsibility, P.O. Box 717, Palo Alto, CA 94301; (415) 322-3778

- International Association of Machinists, 1300 Connecticut Ave. NW, Washington, DC 20036; (202) 857-5200

Further Reading

- Michael H. Goldhaber, *Reinventing Technology: Policies for Democratic Values*, Routledge & Kegan Paul, 1986.

- Michael J. Piore and Charles F. Sabel, *The Second Industrial Divide: Possibilities for Prosperity*, Basic Books, 1986.

- Richard Evan Sclove, "Technology and Freedom: A Prescriptive Theory of Technological Design and Practice in Democratic Societies," Ph.D. dissertation, Massachusetts Institute of Technology, June 1986, unpublished.

Michael H. Goldhaber, author of *Reinventing Technology* and former Director of the Technology and Democracy Project at the Institute for Policy Studies, is currently organizing a new Center for Technology and Democracy in San Francisco (P.O. Box 146516, San Francisco, CA 94114-6516). The Center will be concerned with redirecting technology and related policies so as to promote democracy and social equality. It will also analyze the broad societal implications of the direction of technology. His interest in this subject grew from his earlier experience as a theoretical physicist and his opposition to the complicity of scientists in the Vietnam and other wars.

A Responsible Energy Policy
for the United States and the World

Platform

- The United States must formulate an energy policy predicated on respect for the earth and recognition of the cumulative, often irreversible, danger of doing violence to it.

- This policy must honor the rights of *all* people to a fair share of non-violently acquired energy resources.

- This policy must be supportive of institutions and relations that are democratic, just, and peaceful.

- Encouragement must be directed to the utilization of renewable resources and the transition to solar energy, biomass technologies, and wind, water, and geothermal power.

- Nuclear power should be phased out.

- A public investment fund should be created to provide seed money for imaginative community groups to utilize regional energy technologies to be operated under public management.

- There must be full public access to information about energy resources and technology and their ecological dimensions.

Energy crisis ahead? Why that happened back in... Surely we have solved that one. People in the United States have become somewhat more energy-conscious, although homes still feel overheated and traffic is increasingly bumper-to-bumper with more, if sometimes smaller, vehicles. There may be cutbacks on domestic steel and electronic production, but stores remain crowded with petroleum-based goods that we supposedly need. There is little to suggest that our trillion-dollar war machine has stalled because of an empty tank.

Someplace off in what too readily are labeled utopian green pastures, there are groups warning the public about the dangers of nuclear power and championing safer energy. If, at times, they appear to be as passionate in their divisions among themselves as in their shared dirges about the certain ecological doomsday if we do not reverse our present energy course, they are united in recognizing the imperative for shedding our cultural obsession with thinking that bigger is always better. Meanwhile, scholars and technicians have rather happily discovered energy development as a lucrative field for specialized study and grants, again illustrating how easily we develop a vested interest in our problems, perhaps more readily than in their resolution. Candidates for the presidency and other political offices generally prefer to neglect what seems to be functioning smoothly until the public demands a solution. Energy is rarely cited, and less often debated. An overall policy for energy is viewed as too remote from public concern to elicit more than boredom, if not outright rejection at the polls.

There is some short-run justification for tiptoeing around the subject. A serious and rational approach to our energy predicament would raise a cluster of uncomfortable and complex problems concerning the American way of life. The primary issue is not that the United States is running out of fuel— a conventional response which is somewhat short on conclusive documentation. There is ample room for disagreement as to reserves and potential sources among honorable experts in the corporations, government agencies, and the academy, and not just from those who believe that the specter of a world without adequate fuel is the catalyst that will impel us to act wisely and in time. This country is extraordinarily well endowed, possessing within its own borders an almost unrivalled range of energy options. Oil and natural gas are still the basic source for the United States, and currently there is a glut. More oil from home and abroad is coming on-stream and into the national market than traditional market mechanisms—designed to protect price by ensuring that supply does not exceed market demand—can handle effectively. Despite the quick and shaky charge of being a cartel, OPEC has not been consistent or successful in containing production rivalries and orchestrating overall quotas among member states. The latter's priority is income rather than price. The rise of non-OPEC sources, coupled with the slowing down of conservation efforts in consuming centers, have at least for the immediate future made abundance, rather than scarcity, the prevailing nightmare of oil producers.

But the United States has become a net importer of oil, facing the troubling prospect of extracting oil at a faster rate than it is discovering new fields. Yet even here one needs to be cautious in drawing conclusions. Reserves, ultimately unknown although not unlimited, are related to price. The "right" price will stimulate investment and application of the necessary technology for extending reserves. (Yet when the incoming Reagan administration sought to "turn the industry loose in the marketplace" by cutting back government intervention, the energy barons responded by putting their money where they calculated the best earning opportunities could be found, which happened to be in mergers, takeovers, and non-energy investments in this country and overseas.) Within their traditional arenas, the corporations focused on the fuels that were the most profitable and firmly under their control. They continued to drill and dig for non-renewable fuels, undertook minimum fundamental research on renewables, and downplayed efforts for alternative energy forms, excep where the latter required giant technologies—such as synthetic fuels—which their vast capital and a sympathetic government ensured they could dominate. Thus, American consumers felt relatively little deprivation, and the heaviest social costs were, as usual, shifted to low-income groups and the community.

A critical evaluation of U.S. energy policy must begin with questioning its environmental impact. We have thus far viewed energy primarily as a resource to be dominated, deployed, and disposed of as we use our knowledge to extend mastery over nature. Are we now prepared to recognize ourselves as organically part of the natural order, responsive to its limits, and therefore appreciative of its self-balancing attributes, which depend upon recognizing a scale of activities which the environment can sustain? This appraisal asks how we deal with the earth's resources, not as a master race of Western consumers with impressionable, insatiable appctites, but in terms of the long-run needs of all humankind. It demands that we determine the kind of environmental and social order we wish to leave for the generations that follow. Who is to decide? Energy is an essentially political question of global political dimensions, but it is also an ethical one, containing its own painful questions of definition and resolution.

Three guiding principles for energy policy are offered here. First, energy policy should respect the earth and recognize the cumulative, often irreversible, danger of doing violence to it. Second, this policy must honor the rights of *all* people to a fair share of non-violently acquired energy resources. Third, energy policy should be supportive of institutions and relations that are democratic, just, and peaceful.

Unexamined, these three precepts can be treated as general and bland enough to pass muster in a sleepy Sunday sermon or as warm-up campaign oratory. On closer inspection, it is clear that we have looted the earth of its coal, uranium, oil, and gas. We have done so without seeking to understand the natural limits that would allow us to live in harmony with its rhythms, to think deeply about questions of exhaustion and replenishment. Instead, we have created underground and surface wastelands. In a monied frenzy to extract the most accessible resources, we have bypassed much of the coal and dissipated many of the pressures needed to drive the petroleum to the surface. Taking what is most easily available first, we have inevitably left what is technologically more difficult and costly to extract for future generations. Corporate and government policymakers now covet the energy suspected to be beneath national parks and wildlife refuges, further threatening many species and their already rapidly disappearing wilderness areas. There is also disturbing, if fragmented, scientific evidence that the accelerated burning of fossil fuels is raising atmospheric temperatures, with a possibly major adverse impact upon climate and sea levels. As if in response to such despoiling of our immediate nest, we are ready to implement imperial designs for energy exploitation on heavenly bodies.

All this acquisition is benignly called "development." Energy will help society stay on the supposed frontiers of science and technology. Giant energy schemes, embracing networks of nuclear installations, synthetic fuel plants, coal-fired power stations, and widespread drilling and mining, costing billions of dollars and spread over the continent and beyond, have been proposed as the necessary energy underpinnings for an industrial system, limited in size only by the boldness of human initiative. Indeed, corporate advertisements have suggested that those who challenge such progress are elitists, determined to frustrate the underprivileged, who, for the first time in human history, may have an opportunity to share in the material blessings of modernization. Towering drilling rigs on the continental shelf, in the Arctic, everywhere, operated by heroic workers and directed in laboratories by white-coated scientists (now occasionally female and even black), serve as huckstered symbols for this 20th century pioneering on behalf of the American dream. Less publicized are the huge government subsidies that support these operations, which further the distortion of national investment priorities and the neglect of urgent social needs.

In the past, lands for fulfilling the "manifest destiny" which expanded U.S. boundaries to the Pacific were viewed as unclaimed and occupied only by inferiors—such as Native Americans—who possessed a less arrogant attitude toward their natural environment, and also less firepower. "Backward" inhabitants—as in Appalachia—often signed away their rights to coal and timber, their immediate economic need outstripping their industrial sophistication. They watched helplessly as their "underdeveloped" region was quickly reshaped as a corporate colony and slagheap in the service of their more advanced betters. In Alaska, the native people learned that their loyalty to ancestral lands and hunting patterns was an atavistic impediment to integration with the industrial requirements of the continental United States.

Violence against nature rapidly became aggression against any people wherever their communities limited access to these resources. Outright bribery and armed bullying were once adequate tactics. In Latin America, North Africa, the Middle East, and Southeast Asia, corrupt ruling groups, bought off by dollars and the promise of protection from the ultimate wrath of their own people, leased or sold outright the energy riches of their lands.

Corporations have dug, drilled, and marketed wherever they could possibly gain entry, generally buttressed by the full weight of U.S. diplomacy. This has been the simplest meaning of historical policies called "the open door." U.S. involvement in Latin America has been oil-stained, a conclusion that is easily reached from a review of our historical relations with Mexico, Venezuela, and other Gulf and Caribbean nations which the United States has viewed as its rightful energy reservoirs. The clearest meaning of anti-communism comes into focus when the U.S. government and corporate officials reflexively equate any movement of sovereign nations to control their own resources with Soviet intrigue and communist subversion. For example, when the United States sought to smash the revolution in energy-poor Cuba by instructing U.S. refineries there not to accept oil obtained from Russia, the new government seized the installations and was soon receiving most of its fuel through this route, thereby strengthening the links between the two allies.

In a similar vein, covert and military actions in Iran are also justified as legitimate defenses of U.S. national interests, and few voices at home are raised to dispute the claim that the Middle East is integral to U.S. national security, and that it is appropriate for the Navy to patrol the Persian Gulf in defense of *our* oil. Almost no one has the temerity to question this unilateral declaration. Thus, the unyielding thirst for energy and expanding markets for its products are central factors in the permanent militarization of the American state. U.S. citizens are asked to identify their continued material well-being with acceptance of these exploitative arrangements.

Focusing on the freedom to consume, we have asked few serious questions about how production decisions are made and what are the most efficient energy criteria for such production. To pursue such themes too rigorously would raise uncomfortable questions about that most sacred principle of the business system, the right of private investment. Resources are heavily private and their development is clearly within the province of those who control the corporate structure, always guided by mysterious, impersonal market forces. To suggest otherwise, by raising questions of accountability, would be to shake "business confidence" and impede the flow of capital. To act otherwise, to challenge this decisionmaking power, would be to threaten "national security." And so these twin pillars of the U.S. political economy maintain the rules of the game, protecting giant energy systems and the production of goods and services that sacrifice need for profit.

Still fewer questions are asked about some degree of equity in energy. The only accepted test automatically equates money with the right to acquire and employ natural resources. Whether through travel by Concorde across the Atlantic or chauffeured limousine across Manhattan, time and space are privileges to command and consume, regardless of the social cost. Raising the price of fuel, often promoted as a conservation measure, makes little inroad on such prerogatives. Indeed, it more likely ensures that such perquisites of power remain exclusive, and that the excluded will pay higher prices and taxes. Thus do the rewards go to those who are most adept at shifting risk to the less strategically advised and positioned, and not at taking risks, as our economic ideology would otherwise indicate.

The carefully cultivated myth that corporate supremacy over oil has vanished makes it easier to perpetuate the private control of energy. Multinational corporations still dominate oil distribution throughout much of the world. Under a sympathetic Reagan administration, the takeovers, mergers, and integration of once separate energy concerns have intensified and the development of alternative energy technologies has languished. Under the privileged sanctuary known as "technological readiness," the corporations decide when a new energy form is ready to go on-line, allowing them to protect prices from competition and thwart the development of alternative and renewable fuels. Meanwhile, the consuming public remains hooked on the energy provided by its global connection.

How and where is a beginning to be made in the direction of a sane and humane energy policy?

A program which respects the natural environment would phase out costly energy such as nuclear power, which threatens human life while accelerating the destruction of the earth and the corrosion of democratic processes. It would also challenge the kind of energy dependence which requires the imperial reach of a garrison state and furthers the gross inequities of resource access which now prevail among the peoples of the world. Instead, encouragement must be directed to the utilization of renewable resources and the transition to solar energy, biomass technologies, and wind, water, and geothermal power which give hope for a renewable economy. Such energy forms can stimulate local and regional self-reliance, while empowering citizens in democratic directions, rather than primarily as consumers. Decentralized energy would weaken the justification for a Navy large enough to simultaneously protect energy lifelines around the world, for an Army and Marine Corps that can quickly be moved whenever "our" energy is threatened, and for a foreign policy which arms indigenous troops to keep their country safe for U.S. intervention and exploitation.

If energy policy is to support democratic institutions, a starting point must be public access to full information about energy resources and technologies. Such data—even over the amount and quality of energy reserves on the one-third of the land area of the United States that is publicly owned—are often concealed by corporations and public agencies "so as not to upset competitive relations."

Getting at the truth about shale oil development offers a vivid example of Bertolt Brecht's proposition that "there is not much knowledge that leads to power, but plenty of knowledge to which only power can lead." Most of the shale in the United States, potentially our largest untapped source of hydrocarbon energy, is on western federal lands. The government has sponsored research and experiments for many years but the development has been left to private corporations. The processes examined thus far for converting the organic matter in the rock into petroleum are expensive. Serious ecological questions are posed by the tremendous amounts of water required and the concomitant waste of other resources. Should this fuel source be pursued? Here is a case for independent, reliable information. If the ultimate judgment is to proceed, this should be as a yardstick operation under public control, with every possible institutional safeguard to keep the project safe and accountable. While the Tennessee Valley Authority veered in bureaucratic directions as it grew, there were aspects of its functioning as a democratic planning agency for public power which are worth study and replication. Meanwhile, there should be a moratorium on leasing public lands to private energy interests, including those off-shore, so that an appropriate public agency can evaluate the present stewardship of these resources and develop the standards which ought to prevail.

A corps of scientists, engineers, mechanics, and social scientists dedicated to the public development of renewable energy and to conservation should be created. There are many such people who would respond with full dedication to the challenge of working for social purposes.

A public investment fund should be created to provide seed money for imaginative community groups which appreciate the utility and simplicity of regional energy technologies. They could develop experimental solar, hydroelectric, and conservation projects which could operate under public or cooperative management. There could also be loan and assistance programs for private groups interested in home and farm energy construction. These funds need not be so massive as to attract large businesses and their academic satellites. For example, the Community Services Administration, which was wrecked by the Reagan administration, had stimulated a network of individuals and groups across the nation who created modest but innovative and viable energy and conservation programs. Other related needs include continued research on photovoltaic cells so as to substantially reduce their cost for converting sunlight directly into electricity. And efforts begun to encourage mass transit must be continued, for the private automobile remains a major petroleum devourer. Ultimately, end use planning which asks "energy for what?" must become an integral component of our economic reconstruction if we are to make significant headway in reducing energy consumption patterns.

Underlying these efforts must be caution about all new technologies and a willingness to ask fundamental questions about their likely ecological and human costs. A respect for projects which are in harmony with the natural limits of their environment has much to commend. Without condemning people to backbreaking tasks and drudgery, we should question the rush to replace human energy when it means the abolition of productive jobs that require skill and that render service to the community and satisfaction to the worker. Family-type farming is one example. We should be prepared to set rigorous health and safety standards for energy workers and communities when making decisions about which energy forms to support and which to discourage.

Basic energy choices which affect society must not be the exclusive domain of corporate leaders. The survival of the earth and its people is too fundamental to be resolved by what is judged most profitable. It is unlikely that government can facilitate democratic energy planning if these resources remain privately controlled, treated simply as another commodity. Too often, public leaders have been subservient to private forces, accepting as their major responsibility such assignments as helping to keep prices up and supply down while shouldering some of the risks and generally running interference for the global machinations of the modern energy corporations.

An alternative energy policy is thus an alternative political policy. There is no way of doing an end run around the existing economic forces and the structure of power of which they are part. Too much of the writing, and even the advocacy, about energy is essentially apolitical, focusing upon technological fixes. Energy corporations will not disappear as solar power is explored. More likely, they will move in to dominate it, recreating solar not as a human scale, viable alternative, but as a massive, capital-intensive undertaking once the time is right.

The question remains as to who learns what from the experiences of history. If people wish to end their vulnerability to the present energy system and challenge the assumption of technological determinism upon which it rests, they will have to mobilize to place democratic planning on the political agenda. As the late E.F. Schumacher wrote some 30 years ago, "Instead of forecasting what we 'need,'" we might "attempt to work out what it would be wise and prudent to need."

Resources

Recommended Appointees for a New Administration

- Richard Saul, former energy administrator in the Office of Economic Opportunity and the Community Services Administration. Saul has extensive knowledge about energy and conservation needs and programs and has built a network of community activists around the country.

- Robert Cook, an iron worker, trade unionist, homesteader, and maple sugar producer. Cook lives in Worthington, Massachusetts, where he is an ardent advocate of solar energy and heads his town's planning board. He formerly taught sociology at Yale University, and ran for Congress in New Haven, Connecticut.

- Irving Like, an attorney in Babylon, New York, who has been a leader in the fight against the Shoreham nuclear power installation of Lilco on Long Island, also a leading participant in the Agent Orange case, representing Vietnam veterans.
- Peter Bradford, chairman of New York State Public Service Commission, formerly member of U.S. Nuclear Regulatory Agency and Maine Utility Commissioner, and one of the original Nader Raiders.
- Wendell Berry, farmer, poet, agricultural writer (*The Unsettling of America*), teaches at the University of Kentucky.
- Sidney Plotkin, a political scientist at Vassar College, has made extensive study of land use policy in the United States (*Keep Out*) and is knowledgeable about siting fights over nuclear and energy plants.

Organizations

- Sierra Club, 330 Pennsylvania Ave. SE, Washington, DC 20003; (202) 547-1141
- Friends of the Earth, 530 7th St. SE, Washington, DC 20003; (202) 543-4312
- Natural Resources Defense Council, 1350 New York Ave. NW, Washington, DC 20005; (202) 783-7800
- National Audubon Society, 801 Pennsylvania Ave. SE, Washington, DC 20003; (202) 547-9009
- Citizens Labor-Energy Coalition, 1300 Connecticut Ave. NW, Suite 401, Washington, DC 20036; (202) 857-5153
- Greenpeace, 1611 Connecticut Ave. NW, Washington, DC 20009; (202) 462-1177

Further Reading

- Lewis Mumford, *Technics and Civilization*, Harcourt, Brace, and World, 1934.
- Harrison Brown, *The Challenge of Man's Future*, Viking, 1954.
- *The Global 2000 Report to the President*, U.S. Council on Environmental Quality and Department of State, Penguin, 1982.
- Thorstein Veblen, *Absentee Ownership and Business Enterprises in Recent Times: The Case of America*, B.W. Huebsch, 1923.
- Ruth Leger Sivard, *World Military and Social Expenditures, 1987-1988*, World Priorities, 1987.
- E.F. Schumacher, *Small is Beautiful: Economics As If People Mattered*, Harper and Row, 1973.

Robert Engler is author of *The Politics of Oil: A Study of Private Power and Democratic Directions* and *The Brotherhood of Oil: Energy Policy and the Public Interest.* He has edited *America's Energy: Report from the Nation on 100 Years of Struggle for Democratic Control of Our Resources,* and his article, "Many Bhopals: Technology Out of Control," appeared as a special issue of *The Nation* (April 27, 1985). He teaches at the Graduate School of the City University of New York. In the academic year beginning September 1988, he will hold the professorship of world politics of peace and war at Princeton University.

Paul L. Wachtel

Toward a Quality-of-Life Society: Alternatives to Growth

Platform

- A Universal Employment Act shall initially set at thirty-five the number of hours a week above which employers are required to pay employees time-and-one-half. The number of hours shall be adjusted according to a formula that raises the number of hours as unemployment declines, and lowers it as unemployment increases. Thus, employers will have an incentive to hire new workers and spread the available work more evenly over a larger pool.

- Where, despite job-sharing initiatives, workers are displaced in the transition to an economy not dependent on growth, retraining programs shall be made available, and workers who participate shall receive regular compensation.

- A Leisure and Recreational Development Act shall set aside funds for the expansion and improvement of public recreational facilities and educational opportunities designed to enhance the capacity to enjoy stimulating leisure. This key policy should be explicitly designed to encourage a shift away from using our productive efficiency to purchase more goods and toward taking our surplus in leisure.

- In order to assure an equitable distribution of the costs of transition to a quality-of-life economy, tax rates shall be restored to the progressive rates that existed prior to the tax legislation of the Reagan administration. Individuals whose work falls under the job-sharing initiatives (and who therefore would bear more directly the costs of the transition) shall receive a tax credit in partial compensation.

- More generally, because the market can be both a means of permitting free and efficient deployment of resources and a source of undesirable and socially harmful inequality, tax policy shall be utilized

405

as a supplement to market forces to assure that excessive inequities do not persist and grow.

- A central aim of a quality-of-life society is to preserve the life-sustaining environment that is threatened by an excessive emphasis on growth. Accordingly, environmental standards must be strictly enforced, both through regulation and tax incentives. Recycling and other conservation methods should be promoted as well as stricter standards against pollution of air, soil, and water.

- In order to reduce reliance on energy-consuming and polluting forms of private transit, research on and promotion of a variety of mass transit alternatives should be funded, including the use of computers to route door-to-door jitney services that would combine the convenience of private cars with the energy efficiency of mass transit.

Our society's preoccupying emphasis on economic growth does not effectively address—indeed, it even exacerbates—our two most glaring domestic problems: inequality and poverty in a land of plenty, and the deterioration of the life-sustaining environment. We persist nonetheless on our current course because of two key assumptions: that economic growth will yield us the good life and that growth is essential to generate jobs. These two assumptions are linked; part of why we have not given serious consideration to the obvious road to full employment—job-sharing—is that we have been afraid that such a course will leave us with "less."

But growth does not really lead to greater satisfaction. Indeed, growth as a way of life makes real satisfaction less likely.

In 1958, when the United States was widely and appropriately hailed as "The Affluent Society," 9.5 percent of U.S households had air conditioning, about 4 percent had dishwashers, and less than 15 percent had more than one car. In 1980, when Ronald Reagan's successful bid to replace Jimmy Carter was based on a widely shared sense that people were suffering economically, the percentage of homes with air conditioning had quintupled, the percentage with two or more cars had about tripled, and the percentage with dishwashers had increased more than 700 percent. Economic growth since 1958 has been astounding, yet indicators of Americans' sense of well-being show a significant decline.

There were many reasons for the experienced sense of decline, including inflation confusion and shifting power relations in the world at large that left the United States less overwhelmingly dominant. But one thing should be clear: the relation between economic growth and the experience of well-being is less simple and direct than we are accustomed to thinking. Indeed, the very nature of a growth society works against contentment and satisfaction; people must be made to feel discontent with what they have. The sense of having enough must be like the horizon—seemingly reachable but continually receding as it is approached. We have succeeded all too well in fostering such a psychology. Other countries may be overtaking us in manufacturing goods, but none come near us in manufacturing desire.

On top of this failure to yield the satisfaction it promises, growth presents, of course, an even more severe assault on our well-being. We are all familiar with the serious health threats associated with producing more and more: seepage of deadly chemicals into our water supply; toxic wastes that leach into our soil; acid rain that destroys life in our lakes and now seems to be affecting our own health; destruction of the ozone layer by fluorocarbons that greatly increases the risk of skin cancer and cataracts; pollution of the air by the exhausts of millions of automobiles and smokestacks; poisoning of our rivers by the waste products of industrial manufacture; dangers posed by nuclear power plants, both in disposing of their radioactive wastes and in the ever-present possibility of another Three Mile Island or Chernobyl—the list seems virtually endless. We all know about these dangers, and we probably all know that they are likely to shorten our lives and cause debilitating illness. Yet we have learned to live with them by employing psychological mechanisms of denial and avoidance. What we deny most of all is that it is the very essence of growth that these problems will increase exponentially, that what growth *means* is that we will continue to exploit the environment at a faster and faster rate.

Why do we persist in committing ourselves to a path that brings us little real satisfaction and has such harmful consequences to our health? Why do we continue to support candidates who promise (regardless of their ability to deliver) to foster high rates of growth? There are many complex psychological reasons why the call to "get us moving again" stirs our assent. In large measure, the reason we are unable to let go of the growth imperative is that all of our jobs seem to depend on it. The platform proposals above are designed to sever this deadly connection between jobs and environmental degradation. Promoting employment through sharing available jobs, rather than creating new jobs just to keep people employed, makes it possible for people to participate in the economy, whether it is growing or not.

Most people would agree that the availability of a job for every individual who is able to work is a desirable social goal. People have a need not just for income but for the self-respect and the respect of others that come with being a contributing member of society. Most of us, moreover, feel that the goal should be not just a job but a "full-time" job. With certain exceptions, part-time work is accorded low status and seen as a compromise or a stop-gap solution.

Our conception of what constitutes full-time work, however, has tended in recent years to be rather rigid and short-sighted. By historical standards, most of us work "part-time." At the beginning of the industrial revolution, sixty-, seventy-, even 80-hour weeks were not uncommon. For many years reformers wanted to reduce the work week, and little by little the standard decreased to our present pattern of about forty hours. For several decades, we have been stalled at this level, and have come to regard it as almost a God-given standard.

A slight revision in our notion of what constitutes full-time work would make a substantial contribution to increasing the availability of jobs. Reducing the work week from forty to thirty-six hours, for example, would require 10 percent more workers. Were those presently unemployed properly trained, this reduction in hours would virtually eliminate unemployment without requiring any growth at all, while also providing more leisure to millions of workers.

Such an approach within a steady-state economy would, of course, mean a reduction in income for those whose working hours are reduced. One difference between the present job-sharing proposal and the largely admirable Quality of Life Action Act, sponsored by Representative Charles Hayes (D-IL), which also advocates job-sharing, is that the latter mandates that no loss in weekly wages is to accompany the decrease in working hours. Although the overall program outlined here includes an explicit concern with redistribution, and thus to some degree could accommodate a maintenance of wages at the expense of profits, and although the tax proposal put forward above would provide some compensation through tax credits for those most directly affected by job-sharing, the present proposal, rooted in a challenge to growth, must address directly the limits on the total product to go around.

In the present climate, the number of people willing to forego income for leisure is clearly a minority. The proposals offered here will gain widespread support only if and when large numbers of people begin to recognize the failure of increased material possessions to raise their sense of well-being. The burden on advocates of alternatives to growth is to paint a picture of a life in which increased leisure opportunities will more than compensate for a reduced income.

It is useful to remind ourselves that in 1957, just one year before the publication of *The Affluent Society*, Americans reported a level of satisfaction with their lives that has yet to be surpassed. Given the rate of growth since then, even if the average full-time worker were to reduce his or her working hours from forty to thirty-two, the resulting real per capita income would still be substantially higher than in that year of contentment; and that would be combined with full employment and the enormous improvement in the social climate that would result from everyone being able to have a three-day weekend every week of the year, and with the beneficial effects on our own and our children's health that would follow from a move away from relying on polluting industries to provide jobs.

Along with a shift away from industrial activities that foul the environment, and toward leisure, would be an emphasis on helping people learn to enjoy and enrich their use of those increased leisure hours. In a quality-of-life economy, money would be invested in community facilities considerably more attractive and comprehensive than presently available. Indeed, though job-sharing would be a basic commitment of a quality-of-life society (in order to ensure that socially useless or even harmful activities were not encouraged simply to "create jobs") some of the slack in employment resulting from a deemphasis on environmentally harmful economic activity would be picked up by building parks, public athletic facilities, and theaters, as well by providing instruction in sports, the arts, and other activities associated with productive use of leisure. (Emphasis would be placed on shared and public facilities, in which for the same total outlay many more person-hours of use could be provided.) Even more important, there would be much work to be done in meeting the needs of the disadvantaged.

Some might argue that shifting away from growth could improve the quality of life for middle-class people, but they would maintain that growth is essential if we are to improve the lot of those most in need. It has been a widely shared assumption that only a growing economy can afford to finance the construction of schools, hospitals, and housing for the poor or to provide the services required to correct the results of past discriminations and deprivations. This assumption has two bases. The first is that growth is essential to provide employment for those without jobs. I have already addressed this in suggesting job-sharing as an alternative strategy for achieving full employment. The second is that only if the majority's circumstances are continually improving will they be willing to finance the needed programs. What is ignored is that people don't necessarily feel more comfortable and contented as the economy grows, that in growth-oriented society, discontent is generated instead. More is not enough, and sometimes it doesn't even feel like more. Responsiveness to the needs of others is more likely to flourish in an economy that is not organized around the continuing generation of new needs and desires.

The growth approach to meeting the needs of the disadvantaged is flawed because it is covertly premised on continuing inequality. Historically, the growth solution has been offered as an alternative to redistribution schemes. Whether clothed in liberal or conservative rhetoric, growth is a form of "trickle down" economics, in which continued accumulation by the haves is thought to yield beneficial side-effects for the have-nots. To be sure, under Reagan, even less than usual has trickled down, but failure to confront the key issue of inequality has a long history.

The U.S. poor suffer as much from inequality as from absolute deprivation. There are, of course, significant and real deprivations: people need to be better fed, better housed, to receive better medical care and education, to have better job opportunities. These needs are urgent and real. But they will not be met satisfactorily through general economic growth in which the poor receive the same small portion of the new product that they received of the old one. That results simply in inequality at a higher level.

Some improvements, of course, will result from continued growth, but the sense of deprivation that goes hand-in-hand with being excluded from whatever society views as the standard and expectable comforts will persist if severe inequality persists. Moreover, the improvements that are achieved can be quickly eroded as the despair that inequality breeds spreads through the community, bringing the crime, dirt, and deterioration that are perhaps the most serious scourge of the poor in this country.

Further, the ways our society maximizes growth tend to interfere with directing our resources—even if those resources increase—toward the most pressing human needs. Per capita GNP is considerably higher now than it was in the era of the "War on Poverty," yet today we are far more inclined to say that we "can't afford" social programs.

More recently, the conventional wisdom about stimulating growth has pointed even further away from the needs of the disadvantaged. Whereas somehow we mustered sufficient incentive for quite considerable growth when the highest tax brackets were as much as 70-90 percent, now we are being told that it takes a marginal rate of not more than about 30 percent to induce investors to do anything productive. In the name of the growth that will supposedly benefit the poor, we are left with budget shortfalls whose burden predictably falls precisely on the programs the poor desperately need.

If we are serious about addressing the needs of the disadvantaged in our society, we will have to stop attempting to meet those needs with mirrors, in the largely vain hope that aiming to fill others' needs— mainly of those who command the most dollars—will somehow reflect back to aid the poor. Direct investment in housing, education, and programs that enable the chronically poor to enter the mainstream of society, along with a commitment to assure—through tax credits, subsidies, or other means—that a genuinely living wage is available to all, are the means to end the shame of poverty. If we do not believe that we can accomplish this until we are richer, we will find that we somehow are never quite there. We are rich enough now to do it, over $600 billion dollars a year richer in constant dollars than we were at the time of "The Affluent Society." Insight and commitment are what are lacking—not still greater wealth.

It is not possible to go into detail here about the implications of the proposed policies on the structure of incentives, on the budget and balance-of-trade deficits, and on the U.S. role in the international marketplace. In some ways, the proposed changes introduce new and difficult wrinkles to already serious problems; in other ways, the reduced spending that would accompany this new direction could be helpful. How best to manage the transition once there was support for it would pose considerable challenges to economic policymakers.

If the answer to our problems is not to be dogmatic, short-sighted, and pessimistic, it is essential that the premises of such a transition not be obscured. Many of the objections to these proposals can be seen, on close examination, to incorporate the very growth assumptions that the proposed changes are designed to confront. If the guiding aim of our economy is to remain stable and productive while *not* growing, and to shift our economic efforts away from activities that pollute the environment and from mechanisms that increase inequality, then the success of the economy must be judged on those grounds, not on its ability to compete in a game we have deliberately chosen not to play.

What then of the difficulty in persuading people to follow the course described here? Should we not be "realistic" and advocate policies that are presently achievable in light of the electorate's present views? Such a position reminds me of the old story of the drunk who is looking for his lost keys near a lamppost; when asked if that's where he lost them, he replies "No, I lost them down the block, but the light is better here." Growth is the lamppost to which our politicians, both liberal and conservative, are drawn. But it is not where the solution to our society's problems lies.

Unless we can persuade people that growth-oriented policies have brought considerable pollution and inequality, but precious little contentment, it is our problems—and not our pleasures—that are most likely to grow.

Resources

Recommended Appointees for a New Administration

- Herman Daly, formerly Alumni Professor of Economics at Louisiana State University, presently at the World Bank, is one of the world's foremost proponents of a steady state economy.

- Barry Commoner is Director of the Center for Biology and Natural Systems at Queens College of the City University of New York and former presidential candidate.

- Seymour B. Sarason, one of the founders of the field of community psychology, is presently at Yale's Institute for Social and Policy Studies.

- Robert L. Heilbroner, Norman Thomas Professor of Economics at the New School for Social Research, is one of the few economists to address seriously the dangers posed by our rampant exploitation of the environment.

- Hazel Henderson, environmental activist and author. Henderson has been founder of and advisor to such organizations as Citizens for Clean Air, Environmental Action, Council on Economic Priorities, and the Public Interest Economics Foundation, and has written widely on the economic and moral bases of an ecologically sound and a socially just society.

Organizations

- Natural Resources Defense Council, 122 E. 42nd St., New York, NY 10017; (212) 949-0049
- Environmental Defense Fund, 257 Park Ave. South, New York, NY; (212) 686-4191
- Sierra Club, 730 Polk St., San Francisco, CA 94109; (415) 776-2211
- Environmental Action, 1525 New Hampshire Ave. NW, Washington, DC 20036; (202) 745-4870
- Zero Population Growth, 1400 16th St., 3rd Floor, Washington, DC 20036; (202) 332-2200
- Negative Population Growth, 16 E. 42nd St., New York, NY 10017; (212) 599-2020

Further Reading

- Herman Daly, *Steady State Economics*, Louisiana State University Press, 1977.
- John Kenneth Galbraith, *The Affluent Society*, 4th edition, Houghton Mifflin, 1984.
- Nicholas Georgescu-Roegen, *The Entropy Law and Economic Process*, Harvard University Press, 1971.
- Robert L. Heilbroner, *An Inquiry into the Human Prospect*, Norton, 1975.
- Fred Hirsch, *Social Limits to Growth*, Harvard University Press, 1977.
- William Leiss, *The Limits to Satisfaction*, University of Toronto Press, 1976.
- Ezra Mishan, *The Costs of Economic Growth*, Praeger, 1967.
- Paul L. Wachtel, *The Poverty of Affluence: A Psychological Portrait of the American Way of Life*, New Society Publishers, 1988.

Paul L. Wachtel is Distinguished Professor of Psychology at City College and the Graduate Center of the City University of New York. He is the author of *The Poverty of Affluence: A Psychological Portrait of the American Way of Life*, *Psychoanalysis and Behavior Therapy*, and *Action and Insight*.

About the Editors

Marcus Raskin, political theorist and a major exponent of social reconstruction, is co-founder and Distinguished Fellow of the Institute for Policy Studies. Raskin has served as advisor to the Episcopal Urban Bishops and as co-chair of the Issues Commission of the Progressive Alliance, a group of 150 public interest and labor organizations. He served as a member of a Presidential Commission on Education and advisor to the Bureau of the Budget, as well as to the Office of Science and Technology in the Executive Office of the President. He stood trial for draft resistance during the Vietnam War and was acquitted. He has received the University of Chicago Alumni Award, Johns Hopkins Centenary medal, and served as trustee of Antioch College. He is the author of, among other books, *The Common Good, New Ways of Knowing*, and *The Federal Budget and Social Reconstruction*.

Chester Hartman is a Fellow of the Institute for Policy Studies and founder and chair of The Planners Network, a national organization of progressive urban planners and community organizers. He has taught urban planning at Harvard, Yale, the University of North Carolina, Cornell, and the University of California, Berkeley. He serves on the editorial board of *Urban Affairs Quarterly*, the *Journal of Urban Affairs*, and *Housing Studies*. Among his recent books are *The Transformation of San Francisco* and *Critical Perspectives on Housing*.

About the Institute for Policy Studies and South End Press

The Institute for Policy Studies (IPS) is an independent, non-profit, tax-exempt research and education organization which was founded in 1963 to pose fundamental questions, provide conceptual thought, and develop programs and alternatives to further democracy, peace, and equity in our society and foreign relations. IPS is centered in Washington, DC with a European affiliate, the Transnational Institute, in Amsterdam. IPS staff includes fifteen Fellows and Project Directors and thirty Associate Fellows and Guest Scholars. The work of IPS includes research and action in the areas of national security, intervention, international economics, and domestic reconstruction. Its education and outreach programs include the Washington School, seminars and conferences, and a publications program.

South End Press was founded in 1977 to help give expression to a diversity of progressive social movements in the United States and to provide an alternative to the products of corporate publishing. Today, the press continues into its second decade, with over 140 titles in print on a wide variety of topics: U.S. foreign policy, feminism, education, labor, culture, ecology, political theory. Books are written in broadly accessible language and are intended to reach a wide reading audience with important critiques and creative alternatives for American society. Working to widen the spectrum of debate on questions of power and social justice, South End Press invites your critical support and feedback.